3795

# THE PSYCHOTHERAPIST'S GUIDE
# TO PSYCHOPHARMACOLOGY

# The
# Psychotherapist's
# Guide to
# Psychopharmacology

MICHAEL J. GITLIN, M.D.

**THE FREE PRESS**
*A Division of Macmillan, Inc.*
NEW YORK

Maxwell Macmillan Canada
TORONTO

Maxwell Macmillan International
NEW YORK   OXFORD   SINGAPORE   SYDNEY

The Free Press
A Division of Macmillan, Inc.
866 Third Avenue, New York, N.Y. 10022

Maxwell Macmillan Canada, Inc.
1200 Eglinton Avenue East
Suite 200
Don Mills, Ontario M3C 3N1

Macmillan, Inc. is part of the Maxwell Communication Group of Companies.

Printed in the United States of America

printing number
    4   5   6   7   8   9   10

**Library of Congress Cataloging-in-Publication Data**

Gitlin, Michael J.
    The psychotherapist's guide to psychopharmacology /
Michael J. Gitlin.
        p.   cm.
    Includes bibliographical references.
    ISBN 0-02-911781-X
    1. Psychopharmacology. 2. Psychotherapists. I. Title.
    [DNLM:   1. Mental Disorders—drug therapy.   2.
Psychotropic   Drugs—pharmacology.   3. Psychotropic
Drugs—therapeutic use.]
    RM315.G57   1990
    616.89'18—dc20
    DNLM/DLC
    for Library of Congress                              90-1734
                                                              CIP

To my mother,
*Beatrice Gitlin,*
who showed me the value of sensitivity
and
to the memory of my father,
*Hyman Gitlin, M.D.,*
who demonstrated the art of being a physician

# Contents

## SECTION FOUR

## SECTION FIVE

# List of Illustrations and Tables

## ILLUSTRATIONS

## TABLES

# Preface

With the emergence of medications as viable treatment options for psychiatric/psychological disorders, an unfortunate split has developed between those who prescribe medications—psychiatrists—and those who do not—nonphysician therapists and some psychoanalyst physicians. Widening the split is the lack of accessible information that might close the gap and promote improved communication between the two groups. The problem is not a dearth of psychopharmacology textbooks. These are abundant but are written (with rare exceptions) for professionals who are already familiar with psychiatric disorders and who already have some experience in prescribing medications. For those therapists who have neither training nor experience in the medical model, these textbooks can be alienating in their use of technical language and assumption of basic knowledge of biological aspects of psychiatry.

The purpose of this book is to bridge the gap, to provide a source of information about the medical aspects of modern psychiatry to therapists who cannot or do not often prescribe psychotropic medications. It is written for clinical psychologists, social workers, marriage and family counselors, clinical nurse therapists, and those psychiatrists whose knowledge of psychopharmacology is not up to date or extensive. Some family practitioners or internists may also find it useful. I have attempted to utilize nontechnical language. Some terms derived from the world of medicine, biology, and science, however, are inevitable and are defined when introduced.

It seems useless to describe medication treatments for disorders that may not in all cases be familiar to readers. Therefore a significant portion of the book is devoted to describing disorders for which medications are prescribed. With rare exception, I have drawn on the *Diagnostic and Statistical Manual, Third Edition, Revised* (American Psychiatric Association, 1987), or DSM-III-R as it is called, for this purpose. (See chapter 1 for a more detailed discussion of DSM-III-R.) As I point out repeatedly in the text, by no means does this imply a wholesale acceptance of these criteria. Neither DSM-III-R nor any other manual or textbook can be considered the revealed truth. In many places in the text, I have noted my disagreements with DSM-III-R. The diagnostic manual, however, does offer a set of descriptors and a definition of terms. For example, before we can meaningfully discuss the use of antidepressants for treating depression, we must all have a common definition of depression. DSM-III-R provides this. Although the DSM-III-R diagnostic criteria vary in how well they describe discrete clinical syndromes, they at least give us a starting point for diagnosis.

The book is organized so that the reader can approach psychopharmacology in two ways: focusing on a psychiatric disorder and the medications used in its treatment, or on the medication itself and the disorders for which it is useful. The book is divided into five sections:

Chapter 1 explores concepts of diagnosis and treatment effects.

Chapter 2 provides an overview of brain function. It describes how cells within the brain communicate with each other, how these mechanisms may go awry in some major psychiatric disorders, and how medications may work biochemically. Although the information in this chapter is not directly relevant to the clinical focus of the book, it does provide a background for those interested and, more importantly, it introduces certain terms and concepts regarding medications that are referred to in later chapters.

Chapters 3 through 8 are devoted to the disorders for which medications are currently prescribed. For each disorder, the following issues are addressed: how the diagnosis is made (including, for the major disorders, a list of pertinent questions to ask); the possible genetic components; the natural history of the disorder. Differential diagnosis, that is, of disorders, both medical and psychiatric, that are often confused with the disorder in question, is also treated. The second half of each chapter discusses medication treatment. Here the emphasis is on how decisions on medication can and should be made, with less attention to technical aspects of treatment, such as doses and side effects.

Chapters 9 through 13 focus on the medications themselves: the disorders for which they might be prescribed, their likely mechanisms of action, the names of the different medications, how they are prescribed, the doses used, and the major side effects that might be seen.

Finally, Chapter 14 discusses psychotherapy/psychopharmacology interactions: theoretical considerations, how to evaluate and select a pharmacotherapist in your area, and ways in which two professionals, one of whom prescribes medications and the other of whom provides psychotherapy, can best work together.

Case histories are presented throughout the book. These may illustrate types of disorders not easily recognized or complex situations that are most easily explicated by a specific case, or they may be typical vignettes involving medications. All case histories are real ones, altered to preserve anonymity but with the essential features intact.

Because this book is intended as a clinical guide and not as an exhaustive review, references are provided only intermittently. References are generally given for classic or unique studies, little known findings, the most recent study of its type, or for recent reviews of a topic. For those interested in more extensive reading, suggestions are provided at the end of the book.

Tables that list all medications of a class give both the trade names and generic names. However, within the text, in order to avoid advertising a specific product of a pharmaceutical firm, medications are called by their generic names with trade names only occasionally given in parentheses. The appendix lists all medications referred to in the book alphabetically by generic names, trade names, and medication class. Dosage ranges should be considered as approximate; occasionally patients may respond to smaller doses than expected while other patients will need higher doses than are generally recommended.

The following linguistic conventions are used: (1) Because the concern is with the more severe psychiatric/psychological problems for which the medical model can be applied relatively easily (except for personality disorders), the people we treat will be described as patients, not clients. The use of this term simply acknowledges that the types of problems described for which medications might be prescribed are different from, for instance, marital conflict. (2) The masculine pronoun "he" will be used, except in the discussions on pregnant patients and those with eating disorders (who are overwhelmingly women). (3) The professional prescribing medication will be described as the psychopharmacologist, pharmacotherapist, or consultant, these terms being used interchangeably. The term "therapist" is used for any mental health professional who is treating the patient using some form of talking therapy. This would include clinical psychologists, social workers, marriage and family counselors, clinical nurse therapists, and psychiatrists.

# Acknowledgments

Even a solo authored book is never the work of one person. From the initial idea—a psychopharmacology textbook for therapists who would never touch a prescription pad—to the final touches, various people in my personal and professional life played a part. Not surprisingly, the idea for the book belongs to two friends who are themselves clinical psychologists with whom I had shared a number of patients. It also helped that these two, Drs. Joseph Barber and Cheri Adrian, themselves had experience in writing books.

Professionally, for the past decade, I have been blessed by close working relationships with three psychologists with whom the model of good collaborative work in teaching, administration, research, and patient care came easily and naturally. It is in large part by observing the success of my work with Drs. Kay Jamison, Keith Nuechterlein, and Connie Hammen that I have learned so much about these issues. Learning to collaborate requires the right collaborators. I've had them. My ongoing work in the UCLA Affective Disorders Clinic has always involved a great deal of teaching with both psychiatric residents and psychology interns who elected to spend a year exploring the mysteries, fascinations, and satisfactions of working with patients with mood disorders. If my explanations about psychopharmacology are in any way helpful, it is due to having refined the skill of explaining without resorting to obfuscatory, technical jargon, a skill developed by working with these intelligent, inquisitive students whose primary interests were in patient care, not research. I am indebted to CeeCee Garfinkel who was helpful to me in the library research for the book and in constructing the tables and figures. Dr. Vivian Burt, Chief of Outpatient Psychiatry at UCLA, has provided much appreciated support, encouragement, and friendship. My thinking has been sharpened by an endless series of dialogues with Robert Dworkin, PhD, which have taken place since our college days. Finally, my most important professional debt belongs to Dr. Joel Yager, Professor of Psychiatry at UCLA and Director of Residency Education, who was my supervisor and teacher, and is now colleague, supporter, and close friend.

He demonstrated to me by example that it was possible (but not easy) to develop an academic mind without losing one's clinical soul.

A number of colleagues and friends graciously read earlier drafts of the book and helped improve the content and style. They are: Joseph Barber, PhD; Alexander Bystritsky, MD; Robert Dworkin, PhD; Carole Edelstein, MD; Connie Hammen, PhD; Richard Sandor, MD; Marjorie Schuman, PhD; Dan Siegel, MD; Paula Smith-Marder, PhD; Jerry Tarlow, PhD; Joel Yager, MD. I appreciate their thoughtful suggestions.

Since I am a clinician and teacher first and a researcher and administrator second, it was not possible to take time out from my basic professional responsibilities to write this book. Thus, the time invested in its writing was taken from missed movies with Josh, unbicycled rides with Katie, and unwatched Sesame Streets with Rebecca, my three children who were more patient with me than I would have been in their place. More than anyone, however, this book belongs to my wife, Jean Gitlin, PhD, a clinical psychologist who encouraged me, pushed me, read early drafts of the book, and who, in her clinical work, consistently demonstrates the value of wisdom along with knowledge.

# SECTION
## ONE

# 1

---

# Diagnosis and Treatment: Basic Principles

---

$I$n the last twenty-five years, we in the mental health field have witnessed a veritable explosion of new information that has shifted the emphasis from the more psychoanalytically based models and treatments that dominated psychiatry and psychology for the preceding thirty years to descriptive and biological ones. The new approach is based on a number of assumptions, three of which are relevant to this book. The first is that psychiatric disorders can be reliably classified according to diagnostic methods used in medicine before the introduction of laboratory tests. The second is that pharmacological treatments—medications—are effective in treating a variety of psychiatric disorders. The third is that the efficacy of psychiatric therapies can be evaluated by empirical studies. Not surprisingly, the bulk of these treatment studies have involved medications. In this chapter, these three assumptions—that psychopathology can be described by symptom-based terms, that medications can be used to treat psychiatric disorders, and that scientific methods can be applied to evaluate treatments—will be discussed. The goals of medication treatment and criteria for the selection of appropriate patients for psychopharmacological evaluation will then be presented.

## DESCRIPTIVE PSYCHIATRY AND DSM-III-R

Although the introduction of a descriptive, diagnosis-based approach to psychopathology was a radical shift from the etiologically based language of psychoanalysis, it was far from new. During the late nineteenth and early twentieth centuries, descriptive approaches dominated European psychiatry and resulted

3

in the first diagnostic distinction between manic-depressive illness and schizophrenia (then called dementia praecox) on the basis of their differing clinical pictures. However, the descriptive approach fell into disfavor in this country for many decades, resurfacing only with the emergence of the *Diagnostic and Statistical Manual of Mental Disorders,* Third Edition (DSM-III) in 1980 and, since 1987, the revised edition (DSM-III-R). The goal of diagnosis for DSM-III-R, as for any other classification scheme, is to define disorders reliably, so that both clinicians and researchers agree on what is meant by terms such as depression, and to predict prognosis and treatment response.

Because the first half of this book is organized according to its classifications, it is worth reviewing the essential components of DSM-III-R.

The most important question in the descriptive approach used by DSM-III-R is "what," in contrast to the centrality of "why" in psychoanalysis. It attempts (with only varying degrees of success) to be atheoretical with regard to etiology. Thus, when a 37-year-old man goes through a period of depressed mood with alterations in sleep, appetite, energy, and concentrating ability, the reason *why* is irrelevant for making the diagnosis of depression. Whether this patient's depression is best understood by his poor introject of a maternal object, depressogenic assumptions (using a cognitive framework), or by an alteration in the regulation of norepinephrine in certain parts of the brain does not alter the diagnosis.

Among the objections to the descriptive approach is that patients are pigeonholed into diagnostic boxes and not understood for the unique constellation of intrapsychic, historical, and environmental variables that set each one apart from others. This objection is valid *if* clinicians view the patient's identity as synonymous with his diagnosis. Is the patient viewed as a person with manic-depressive disorder or is he a manic-depressive? The difference is far from semantic. Although the descriptive approach can be misused to objectify and distance patients, that is neither its purpose nor its proper use.

The second essential feature of DSM-III-R is its multiaxial approach. Patients are rated along five axes simultaneously, each of which utilizes different types of information. Psychiatric disorders are listed on Axes I and II while Axes III, IV, and V describe associated medical conditions, psychosocial stressors, and level of functioning. Axis I disorders comprise all clinical syndromes except for personality disorders and developmental disorders arising in childhood, which are listed on Axis II. Thus, Axis II disorders are, in general, more stable and long lasting. When a clinician describes a patient as having an Axis I disorder, he is referring to the presence of a symptom-based disorder, such as depression, phobias, or schizophrenia. Describing an adult patient as having an Axis II disorder is equivalent to saying he has a personality disorder. Among the goals of separating Axis I from Axis II is to encourage clinicians to conceptualize coexistent disorders. Instead of deciding whether the patient suffers from major depression *or* narcissistic personality disorder, the clinician can diagnose both disorders. This approach makes evaluation more difficult, but also more accurate. In this way, either/or formulations can be replaced by richer, more complex models.

It is in the evaluation and diagnosis of personality disorders that the descriptive, atheoretical approach of DSM-III-R is most problematic. Inherently, personality features are difficult to describe using the language of symptoms and signs. As an example, criteria used to diagnose personality disorders such as lack of empathy or persistent identity disturbance simply do not fit well into a classification system that is defined as atheoretical and descriptive. For the purposes of this book, however, it is a minor problem since the vast majority of patients who should be considered for medication have Axis I disorders. Chapter 7 reviews the little that is known about pharmacotherapy of personality disorders.

One of the major stumbling blocks for the acceptance of the descriptive approach has been an understandable concern that this new model would replace and discount all other ways of understanding psychopathology. Descriptive models, however, should *never* preclude other ways of understanding psychological phenomena. For any clinical disorder, for any individual patient, different models will each have advantages and disadvantages in explaining the psychopathology. The clinical phenomenon of acute mania may be best viewed using the descriptive model, while adjustment disorders or narcissistic personalities will be better understood by an interpersonal or psychoanalytic perspective. A patient with a mild to moderate depression triggered by a loss, however, might be best understood using both medical (really, descriptive) and psychological concepts, with each model clarifying only a piece of the puzzle. It would be redundant and disruptive to point out continually in this text that other ways of understanding patients are helpful and, at times, mandatory. The use of multiple conceptual models should be considered a basic prerequisite for the full understanding of patients.

## PHARMACOTHERAPY AND ITS IMPLICATIONS FOR OTHER THERAPIES

The second assumption of the medical model in psychiatry, that some psychiatric disorders are effectively treated by medications, has been established through the astonishing amount of research over the last thirty years devoted to the discovery, development, and documentation of psychopharmacologically active drugs. Initially used for severe depressions and psychotic disorders, medications have now been demonstrated to be useful for at least some patients with a wide variety of disorders. The simple existence of this book is testimony to the extent to which medications have been established as a treatment modality for psychiatric disorders. Two observations, however, have tempered some of the early, unrealistic hopes of the more biologically oriented clinicians. First, despite the dramatic effect of medications in reducing or preventing psychopathology, their limitations have become apparent. In a variety of disorders, medications are profoundly effective, yet still leave untouched some core aspects of the disorder which must be treated with other modalities. These limitations are most obvious in schizophrenia (see chapter 5), but are apparent also in panic disorder, manic-depressive illness, and others. Second, the initial pace with which effective medications were discovered has slowed considerably. Despite the regular release of new drugs, too often they offer few advantages over similar existing medications. Certainly, some advantages of the newer medications exist—side effects may be lessened, risk of lethal overdose diminished, choices for allergic or particularly sensitive patients have been expanded. But medications that are more effective than older similar agents are few.

Because of the proliferation of medications in psychiatric treatment, many therapists and interested laypeople have been concerned that prescribed drugs would become the quick fix for all problems, that any patient suffering distress would be given a medication to feel better with little regard to psychological and psychosocial factors. Would pills become a treatment for a bad day or problems with intimacy? Yet, despite the astonishing amount of press given biological treatments over the last number of years, the evidence is that neither patients nor clinicians are "medication crazy." As an example, in a recent large-scale study examining the types of treatments received by patients at major university medical centers, almost one third of outpatients with major depressive disorder received no antidepressants at all, while over half received either no or very small amounts of antidepressants (Keller, Lavori, Klerman, et al., 1986). Similarly, in a recent epidemiological study, less than one third of those with a DSM-III defined mood disorder had sought treatment of any type for their psychiatric problems (Regier and Burke, 1987). There is even evidence that only one quarter of chronically anxious patients use tranquilizers (Uhlenhuth, Balter, Mellinger, Cisin, and Clinthorne, 1983). Together, these studies suggest that we are far from being an overmedicated society.

Another concern of psychotherapists about the advent of medications was their implication for the etiology of psychiatric disorders. There is a natural assumption that if medications are helpful, they must be correcting some biochemical abnormality which would then be viewed as the sole cause of the disorder. Despite a remarkable amount of research over the last twenty-five years, however, there is still no definitive biological explanation for any psychiatric disorder (see chapter 2). Furthermore, even if a biological cause might be found for one or a number of disorders, it would not, by itself, imply the proper or effective methods of treatment. For example, coronary artery disease culminating in heart attacks has genetic and biological causes. Yet its course and outcome can be altered by life-style changes, such as diet, smoking, exercise, and the like. Similarly, even if depression were shown to be caused by a specific neurotransmitter abnormality, this would have no necessary implication for the efficacy of psychotherapy in treating it.

In summary, just as descriptive models of psychopathology, as exemplified by DSM-III-R, must be supplemented by other models to best understand our patients' problems, pharmacotherapy *never* precludes other methods of treatment. For some disorders, such as mild to moderate depression or obsessive compulsive disorder, there may be a variety of different, valid therapeutic approaches. As discussed in more detail in chapter 14, even with those disorders for which medications are the most effective treatments available, such as manic-depressive illness, psychotherapy is likely to enhance the treatment and help patients in ways not measured in research studies. Moreover, since there is no evidence that, when utilized together, medication and psychotherapy interfere with the efficacy of each other, combination treatment should always be considered. Because this book focuses on pharmacological therapies, it will often not discuss the use of other valid treatments. Nonetheless, it should be assumed that other approaches do exist and may at times be preferable to medications for specific patients with certain disorders.

## EVALUATING TREATMENTS:
## THE MEANING OF THE WORD EFFECTIVE

The application of scientific methods of evaluating treatment is the third important assumption inherent in the medical model approach to psychiatric disorders. An in-depth discussion of statistics is hardly necessary or relevant for this book. What is important, however, is a clarification of the use of the word "effective," since throughout the book statements will be made referring to a medication's effectiveness in treating a psychiatric disorder. At first glance, the meaning of the word "effective" seems clear—that the medication is useful in diminishing the manifestations of the disorder being treated. However, a number of questions about the use of this word must be addressed.

First and most important, how does this treatment compare to others? As already noted, the effectiveness of a medication does not bear on that of another type of treatment. For instance, the efficacy of certain antidepressants in diminishing the symptoms of obsessive compulsive disorder (see chapter 4) does not, in any way, negate the well-documented efficacy of behavior therapy for the same disorder. Similarly, the effectiveness of a medication does not bear on the potential value of other treatments administered simultaneously. In the treatment of schizophrenia, for instance, antipsychotics, although vital, are rarely sufficient for maximal response. A combination of medication with psychotherapy is likely to be the best treatment.

Another important question is that of assessment: how is effectiveness evaluated? During the twentieth century, and increasingly over the last thirty years, the hallmark of efficacy is that the medication has been shown to be effective in research studies using a double-blind, placebo-controlled design. In these studies, patients are randomly assigned to receive either the medication or an identical looking placebo. Patients and investigators are unaware of (i.e., blind to) the identity of the treatment actually received. In this way, the enthusiasm of the investigator as well as that of the patient ("I'm receiving a new pill that will make me all better") is similar for both the real medication and the placebo. If a drug is consistently associated with more improvement than a placebo in these studies, it is considered an effective treatment. For new drugs to be released in the United States, efficacy in double-blind studies (along with numerous other requirements) must be demonstrated.

The demand for demonstrating efficacy is far less rigorous when medications already available for one disorder are introduced to treat another. As an example, antipsychotics, long available in the treatment of schizophrenia, were used for years to treat patients with borderline personality disorder who were in crisis before double-blind studies to support this type of treatment existed (see chapter 7). Numerous similar examples exist, since a great deal of the psychopharmacological research done in the last twenty years has been in discovering new uses of already available medications.

The last important question is that of relativity: what is meant when one active treatment is described as more effective than another? As a generalization, this means that a larger percentage of patients responded (or improved to a greater degree) to one treatment compared to another. The magnitude of this difference may be relatively small (e.g., 60 percent vs. 50 percent) or large (70 percent vs. 30 percent). In both examples, however, *some* patients responded to the less effective treatment. (The inclusion of a placebo group would help evaluate whether the less effective treatment was superior to a placebo.) In a number of clinical situations, it is entirely appropriate to use the less effective treatment. If the more effective of two treatments has significantly more side effects, the less effective medication might be preferable. Furthermore, statements of comparative efficacy do not predict the response of an individual patient to either treatment since studies refer to groups, not individuals. Thus, a number of individual patients may respond better to the less effective treatment. The comparison statement simply states that a greater number of patients will respond to one medication than another.

Furthermore, even if a methodologically careful study demonstrates the effectiveness of a medication (compared to a placebo or to another drug), it should never be accepted as conclusive or proven. The recent history of medicine in general, and psychiatry specifically, is filled with carefully executed initial studies, the results of which are never replicated. There are a variety of explanations for this phenomenon, including subtle biases in the study design or selection of unusual patients (for instance, depressed patients seen at a university medical school may not be representative of the types of patients seen in the community and might respond to treatment differently). Despite the occasional story in the press, fraud is rarely responsible for contradictory findings in research. In general, any finding that is valid will be demonstrated in a number of different studies. Unfortunately, in their zeal for "hot" news, television and newspapers quote single studies as if they discovered the revealed truth. Patients who read these reports often look for this new magic. Therapists as well as psychopharmacologists need to help keep our patients from being swayed by these distortions.

Finally, the relationship between starting an individual patient on a medication (or any new treatment) and the resulting clinical response is not always as clear as it may seem. A patient's improvement may be due to one of three variables. First, the medication itself may have a pharmacological effect. Second, a placebo response may occur, defined here as improvement from any and all aspects of treatment that have no specific value for the condition being treated. Thus, a patient who is given a medication may improve because of increased hope, the magic of taking a pill administered by a societally sanctioned healer, or positive transference to a parental figure. This would be described as a placebo response insofar as the clinical change was unrelated to the pharmacological effects of the specific medication. A third variable is spontaneous remission. A variety of psychiatric disorders for which medications are prescribed are self-limited by nature, with or without treatment. As an example, major depressive disorder lasts an average of six to eight months. Thus, if a medication is started during the eighth month, it might be difficult to know whether the improvement seen was due to the treatment or the lifting of the depression that would have occurred anyway at that time.

## GOALS OF PHARMACOTHERAPY

Pharmacological treatments can be considered to have more than one goal. Specifically, medications may be prescribed to (1) treat an acute disorder, (2) prevent a relapse soon after clinical improvement, or (3) prevent future episodes of the disorder. These three goals or phases are termed acute, continuation, and maintenance treatment.

Acute treatment is used to alleviate the symptoms of an actively occurring disorder. When most people think of treatment as necessary, they are referring to acute treatment. A depressed patient is given antidepressants to alleviate the active symptoms of the disorder; lithium is prescribed to diminish the symptoms of an acute manic episode.

The goal of continuation treatment is to prevent a relapse into the same episode for which treatment was begun. As an example, the depressed patient who is given an antidepressant may improve over four weeks. Once the symptoms of the disorder have remitted, acute treatment ends and continuation treatment begins. If the antidepressant is stopped at this point, when the patient has only recently become asymptomatic, the risk of relapse is high. The analogy in general medicine is the standard recommendation to continue antibiotics after the cough of a respiratory infection has stopped. The cough may remit after three to four days, but the antibiotics are typically prescribed for an additional ten to fourteen days as a continuation treatment. For psychiatric disorders, continuation treatment is typically extended for many months. Recommendations as to the length of continuation treatment are slightly different for each disorder. These will be covered in the chapters on the individual disorders. Unfortunately, there is an astonishing paucity of research regarding the appropriate length of continuation treatment. Thus, the recommendations given will reflect clinical wisdom more than validated research findings.

Maintenance treatment is synonymous with preventive treatment. Because many psychiatric disorders occur in episodes throughout a person's lifetime, a decision can be made whether to treat each episode only when it arises (acute treatment), or to prevent recurrences by the ongoing, maintenance use of a medication. The two most common examples of medication maintenance treatment in psychiatry are lithium for bipolar disorder and antipsychotics for schizophrenia. In both disorders, there is an overwhelming likelihood of repeated recurrences. The decision to institute a psychopharmacological maintenance treatment is based on a judgment that takes into account such factors as the length of time between episodes, the severity and destructiveness of the episodes, the ease of treating acute episodes, the rapidity with which the episodes begin, patients' capacity for insight into the beginning of an episode (that is, can they recognize the warning signs so that acute treatment can begin quickly?), the potential toxicity of the treatment, and alternative preventive therapies. Thus, for each patient and for each disorder, somewhat different considerations apply. Maintenance treatment is discussed further in the chapters covering individual disorders.

## WHO SHOULD HAVE
## A MEDICATION CONSULTATION?

In deciding whether a psychotherapy patient should be referred for medication consultation, the most difficult problem is to elicit the relevant information needed to make the decision. Typically, the interviewing style in psychotherapy, in initial sessions and even more during the course of the therapy, is open-ended and nondirective. What is easily missed using that technique is the presence of symptoms that the patient is either unaware of or whose significance the patient does not grasp. In the past, the mental status examination, in which the patient's behavior in the interview setting was observed and systematically evaluated, was emphasized. To a great degree, this has been replaced by a heightened emphasis on obtaining an accurate history. With the current focus on longitudinal data (what symptoms are present and for how long?), it is less important (though not unimportant) to accurately describe the patient's affect in the interview or to distinguish between flight of ideas or loose associations than to find out how long the patient has been unable to concentrate or felt depressed. Thus, in evaluating patients for pharmacological consultation, the therapist may need to shift into a more directive style of questioning. The timing of these questions—whether in the first session or later—will depend, in great part, on the therapist's suspicion about the presence of a pharmacologically treatable disorder.

A series of clinical clues that are nonspecific with regard to diagnosis but that suggest the presence of the type of Axis I disorder for which medication might be appropriate are listed in Table 1–1. These items are broad-based and do not substitute for specific questions that are needed to diagnose specific disorders. Sample questions that will help diagnose specific disorders such as depression, manic-depressive illness, a variety of anxiety disorders, or schizophrenia are given in the individual chapters.

Most important among the general items that should suggest a consultation is the ability to describe the patient's difficulties using the language of symptoms, such as insomnia or fatigue, as opposed to psychological feelings or interpersonal interactions. Marital conflict, as an example, can usually be described only using interactive terms. Similarly, a personality disorder characterized by self-esteem and interpersonal difficulties is not easily described by symptoms. Axis I disorders, for which medications are most commonly prescribed, are defined by these

TABLE 1–1

*Clinical Characteristics That Should Suggest a Psychopharmacological Consultation*

Psychiatric symptoms:
    Sleep or appetite disturbances, fatigue, panic attacks, ritualistic behavior
    Cognitive symptoms, such as poor memory, concentration difficulties, confusion
    Psychosis, such as delusions, hallucinations
Prominent physical symptoms or significant medical disorder
Significant suicidality
Family history of major psychiatric disorder
Nonresponse to psychotherapy

types of symptoms. Therefore, the more the patient's problems or complaints focus on sensations or bodily feelings, the more a consultation should be considered. This is especially true when the symptoms involve cognitive capacities that have changed. Common examples include a new-onset memory disturbance or a diminution in concentrating ability. Psychotic symptoms, that is, those that involve a gross impairment in reality testing, comprise another group of important symptoms that usually require pharmacological intervention.

The presence of medical symptoms or disorders is another clue for consultation. New or recent-onset medical symptoms, such as headaches, abdominal pain, or clumsiness may reflect a medical or a psychiatric disorder. If the patient has an ongoing medical problem that has not been recently reevaluated, or takes medication and has symptoms or physical complaints, an evaluation, either by a psychopharmacologist or an internist, should be done.

Patients who are significantly suicidal are also candidates for psychopharmacological consultation. The most important reason for this is that the majority of people who commit suicide suffer from types of Axis I disorders (the most common of which is depression) for which medications can often be helpful (Robins, 1986). Second, with the medicolegal climate as it currently exists, if a patient commits suicide without having been evaluated (but not necessarily treated) for medication, the therapist may be considered negligent and at higher risk for being sued.

As will be highlighted during the course of the book, the types of disorders for which medications are useful tend to run in families. It is usually impossible to tease apart early environmental variables from genetic ones, since the parent who may have transmitted the genetic vulnerability is usually the same one who raised the patient. Nonetheless, a patient who describes mood swings that are mild but whose mother and brother have clear-cut manic-depressive illness is more likely to have a pharmacologically treatable disorder than is another patient with no history of mood disorders in the family.

Finally, nonresponse to psychotherapy might also suggest a consultation. This often takes the form of patient and therapist acknowledging that the work of the therapy has gone well—a therapeutic alliance has been established, the patient has gained significant insight into the source and context of his problems—yet the depressed mood, or the chronic anxiety, or the exaggerated response to rejection is unchanged. Certainly, an unsatisfactory response to psychotherapy does not by itself imply a pharmacologically treatable disorder, but it may be worth considering.

# SECTION
# TWO

# 2

## Biological Basis of Psychopharmacology

Understanding the brain and the intricate nuances of its function has been among the major goals of modern research. The ultimate hope is that greater understanding will enhance our ability to accurately diagnose and treat those disorders characterized by brain dysfunction. Until now, however, virtually all the major advances in psychopharmacology—the discoveries of the first antipsychotics, antidepressants, antianxiety agents, and lithium—have depended far more on chance than on a detailed understanding of brain chemistry that then led to the synthesis of drugs capable of correcting known abnormalities. Furthermore, in the thirty to forty years since the introduction of these original medications, almost all subsequent additions have similarly been based either on refining the already known drugs or on discovering new uses for previously available agents.

Why, therefore, should any therapist spend the time to understand the basics of brain biology? There are two important reasons: First, it is helpful for clinicians working with patients who may be taking psychiatric medications to understand the ways in which they alter brain function. To do that, some knowledge of brain biology is necessary. Second, in the foreseeable future, current research is highly likely to yield the fruits of new, more specific and effective biological treatments for the major psychiatric disorders. It will be important then for all clinicians to have at least a passing familiarity with this body of knowledge.

In this chapter, we will examine the ways in which neurons (nerve cells) function, the way they communicate with each other, how medications exert their therapeutic effects, and the role of the most important brain chemicals (neurotransmitters) in the regulation of mood and thinking. We will then briefly review current theories of the biology of the major psychiatric disorders for which medications are typically prescribed.

17

## NEURONS AND NEUROTRANSMISSION

In keeping with the variety and subtleties of its functions, the brain is the most sophisticated of our organs. Yet the billions of neurons of the brain interact with each other in rather predictable characteristic ways. The complexities are due to the extraordinary number of interconnections that work in synchrony, creating the possibility of graded responses. Clinically, this translates into a wide repertoire of cognitive, affective, and behavioral capacities.

The essential unit of function in the brain, as shown in Figure 2–1, is composed of two neurons and the physical gap between them, called the synapse (derived from the Greek work *synapto,* meaning "to join"). Messages are transmitted in this system both electrically and chemically. Electrical impulses travel through the cell to the axon culminating at the nerve terminal. Since electrical impulses cannot bridge the physical gap between neurons, further propagation of the messages is dependent on chemical messengers, called neurotransmitters. When the electrical impulse reaches the nerve terminal on the presynaptic neuron, it causes the release of a neurotransmitter into the synaptic cleft. The neurotransmitter then diffuses across the synapse where it comes into contact with the postsynaptic neuron via an area on the surface of the neuron called a receptor site. These sites are specifically structured to bind with neurotransmitters. Depending on the neurotransmitter and the specific receptor site, the postsynaptic cell is "instructed" to either continue the electrical impulse (an excitatory response) or to retard the impulse (an inhibitory response).

**Figure 2–1** The Synapse

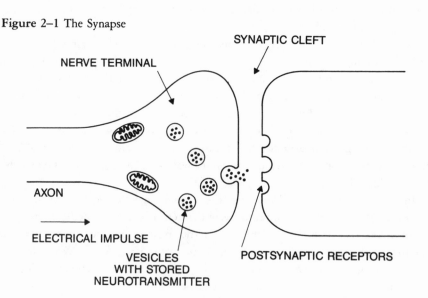

Once the postsynaptic cell has received the message, the neurotransmitter is inactivated in order for the cell to be able to receive new messages.

## NEUROTRANSMITTERS AND RECEPTORS

The brain utilizes a variety of neurotransmitters. Since new neurotransmitters are discovered regularly, their exact number will continue to change, but the list now numbers more than fifty (Hyman, 1988). Although different parts of the brain utilize different neurotransmitters, they are all synthesized, stored, released, and inactivated by the same general principles given above. Some are widely distributed, found over large areas of the brain. Others are found only in very specific parts, utilized in the regulation of just a few brain functions. As an example, the neurotransmitters that seem most involved in the regulation of mood, cognition, and sensory experiences (and therefore are the most likely to be disturbed by psychiatric disorders)—norepinephrine, serotonin, and dopamine—are each found in less than 2 percent of the synapses in the brain (Snyder, 1988). In these cases, it is helpful to think of neurotransmitter tracts, composed of groups of neurons all utilizing the same neurotransmitter and usually regulating a few specific functions.

Neurotransmitters can also be characterized as having predominantly excitatory (enhancing transmission of electrical impulses) or inhibitory properties. A good example of the latter is gamma-aminobutyric acid, called GABA, which is widely distributed but may have a very specific role to play in the regulation of anxiety and the mechanism of action of most effective tranquilizers (see chapter 11).

Neurotransmitters are synthesized within the neuron from precursors delivered to the cell from the outside. Enzymes within the neuron break down and alter these precursors, ultimately forming neurotransmitters, which are then stored in vesicles at the nerve terminals, ready for release into the synapse when an electrical impulse surges through the cell. Each vesicle contains from dozens to thousands of molecules of one type of neurotransmitter. In general, each neuron will contain only one type of neurotransmitter, although exceptions to this rule have recently been found (Bloom, 1985).

Once the neurotransmitter is released and affects the postsynaptic neuron, it must be quickly inactivated. This can be accomplished in a number of ways. The most important of these for understanding how medications work is called reuptake. In this process, the neurotransmitter is transported back into the presynaptic neuron where some of it is repackaged into the vesicles—recycled, as it were.

A receptor is the lock for which the neurotransmitter is the key. Receptors are specific discrete countable structures located on the outside of the cell. The neurotransmitter molecules fit into receptors specifically shaped to receive them. Once the neurotransmitter binds to the receptor, the message is translated either by changing electrical characteristics of the cell or by initiating some biochemical action within the cell. The biochemical changes are initiated via what are called "second messengers."

For any neurotransmitter, there may be subpopulations of receptors. These subpopulations are usually labeled by Greek letters and numbers such as alpha-one, alpha-two, beta-one, and so on. When stimulated, each receptor subtype will precipitate a slightly different effect. For instance, stimulation of beta adrenergic receptors in the brain will enhance neurotransmission via one of the second messenger systems, whereas activating alpha receptors will either have no effect or inhibit it (Janowsky and Sulser, 1987). A neuron can contain a variety of receptor subtypes for the same neurotransmitter. Figure 2–2 shows this. Additionally, receptors are found on both the pre- and postsynaptic neurons. The simultaneous existence of all these receptor types—some excitatory, others inhibitory, some presynaptic and others postsynaptic, with subpopulations for each neurotransmitter—as well as the multiple synapses that any one neuron may make with other neurons, reflect a system that is complex not only in the sheer volume of inputs but also in the competing nature of these inputs. Finely tuned regulation and the need for maintaining sameness despite a variety of influences is vital for the brain to function correctly. The final effect, then, is a summation of the individual influences.

**Figure 2–2** Receptor Sites

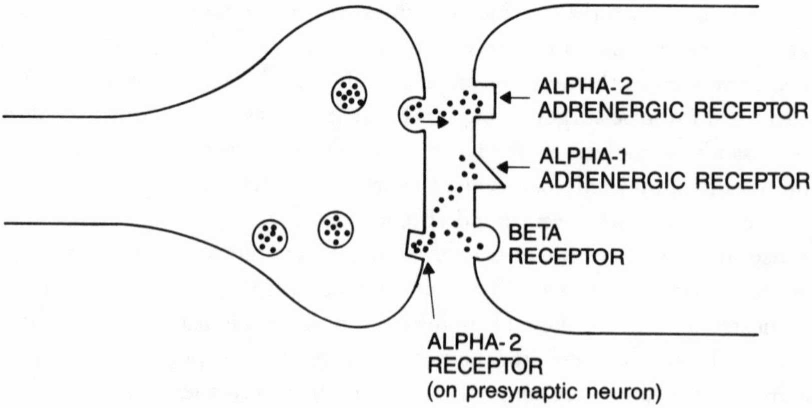

## HOW MEDICATIONS WORK

All medications discussed in this book work by affecting some aspect of the neurotransmitter/receptor system and not by altering electrical conduction. The mechanisms of action of currently available medications are explainable by one or more of seven different effects on this system. These are shown schematically in Figure 2–3.

The simplest way that medications work is by directly binding to the receptor site (no. 1 in Figure 2–3). If the medication mimics the neurotransmitter by stimulating the receptor, it is described as being a receptor agonist. Morphine is a direct agonist for endorphin receptors, causing a diminution of pain as does the naturally occurring neurotransmitter. Conversely, some medications, called receptor antagonists, bind to the receptor site but cause no response, thereby blocking the effect of the naturally occurring (also called endogenous) neurotransmitter. Antipsychotics, which block postsynaptic dopamine receptors, are examples of this type of medication. A second method by which medications act is by causing the release of more neurotransmitter, thereby functionally increasing the effect of the system (no. 2). Stimulants, such as d-amphetamine, work in part by stimulating the release of dopamine and norepinephrine. Further complicating the picture, some medications are partial agonists, causing some biological effect but less than the endogenous neurotransmitter.

Blocking the reuptake of neurotransmitters back into the presynaptic neuron (no. 3) allows the chemicals more time in the synapse, enhancing the possibility of stimulating the postsynaptic receptor. The effect is to increase the neuro-

**Figure 2–3** How Medications Work

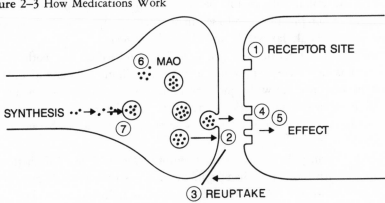

transmission. Cyclic antidepressants work, in part, by blocking the reuptake of norepinephrine, serotonin, or both.

Two other ways (nos. 4 and 5) by which medications may work are via their effects on receptor mechanisms. Antidepressants all cause changes in either the number of receptor sites (called down or up regulation for decrease or increase in the number respectively) or the sensitivity of receptors (i.e., altering the magnitude of response resulting from stimulation of the receptor). It is also possible to effect changes through the second messenger system. Lithium may exert its mood stabilizing effects by "dampening" the effects of one of these systems.

Altering the metabolism of a neurotransmitter will also change the amount available for release (no. 6). The class of antidepressants called monoamine oxidase (MAO) inhibitors exert their effects, in part, by diminishing the metabolism of a wide variety of neurotransmitters, all of which are metabolized by the enzyme MAO. Finally, the amount of neurotransmitter available could theoretically be altered by providing more or less of the precursor ingredients (no. 7). L-tryptophan is a naturally occurring amino acid that is metabolized into serotonin. Thus, ingesting large amounts of l-tryptophan might result in an increase in serotonin.

Focusing on one major biological effect of a medication and then correctly predicting its clinical effect, however, is rarely possible. One reason is that the brain's system of checks and balances works as much in response to outside influences as it does for the competing internal influences. Thus, taking a medication that blocks a neurotransmitter receptor—for example, taking an antipsychotic that blocks dopamine—will immediately cause an increase in dopamine release, as if the brain were trying to overcome the blockade by increasing the neurotransmitter blocked (Creese, 1985). Similarly, taking an antidepressant that blocks the reuptake of norepinephrine, thereby functionally increasing the amount of available neurotransmitter, results in the decrease in the amount of norepinephrine released in another attempt to provide sameness or homeostasis (Paul, Janowsky, and Skolnick, 1985).

Other than direct-acting agonists, how then can medications work at all if the system is designed to prevent changes? No single answer satisfies, but ultimately, it seems that with continual influences such as taking a medication regularly over an extended period of time, the regulatory mechanisms themselves are altered. Slowly, over the many weeks, a new balance between competing influences can emerge.

Another difficulty that confuses our attempt to correlate the clinical effects of medications with biological changes in the brain is that virtually all medications have broad-based effects. If medications were tailor made for the specific purpose we desired, instead of being discovered by chance (as all our basic psychopharmacological medication classes have been), we might have a "pure" drug that hits the receptors we desire and none others. Since this isn't so, our current pharmacopoeia consists of medications that have one desired effect but also a host of other unwanted ones. In the case of antipsychotics, dopamine blocking in the area controlling psychotic versus nonpsychotic thinking is wanted but the other biological effects, whether through dopamine blocking in other tracts or via interactions with other neurotransmitters, simply cause side effects. Thus, side effects can be considered to be due to the broad effects of medications and not central to their capacity to cause the desired clinical change.

## NEUROTRANSMITTERS THAT HELP REGULATE MOOD AND BEHAVIOR

Some knowledge of the brain's limbic system is needed in order to understand how and where the neurotransmitters exert their major effects. Composed of a variety of discrete sections of the brain, such as parts of the temporal lobe including the amygdala and hippocampus, the limbic system is one of the oldest (in terms of evolution) sections of the brain. The group of structures that compose the limbic system are all connected to each other and seem to form a circuit that plays a key role in the regulation of emotions (Snyder, 1988). It is closely linked to the hypothalamus, which serves as a coordinating structure for many different brain structures. The limbic system also has many connections to the frontal lobe, the area of the brain involved with speech and the coordination of feelings and perceptions. In animal experiments, alterations of function in the limbic system cause changes in emotional responses such as rage or calm as well as changes in alertness, memory, and sexual behavior. Human neurological disorders in this area are characterized by a variety of psychiatric symptoms often mistaken for depression or schizophrenia. Personality changes or peculiar perceptions, such as déjà-vu phenomena, are also commonly seen.

Dopamine, norepinephrine, and serotonin are the three neurotransmitters which seem most involved in the regulation of mood and thinking and for which there is evidence of disturbed functioning in major psychiatric disorders. (A fourth neurotransmitter, GABA, may be very important in the regulation of anxiety. Since much of what we know about the role of GABA in psychiatric disorders is linked to the mechanism of action of tranquilizers, it is discussed in chapter 11.)

Dopamine is derived from the amino acid tyrosine (available in health food stores), which is converted into dopa and then into dopamine. It is ultimately metabolized into homovanillic acid (HVA). Dopamine is utilized as a neurotransmitter in two tracts involved in thinking and feeling processes, called the mesolimbic and mesocortical tracts (so named because they connect the midbrain with the limbic system and the cerebral cortex, respectively) (Pickar, 1986). Two other areas that are rich in dopamine are the nigrostriatal tract that regulates motor movements and the tract that connects the pituitary gland with the hypothalamus. Dopamine blockers, prescribed to decrease psychotic thinking, therefore cause a number of movement and endocrine side effects related to their effects in these two areas.

Like dopamine, norepinephrine is derived from tyrosine. The direct precursor of norepinephrine is dopamine, while its major metabolite in the central nervous system is initialed MHPG (3-methoxy-4-hydroxyphenylglycol). Together, norepinephrine and dopamine are described as catecholamines (referring to an aspect of their chemical structure). Because norepinephrine is also called noradrenaline, pathways utilizing this neurotransmitter are called noradrenergic or adrenergic. The single greatest concentration of norepinephrine in the brain is found in an area of the brainstem called the locus ceruleus. Neurons in this area seem to be involved in the regulation of alertness, arousal, and anxiety (Snyder, 1988). The other major adrenergic tract connects the brainstem with a number of areas of the limbic system, including the part of the hypothalamus that regulates pleasure. Not surprisingly, there is much speculation that abnormalities in this area may manifest in mood disturbances. Norepinephrine also seems to be involved in the biological response to new stimuli.

As noted above, l-tryptophan is a precursor amino acid which, after one intermediate step, is converted into serotonin, properly known as 5-hydroxytryptamine (or 5-HT). Serotonin's metabolic endproduct is 5-hydroxyindoleacetic acid (5-HIAA). The most important serotonergic tracts extend from the midbrain into the hypothalamus and the limbic system. These tracts play a role in the sleep-wakefulness cycle, appetite regulation, as well as mood regulation. Low serotonin may also be implicated in a tendency towards violent behavior and suicidality without regard to specific diagnosis (Stanley and Mann, 1988).

## BIOLOGICAL HYPOTHESES OF THE MAJOR PSYCHIATRIC DISORDERS

Despite over twenty years of energetic effort, no biological hypothesis has yet marshalled enough supporting evidence to definitively explain any psychiatric disorder. (Of course, the same could be said about *any* model of psychopathology, be it psychoanalytic, behavioral, or cognitive.) What has precluded better biological hypotheses and more definitive answers has been the slow progress in developing the necessary tools of investigation, such as biochemical tests (e.g., measurements of various neurotransmitters and their metabolites, of receptor number and sensitivity) and imaging techniques, including the various types of brain scans. As our tools become more refined, so will our understanding of the biological underpinnings of some forms of psychopathology.

On the other hand, there is little doubt that disturbed biology plays a part in the vulnerability towards the major psychiatric disorders and that biological abnormalities are evident in the major disorders. Overall, the most persuasive evidence for the biological hypotheses rests on the twin pillars of genetic studies and the efficacy of medications in treating those disorders. Numerous investigations have confirmed not only that schizophrenia, bipolar and unipolar mood disorders, and panic disorder run in families, but also that genetic transmission specifically is involved to some degree. Whether the genetic contribution is investigated by comparing rates of disorders in monozygotic (identical) versus dizygotic (fraternal) twins, by adoption studies in which the rates of psychiatric disorders in families of adopted patients can be compared with those of the relatives of adopted controls (nonpatients), or by examining the rates of disorders in the families of patients, the evidence is consistent.

Similarly, the documented efficacy of medications in experiments that have controlled for the effects of expectation—double-blind, placebo-controlled trials—also adds to the weight of biological evidence. This is especially true for those disorders such as schizophrenia or acute mania for which no other modalities of treatment are consistently effective. It is not unreasonable to assume that the effectiveness of a biological treatment such as medication reflects the presence of a biological abnormality (although not necessarily a biological etiology—see below). This line of thinking is further strengthened when there is consistent evidence from a number of directions, all of which agree with each other. For instance, since drugs that increase dopamine cause psychosis and dopamine blockers diminish psychosis, a theory that explains psychotic processes by abnormalities in the dopamine system is supported.

However, examining the arguments just set forth with a critical eye reveals the shaky ground upon which the biological hypotheses rest. Yes, monozygotic twins are more likely to have the same disorders than are dizygotic twins, but the chances are never 100 percent for these genetically identical relatives. Even if the risk is 50 to 75 percent as it is for major mood disorders or schizophrenia, there is still the 25 to 50 percent chance that the twins will not both express the same disorder, thereby implicating other nongenetic mechanisms. Examining the evidence for efficacy of medications, one must confront the fact that placebo response rates for many disorders, although less than that for active medications, are virtually never zero. As an example, 20 to 40 percent of depressed patients will respond to placebo (Klein, Gittelman, Quitkin, and Rifkin, 1980). Furthermore, the rate of response of depressed patients to some short-term psychotherapies, such as interpersonal therapy or cognitive therapy, is significant, in some studies comparable to that for antidepressants (Elkin et al., 1989). Does this imply that those patients who are placebo responders or who respond to nonbiological treatment have a different disorder? Herein lies the weakness in extrapolating from a treatment response to a theory of causation. The observation that a biological treatment is effective implies very little about the "cause" of the disorder, nor does it preclude other modalities from being equally or more effective. Theoretically, there may be many pathways, biological or psychological, towards the same result—that of clinical improvement.

With the caveats just noted, it is worth reviewing the major biological hypotheses of schizophrenia, mood disorders, and panic disorder. Much evidence both supporting and contradicting these theories is integrally linked to clinical and biological effects of the medications used to treat these disorders. Further details on the medications are presented in subsequent chapters.

## Mood Disorders

From the time of the ancient Greeks, who believed that melancholia resulted from the biochemical effects of toxic humors such as black bile, and the tendency of mania and depression to run in families, thereby implicating possible genetic factors, it has long been suspected that mood disorders have a biological basis. The most important of the modern biological explanations, which dominated research from the mid-1960s for the next twenty years, is the monoamine hypothesis. Simply put, it states that depression is characterized by a deficiency of monoamines, the class of neurotransmitters that includes norepinephrine and serotonin, while mania is associated with overactivity. As so often happens, the initial evidence supporting the hypothesis derived from two observations related to medication effects. First, the two antidepressant classes discovered in the 1950s both functionally increase the amount of norepinephrine or serotonin, albeit by different mechanisms. Tricyclic antidepressants block the reuptake of the neurotransmitters, thereby increasing their availability to the postsynaptic receptor (see Figure 2–3) while the MAO inhibitors prevent their metabolism. Second, reserpine, used to treat hypertension (high blood pressure), was found to cause severe depression in some patients. Reserpine releases neurotransmitters from the intraneuronal vesicles where they are stored, thereby making them easier to metabolize. Thus, two medication classes that increase monoamines alleviate depression while another which decreases them causes depression. Although the initial hypothesis focused on the role of norepinephrine, it was also postulated that either neurotransmitter or the interaction between the two could be abnormal in mood disorders (Bunney and Davis, 1965).

From the late 1960s through the early 1980s, biological research in depression focused on evaluating the monoamine hypothesis. An early hope was that it would be possible to characterize depressions as norepinephrine deficient or serotonin deficient. Hypothetically, the former would then respond to norepinephrine-enhancing antidepressants while the latter would improve when treated with serotonergic antidepressants. Preliminary evidence supported this idea.

As is so common in research, the satisfying nature of the monoamine hypothesis and the early experimental research in support of its clinical applicability unfortunately represented a triumph more of hope and excitement than of replicable clinical science. Multiple methodological problems cast doubt on the original hypothesis and on the early supporting data. Additionally, the findings of the early studies have not been consistently replicated. In the largest study to date, measuring a variety of neurotransmitters and their metabolites, no consistent differences between depressed patients and controls were found at all (Koslow et al., 1983). In that same study, no evidence was found for the existence of subgroups of norepinephrine deficient or serotonin deficient patients (Davis et al., 1988).

Experimental findings aside, a larger objection to the original monoamine hypothesis focused on the time course of response to antidepressants. It may be remembered that antidepressants have the effect of functionally increasing the amount of norepinephrine, serotonin, or both, thereby implying a possible correction of a deficiency of these neurotransmitters. The functional increase in the neurotransmitters occurs within the first day of treatment with the antidepressant. Unfortunately for the hypothesis, patients don't improve with antidepressants for many weeks (see chapter 3). If simple increases in important neurotransmitters were sufficient to correct the presumed deficiency, why do the medications take weeks to work? Additionally, how do we explain the efficacy of certain antidepressants, such as bupropion and others available only in Europe, which have little or no effect on these neurotransmitters? In exploring these questions, it was discovered that antidepressants have different biological effects when taken chronically (e.g., over a number of weeks) than acutely. These chronic effects therefore correlate with the time course of antidepressant response. One such effect of antidepressants is that they alter the number and/or sensitivity of the receptors (Heninger and Charney, 1987). So far, it has not been possible to describe a universal, consistent effect of all antidepressants on one or a group of receptors. At this point, it is not even clear that the receptor changes caused by antidepressants are the mechanism by which antidepressants exert their effects. And if they are, the implications this has for understanding the core biological abnormalities of depression are also unclear.

Along these lines, much of the recent research has been to evaluate the number and sensitivities of receptors in depressed patients prior to treatment with antidepressants. Here too, the research is still preliminary and no consistent findings have been found that allow for coherent theorizing.

Although it has been an integral part of the hypothesis, the biology of mania has been relatively ignored. In part, this has been due to the difficulty in recruiting manic patients for research (they are not very cooperative for activities such as blood drawing and urine collections) but also because the effects of the medications used to treat mania, such as lithium, do not fit easily into the model. Additionally, whatever studies in mania have been done are not consistently in favor of the biogenic amine hypothesis.

Where, then, does that leave the monoamine hypothesis of mood disorders? With the benefit of twenty years of research and powerful hindsight, the hypothesis as originally formulated has more evidence against it than for it. No consistent evidence yet exists to support the notion of either a decrease of norepinephrine or serotonin in depression or an increase in mania. Even the likely mechanism of action of antidepressants, the cornerstone of the hypothesis, is different than initially thought. Yet, the evidence that *something* is awry in the amount or regulation of these two neurotransmitters in mood disorders is still impressive. It is also likely that there are multiple pathways, both biological and psychological, to the state of clinical depression. As one small example, destruction of serotonergic neurons prevents the decrease in adrenergic receptors seen with chronic use of antidepressants, indicating the interdependencies of two supposedly separate neurotransmitter systems (Janowsky, Okada, Applegate, Manier, and Sulser, 1982). This serves as a reminder that the brain is easy to understand when viewed simplistically using "too much, too little" concepts—but such models are wrong. A richer, more accurate comprehension will only come with a deeper understanding of brain biology and the development of more complex models of normal and abnormal states such as depression.

## Schizophrenia

The dopamine hypothesis has been the predominant biological theme of schizophrenia over the last twenty-five years. In its simplest form, this hypothesis postulates that the disorder results from a functional excess of dopamine in the central nervous system. The term "functional excess" implies that the enhanced activity could result from a variety of means, such as hypersensitive receptors, decreased inhibitory influences, as well as a sheer increase in the amount of dopamine released at synapses. As initially proposed, the hypothesis rested on two lines of evidence (Wyatt, 1986): First, amphetamines when ingested in large amounts ultimately lead to a paranoid psychosis, resembling paranoid schizophrenia. Also, some schizophrenics will show a marked worsening of their psychosis if given amphetamines. As one of their major effects, amphetamines cause an increase in the release of dopamine at the synapse, thus potentially linking the symptom change with a biological effect. Second, although their clinical effects were discovered serendipitously, antipsychotics, which are the mainstay of treatment in schizophrenia, seem to work by blocking postsynaptic dopamine receptors (see chapter 12). Furthermore, there is a strong inverse correlation between the capacity of an antipsychotic to block dopamine and the dose of the antipsychotic needed for a clinical effect. In other words, a medication that is a powerful dopamine blocker is usually prescribed in low doses (e.g., 5 mg) to be effective whereas a weaker dopamine blocker must be given in larger doses (e.g., 100 mg) for the same clinical effect.

These lines of evidence supporting the dopamine hypothesis, linking response to treatment with documented effects of the medications and understanding the biology of abused drugs, are powerful indeed. Unfortunately, much of the research investigating further evidence for dopamine hyperactivity in schizophrenia has been hampered by the biological effects of the medications. A great deal of investigation has focused on the levels of dopamine metabolites in the central nervous system, with the assumption that if an increase is found, it would support the notion of abnormal amounts of the neurotransmitter present. But if increased dopamine metabolites are found in schizophrenic patients recently treated with dopamine blockers, does this reflect the disorder or the lingering effect of medication? Similarly, it is now possible to count dopamine receptors in certain parts of the brain. Here too, it has not yet been possible to distinguish between the effects of antipsychotic treatment (which may change the number of receptors permanently or at least for a long time) and that of the disorder being treated (Martin, Owen, and Morihisa, 1987).

Even without these methodological dilemmas, other problems related to the dopamine hypothesis, both clinical and biological, remain. First, there is still no direct consistent evidence for dopamine overactivity in schizophrenics as measured in a variety of ways (Martin et al., 1987). Second, antipsychotics are effective in a number of clinical states (see chapter 12), not just schizophrenia. Third, amphetamines do not worsen clinical symptoms in all schizophrenics. In fact, some seem to improve (Van Kammen et al., 1982). Fourth, since antipsychotics block dopamine quickly, why does it take many weeks to see maximal improvement with the medication? Finally, a whole body of evidence and thinking has more recently focused on the possibility of *decreased* dopamine activity in certain parts of the brain, in certain schizophrenic symptoms or subtypes, or in certain phases of the disorder. The so-called negative symptoms of schizophrenia such as social withdrawal, blunted affect, and poor motivation (see chapter 5 for details) may, for instance, represent dopamine deficiency symptoms. This may explain findings such as the improvement of some schizophrenic patients with dopamine agonists, the lack of improvement of some patients with dopamine blockers, or the relative lack of response of negative symptoms to antipsychotics (Crow, Ferrier, and Johnstone, 1986). One could even postulate that a dopamine deficiency in one area of the brain responsible for the affective and cognitive deficits of schizophrenia could result in overactivity in a different dopamine tract in the brain through overcompensation or disinhibition, thereby explaining dopamine excess and deficit simultaneously (Weinberger, 1987). Clearly, our current body of knowledge cannot easily reconcile all of the problems in the dopamine hypothesis.

## Anxiety

The two anxiety states that have been the subject of the most intensive biological research over the last decade have been generalized anxiety—including both the nonspecific quality of anxiety seen in a variety of disorders as well as generalized anxiety disorder—and panic disorder. (See chapter 4 for a discussion of the different anxiety disorders.) Unfortunately, compared to the investigations into the biology of schizophrenia and depression, anxiety research is in its infancy. Therefore, even the most current hypotheses must still be considered tentative. Since the most prominent biological theory of generalized anxiety rests almost entirely on the mechanism of action of the benzodiazepine tranquilizers, which include medications such as diazepam (Valium) and alprazolam (Xanax), it will be discussed in chapter 11 which focuses on these medications.

From the early investigations in the beginning of this century, it has long been suspected that adrenergic chemicals such as epinephrine and norepinephrine play a role in the generation of acute arousal and panic. The symptoms of panic resemble those feelings triggered by acute fear or sudden excitement colloquially known as "the adrenaline rush." Clinical observations during World War I suggested that patients who in retrospect probably had panic disorder showed unusual sensitivity to injected epinephrine (Jefferson, 1988). Our current hypotheses may be more elaborate given our increased level of biological sophistication but agree with the older observations: panic disorder seems to be most related to a "dysregulation" of the noradrenergic system in the brain, causing a functional hyperactivity of the system and consequent symptoms of anxiety.

Most of the attention has focused on the workings of the locus ceruleus, noted above as the part of the brain with the highest concentration of cells utilizing norepinephrine as a neurotransmitter. Animal experiments have demonstrated that when this area of the brain is stimulated, fear responses are provoked; destruction of the locus ceruleus abolishes these responses (Martin et al., 1987).

Observations of patients undergoing panic attacks have, unfortunately, not shed significant light on the disorder itself. For instance, panic attacks are usually but not always accompanied by increases in heart rate, blood pressure, and skin temperature. Patients with panic disorder tend not to show heightened cardiac activity (such as high pulse or blood pressure) throughout the day although they may have more frequent intermittent rises in pulse during the course of the day (Shear, 1986).

A major focus of recent research has been the study of panic attacks provoked by external agents. A variety of pharmacological agents will reliably provoke panic attacks in panic disorder patients but not in control subjects. Surprisingly, epinephrine seems not to provoke panic. The most well documented panic-producing technique is the infusion of intravenous lactate, which provokes clear panic attacks in 70 percent of panic patients but only rarely in normal controls (Shear and Fyer, 1988). When patients are successfully treated for panic with medications, lactate no longer provokes attacks. Other agents that seem to provoke significant anxiety or panic are caffeine, yohimbine (a medication used in the treatment of impotence), and carbon dioxide that is inhaled in high concentrations.

Unfortunately, the mechanisms by which most of these agents provoke panic are unknown. There is some indication that a dysregulation of the locus ceruleus is involved. Moreover, most medications that block panic, such as the cyclic antidepressants (see chapter 4), decrease locus ceruleus activity. This provides some consistent evidence that the locus ceruleus may be involved in the genesis of panic. Direct evidence of abnormalities of the adrenergic system in panic disorder, however, is lacking.

As must be obvious from the above, there is no coherent explanation of the biology of panic. It does seem likely that a heightened biological sensitivity to internal and/or external stimulation exists in panic patients, although consistent proof of this does not exist. Thus, symptoms such as spontaneous panic attacks or phobic fear may reflect exaggerated biological responses in the noradrenergic system to normal stimuli (Heninger and Charney, 1988). Aside from our lack of understanding of the mechanisms of provoked panic, it is also not clear that these induced attacks, which provide much of the research data, are valid models for spontaneous episodes. Certain somatic cues during a lactate infusion, for instance, may trigger a learned anxiety response because of prior naturally occurring panic, and not because of the specific provoking agent, thereby making the exploration of the "cause" of the provoked panic attack spurious. As the research progresses, hypotheses encompassing the role of learning, using both biological and psychological constructs, will undoubtedly enhance the richness and validity of the models (Gorman, Liebowitz, Fyer, and Stein, 1989).

# SECTION
# THREE

# 3

## Mood Disorders

### DIAGNOSIS

#### Major Depression

The evaluation of abnormal moods, especially depression, is the most common reason for psychopharmacological consultation. This stems from a number of different factors. First, mood disorders are relatively common, having six-month and lifetime prevalences of 5.8 and 8.3 percent respectively in this country (Regier et al., 1988). Second, mood disorders are among the most pharmacologically treatable disorders in psychiatry, with extensive documentation of success for over thirty years. But the frequency of consultations stems just as much from the semantic confusion surrounding the word *depression*. Before this century, the term *melancholia* was used in a variety of ways, referring to the brooding aspects of character—"a melancholy person"—as well as to a number of different psychiatric disorders. To help remedy this confusing situation, Adolph Meyer, a leading psychiatrist in the first part of this century, suggested substituting the term *depression* for *melancholia,* with subtypes used to define the meaning of the term. Unfortunately, little further progress toward this goal has been made (Snaith, 1987). Now, eighty years later we have the same quandary as in the past, except that *depression* is used in the same imprecise ways as was *melancholia!*

Understandably, using one word—depression—in two separate ways guarantees both muddled conceptualization and fuzzy communication. The first and colloquial use of the term *depression* treats it as equivalent to or synonymous with the terms *sad, blue, down in the dumps, unhappy, miserable,* and so on. This use of

35

the term, therefore, defines a symptom or feeling state. The second use refers to the depressive syndrome—major depressive episode or disorder (MDD) in DSM-III-R—which is manifested not only by a mood disturbance but also by other signs and symptoms noted below.

Depression as a symptom (also called dysphoric mood) is ubiquitous in virtually all psychiatric disorders. Almost everyone who walks into a therapist's office is unhappy to some degree or they wouldn't seek treatment. The only possible exception to this are patients with mania and certain forms of schizophrenia and dementia, all of which are disorders in which insight is lost as part of the psychopathology and the severe disturbance may be unrecognized by the patient. Traditionally, antisocial patients (or psychopaths as they were called in the past) were thought to be guilt free as part of their core pathology, but more recent studies indicate that these patients frequently experience depressed mood, whether they view their problems as consequences of their own behavior and feelings or because of the unfairness of the world (Perry, 1985). All other forms of Axis I and II psychopathology (see chapter 1 for definitions) involve clear measures of distress or depressed mood.

If depressed mood, then, were synonymous with depression, virtually all patients seeking psychological treatment would be seriously considered for antidepressant treatment. Clearly, this is a foolish notion. In the vast majority of cases, antidepressants are useful for treating depressive disorders and not depressed moods. In this chapter, therefore, the focus will be on patients with major depression, since they are the most likely to respond to antidepressants. The other important group of patients to be discussed are those with atypical depressions who appear to suffer from chronic misery or other syndromes but who may still respond to somatic treatment.

Table 3–1 shows the DSM-III-R criteria for major depressive episode. Although patients with more than one major depression are described as having major depression, recurrent, in DSM-III-R, they are also commonly referred to as unipolar depressives (as distinguished from bipolars who suffer from both manias and depressions—see below). Implicit in the five-of-nine-symptom criterion is the lack of a pathognomonic symptom for MDD (i.e., a symptom or sign that is specific for the disorder in question, seen only in that disorder and in no others). The clearest way of using these criteria is to think of depression as a syndrome characterized by (1) an alteration in mood and (2) a cluster of signs and symptoms reflecting alterations in basic biological functioning (sleep, appetite, psychomotor changes) and subjective/psychological functioning (change in cognition, suicidal ideation, guilt, apathy, and fatigue) lasting two

TABLE 3-1

*Diagnostic Criteria for Major Depressive Episode*

A. At least five of the following symptoms have been present during the same two-week period and represent a change from previous functioning; at least one of the symptoms is either (1) depressed mood, or (2) loss of interest or pleasure. (Do not include symptoms that are clearly due to a physical condition, mood-incongruent delusions or hallucinations, incoherence, or marked loosening of associations.)

(1) depressed mood (or can be irritable mood in children and adolescents) most of the day, nearly every day, as indicated either by subjective account or observation by others

(2) markedly diminished interest or pleasure in all, or almost all, activities most of the day, nearly every day (as indicated either by subjective account or observation by others of apathy most of the time)

(3) significant weight loss or weight gain when not dieting (e.g., more than 5% of body weight in a month), or decrease or increase in appetite nearly every day (in children, consider failure to make expected weight gains)

(4) insomnia or hypersomnia nearly every day

(5) psychomotor agitation or retardation nearly every day (observable by others, not merely subjective feelings of restlessness or being slowed down)

(6) fatigue or loss of energy nearly every day

(7) feelings of worthlessness or excessive or inappropriate guilt (which may be delusional) nearly every day (not merely self-reproach or guilt about being sick)

(8) diminished ability to think or concentrate, or indecisiveness, nearly every day (either by subjective account or as observed by others)

(9) recurrent thoughts of death (not just fear of dying), recurrent suicidal ideation without a specific plan, or a suicide attempt or a specific plan for committing suicide

B. (1) It cannot be established that an organic factor initiated and maintained the disturbance

(2) The disturbance is not a normal reaction to the death of a loved one (uncomplicated bereavement)

**Note:** Morbid preoccupation with worthlessness, suicidal ideation, marked functional impairment or psychomotor retardation, or prolonged duration suggest bereavement complicated by major depression.

C. At no time during the disturbance have there been delusions or hallucinations for as long as two weeks in the absence of prominent mood symptoms (i.e., before the mood symptoms developed or after they have remitted).

weeks or more. It is unusual for a patient to exhibit all the signs and symptoms listed in Table 3–1. DSM-III-R requires the presence of only five of the nine symptoms to meet the criteria. But there is nothing magical about the threshold of five symptoms. Many patients whose clinical presentations are entirely consistent with a diagnosis of depression (by natural history, family history, response to treatment, etc.) may have a mild episode in which only four symptoms are present. For clinical work, the diagnostic criteria are guidelines, not rigid rules.

Because a patient can meet the criteria for MDD and still be only mildly depressed, DSM-III-R also has a depressive subtype called melancholia, which is a more severe form of MDD (see Table 3–2). The clinical picture of melancholic depression is that of a patient with discrete episodes of severe depression during which the mood tends to be autonomous—that is, impervious to environmental stimuli such that the person is not cheered up even when a usually pleasurable event occurs. In general, the closer the clinical picture fits that of melancholic depression, the more seriously a therapist should consider a psychopharmacological consultation.

Another more severe subtype of major depression is MDD with psychotic features. Patients with psychotic depression are usually profoundly dysfunctional and severely depressed. In its most typical form, the psychotic features

TABLE 3–2

*Diagnostic Criteria for Major Depressive Episode, Melancholic Type*

The presence of at least five of the following:

(1) loss of interest or pleasure in all, or almost all, activities
(2) lack of reactivity to usually pleasurable stimuli (does not feel much better, even temporarily, when something good happens)
(3) depression regularly worse in the morning
(4) early morning awakening (at least two hours before usual time of awakening)
(5) psychomotor retardation or agitation (not merely subjective complaints)
(6) significant anorexia or weight loss (e.g., more than 5% of body weight in a month)
(7) no significant personality disturbance before first major depressive episode
(8) one or more previous major depressive episodes followed by complete, or nearly complete, recovery
(9) previous good response to specific and adequate somatic antidepressant therapy, e.g., tricyclics, ECT, MAO inhibitors, lithium

Reprinted with permission from the *Diagnostic and Statistical Manual of Mental Disorders, Third Edition, Revised.* Copyright 1987 American Psychiatric Association.

are mood congruent; that is, the psychotic themes are depressive in content. The importance of making this diagnosis is that the presence of psychotic features predicts a relatively poor response to antidepressants alone and a better response to a combination of antidepressants plus antipsychotics or electroconvulsive treatment (ECT) (Joyce and Paykel, 1989).

A final depressive subtype recognized by DSM-III-R is seasonal affective disorder (SAD). Patients with SAD have depressions almost exclusively in the winter months that typically remit in springtime. These depressions are usually characterized by increased sleep, increased appetite, and feeling slowed down, not agitated (Rosenthal et al., 1984). Since SAD has a unique form of treatment—light therapy—an accurate diagnosis is important.

The criteria for depression are mostly self-explanatory. However, a few key points are worth highlighting. The most important is the DSM-III-R equivalence of sadness (depressed mood) and lack of interest (apathy) as the mood disturbance. If a patient is very sad, the notion of a depressive disorder suggests itself quickly. It is less obvious when the patient complains of feeling flat, distant, removed, or disinterested. Yet this is the most prominent symptom for many depressed patients. With further probing, these apathetic patients will describe the same depressive symptoms (sleep, appetite disturbance, etc.) as those who are sad.

The second important diagnostic point is the cognitive deficit of depression. Although characterized as a mood disorder, depression is also a cognitive disorder. From indecisiveness to poor concentration to feeling that one's brain is going at half speed, virtually all depressed patients have some change in cognition. Occasionally, this will be the presenting complaint. Therefore, if an indecisive apathetic person comes to therapy, the possibility of a depressive disorder must be considered seriously.

For the many therapists who are not experienced in interviews that focus on symptoms (as opposed to the more open-ended psychodynamic approach), the following questions are examples of how to elicit information needed to diagnose major depression.

---

Have you been feeling down, blue, or depressed lately? Does this feeling wax and wane a great deal within the course of the day or is this feeling present pretty much all of the time? How long has this feeling been going on?

Do you feel as interested as you usually are in activities that are enjoyable to you? (If you know what the patient likes to do, asking about that activity may be very helpful; e.g., Do you feel less like bicycling lately? How long has that been going on?)

Has your appetite or weight changed during this time? In what way? (If the patient lost weight, make sure it was not from conscious dieting.) Over what period of time did you gain (lose) the weight?

Has your sleep pattern changed? (If decreased sleep, is the problem getting to sleep or waking during the night? If the patient wakes up during the night, can he get back to sleep? What time does he wake up? If increased sleep, how many hours of sleep does the patient get? It is important to distinguish this from lying in bed awake.)

Do you feel physically slowed down such that you are really moving more slowly? Do other people notice it? (DSM-III-R requires observable changes, not just the self-perception of being slowed down.) Do you feel agitated or restless so that others might notice it?

What's your energy like? Are you tired most or all of the time?

Have you been feeling bad or guilty about yourself lately? Do you feel like a failure? What kinds of things do you feel guilty about? (Guilt about being depressed should not be considered. The content of the guilt is also a probe as to whether the patient has psychotic guilt, a consideration with treatment implications.)

Have you had difficulty concentrating? (Probe to clarify the patient's concentrating capacity—can he do his work, can he read, can he follow television programs?) Is it hard for you to make decisions? Does it feel as if you are thinking more slowly?

Have you been thinking about dying or focusing on morbid thoughts? Do you find yourself wondering if life is worth living? Have you had thoughts of killing yourself? (If yes, ask how specific those thoughts are. Does the patient have a plan? When? How?)

If you do something you usually enjoy, can you still enjoy it? (As with questions about interest, use an example from the patient's own experience.)

If something good happens to you, can you snap out of your mood, even if only for a while?

Is there a particular time of day in which you feel worst? When is that? (Make sure that the diurnal variation, if it occurs, exists on weekends *and* weekdays. Not looking forward to weekday mornings because you hate your job but feeling fine on weekends is *not* melancholia.)

---

## Bipolar Disorder

The other major mood disorder is bipolar disorder (or manic-depressive illness as it was previously called). By definition, patients with bipolar disorder have episodes of mania and depression. The diagnostic criteria for bipolar depression and major depression are the same. When depressed, however, bipolar patients, especially younger ones, are more likely to exhibit hypersomnia (increased sleep), hyperphagia (increased appetite), and psychomotor retardation, in contrast to the more common insomnic, decreased appetite, and agitated depressions seen in unipolar depressions (Caspar et al., 1985).

The DSM-III-R criteria for a manic episode are shown in Table 3–3. As can be seen, the diagnostic principles used are the same as for MDD; that is, mania is defined as a period of time in which there is an abnormal mood and a cluster of signs and symptoms. The major difference is that there is no time criterion for mania (as opposed to depression in which the symptoms must be present for two weeks.)

TABLE 3–3

*Diagnostic Criteria for Manic Episode*

---

**Note:** A "manic syndrome" is defined as including criteria A, B, and C below. A "hypomanic syndrome" is defined as including criteria A and B, but not C, i.e., no marked impairment.

A. A distinct period of abnormally and persistently elevated, expansive, or irritable mood.

B. During the period of mood disturbance, at least three of the following symptoms have persisted (four if the mood is only irritable) and have been present to a significant degree:

   (1) inflated self-esteem or grandiosity
   (2) decreased need for sleep, e.g., feels rested after only three hours of sleep
   (3) more talkative than usual or pressure to keep talking
   (4) flight of ideas or subjective experience that thoughts are racing
   (5) distractibility, i.e., attention too easily drawn to unimportant or irrelevant external stimuli
   (6) increase in goal-directed activity (either socially, at work or school, or sexually) or psychomotor agitation
   (7) excessive involvement in pleasurable activities which have a high potential for painful consequences, e.g., the person engages in unrestrained buying sprees, sexual indiscretions, or foolish business investments

C. Mood disturbance sufficiently severe to cause marked impairment in occupational functioning or in usual social activities or relationships with others, or to necessitate hospitalization to prevent harm to self or others.

D. At no time during the disturbance have there been delusions or hallucinations for as long as two weeks in the absence of prominent mood symptoms (i.e., before the mood symptoms developed or after they have remitted).

---

Reprinted with permission from the *Diagnostic and Statistical Manual of Mental Disorders, Third Edition, Revised.* Copyright 1987 American Psychiatric Association.

A severe manic syndrome is called mania; a milder syndrome in which impairment is less marked is called hypomania (i.e., "under" mania). The hallmark of mania is increased energy/activity. This energy may be reflected in a euphoric, expansive mood, by irritability, or by a combination of the two. It is helpful to think of someone taking amphetamines who can feel focused, intense, and good, or irritable, paranoid, and uncomfortable. As with major depression, the criteria for mania include physical, observable symptoms (decreased sleep, increased activity and talking), subjective/psychological symptoms (increased self-esteem, racing thoughts), and mixed symptoms (distractibility and poor judgment).

When a florid manic syndrome exists, it is impossible to miss; the person's energy is alternately infectious to those around him and exhausting, irresistible, and obnoxious. However, in its subtler form, hypomania, it is easily missed. The patient may simply seem to be functioning exceedingly well. If a switch into hypomania occurs while the patient is in therapy, it is easy to assume that the therapy has "clicked." Since virtually all manic or hypomanic episodes are time-limited, however, the period of high energy and functioning will end, and a depression will frequently follow. This pattern—cycles of expanding activities, new plans, and a spurt of self-confidence followed by a collapse of these changes—should make the therapist consider the diagnosis of bipolar disorder.

Patients will sometimes present with features of both mania and depression simultaneously, called mixed bipolar disorder. Intense dysphoria will be present along with racing thoughts, suicidal ideation with increased energy, depressive delusions with grandiose delusions. These states can be explosive and destructive—the combination of suicidal despair and manic irritable energy is a dangerous combination for suicide risk. In general, these patients are treated as severe bipolars; the first goal of the pharmacological treatment is to decrease the irritable energy and possibility of impulsive behavior.

Often, it is vital to obtain information from significant others in the patient's life to evaluate a possible manic episode. Because denial and lack of insight are very common in mania and hypomania, others may observe clear dysfunctional symptoms that the patient denies. It is impossible to overemphasize the seductive qualities of mania or hypomania. Manic patients can be wonderfully coherent for short periods of time and fool even experienced therapists. The use of outside observers (e.g., friends, family members) can be crucial for making an accurate diagnosis.

The questions that follow may help the therapist identify manic symptoms:

---

Have you been feeling much better than usual? Would you describe your mood as euphoric? Have others commented on how happy you seem? Is this the best you've ever felt? or, Have you been irritable in a speedy way lately, such that you've gotten into more fights than usual?

During this time, have you been feeling terrific about yourself? Did you feel as if you had special powers? (Ask about new-onset "creativity," or telepathy or a new ability to make people do things.)

Have you been sleeping less than usual? How much less? Are you tired?

Have you been talking more than usual?

Do you have the sensation of thoughts racing in your head? Does it feel like you are going at 78 rpm while the rest of the world is at 45 rpm?

Have you had trouble following through on tasks because you were easily diverted to other tasks or because you felt that there were so many interesting things to do you wanted to do them all at once?

Have you been more active than usual—doing more things for longer hours? Like what?

Have you gotten into trouble lately? For example, have you been speeding in your car, having more sexual affairs than usual, or spending more money than usual? (It is always important to compare these activities to the person's *usual* behavior.)

Have these symptoms or activities had a major impact on you, on your job, your relationships?

Have you been making long distance phone calls? Have you been buying lots of things you don't need or have you been buying more items than you need, like six pairs of shoes when you need only one?

---

## NATURAL HISTORY, EPIDEMIOLOGY, AND GENETICS

It is likely that the disorder we call major depression is heterogeneous in nature; that is, it is composed of a number of different subtypes, all of which share the same cluster of signs and symptoms. Because of the presence of multiple subtypes, it is difficult to describe accurately the natural history of major depression. Until recently, the mean age of onset for a first depressive episode was around age 40. Studies over the last few years, though, indicate that depressions are increasingly seen in younger people, with the age of onset approaching the twenties (Klerman, 1988). Classically, it was thought that the mean length of a depressive episode was six months. Here too, recent studies have altered our thinking, with increasing evidence that a substantial proportion of patients have episodes lasting one year or more (Keller, Shapiro, Lavori, and Wolfe, 1982). Additionally, 20 percent of depressions may become chronic (Keller, Lavori, Rice, Coryell, and Hirschfield, 1986). Approximately half the patients with depression will have only one episode in a lifetime (Coryell and Winokur, 1982). Those with recurrent depressions average approximately five to six episodes in a lifetime without preventive treatment (Angst, 1973; Grof, Angst, and Haines, 1973).

Bipolar disorder, on the other hand, is more homogeneous in nature. The major subtypes are generally called Bipolar I disorder (bipolar disorder in DSM-III-R) and Bipolar II disorder (given the misnomer of bipolar disorder NOS—not otherwise specified—in DSM-III-R) in which the patient suffers from recurrent hypomanias and depressions but never has manic episodes. In comparison with Bipolar I disorder, Bipolar II disorder has depressions equal in severity, but manic episodes of lesser intensity. The mean age of onset in bipolar disorder is the mid-twenties, with approximately 20 percent of patients having a first episode in the teenage years (Goodwin and Jamison, 1984). An average manic episode lasts approximately three months. All the possible sequential patterns of episodes—depression followed by mania followed by euthymia, mania leading into depression, mania alone, and depression alone—can be seen.

Bipolar disorder is almost always recurrent, with more than 95 percent of patients having more than one episode in a lifetime (Goodwin and Jamison, 1984). In one of the best of the recent studies, the average number of episodes for bipolar patients was twelve (Angst, Felder, and Frey, 1979).

Both unipolar and bipolar mood disorders unquestionably run in families. That is, in the families of both bipolar and unipolar patients, more relatives have mood disorders than are seen in the general population. The risk to the relatives differs, depending on the subtype of the disorder of the patient. The families of bipolar patients show a marked increase in both bipolar (Bipolar I and Bipolar II) and unipolar disorder. In the families of unipolar patients, the increased risk is strongest for unipolar disorder, less so for Bipolar II, and minimal for Bipolar I disorder (Rice et al., 1987). A possible explanation for these findings is that bipolar disorder is the most severe form of mood disorder (resulting from greater genetic vulnerability), conferring a higher risk for all forms of the disorder, whereas the milder unipolar type confers higher risks for only the milder subtypes. Earlier onset of the disorder is usually associated with increased risks in family members (Weissman et al., 1984). Unipolar patients with recurrent episodes are more likely to have relatives with mood disorders than are those with only one episode (Bland, Newman, and Orr, 1986).

## PRESENTATIONS OF MILD MOOD DISORDERS

There are three major syndromes that, although they do not necessarily meet the criteria listed above for either major depression or bipolar disorder, should cause a therapist to consider psychopharmacological consultation and treatment. These are dysthymia, cyclothymia, and atypical depression.

### Dysthymia

The core concept underlying the definition of dysthymic disorder is that of a low-grade chronic depression in which the symptoms are inseparable from what appears to be a personality type. Dysthymia has its roots in the depressive personality described in the past. Although DSM-III-R classifies dysthymic disorder as a mood disorder and not a personality disorder, this is a conclusion not yet warranted given how little we know about the disorder. The DSM-III-R definition requires at least two years of depressed mood most of the time with at least two of the following: (1) poor appetite or overeating; (2) insomnia or hypersomnia; (3) low energy or fatigue; (4) low self-esteem; (5) poor concentration or difficulty making decisions, (6) feelings of hopelessness.

These are the patients who frequently say they cannot remember a time when they weren't depressed, that they were probably depressed from the time they emerged from the womb! They complain of a chronic lack of feeling joy in living and perceive the rest of the world as being happier than they are. They often describe themselves as feeling they have a cloud over their heads. Despite this, dysthymic patients may be very successful measured in occupational and financial terms.

Many dysthymic patients also suffer from recurrent major depressions. This pattern, with the boundaries between dysthymic disorder and the major depression frequently blurred, is called double depression (Keller, Shapiro, Lavori, and Wolfe, 1982). There are surprisingly few psychopharmacological treatment studies on dysthymic patients. Most of the attention has been on patients with double depression, not on dysthymics who never have had a major depression. Whether this is because pure dysthymics do not seek medication treatment or because there aren't many dysthymics who never get depressed is unclear. As an example of the difficulty of finding "pure" dysthymics, in a recent study for which the investigators were seeking dysthymic patients, 96 percent of the patients who were ultimately selected were double depressives (Kocsis et al., 1988).

We can currently make two generalizations about dysthymia: First, patients with dysthymia alone (who have never had a major depression) sometimes respond to antidepressants. Since no validated predictors of medication response exist for treating dysthymia, an empirical trial of antidepressants may be the only way. A specific indication for antidepressants with these patients may be a lack of progress in psychotherapy, especially for those who are working well in the treatment, attaining insights and shifting cognitions, yet feeling no better in their mood or energy. Second, patients with double depression have a waxing and waning course to their disorder with major depressions that are comparatively shorter than those of classic depressives (Keller, et al., 1982). These patients may also be more likely to respond to antidepressants than pure dysthymics (Akiskal et al., 1980). When treated with antidepressants, some double depressives will show improvement only in the superimposed major depression (leaving the underlying dysthymia unchanged), while others will show amelioration of both disorders.

> From the time he was a child, Noah had always been quiet. When other children were boisterous, he sat well-behaved, rarely displaying age-appropriate animation. He did well in school, had a few friends, and attracted little attention. Through high school and college the pattern continued unchanged. Noah always functioned and had a few relationships, but a spark seemed to be missing from his life. As an adult, he became an accountant and achieved occupational success because of his intelligence, conscientiousness, and responsible nature.
>
> Noah first came into therapy in his thirties. By that time, he was married with children and a successful career but felt that his life was joyless. He could clearly experience pleasure, but the positive feelings receded quickly following a happy event. He brooded over problems and felt paralyzed at times in making decisions. On weekends, he took naps as often as he could, declaring that he was happiest when sleeping. He could see the parts of his life that were successful, but still felt inadequate.
>
> After three years of psychodynamic therapy, Noah was more aware of his feelings and the sources of his depressed mood, having explored his experiences of emotional deprivation as a child. His basic mood, however, was unchanged. A psychopharmacological consultant felt that Noah was dysthymic and was not very likely to improve with antidepressants, but acknowledged that there was a possibility of response. Noah ambivalently decided to try medication, quickly experienced a few side effects, and elected not to pursue pharmacological treatment. When last seen, he was planning to work with a new therapist who used more cognitive and behavioral techniques. The door to using medications at a later time was left open.

Like Noah, Ernie, now 60, had always felt a spark missing from his life. He was a successful businessman, having worked his way to a high management position in a large firm. His marriage of thirty years had always been conflictual, in part because his wife correctly felt he was resistant to any spontaneity in their lives. She was also resentful of the recurrent depressive episodes that Ernie suffered. Multiple times during his life, often but not always in response to an external stressor, Ernie would become seriously depressed with anhedonia, sleep and appetite difficulties, and fatigue. Twice in the past, he had needed to be hospitalized because of a serious risk of suicide. Ernie had been in psychotherapy for twenty years and had developed a significant dependency on his therapist. Yet neither his baseline dysthymic disorder nor his recurrent major depressions were altered with treatment. Eight years ago, during a hospitalization for another depression, a consultant strongly recommended antidepressants. Desipramine was started and increased to 150 mg daily. The effect on Ernie's depression was unequivocal—his suicidal ideation dissipated, he began to eat and sleep normally, his mood brightened. Because of the frequency and seriousness of his depressions, Ernie and his therapist agreed with the psychopharmacologist that maintenance, preventive treatment with the antidepressant was appropriate. Over the last eight years, Ernie has continued to brood and be restricted in his affect, but has had no major depressions.

## Cyclothymia

Patients described as cyclothymic have a disorder characterized by rapid and frequent bipolar mood swings—that is, they have frequent hypomanic and depressive periods. What distinguishes them from patients with Bipolar II disorder is that the depressions are neither long enough nor severe enough to meet criteria for major depression. As such, cyclothymia can be thought of as a clear bipolar disorder, but that does not fit our other diagnostic "boxes."

Cyclothymic patients, like Bipolar II patients, tend to lead chaotic lives. It may be easy to miss the cyclothymic mood swings and ascribe the cycles of mood and energy to narcissistic disturbances, or flights into health. The key point in distinguishing cyclothymics from patients with personality-based mood swings is the presence of clear behavioral signs of mania (Akiskal, Djenderedjan, Rosenthal, and Khani, 1977). Cyclothymics tend to have cycles with shortened sleep, increased spending, increased rapidity of talking, and the grandiose plans of mania which are then followed by a collapse—the hypersomnia, fatigue, apathy, and suicidal ideation of depression. Thus, the patient who spends excessively and compulsively constantly is less likely to have cyclothymia than the patient who spends in spurts and in conjunction with other typical hypomanic symptoms.

Cyclothymics frequently show excellent responses to pharmacological treatment. Treatment strategies are akin to treating bipolar patients (see below). Because cyclothymic episodes tend to be short-lived, the focus of treatment must be prophylactic, to prevent these rapid frequent cycles of highs and lows.

> When first seen at age 28 for psychopharmacological consultation, Judy complained of being tired of the chaos in her life. She had been in and out of psychotherapy for years, never staying in treatment for more than a few months. Family members, friends, and lovers had always characterized her as moody and unpredictable, descriptions she felt were accurate. Her usual self was energetic, active, and talkative. However, she described frequent episodes of what she called her "demons," a term she used with both affection and fear. During these episodes, she would become much more energetic than usual, having new ideas and often staying up nights organizing her thoughts for a career change. She would become absolutely focused on these plans and became enraged at anyone (typically her boyfriend or family) who wasn't completely supportive. She would spend hours on the telephone, calling old acquaintances, telling them of her ideas. After a few days of this, Judy seemed to collapse. She would be unable to sustain interest in the very ideas that had so recently possessed her. Although she was able to work, she simply dragged herself around, feeling depressed, guilty, and sleeping ten hours or more nightly. The depressive phases lasted no more than a week, following which she would return to her normal self and try to undo the damage in her relationships. It was at these times that she entered therapy, typically quitting during the next hypomanic phase.
>
> Following a recent episode, Judy saw a new therapist who elicited a family history of bipolar disorder and referred her for a consultation. Two weeks after starting lithium, Judy had another cyclothymic episode during which she stopped treatment. Four months and two episodes later, she restarted lithium. Although she had a number of cyclothymic episodes during the next few months, they were markedly attenuated in severity. Gradually, the episodes became less frequent. Judy then restarted therapy and worked productively and consistently on issues of relationships and self-esteem.

## Atypical Depression/Hysteroid Dysphoria

Although it is unrecognized by DSM-III-R, clinicians frequently recognize a particular subtype of mood disorder, usually called *atypical depression*. Unfortunately, since this is a colloquial, clinically based term, different clinicians have different meanings. The most consistent recent use of the term has been to describe a type of depression characterized by mood reactivity (the ability to be cheered up, albeit temporarily, by pleasant events), overeating (especially sweets and most notable chocolate), oversleeping, fatigue, and chronic rejection sensitivity (Liebowitz, Klein, Quitkin, Stewart, and McGrath, 1984). A postulated subtype of atypical depression is additionally characterized by depressive episodes triggered exclusively by narcissistic insults, usually romantic. Because these patients represent an exaggerated stereotype of the overly romantically preoccupied female, the term *hysteroid dysphoria* has arisen to describe these patients of either sex. A better way of conceptualizing these patients is to consider them as having rejection-sensitive nonautonomous depressions in narcissistic/borderline character structures. (Even if poorly named, hysteroid dysphoria is simpler to say!)

The importance of recognizing both atypical depression and hysteroid dysphoria is twofold. First, since these patients frequently are in psychotherapy for their fragile self-esteem and typically poor interpersonal relationships, and because their symptoms are clearly and inextricably intertwined with their personality disorders, it is easy to miss their psychopathology as a type of depression. Second, these patients often respond very well to monoamine oxidase (MAO) inhibitor antidepressants with a marked diminution of their depressive response to narcissistic slights (Liebowitz, Quitkin, et al., 1988).

> Eileen had always been moody and difficult. With friends, she was demanding and exquisitely sensitive to rejection. Slights such as not being invited to every social gathering would enrage her. When with her friends, Eileen had to be the center of attention. In her relationships with men she was intense and sexually seductive. Her tendency to idealize new boyfriends made her initially attractive to the many men she dated. Once in a romantic relationship, however, if she felt she was not being treated specially, she would become irate and belittle the men in ways that would confuse or more typically alienate them. At that point, they usually ran from the relationship, leaving Eileen with the rejection and abandonment she most dreaded. When this happened, she seemed to fall apart for a short period of time. Often, she would miss a day or two of work, spending the day in her apartment, watching soap operas

and eating junk food, especially chocolate ice cream. She would call people (including her therapist) for support incessantly during this time, seeming to derive some comfort from the sympathy of others.

By the time she was 30 years old, Eileen had been in therapy intermittently for seven years. She had become aware of the contribution of her early family relationships in creating her narcissistic fragility. Yet understanding more about herself and her feelings seemed to provide little buffering from her desperate fears of rejection and responses to them when they occurred. Her current therapist, with whom Eileen had a good relationship, suggested the possibility of medication as an aid to their work. The consultant prescribed the MAO inhibitor phenelzine, which Eileen found too sedating. Tranylcypromine, a more stimulating MAO inhibitor, was then prescribed. Three weeks after starting the medication, Eileen noted a decrease in her day-to-day moodiness. Over the next six months, during which time she stayed on the medication, there was an unquestionable improvement in her capacity to tolerate bad feelings in a relationship. Although she still felt like screaming at men she felt were not attentive enough, she was able to ask for what she needed without completely alienating them. This sense of mastery heightened her self-esteem and allowed her to deal with other painful issues related to abandonment in her therapy. Although her relationships were still far from smooth, Eileen and her psychotherapy had taken a great step forward.

## POSTPARTUM DEPRESSION

Just as the term *depression* has been blurred by multiple definitions, so too has *postpartum depression*. It is important to distinguish among the three common uses of the term, since the need for medical intervention differs among them.

1. Postpartum blues is a common (50 to 80 percent of all women giving birth) mild depressive syndrome occurring within the first ten days postpartum and characterized by rapid mood swings, crying spells, and a sense of confusion (but without disorientation or serious cognitive changes). The blues are self-limited. The appropriate treatment is support and reassurance that the feelings experienced are normal.

2. Severe postpartum psychosis/depression occurs in 2 per 1,000 births usually starting within the first month postpartum and frequently within the first two weeks. A full depressive syndrome may be present (although it

is difficult to evaluate sleep and energy symptoms in a woman who has just given birth) and psychotic features are common. It is vital to diagnose postpartum psychosis because suicidal and infanticidal ideation and acts can occur. Therapists should look for an inability to function, unusual feelings of worthlessness and hopelessness, suicidal or homicidal statements, or any psychotic symptom. This type of psychosis constitutes a potential psychiatric emergency; hospitalization is commonly indicated.

3. Mild postpartum depression is seen in 10 to 15 percent of women within six months after giving birth. These depressions look like mild to moderate major depressive episodes. Some of these women will do well with psychotherapy, education (about being a mother), and support while others need antidepressants in addition (Gitlin and Pasnau, 1989).

## MEDICAL DIFFERENTIAL DIAGNOSIS AND EVALUATION

The list of medical disorders that can mimic depression is very long (see Table 3–4). Therapists do not need to make specific medical diagnoses or recognize subtle medical problems that might be contributing to patients' psychiatric problems. It is important, however, to recognize when an evaluation is necessary. When a patient has a mood disorder, the following signs and symptoms should suggest a medical evaluation by an internist or family practitioner: (1) prominent

TABLE 3–4

*Medical Disorders That May Cause Depressive Syndromes*

*Central Nervous System:* Alzheimer's disease, brain tumors, brian abscesses, aneurysms, encephalitis, intracranial hemorrhages, general paresis (syphilis), subdural and epidural hematomas, epilepsy, brain contusion (from head injury), normal pressure hydrocephalus, multiple sclerosis, Parkinson's disease, Huntington's disease, stroke, AIDS

*Endocrine:* Hyperthyroidism, hypothyroidism, hyperparathyroidism, hypopituitarism, Cushing's disease, Addison's disease

*Vitamin Deficiency:* $B_{12}$ (pernicious anemia), niacin (pellagra), thiamine

*Toxins:* Heavy metals (lead, manganese, mercury), toxic wastes

*Intoxications:* alcohol, sedatives, hypnotics, tranquilizers, opiates, marijuana, withdrawal syndromes (especially from stimulant drugs)

*Metabolic and Others:* Remote effects of carcinomas, Wilson's disease, uremia (renal failure)

*Chronic fatigue and other postviral syndromes*

vegetative symptoms, such as weight and sleep disturbances; (2) no prior history of depression, that is, a first episode; (3) older age; (4) ongoing treatment for a current medical disorder.

Of the medical disorders listed in Table 3–4, the most commonly confused with depression are hypothyroidism, Parkinson's disease, certain cancers, chronic fatigue syndrome, acquired immune deficiency syndrome (AIDS), and disorders related to drug and alcohol ingestion and withdrawal.

Hypothyroidism is a low thyroid condition in which patients may look as if they have a psychomotor retarded depression with hypersomnia, weight gain, and fatigue. They may also have dry skin and hair and a lower voice. The diagnosis is confirmed by blood tests for circulating thyroid hormone (called T4, T4 index, or free T4 index) and the pituitary hormone that regulates the production of thyroid hormone (called thyroid stimulating hormone or TSH).

Parkinson's disease is diagnosed primarily by history and a neurological examination. Parkinsonian patients are most likely to be over 50. The most prominent symptoms are a tremor of the hands that is most noticeable when the patient is at rest but which increases with anxiety and disappears during sleep, and stiffness/rigidity affecting the whole body. These patients have marked psychomotor retardation. When they move, they do so slowly. Parkinson's disease can be confused with depression, and the two disorders are often present simultaneously. The common coexistence of these two disorders may be related to the changes in brain neurotransmitters inherent in Parkinson's disease.

Certain cancers such as pancreatic and some lung cancers cause depression far more often than other equally severe illnesses. Presumably, this is due to biological changes caused by the cancer. These cancers tend to appear in older patients who also show significant weight loss, breathing difficulties, or other medical symptoms.

Chronic fatigue syndrome has been increasingly implicated over the last five years as a possible cause of depression. Allegedly viral in origin, the syndrome is characterized by profound fatigue, muscle aches, and depression, and frequently begins with a typical viral syndrome (fever, sore throats, swollen glands, etc). Unfortunately, it isn't clear whether chronic fatigue syndrome exists as a discrete entity. There are no validated diagnostic criteria and no blood tests to confirm or deny its existence. Antidepressants may be somewhat helpful in treating this mysterious disorder.

As AIDS becomes more prevalent, it is clear that central nervous system involvement with the AIDS virus is both more common and occurs earlier than previously thought. Depressive syndromes, dementia syndromes, and a combination of the two are the most common manifestations. Weight loss, night sweats, infections, and fevers should suggest an immediate consultation, especially if the patient is in a high-risk group—male homosexuals or intravenous drug abusers—or has tested positive for the antibody to the AIDS virus (HIV).

Excessive alcohol and/or drug use, especially barbiturates and high-dose tranquilizers, can mimic depression. Taking an accurate history is, of course, mandatory; often a urine test for drugs can be helpful. It is *impossible* to evaluate an underlying depression while the patient is using street drugs and/or alcohol chronically. The alcohol and drugs need to be stopped for weeks to months before any evaluation of an underlying depression can be made. (See chapter 6 for further discussion.)

Withdrawal syndromes that occur after stopping stimulating drugs can result in a transient depressive syndrome. Of these stimulating drugs, the most notorious are cocaine and amphetamines. A good history is, as always, vital. As with acute drug-induced mood disturbances, the need for antidepressants cannot be assessed until the patient has been drug-free for at least a few weeks. (See chapter 6 for medications to help reduce drug craving.)

For mania, the most common medical mimics are hyperthyroidism and drug use. Hyperthyroidism is the opposite of hypothyroidism and is characterized by an increased metabolic rate. Hyperthyroid patients have difficulty sleeping, are irritable, restless, and may show poor concentration; they sweat profusely and hate hot weather; their hands tremble and they may lose weight despite eating more than usual. In a specific form of hyperthyroidism called Graves' disease, patients may have bulging eyes. The diagnosis is made by testing for the amount of thyroid hormone in the blood (T4) and sometimes by a thyroid scan.

Street drugs such as cocaine and amphetamine can easily mimic mania. The diagnosis is made by history and urine tests, if needed.


## MEDICATIONS CAUSING DEPRESSION


The list of medications that have been reported to cause depression occasionally is endless. But some medications are more likely to cause depression than others. It is most important that the therapist ask all depressed patients whether they are taking any medications. If the answer is yes, a consultation regarding that particular medication's capacity to cause depression is in order.

The medications most likely to cause or exacerbate depressions are antihypertensives (blood pressure medications). Many of these medications work by decreasing the amount or effect of epinephrine or norepinephrine. Since, as explained in chapter 2, norepinephrine may be important in the regulation of mood, predisposed individuals may become sluggish or depressed when given certain antihypertensives. The names of the most likely depressogenic antihypertensives are listed in Table 3–5.

Table 3–5

*Antihypertensives Associated with Depression*

Reserpine (Ser-Ap-Es)
Methyldopa (Aldomet)
Beta-blockers, especially propranolol (Inderal)
Clonidine (Catapres)
Thiazides (Hydrodiuril, Diuril, Dyazide)

The other medications most likely to cause mood symptoms, either depression, mania, or nonspecific psychotic thinking, are steroids, such as cortisone or prednisone.


## LABORATORY EVALUATION


No agreement exists among psychopharmacologists regarding the minimum mandatory blood tests to be obtained before antidepressants can be safely prescribed. As described previously, certain aspects of the patient's history may suggest a more extensive medical evaluation. For the medically healthy patient who has no history, signs, or symptoms suggestive of a medical disorder, a general screening blood test (an SMA-C panel, for example, or a Chem 24, which both include measures of liver and kidney function and of chemicals called electrolytes), a blood test for thyroid function, and an electrocardiogram if the patient is over 40, will suffice. The purpose of these simple and inexpensive screening tests is to ensure that there are no unrecognized medical problems that will either cause depression or mania or interfere with the treatment of either disorder. For instance, if the blood test indicated a subtle abnormality in kidney function, the use of lithium (which can adversely affect the kidneys) would be considered more cautiously.

A number of lab tests are currently promoted as being able to diagnose depression. At present, none of these tests has been validated as clinically useful in diagnosis. The dexamethasone suppression test (DST), which was used extensively in the early 1980s, adds little of value to a careful history. The TRH (thyroid releasing hormone) stimulation test has also been used to evaluate depression. Except in rare circumstances (patients with unusual subtle thyroid disorders), it is not helpful. Similar conclusions apply to the urine measurements of MHPG, the major metabolite of brain norepinephrine (see chapter 2), and the more recent computerized EEG (electroencephalogram) studies. PET (positron emission tomography) scans may be helpful in the future but are not currently. Certain abnormalities in sleep EEG studies may suggest depression, but the cumbersomeness and expense of the test rarely justifies its use in everyday clinical work. All of these tests are important windows into understanding the abnormal biology of depression and are appropriately utilized in research studies. However, none of them is reliable, valid, and inexpensive enough to be used in everyday clinical situations.

## PSYCHIATRIC DIFFERENTIAL DIAGNOSIS

### Depression

Since, as previously noted, depressive mood (as opposed to major depression) is so prevalent in patient populations, it is important to distinguish depressions for which psychopharmacological treatment should be considered from other dysphoric states. The three most important general diagnostic cues that can help make this distinction are (1) the episodic nature, (2) the tendency towards cyclicity, and (3) the characteristic genetic pattern of depression. Therefore, in trying to evaluate whether a particular patient has a disorder that might be treatable by antidepressants, a psychopharmacologist will focus on the timing of symptoms: When did it begin? Have you ever had this before? How many times? How long did it last? Are there particular times of year that you tend to feel like this? The psychopharmacologist will also ask a somewhat detailed family history that focuses not so much on the relationship between the patient and his relatives but on the individual characteristics of the family members. In obtaining a family history, care must be taken to remember the dual nature of the word depression: when a patient describes his mother as depressed, it is vital to know whether this refers to the miserable life she had with her husband, a chronic sadness but with normal functioning (suggestive of dysthymia or a depressive personality), or a pattern of discrete episodes of apathy, poor functioning, and suicidality.

Among the dysphoric states that, in general, will not respond to antidepressants are mourning, demoralization, personality disorders, adjustment disorders with depressed mood, premenstrual syndrome, and dementia syndromes (including Alzheimer's disease). These states can coexist with major depression, in which case only those depressive symptoms associated with the depression may be alleviated by antidepressant treatment.

#### Mourning

Patients who are mourning frequently complain of the same symptoms as those seen in major depression. Early in the mourning process, therefore, the distinction is difficult. There are no tried and true ways to distinguish between the two. It is generally thought that in mourning (known as uncomplicated bereavement in DSM-III-R), the preoccupation revolves around the person who has died with self-references focusing on the effect of the loss. In depression, the person becomes obsessed with his own feelings to the exclusion of thinking about the person who has died. Mourning also decreases in intensity after a number of months whereas depression may not. Finally, functional impairment is generally worse in depression. Mourning may evolve into depression, at which point treatment for the depression (i.e., with antidepressants) may become appropriate.

### Demoralization

The person in a state of demoralization has given up hope of improvement. This is frequently seen in association with a variety of chronic medical and psychiatric disorders. At first glance, it is easily confused with depression. The key difference is that demoralization is not necessarily associated with vegetative symptoms, but more with depressive cognitive distortions and attitudinal symptoms. Patients who become demoralized following a major depression from which they have recovered may present an extremely difficult therapeutic problem. Demoralization does not respond to antidepressants. Because of the similarity between the two disorders, however, an empirical trial of antidepressants is often necessary.

> John was a 38-year-old man who came for treatment of his chronic depressive state, which had lasted for five years. He had been a highly successful businessman in his twenties until a cocaine addiction eroded his judgment. During his years of business success, he lived in a grand manner and exhibited many features of a narcissistic character. His first manic episode seems to have been precipitated by his cocaine use. Over the next four years, despite his not using any street drugs, he had two manic and one depressive episodes by which time his fortune and his marriage were gone. After the second manic episode, he was started and continued on maintenance lithium. In the four years before seeing me, he had experienced a constantly depressed mood, despite continuing on his lithium treatment, supplemented by a variety of antidepressants, none of which were effective. He lived in a small apartment, subsisting on money begrudgingly given to him by his parents. His only attempt at working was interrupted by a manic episode during which he was hospitalized. This last episode humiliated him and he lived in constant fear of another episode.

In discussing his current state, John noted that he ate and slept normally and was capable of enjoying things, although not to the degree he experienced previously. He had no diurnal variation and could concentrate well enough to read novels, although he claimed to be unable to read journals relating to business. He could not imagine starting his career again at the bottom and building his way back up. He continually mourned his past—his financial success, his marriage, and his status—feeling that he would never be able to be successful again. He was additionally terrified that any attempt to work would precipitate another manic episode.

It was clear that John did indeed suffer from bipolar disorder (as well as narcissistic personality disorder) but that his current state was more consistent with demoralization, rather than a major depression. For John, the appropriate treatment at this point would be psychotherapy, along with his maintenance lithium. Had he not been previously treated with antidepressants (albeit unsuccessfully), a trial of antidepressants, despite the lack of vegetative signs, would have been appropriate.

## Personality Disorders

Patients with some personality disorders may complain of a constant and severely depressed mood that in the short run seems impervious to psychotherapeutic intervention. In general, these patients do not exhibit the characteristic symptoms (e.g., sleep, appetite, and energy disturbances) of a full depressive syndrome. The most difficult cases, however, are those in which the patient has both depression and personality-disorder-induced dysphoria. Chapter 7 focuses on psychopharmacological evaluation and treatment of personality disorders in greater detail.

## Adjustment Disorder with Depressed Mood

This dysphoric state is distinguished from depression by its relative paucity of vegetative symptoms, nonautonomous mood (i.e., the mood is responsive to events in the environment), and temporal proximity to the obvious major stressor. Similar to mourning, a disorder that initially presents as an adjustment disorder may evolve into a major depression.

## Premenstrual Syndrome

The most obvious feature of premenstrual syndrome (called late luteal phase dysphoric disorder [!] in DSM-III-R) is its relationship to the menstrual cycle. Since it is surprisingly difficult for patients to accurately assess their moods retrospectively, a mood chart filled out prospectively over two cycles is often helpful to ascertain whether the depressive syndrome varies according to the menstrual cycle.

### Dementia Syndromes

Dementia generally and Alzheimer's disease specifically have been the object of increased scientific and public interest as part of a growing awareness of psychiatric disorders of the elderly. One of the most important distinctions that must be made is between "true" dementia, such as Alzheimer's disease, and "pseudodementia," the reversible cognitive symptoms seen in depressions in the elderly. The features that help distinguish between depression and dementia are shown in Table 3–6. No single sign or test reliably distinguishes between the two disorders. When dementia and depression coexist, as occurs in 10 to 20 percent of cases of Alzheimer's disease (Wragg and Jeste, 1989), the correct diagnosis is particularly difficult. If diagnostic doubt still remains after a thorough evaluation, as is common, most psychopharmacologists would elect to treat patients as if they were depressed, since withholding treatment for a treatable disorder (depression) will cause more suffering than treating the untreatable disorder. Therefore, until treatments for Alzheimer's disease are comparable in efficacy to those for depression, the disorder should be first treated as depression.

## Mania

A personality type recognized earlier in the century but not described in more recent texts is that of hyperthymic (or hypomanic) personality in which the symptoms of mania exist as personality attributes. These people are the pro-

TABLE 3–6

*Differentiating Pseudodementia (of Depression) from Dementia*

| Depression | Dementia |
| --- | --- |
| Past personal history of depression | No past personal history of depression |
| Family history of depression | Family history of dementia |
| Vegetative signs prominent (sleep and appetite disturbance) | Cognitive deficits out of proportion to vegetative signs |
| Diurnal variation (symptoms worse in morning) | Sundowning (symptoms worse in the evening) |
| Gives up easily during cognitive testing | Attempts to cover up deficits during cognitive testing |

verbial used car salesman types—talkative, bombastic, grandiose, optimistic, and cheerful. Since there is no research on these patients, it is unclear whether this represents a personality type or a subsyndromal mania.

The other personality types that look like bipolar disorder are the chaotic personality disorders—histrionic, narcissistic, borderline, and antisocial types in which "bipolar" (i.e., high and low) mood swings are typical. As with distinguishing misery from depression, the most difficult cases are those in which a chaotic personality *and* a bipolar disorder coexist. Chapter 7 examines this issue in greater detail.

Describing the characteristics of happiness in order to distinguish it from hypomania may seem peculiar. Yet the question arises frequently, especially in the ongoing treatment of bipolar patients. Most typically, the patients' spouse will call the therapist complaining that the patient is exhibiting signs of hypomania. The patient will then angrily deny it, blaming the spouse for not wanting him to be happy. Table 3–7 lists some ways to distinguish between the two states.

> Barbara was a 29-year-old married woman with a clear history of bipolar disorder. Prior to a course of maintenance lithium therapy, she had a number of very severe depressions, one manic and one hypomanic episode, and many short-lived mood swings. During her manic episode, which occurred in September, she left her husband and moved to a different city, citing marital discontent. After the episode resolved, she returned to the marriage. During the hypomania, which also occurred in September two years after the mania, marital relations were severely strained but no separation ensued. Barbara started lithium treatment in January of the next year and initially did well, with a clear diminution

TABLE 3–7

*Distinguishing Hypomania from Happiness*

| Hypomania | Happiness |
| --- | --- |
| Cheerfulness switches easily to irritability when the person is crossed | Mood is even and not so easily perturbed |
| Drivenness in energy | Able to settle down |
| Less sleep than normal | Full night's sleep |
| Grandiosity leading to poor judgment | Good judgment |
| Frequently preceded by or followed by depression, usually of psychomotor retarded hypersomnic type | No predictable relationship to depression |
| Typically cyclical, frequently timed to a specific time of year | Generally not seasonal |

of her short mood swings. In September, nine months after starting lithium, she became increasingly dissatisfied with her marriage, pointing to a number of problems which, she correctly pointed out, had existed for many years. She made plans to move to a different city, insisting that the relationship was untenable and she could never be happy with her husband. At this time, she was compliant with lithium, slept seven hours a night, denied racing thoughts, and showed no obvious signs of mania. Because this marital crisis occurred in September, Barbara's husband was concerned that the problems were due to another hypomanic episode, a conclusion that understandably infuriated her. Because of logistical problems, Barbara did not plan to move until February. By January, however, her anger had substantially dissipated and she abandoned her plans for separation. The quality of the marriage returned to its baseline. By February, she felt strongly that she had experienced a mild hypomania (which had been partially muted by the lithium) during which her dissatisfactions with the marriage were fueled by a manic irritability and anger. She has had no subsequent hypomanias in the last three years and the marriage has continued as before.

## PSYCHOPHARMACOLOGICAL TREATMENT

The large number of medications available for treating mood disorders is impressive—thirteen cyclic antidepressants, three MAO inhibitors, three mood stabilizers, electroconvulsive therapy, and more. Yet this broad range of options masks the fact that the "correct" treatment in any clinical situation is rarely clear. For some clinical problems there may be one, or at most a few, rational treatment options; for example, when a bipolar patient on an antidepressant becomes acutely manic, the only reasonable initial approach would be to stop the antidepressant. But for other clinical situations, a variety of alternatives may be equally valid, with the choice of one medication over another based on the nuances of that particular situation; for instance, a first major depressive episode can be treated with any of the cyclic antidepressants with equal likelihood of success.

Moreover, since the diagnosis of depression is often difficult, especially in its milder forms or when it coexists with another source of depressed mood (e.g., dysthymia or many personality disorders), medication is often suggested by the process of exclusion. That is, since other therapeutic strategies have been unsuccessful, medication is utilized, sometimes as a last resort. The strength of conviction that the disorder being treated is indeed a depression—regardless of whatever other disorders may also exist—often determines the extent or aggressiveness of the medication trial. If the first two trials of cyclic antidepressants have been cut short because of side effects, should a third be tried? Should combination treatments be utilized (see below)? As with the choice of initial treatment, these questions can only be answered using the specific circumstances of each clinical situation.

In the organization of this section, the treatments for unipolar and bipolar disorders are separated. Although the symptoms of unipolar and bipolar depression are phenomenologically similar and the therapeutic options are identical, the "drug decision trees" for these two major types of depression differ. This stems from two clinical observations: First, bipolar and unipolar depressives differ somewhat in their response to mood stabilizers (see below). Second, and more important, antidepressants have the potentially adverse effects of causing mania or rapid cycling in bipolar patients, a risk not shared by unipolars.

## Acute Treatment of Major Depression (Unipolar Depression)

Table 3–8 shows the broad classes of psychopharmacological treatment options for an acute depressive episode.

### Cyclic Antidepressants

For the majority of patients, the first line of treatment will be one of the tricyclic or newer heterocyclic antidepressants. Since, as discussed in more detail in chapter 9, the number of rings (three for tricyclics or other than three for the heterocyclics) does not determine efficacy, in this chapter tricyclic and heterocyclic antidepressants will be discussed together under the general class of cyclic antidepressants. All the cyclic antidepressants are equally effective in *groups* of depressed patients, with approximately 70 percent of patients showing marked improvement in controlled studies (Baldessarini, 1989). Thus, the questions "which is the strongest antidepressant?" and "which is the mildest antidepressant?" are unanswerable. Efficacy is equivalent; the medications differ

TABLE 3–8

*Psychopharmacological Treatment Options for Depression*

Tricyclic and heterocyclic antidepressants
Monoamine oxidase inhibitors
Lithium (and other mood stabilizers)
Electroconvulsive therapy (ECT)

primarily in their side effect profiles. Sometimes, patients (and clinicians) tend to equate bothersomeness of side effects with efficacy, so that a very sedating medication will be thought of as more powerful, or an antidepressant well tolerated will be considered mild. The capacity to cause side effects does not correlate with efficacy. If any generalization is appropriate, it is that the more powerful the side effects, the less likely it is that the patient will comply with treatment. Decreased efficacy will then ensue.

Table 3–9 shows the major factors that are considered in deciding which cyclic antidepressant to prescribe. Current clinical psychopharmacological strategies are still based more on practical and historical variables than on theoretical or laboratory considerations. Thus, the most important consideration in choosing a cyclic antidepressant is the history of past response. One exception to this rule might be if the link between the past treatment and the remission of a prior episode is unclear. For instance, a patient who "responded" to imipramine after one day is likely to have had a placebo response, while improvement six months after beginning an antidepressant suggests a spontaneous remission (see chapter 1 for further discussion). Another exception might be made if the past successful treatment caused significant side effects. As an example, a patient's depressive episode seven years ago may have responded to amitriptyline (Elavil) but with sedation as a very unpleasant side effect. In that case, the current episode might be best treated with an antidepressant that is chemically similar to amitriptyline (trying to repeat its therapeutic effect) but which is less sedating—such as nortriptyline.

It is unusual for a psychopharmacologist to have the luxury of knowing that a close relative of the patient has responded well to a specific medication for the same depressive syndrome, but if this information is available, it should be considered strongly. The research evidence for this approach is sparse but a great deal of common sense suggests it highly.

In most situations, though, the choice of one cyclic antidepressant over the others will rest primarily on side effect considerations. Noncompliance to med-

TABLE 3–9

*Factors Used in Choosing a Specific Cyclic Antidepressant*

History of past response
Family history of response
Side effect profile
Safety/medical considerations
Neurotransmitter specificity
Blood level considerations
Cost

ication regimens is startlingly high for both psychiatric and nonpsychiatric treatments (see chapter 14), and side effects are a major (although not *the* major) cause of noncompliance. The appropriate strategy, then, is to find a medication the patient can and will tolerate at sufficiently high dose for a sufficiently long time to cause a positive clinical response. Since all antidepressants have potential side effects and are equally effective, the psychopharmacologist's task is to ascertain the side effects that will be most disruptive *for that particular patient,* and then choose an antidepressant that is least likely to cause them (see Chapter 9 for details on side effects of specific antidepressants). Examples of this approach would be:

1. A 54-year-old trial lawyer might well find dry mouth a great liability. Therefore if some sedation is needed (because of insomnia and agitation), trazodone (Desyrel), a sedating antidepressant that rarely causes dry mouth, might be preferable to doxepin (Sinequan), which is equally sedating but far more drying.
2. For a 27-year-old dancer, weight gain would be far more distressing than a dry mouth would. Fluoxetine (Prozac), which is least likely among the cyclic antidepressants to cause weight gain, might therefore be the treatment of choice.
3. A 70-year-old retiree with postural unsteadiness and poor balance from arthritis and other causes is at high risk to fall if he is on a medication that causes postural hypotension (a drop in blood pressure upon standing up). An appropriate initial choice for treatment might be nortriptyline (Pamelor, Aventyl), which is far less hypotensive than imipramine (Tofranil) but is otherwise similar in side effect profile.

Naturally, this approach, logical though it may be, does not always work. The dancer may not gain weight on fluoxetine, but if she becomes unmanageably tremulous and insomnic, a different antidepressant may need to be prescribed. The trial lawyer may find trazodone too sedating and need to be switched to a less sedating antidepressant that has slightly greater drying properties.

The different capacities of the cyclic antidepressants to cause or interact with medical conditions is also important. Trazodone may cause increased premature heart beats; for patients with normal hearts, this is probably irrelevant. For a patient with a history of premature beats, the psychopharmacologist may decide to pick a different medication.

Lethality in overdose is sometimes a consideration in antidepressant choice. Trazodone, fluoxetine, and bupropion are less lethal in overdose than the other cyclic antidepressants. However, if the possibility of overdose is high, hospitalization should be given serious consideration, regardless of the medication's safety.

At one time, it was thought that it might be possible to subtype depressions as norepinephrine-deficient or serotonin-deficient. (See chapter 2 for a review of neurotransmitters and biological theories of depression.) The choice of medication could then be based on the different capacities of each antidepressant to enhance norepinephrine or serotonin to increase the neurotransmitter that was abnormally low. This approach ultimately was demonstrated to be clinically not viable. Nonetheless, patients who fail to respond to a norepinephrine-active antidepressant (see Table 9–2), should not be given a second cyclic antidepressant with the same neurotransmitter effect. Thus, if desipramine, which is norepinephrine-specific, is ineffective, and a second cyclic antidepressant is prescribed, trazodone (which has specific effects on serotonin) would be a more logical next agent than maprotiline which is similar to desipramine in its neurotransmitter effects.

The relationship between blood levels of most cyclic antidepressants and therapeutic response is inconsistent (see chapter 9 for details). Only three of the cyclic antidepressants—imipramine, nortriptyline, and desipramine—show any consistent correlation between blood level and efficacy. If a patient does not improve while taking one of these three medications, measuring the blood level can tell the psychiatrist whether the patient metabolizes medications very quickly (and thus needs higher doses) or is on too much medication with the possibility that a lower dose would help. One of these three antidepressants might therefore be prescribed if the patient is likely to be treatment resistant so that the dose can be adjusted more accurately. Because blood levels of antidepressants are *not* always helpful (since for most antidepressants the range of therapeutic values has not been established), they are not drawn routinely.

Finally, medication cost is an occasional factor in antidepressant choice. This may be especially true with the newer medications which tend to be more expensive than the older ones.

### Monoamine Oxidase (MAO) Inhibitors

Although prescribed far less commonly than the cyclic antidepressants, MAO inhibitors are used with increasing frequency. Both patients and mental health professionals who are unfamiliar with MAO inhibitors tend to view them as strange and dangerous drugs, to be prescribed only in emergent and desperate situations in which the risks of these medications are warranted. The risks of hypertensive reactions with MAO inhibitors are real and worthy of detailed explanation and concern (see chapter 9 for details). Yet with proper patient preparation, these medications are no more dangerous than the cyclic antidepressants. The lore of the MAO inhibitors' danger stems from the 1960s, before the cause of the hypertensive reactions (ingestion of tyramine-containing foods) was known. Without the basic dietary restrictions necessary with these medications, a number of patients during that time had strokes and died. At that time, both psychiatrists and patients appropriately viewed MAO inhibitors as dangerous. Today, it is simply not true. A psychiatrist knowledgeable about these medications treating a reasonably cooperative patient is a safe combination that confers few special risks.

Our ability to predict response to one class of antidepressants compared with the other is in its infancy and no well-validated predictors exist. Table 3–10 lists the reasons a psychopharmacologist might consider prescribing an MAO inhibitor.

As with the cyclic antidepressants, a history of past or family response should be given consideration in favor of MAO inhibitors. The most common reason MAO inhibitors are prescribed is nonresponse to cyclic antidepressants. Typically, no more than two full trials of cyclic antidepressants are given before an MAO inhibitor is prescribed. Some psychopharmacologists, myself included, will prescribe an MAO inhibitor if a patient does not respond to one cyclic antidepressant at adequate dose for six weeks. Anecdotally, and in uncontrolled trials (since so few controlled treatment studies on this topic exist), a significant proportion of cyclic antidepressant nonresponders will show a clear response to MAO inhibitors (McGrath, Stewart, Harrison, and Quitkin, 1987).

Patients with one of two depressive subtypes may show a preferential response to MAO inhibitors. One is atypical depression and its subtype, hysteroid dysphoria (discussed earlier in this chapter). A related group, those depressed patients who show marked interpersonal sensitivity, may also respond well to MAO inhibitors (Davidson, Giller, Zizook, and Overall, 1988). The other subtype consists of patients with a mixed panic disorder and depression. For these patients, cyclic antidepressants may be helpful but there are suggestions in controlled studies that MAO inhibitors may be more effective (Kayser et al., 1988).

TABLE 3–10

*Factors Used in Deciding to Prescribe a*
*Monoamine Oxidase Inhibitor*

History of past response
Family history of response
Nonresponse to a cyclic antidepressant
Mixed panic disorder and depression
Atypical depression; hysteroid dysphoria (or
    marked interpersonal sensitivity)

When choosing between the three MAO inhibitors for treating depression (see Table 9–8), the choice of medication rests on clinical lore and side effect considerations. Chapter 9 details the differences among these three medications.

### Lithium

Lithium is occasionally prescribed for acute unipolar depression. However, it is clearly not the equal of the cyclic antidepressants or the MAO inhibitors in this regard (Jefferson, Greist, Ackerman, and Carroll, 1987). Despite this, there are two clinical situations in which lithium is considered to treat an acute unipolar depression: When patients present with a history of hypersomnic, hyperphagic depressions—the type that are more typically seen with bipolar depression—and have family histories of bipolar disorder, one may hypothesize that these patients have an unexpressed bipolar disorder, that is, they are genetically bipolar but have not yet had a first manic episode. This type of patient might respond to lithium as a bipolar depressive would, with some reasonable chance of clinical response. Lithium may also be considered when patients do not respond to cyclic or MAO inhibitor antidepressants.

The other mood stabilizers used in treating bipolar disorder, carbamazepine and sodium valproate, are similarly prescribed for acute unipolar depression, although the evidence for their efficacy is rather small (see chapter 10). Typically, these medications are tried after an unsuccessful lithium trial.

### Alprazolam

Among the newer treatment strategies for unipolar depression is prescribing alprazolam (Xanax), a benzodiazepine best known for its effect in panic disorder, generalized anxiety disorder, and insomnia. A number of studies over the last five years have demonstrated alprazolam's antidepressant effect (Rickels et al., 1987). It is probably most effective for mild to moderately depressed patients. Alprazolam's effect in treating more severe, melancholic depression is less clear. Some melancholic patients do indeed respond but the response is less consistent than that seen in milder depressions.

Alprazolam should be strongly considered as an antidepressant for two groups of depressed patients: (1) those for whom the side effects of the cyclic antidepressants are intolerable, and (2) patients with mixed depression and panic disorder. The other important consideration is that since there is a potential for dependence with alprazolam not shared by the cyclic antidepressants, it should be only given with extreme caution to those with a history of alcohol abuse or drug dependence.

## Electroconvulsive Treatment (ECT)

Without question, the controversy surrounding ECT continues to be the most sensitive in psychiatry's attempt to present somatic treatments of psychiatric disorders to other mental health professionals and the general public. (I am ignoring the debate about psychosurgery for intractable depression and obsessive compulsive disorder since these surgeries are rarely performed in this country and thus engender little debate.) As with the MAO inhibitors, the residue of past problems with ECT has obscured the vast body of data collected over the last fifteen years documenting ECT's efficacy and safety. Chapter 13 discusses ECT in detail.

For patients with acute unipolar depression, there are a few specific indications for ECT. The most well-documented of these is psychotic depression (DSM-III-R major depressive episode with mood-congruent psychotic features) for which ECT is highly effective (Consensus Conference, 1985). The second indication for ECT in unipolar depression is in treating patients with severe depressions, typically with melancholic features, who have failed to respond to adequate trials of at least one cyclic antidepressant and one MAO inhibitor. A third indication for ECT is a depression characterized by profound, obsessional suicidality. Even when these patients are hospitalized, they may still pose a major risk to themselves, managing to hurt themselves no matter how closely they are watched (e.g., by stabbing themselves with eating utensils). Although controlled studies do not exist, substantial clinical evidence suggests that ECT seems to interrupt the life-threatening suicidal obsession. Finally, patients with certain medical problems may be treated more safely with ECT than with antidepressants. An example of this would be a patient with unstable cardiac disease for whom the potential risk of blood pressure changes or alterations in cardiac rhythms seen with antidepressants is unacceptable. Since ECT is administered under controlled conditions (see chapter 13), including the presence of an anesthesiologist and anesthesia lasting only minutes, it is likely to be safer.

> For most of her 69 years, Ethel had been energetic, optimistic, capable. Three times during her life, however, she had become profoundly depressed—once after giving birth to her first baby (but not after the second), once in her early forties, and six months ago. During each of these episodes, she became completely dysfunctional. She would lose 10 to 15 pounds, have classic early morning awakening, be unable to see friends, and would spend most of her time agitated and complaining of intolerable anxiety that was not significantly relieved by tranquilizers. Although insisting she wanted to die, Ethel made no suicide attempts. Her first episode had not been treated; a nanny took care of her new-

born while family members watched over Ethel for ten months until she spontaneously improved. When she became depressed a second time, the family sought psychiatric help. Inpatient treatment in a hospital was unhelpful until she was given ten ECT treatments to which she responded completely. However, the ECT experience was disturbing to both Ethel and her family; they resented the lack of communication with the doctor, the lack of careful supervision they had expected, and the memory loss she experienced. (See chapter 13 for a discussion of ECT and memory loss.) Now, with a third depression, they reluctantly sought out a psychiatrist specializing in psychopharmacology.

At the initial consultation, the psychiatrist felt ECT was one of many options. Because of their past experience, both Ethel and her family wanted to try antidepressants. Over the next four months, nortriptyline, a cyclic antidepressant, and then phenelzine, an MAO inhibitor, were prescribed at adequate dose for six weeks each. (Two other antidepressant trials had been cut short by side effects.) By this time, Ethel had lost more weight and was talking increasingly of dying. It was explained to Ethel and her family that, although other medications, either individually or in combination, could be tried, the likelihood of a good response was now far less than with ECT. After a great deal of discussion with the psychiatrist and education about the techniques and possible side effects, Ethel ambivalently agreed to ECT. A series of eight ECT treatments again resulted in a complete remission. With the use of unilateral ECT (see chapter 13), the memory loss was significantly less than during her previous ECT treatments. Nortriptyline was restarted as a continuation treatment (see below) for the next six months and then tapered without incident.

### Light Therapy

When light therapy is described, it may sound like the fringiest of fringe treatments, but it is well documented as an effective treatment for seasonal affective disorder (Rosenthal, Sack, Skwerer, Jacobsen, and Wehr, 1988). Patients sit three feet from high-intensity, full-frequency lights (similar to the lights used to grow indoor plants or, of course, sunlight) for two to four hours daily. During this time, they may read, watch TV, pay bills, or anything else as long as they glance at the light source frequently—usually once or twice a minute—and do not keep their eyes closed. Typically, a marked reduction of the depressive symptoms is seen within days, far shorter than the usual two- to three-week lag time for antidepressants to work. There is controversy as to whether the lights need to be administered during a specific time of day, with inconsistent evidence that light therapy administered in the morning may be more effective than that given in the evening (Blehar and Rosenthal, 1989). If the morning use of lights does not help (or is not practical because of the patient's work schedule), it is reasonable to switch to evening light before abandoning light as a viable treatment.

## Strategies Used in Treatment-Resistant Depressions

Although a thorough review of the unusual treatments and treatment combinations sometimes employed with patients whose depressions don't respond to more conventional treatment is beyond the scope of this book, it is worth describing a few of the more commonly used strategies.

Among the most common of these strategies is combining a cyclic antidepressant with an MAO inhibitor. The *Physicians' Desk Reference* loudly announces that this combination should not be utilized. Yet it has been used for many years by many practitioners and examined in a few careful studies. When combined properly, there are no more side effects than when the individual medications are prescribed and there is no increased danger of a hypertensive episode (Razani et al., 1983). Among the MAO inhibitors, tranylcypromine must be used with increased caution in combination treatment. The two antidepressants may be started together or the MAO inhibitor may be added cautiously to the cyclic antidepressant. Adding the cyclic antidepressant to the MAO inhibitor should not be done, since this confers the risk of provoking a hypertensive or hyperthermic (high-temperature) toxic reaction (see chapter 9). Double-blind studies have not shown increased efficacy for combination treatment over single-agent treatment, suggesting that it may be significantly effective for only a minority of patients. Nonetheless, enough anecdotes attest to its effect to consider it a prime strategy for treatment-resistant depression.

Adding lithium to either a cyclic antidepressant or an MAO inhibitor that has been ineffective is another common treatment (Price, Charney, and Heninger, 1986). Using lithium in this adjunctive way can cause a marked clinical improvement within days to two weeks, further demonstrating lithium's beneficial effects in patients with unipolar depressions. The adjunctive effect of lithium seems to occur at lower blood levels than are usually needed when it is used as a single treatment.

$T_3$, a thyroid hormone, has been used with variable success to effect a response when added to a previously ineffective antidepressant. Although it is always mentioned prominently as an effective adjunctive treatment, the evidence for its efficacy for large numbers of patients is rather slim (Gitlin, Weiner, Fairbanks, Hershman, and Friedfeld, 1987). Still, it does seem to work in some treatment-resistant patients within three weeks and frequently sooner. There are no established predictors of response to adjunctive $T_3$. Side effects are virtually nonexistent, therefore making it a low-risk strategy.

Stimulants such as methylphenidate (Ritalin) or d-amphetamine (Dexedrine) are sometimes prescribed, either alone or in combination as an adjunctive treatment. Although they are less effective than standard antidepressants, they are frequently prescribed for treatment-refractory patients, apathetic elderly patients, or those with significant medical problems which make the use of antidepressants hazardous (Satel and Nelson, 1989). When used with these patients, low-dose stimulants give increased energy and mood, fostering a reconnection between the patient and his environment. Stimulants are also sometimes added to a cyclic antidepressant to which the patient has not responded. Stimulants should not be used with MAO inhibitors except in extraordinary circumstances (and even then, with extreme caution) because of the risk of hypertensive episodes.

Finally, antipsychotics and antidepressants are often combined. The appropriate use of this combination is for psychotic depression and for depressed patients with profound agitation or anxiety. Unfortunately, this particular combination treatment is frequently inappropriately prescribed, especially by primary care physicians, for treating patients with mildly agitated or anxious depressions. Two combination pills, Triavil and Etrafon, both of which contain perphenazine, an antipsychotic, and amitriptyline, an antidepressant, are often used for this purpose. Presumably, the antipsychotic decreases the agitation while the antidepressant decreases depression. Since antipsychotics confer the risk of tardive dyskinesia (see chapter 12), it is rarely justified to treat patients in this way until more benign treatments have been tried. Furthermore, if both an antipsychotic and an antidepressant are needed simultaneously, it is far better to prescribe two separate medications so the ratio of the two doses can be varied and one can be discontinued while the other is maintained if needed.

### Continuation Treatment of Unipolar Depression

Once a depressed patient treated with somatic therapy improves, how long should the treatment continue to prevent a relapse? Compared to acute treatment, appropriate techniques of continuation treatment have been virtually ignored in clinical research. Of the handful of studies published, all agree that patients switched to a placebo after remission of clinical symptoms relapse at a far higher rate than patients continued on antidepressants (Prien, 1987). Although almost all continuation studies have used cyclic antidepressants as the active treatment, it is reasonable to assume similar results for MAO inhibitors. Unfortunately, the majority of these studies do not help answer the question of the appropriate length of continuation therapy. Clinical wisdom has long suggested that the medication be maintained until the episode would have ended without treatment. Since the mean length of a depressive episode is six to eight months, a tradition of treatment extending for that length of time has been established, again with virtually no studies validating this practice. One study, however, demonstrated that patients who were symptom free for at least sixteen weeks (four months) did not relapse significantly when switched to placebo, thus indicating that four months of euthymia was sufficient for most patients (Prien and Kupfer, 1986). Generally, doses used in continuation treatment are the same as for acute treatment, although some clinicians lower the dose by up to one third. No good studies exist that examine this practice.

Similarly, successful treatment of acute depression with ECT should be followed by continuation therapy with either antidepressants or lithium since ECT alone is followed by an unacceptably high rate of relapse (Fink, 1988).

If maintenance treatment is deemed not appropriate at the time continuation treatment is ending, the medication should be tapered and discontinued, not stopped suddenly. Sudden discontinuation of antidepressant treatment may precipitate an unpleasant (but not dangerous) withdrawal syndrome, characterized by nausea, insomnia, increased dreaming, sweating, nervousness, diarrhea, and flu-like symptoms lasting two to six days. Tapering the medication over at least one week and preferably two to three weeks will minimize or eliminate the possibility of this syndrome occurring. More importantly, though, a tapering of the antidepressant (compared to sudden discontinuation) will afford the opportunity of observing whether a relapse will occur *before* the medication is completely withdrawn. When an antidepressant is tapered over six weeks, a depressive relapse will generally be manifested as a mild, gradual return of symptoms, following which the medication dose can be raised. If the medication is stopped suddenly, a full depressive syndrome may result.

## Maintenance Treatment of Unipolar Disorder

Table 3–11 lists the most important factors to be considered in deciding whether maintenance treatment is appropriate for patients with unipolar depression. Unlike bipolar disorder, in which the likelihood of a patient experiencing just one episode in a lifetime is minimal, a substantial number of unipolar patients may have just one lifetime episode. Therefore, there is virtually no justification for maintenance treatment after a first unipolar depressive episode. Once the patient has a second episode (as happens in 50 percent of patients), a first crude estimate of cycling frequency can be made. In utilizing the factors in Table 3–11, certain clinical situations are clear: Ernie, for in-

TABLE 3–11

*Factors Used in Considering a Maintenance Treatment in Unipolar and Bipolar Mood Disorders*

Frequency of recurrences
Severity of episodes, in functioning, suicidality, effects on relationships and/or job
Responsivity of the episodes to treatment
Speed of onset or episode: Does it gradually get worse over weeks or explode into profound depression or mania within days?
Capacity of patient to retain insight (ability to self-monitor) as episode begins

stance, who was presented earlier in this chapter, had multiple major depressions over thirty years, three of which required hospitalizations, and during two of which suicide was a major risk. He was thus a likely candidate for maintenance treatment. Just as clear would be the 52-year-old man who has had two depressions separated by fourteen years, both of which were precipitated by major life events (one divorce, one death of a parent); both depressions responded well to a combination of psychotherapy and antidepressants without hospitalization or loss of ability to function. Would anyone seriously consider having this patient take medication for the rest of his life to prevent another episode?

Other clinical situations, of course, are more complicated. Patients with infrequent episodes may have depressions that are life-threatening in their suicidal severity, or may respond to no treatment except ECT. What if the patient has had only three episodes in fifteen years but developed psychotic thinking early in each episode, with profound loss of insight and then resistance to treatment until it was involuntary and much psychological, interpersonal, and vocational destruction has ensued? The factors in Table 3–11 are guidelines to be discussed by the patient, the psychotherapist, and the psychopharmacologist. Exploring the possibility of maintenance treatment should provoke the discussion of the early warning signs of depressive (or manic) episodes. Using patients' experiences and teaching them to be better self-monitors promotes mastery and diminishes the helplessness that is frequently experienced when they consider taking a medication to prevent psychiatric problems that are not controlled by psychological means.

Both cyclic antidepressants and lithium are effective preventive treatments in unipolar depression (Prien, 1988). Because the medication that was effective as an acute antidepressant will usually be prescribed as the maintenance treatment, lithium is less commonly prescribed and may be underappreciated as an effective preventive therapy. There are no good studies that examine the appropriate doses to be used in maintenance treatment. Guidelines based on clinical experience suggest that from half the acute dose up to the full acute dose is reasonable.

Rarely, a patient who responds well to ECT acutely and then relapses regularly when treated with prophylactic antidepressant is given maintenance ECT, typically administered as one treatment per month.

## Bipolar Depression—Acute and Continuation Treatment

Although bipolar and unipolar depression shows great clinical similarity, treatment decisions between the two groups differ, because of the risks of treating bipolar patients with antidepressants. When bipolar patients are given antidepressants, a significant proportion will become hypomanic or manic (Wehr and Goodwin, 1987). (The risk is difficult to quantify since some bipolar patients would shift from depression to mania as the natural course of their disorder, regardless of whether antidepressants were prescribed.) In addition to the potentially destructive effects of the manic episode, the patient is also put at risk for a postmanic depression. A further risk for some bipolar patients is that the use of antidepressants may cause rapid cycling, a difficult to treat condition characterized by short frequent episodes of mania and depression, typically with only brief euthymic periods between episodes (Wehr, Sack, Rosenthal, and Cowdry, 1988).

Most experienced clinicians would initially treat Bipolar I patients with mild to moderate depression with lithium. Some bipolar patients will respond to lithium with an acute antidepressant response. Even if the patient does not improve on the lithium, an antidepressant can then be added. The lithium will decrease the risk of an antidepressant-induced mania, although not completely.

For those bipolar patients who are severely depressed, lithium and an antidepressant can be started simultaneously. This strategy increases the risk of precipitating mania (since the lithium is not given the same chance to work before antidepressants are administered) but may accelerate the antidepressant response. As in the treatment of unipolars, no evidence exists that one cyclic antidepressant is superior to another, although common sense suggests prescribing less sedating antidepressants (such as fluoxetine or desipramine) if a patient is significantly slowed down.

If the combination of lithium with a cyclic antidepressant is ineffective, most clinicians would prescribe lithium and an MAO inhibitor together. Although some investigators feel that MAO inhibitors may be more effective than cyclic antidepressants in treating bipolar depression, no data exist yet to substantiate this.

Finally, as with unipolar depression, ECT is an important viable alternative for severe bipolar depression. Lithium must be stopped during the time of ECT treatment to avoid a neurotoxic reaction (confusion, disorientation, marked memory loss) seen when these two treatments are used simultaneously.

The only difference in strategies for treating depressions in Bipolar II versus Bipolar I patients is that many clinicians are less likely to treat Bipolar II patients with lithium alone, preferring lithium plus an antidepressant as a first option. Some clinicians prescribe antidepressants alone to treat Bipolar II depression. Unfortunately, even though hypomania is by definition less destructive than mania, Bipolar IIs are probably at equal risk to experience pharmacological (hypo)mania compared to Bipolar I patients. They also share equally the risk of postmanic depression or rapid cycling.

Continuation treatment is as important for bipolar depression as it is for unipolar depression. However, most unipolar patients will be taking one medication—an antidepressant—during continuation treatment, whereas most bipolar patients will be on either lithium or, more likely, lithium plus an antidepressant. If the patient is taking lithium alone, continuation treatment should extend six to eight months, similar to unipolar patients before the decision regarding maintenance treatment is made. If the patient is on lithium plus an antidepressant, it is reasonable to attempt to decrease or discontinue the antidepressant before six months, since the lithium may have its own continuation effect. This strategy would also minimize the amount of time a bipolar patient takes antidepressants with the attendant risks.

## Treatment of Acute Manic Episodes

There are a variety of reasonable, appropriate strategies for the treatment of a manic or hypomanic episode. It is important to remember, though, that a substantial number of manic (not hypomanic) episodes will need to be treated in hospital because of the destructive aspects of mania—its damaging effect on jobs, relationships, and savings, and the high likelihood of profound social embarrassment and potentially dangerous actions based on impulsiveness, irritability, and poor judgment.

Table 3–12 lists the somatic treatments for acute mania. Lithium and the antipsychotics are approximately equal in efficacy and are the most well-documented treatments (Goodwin and Zis, 1979). More recently, both clonazepam and carbamazepine have shown consistent efficacy and are being prescribed with greater frequency (see below).

Lithium's greatest advantage in the treatment of mania is its quality of "normalizing" the patient's mood. Patients will rarely complain of feeling "drugged" from lithium when it is prescribed in appropriate doses. It is non-

TABLE 3–12

*Treatments for Mania and Bipolar Disorder*

| Treatment | Acute | Maintenance |
|---|:---:|:---:|
| Lithium | * | * |
| Antipsychotics | * | 0 |
| Carbamazepine | * | * |
| Sodium valproate | * | * |
| Clonazepam | * | 0 |
| Lorazepam | * | 0 |
| Verapamil | * | ? |
| ECT | * | 0 |

* = evidence of efficacy
? = possible efficacy
0 = no evidence of efficacy

sedating and is reasonably well tolerated. Lithium's disadvantage is its relatively slow onset of action. Few therapeutic effects are seen within the first week, and it may take up to three weeks for a full therapeutic effect to be manifested. This is especially true in outpatient settings where lithium blood levels (blood tests that are vital in regulating the appropriate lithium dose—see chapter 10) cannot realistically be obtained on a daily basis, as they can in hospital. Without the capacity for very frequent lithium levels, dose adjustments—and therefore clinical response—proceed more slowly. For acute mania, lithium levels of 0.7 to 1.2 mEq/L (milliequivalents per liter—see chapter 10) are most helpful. (See chapter 10 for further discussion on lithium levels.)

Antipsychotics have been used for decades to treat acute mania. Their major advantage is speed of efficacy, with therapeutic effects seen within hours to days. However, they cause many more side effects than lithium (see chapter 12)—sedation, neurological symptoms, dizziness, neuroleptic malignant syndrome, and so on. Additionally, patients have a more negative subjective response to antipsychotics than to lithium, often describing the feeling as having a "blanket on their brain." One frequently sees a manic patient on, for instance, chlorpromazine (Thorazine) who is sedated, stiff, and motorically slowed while still trying to talk at excessive speed and in a scattered speech. This contrasts pointedly with lithium's greater "normalization of mood," and patients' satisfaction with it.

Sedating antipsychotics, such as chlorpromazine, and nonsedating antipsychotics, such as haloperidol (Haldol), are equally effective in treating mania. Higher doses of the nonsedating medications can be used since the dose is not as limited by the sedation. However, there is no good evidence that very high doses of antipsychotics are more effective than moderate doses in treating mania.

Often, a severely manic patient will be started on lithium and antipsychotics simultaneously. In these situations, an attempt is made to lower the dose of the antipsychotic or to stop it completely during the second through fourth week of treatment as the lithium takes effect.

Over the last few years, clonazepam (Klonopin), a sedating benzodiazepine (see chapter 11), has been increasingly utilized as an effective, rapidly acting antimanic medication which does not cause the side effects of the antipsychotics (Chouinard, 1988). Patient acceptance of clonazepam is relatively high, with sedation its main side effect. It is not known whether clonazepam's antimanic properties are shared by all the other benzodiazepines. Lorazepam (Ativan), though, has also been shown to have antimanic properties (Modell, Lenox, and Weiner, 1985).

Two anticonvulsants—carbamazepine (Tegretol) and sodium valproate (Depakene or Depakote)—can also be used to treat acute mania (see chapter 10 for details). Of the two, the evidence for carbamazepine's effect in acute mania is far greater (Post, 1988). Like lithium, they normalize mood but take one to three weeks to work.

A number of other medications have been used occasionally to treat mania, such as clonidine (Catapres) and propranolol (Inderal). The most promising of these at present is verapamil, a calcium channel blocker, used in the treatment of angina and migraine headaches.

Electroconvulsive treatment is an extremely effective treatment for acute severe mania. However, it is a rare manic patient who will agree to take ECT; thus it is rarely used.

## Continuation Treatment of Manic or Hypomanic Episodes

Following the guideline of continuing treatment for the same length of time as the natural history of the episode, manic episodes should be treated for approximately four months. After that time, if maintenance treatment is not appropriate, the medication should be tapered and discontinued. During continuation treatment, however, it is often possible to decrease the amount of medication. If not done previously, antipsychotics or clonazepam may be tapered and withdrawn while lithium or another mood stabilizer is continued. Also, the lithium level needed to treat acute mania (usually 0.8 to 1.2 mEq/L) may be lowered to 0.8 or less.

## Maintenance Treatment of Bipolar Disorder

Compared to unipolar patients, bipolar patients are far more likely to be treated with maintenance pharmacotherapy. The reasons for this are rooted in the known natural history of the disorder, reviewed earlier in this chapter: (1) the increased cycle frequency in bipolars versus unipolars, (2) the rarity of bipolar patients who suffer just one episode in a lifetime, (3) the more destructive effects of manic or hypomanic episodes on relationships, jobs, bank accounts, self-esteem. Because of these factors, virtually all Bipolar I patients and most Bipolar II patients should properly be on maintenance pharmacotherapy at some point in their disorder. But when?

The same factors used to evaluate maintenance treatment in unipolar disorder (see Table 3–11) are used for bipolar disorder. However, since bipolar disorder is more recurrent and destructive, the same evaluative process will generally suggest a preventive treatment. The most difficult clinical decisions in treating these patients occur early in the course of the disorder after the first or second episode. Most psychopharmacologists would not recommend a maintenance treatment after the first episode. Yet recently a panel of experts examined this issue and concluded "the occurrence of a manic episode should always raise the question of preventive therapy" (Consensus Development Panel, 1985, p. 471). Their rationale is clearly based on the assumption of a second potentially highly destructive episode in the life of a young person (the mean age of onset of bipolar disorder is the mid-twenties) whose self-esteem and social reputation are not established and are subject to major disruption. As an example, a second-year medical student who has had a hospitalized manic episode that was embarrassingly obvious to the faculty, nurses, and staff at the hospital in which he was training may be able to avoid having that episode affect his dean's letter (written to potential residency programs). But if he suffers a second episode before the end of medical school, it may well have an irreversible effect on his career path.

For most patients, however, it is generally after the second episode that the discussion of preventive treatment arises. At that time, the patient can no longer be so sure that the first episode was an extraordinary fluke that could never happen again (as many patients want to believe). Also, the cycling frequency—the length of time between the onset of the first and second episodes—can be calculated. While the decision about maintenance treatment rests on a best judgment using the factors outlined in Table 3–11, in general, patients who experience two major episodes, especially if they occur within a few years, are serious candidates for preventive pharmacotherapy.

Without question, lithium is the mainstay of preventive treatment for bipolar disorder. Although many patients continue to experience either persistent mood swings or manic or depressive episodes while taking lithium, it is effective in the majority of cases in diminishing manifestations of the disorder. Lithium's efficacy can be shown by its effect in (1) decreasing the number and frequency of episodes, (2) diminishing the intensity of the episodes, (3) shortening the length of episodes, and (4) decreasing the more subtle and transient mood swings seen between episodes. Approximately two thirds of patients will show a good to excellent response to lithium (Prien and Gelenberg, 1989).

Since lithium treatment is monitored by lithium levels (the concentration of lithium in the blood), it is imperative that the maintenance level be established and followed consistently (see chapter 10 for details). Lithium levels between 0.6 and 0.8 are recommended for most patients (Consensus Development Panel, 1985). Some patients require higher levels (e.g., 1.0 to 1.2) for effective prophylaxis and tolerate these higher levels, while other patients, especially the elderly, may show a good response at levels of 0.4.

For the one third of bipolar patients who show an inadequate response to lithium and for whom other pharmacotherapies are indicated, carbamazepine (Tegretol) is the clear second-line treatment. Valproate (Depakene or Depakote) is another alternative preventive treatment, used with increasing frequency. Both medications have been available for over a decade, used primarily by neurologists in the treatment of seizure disorders. Although the evidence for carbamazepine's effectiveness in preventing both manias and depressions is greater than that of valproate, neither drug can approach lithium in its sheer documentation of usefulness (Prien and Gelenberg, 1989). No studies have directly compared the efficacy of carbamazepine versus valproate and their comparative efficacy is unknown.

Another strategy used occasionally in the maintenance treatment of bipolar patients is to combine two or more partially effective treatments. Lithium and carbamazepine are sometimes prescribed together (as opposed to substituting one for the other) when a patient has a partial response to lithium.

Patients with frequent breakthrough manic or psychotic symptoms are often treated with adjunctive maintenance antipsychotics with some success. Yet this approach must be used with caution because of the risk of developing tardive dyskinesia (see chapter 12) when a mood-disordered patient takes antipsychotics for a significant length of time.

Less commonly, bipolar patients with frequent breakthrough depressions are, by necessity, treated with maintenance antidepressants—either cyclic antidepressants or MAO inhibitors, typically added to a mood stabilizer such as lithium. Although this approach is sometimes effective, it confers the risks of increasing the number of manic episodes and potentially inducing rapid cycling. Both the psychopharmacologist and the psychotherapist *must* be alert to these possibilities and intervene quickly if a manic episode or rapid cycling emerges.

# 4

## Anxiety Disorders and Insomnia

Like the word *depression, anxiety* refers to a number of different entities. Anxiety may be considered a normal, transient feeling that has adaptive properties when it signals danger; it is a symptom seen in a wide variety of disorders; and it refers to a group of disorders in which the symptom of anxiety forms a dominant element. Concepts regarding pathological anxiety have shifted continuously over the last hundred years depending on both the types of patients studied and the causal models of the investigators. As concepts of anxiety have changed, so, of course, have our notions of how best to classify these disorders. Freud, for instance, shifted the focus from physical to psychological symptoms and distinguished anxiety neurosis from the more global disorder, neurasthenia. In Freud's use of the term, anxiety neurosis consisted of what we would now call both panic disorder and generalized anxiety. In modern times, the most important distinction was made during the 1960s when anxiety neurosis was split into panic disorder/agoraphobia and generalized anxiety because of the evidence of differential response to both behavioral and pharmacological treatments.

What all of the currently classified anxiety disorders have in common are anxiety as a major symptom and/or avoidance as a predominant behavior. It would be premature, however, to assume that the diverse disorders currently classified as anxiety disorders really form a single related group of entities. In striving for the goal of increasing diagnostic specificity, syndromes have been "split" into related but officially separate disorders. The split of anxiety neurosis into panic/agoraphobia and generalized anxiety is an example. Two classification schemes later, in DSM-III-R, panic has been divided into panic with and without agoraphobia. As more information on anxiety disorders emerges, our diagnostic scheme is likely to shift yet again. When this occurs, disorders currently classified as anxiety disorders may also be reclassified into a different category. In the recent discussion preceding the adoption of DSM-III-R, for instance, post-traumatic stress disorder was seriously considered for transfer into dissociative disorders. Classification is clearly a process in evolution.

In this chapter, the disorders to be considered are panic disorder with or without agoraphobia, generalized anxiety disorder, simple and social phobias, obsessive compulsive disorder, and post-traumatic stress disorder. More detail will be provided for those disorders for which medications play a more prominent role in treatment. Since the same medications are used to treat insomnia and anxiety disorders (especially generalized anxiety), this chapter will also briefly cover the common causes of and pharmacological approaches to insomnia.

## DIAGNOSIS

Among all the anxiety disorders, panic disorder has received the most clinical attention over the last decade. This attention stems not only from the relatively recent distinction between panic and other types of anxiety, and the potential incapacitating nature of panic, but also because of the increasing numbers of successful treatments, especially medications. In its classic form, panic disorder is characterized by intense episodes of overwhelming anxiety or panic lasting from minutes to an hour, accompanied by a variety of symptoms, both physical and psychological. Table 4–1 shows the DSM-III-R diagnostic criteria. By definition, a panic attack is not triggered exclusively by a specific situation. This exclusion criterion thus attempts to distinguish between "spontaneous" panic attacks and those disorders in which the intense anxiety is situation specific, such as phobias. DSM-III-R requires either four attacks during a four-week period or one attack followed by a month of anticipatory anxiety about having another. Clinically, however, the specific number of attacks may not be relevant since many patients have fewer than four attacks per month but are otherwise indistinguishable from DSM-III-R diagnosed panic disorder patients (Fyer, Mannuzza, and Endicott, 1987).

Those panic patients who constrict their activity, usually to avoid situations from which they fear they cannot escape or get help or in which they feel another panic attack might occur, are diagnosed as having panic disorder with agoraphobia. Examples of commonly avoided situations include being in a car or in crowded areas such as movie theatres or supermarkets. It is presumed that in these patients, who comprise the majority of panic patients, agoraphobic symptoms develop after the panic attacks (Breier, Charney, and Heninger, 1986). Other patients with no history of panic describe clear agoraphobic

TABLE 4–1

*Diagnostic Criteria for Panic Disorder*

---

A. At some time during the disturbance, one or more panic attacks (discrete periods of intense fear or discomfort) have occurred that were (1) unexpected, i.e., did not occur immediately before or on exposure to a situation that almost always caused anxiety, and (2) not triggered by situations in which the person was the focus of others' attention.

B. Either four attacks, as defined in criterion A, have occurred within a four-week period, or one or more attacks have been followed by a period of at least a month of persistent fear of having another attack.

C. At least four of the following symptoms developed during at least one of the attacks:

(1) shortness of breath (dyspnea) or smothering sensations
(2) dizziness, unsteady feelings, or faintness
(3) palpitations or accelerated heart rate (tachycardia)
(4) trembling or shaking
(5) sweating
(6) choking
(7) nausea or abdominal distress
(8) depersonalization or derealization
(9) numbness or tingling sensations (paresthesias)
(10) flushes (hot flashes) or chills
(11) chest pain or discomfort
(12) fear of dying
(13) fear of going crazy or of doing something uncontrolled

Note: Attacks involving four or more symptoms are panic attacks; attacks involving fewer than four symptoms are limited symptom attacks.

D. During at least some of the attacks, at least four of the C symptoms developed suddenly and increased in intensity within ten minutes of the beginning of the first C symptom noticed in the attack.

E. It cannot be established that an organic factor initiated and maintained the disturbance, e.g., amphetamine or caffeine intoxication, hyperthyroidism.

---

Reprinted with permission from the *Diagnostic and Statistical Manual of Mental Disorders, Third Edition, Revised.* Copyright 1987 American Psychiatric Association.

symptoms, although many of them relate fears of having panic-like symptoms in the avoided situation. In patients who enter treatment, though, it is unusual to see agoraphobia without evidence of at least some panic symptoms. Yet epidemiologic studies, which evaluate patients without regard to whether or not they have sought treatment, document a relatively large number of people with agoraphobia without panic symptoms (Robins et al., 1984). Whether this discrepancy is due to the effects of panic symptoms on help-seeking behavior or to the differing methodologies of epidemiological studies as opposed to clinical studies is not known.

Generalized anxiety disorder (GAD) is the least specific of all the anxiety disorders. The DSM-III-R criteria require at least six months of excessive anxiety about two or more life circumstances in combination with six of eighteen physical symptoms such as muscle tension, easy fatigability, shortness of breath, irritability, and insomnia. The focus of the anxiety cannot be the symptoms of another Axis I disorder for GAD to be diagnosed. Thus, the anticipatory anxiety that typically develops during ongoing panic disorder would not be classified as GAD. Because it is often seen coincident with other anxiety disorders (except possibly with simple phobias), some experts feel that GAD is simply a nonspecific complication of all anxiety disorders and therefore should not be delineated as a separate category. Other observers object to the diagnostic separation between panic and GAD, noting that the differences between the two may be more quantitative than qualitative (Jablensky, 1985).

Yet, most clinicians, myself included, have seen patients without panic or other anxiety disorders who are chronic worriers with many somatic anxiety symptoms. Furthermore, there is a subgroup of patients who suffer from both panic with anticipatory anxiety as well as generalized anxiety. Even if the panic and anticipatory anxiety are successfully treated in these patients, the more pervasive generalized anxiety frequently persists, implying that there may be another chronic anxiety disorder that is separate from the more acute panic disorder.

Simple phobia is a fear of a specific object or situation. When confronted with the stimulus, the patient becomes markedly anxious in a manner indistinguishable from a panic attack. Blood-injury phobia (fear of witnessing blood or injuries), claustrophobia, or fears of airplane travel are typical examples.

DSM-III-R designates social phobia as a distinct category, separate from simple phobias. Patients with social phobias specifically fear situations involving observation or scrutiny by others to a degree that interferes with social or occupational functioning. Common fears are those of public speaking, urinating in a public lavatory, or of hand trembling while writing a check. Although DSM-III-R describes social phobia as one clinical syndrome, it may be helpful to distinguish between two subtypes (Liebowitz, Gorman, et al., 1988). In the limited form, usually described as performance anxiety, patients fear public speaking or performing. As an example, a professor's career would be limited by a phobia of speaking at conferences or of lecturing. The second type of social phobia is a generalized social anxiety which interferes with a broader range of social activities such as meeting new people, talking to salespeople, or discussing a work-related issue with the boss. In both types of social phobia, being in the feared situation brings on anxiety similar to that seen in simple phobias or panic. Anticipatory anxiety and avoidant behavior are common. Thus, a patient with a social phobia manifested by fear of urinating in a public place may completely restrict any sort of significant travel, thus seeming agoraphobic when the primary fear is that of urinating in public, not of being away from home.

Obsessive compulsive disorder is characterized by obsessions, defined as persistent ideas, thoughts, or impulses, and/or compulsions which are repetitive, ritualized behaviors typically in response to an obsession. Most patients have both obsessions and compulsions. At its core, these patients are afflicted by pathological doubt. They fear that they haven't done something properly, that they may hurt someone. Shame commonly accompanies these symptoms. Because of this, patients often come into treatment complaining of other symptoms and, unless specifically asked, only reveal their secret obsessions and compulsions many months later. Remarkably, the time from beginning of symptoms to first treatment is frequently more than ten years (Rasmussen and Tsuang, 1986).

According to the DSM-III-R definition, both the obsessions and compulsions are recognized as the product of the person's own thinking (in contrast with psychotic thoughts which are experienced as alien). Attempts are made to neutralize or undo the thoughts, typically by a compulsion that is grossly excessive compared to the fear. Patients who are obsessed by the thought that they have run someone over with their car may return to the spot fifty or more times, consuming incredible amounts of time to reassure themselves that no body is lying in the street. Unfortunately, the compulsions that attempt to relieve the obsessional anxiety are never more than trivially and transiently successful.

Among the obsessions, fear of contamination by dirt, poisons, or toxins is the most common (Rasmussen and Eisen, 1989). Not surprisingly, these patients tend to have cleaning rituals. The second most common obsession is that of having harmed or cheated others; a mother may be afraid of hurting her baby or a man of having left the gas on while using the stove. Common compulsions are those of checking, counting, or cleaning. For instance, patients may be unable to get dressed unless all their clothes are lined up perfectly and grouped in clusters of seven (which they believe has some magical ability to ward off bad events). This type of ritual could consume an hour or more every morning. Obsessions and compulsions may shift over time such that a compulsive handwasher during one episode of the disorder may present with counting rituals during a subsequent episode.

Post-traumatic stress disorder (PTSD) is defined by a cluster of symptoms following an event that would be extremely psychologically distressing to almost anyone. These symptoms, which must last at least one month, are grouped into three types: (1) re-experiencing of the event, such as flashbacks or recurrent dreams; (2) numbing of general responsiveness, such as avoiding thoughts, feelings, or activities reminiscent of the event, general decreased feelings of connection to others, or an inability to have loving feelings; and (3) signs of increased arousal, such as hypervigilance and increased startle response.

Eliciting symptoms of anxiety disorders is often easy, as with simple phobias or generalized anxiety. Sometimes, though, patients will present for treatment and focus on other problems, leaving disabling syndromes a hidden, embarrassing part of their lives. As previously mentioned, obsessive compulsive disorder frequently stays hidden. Panic disorder is always recognized by patients as a problem, but not always as a psychiatric one (see below). To help elicit information relevant to diagnosing the anxiety disorders, the following questions may be helpful.

---

*Panic Disorder:* Have you ever had sudden attacks of anxiety or fear that were extremely uncomfortable? Describe what it felt like. (At that point, one can ask about specific panic symptoms, such as shortness of breath, trembling, and the like.) How long did it take until the symptoms peaked? How long did the entire episode last? How often has this occurred? Is there one specific situation in which these episodes occur or do they occur seemingly out of the blue?

*Agoraphobia:* Have these episodes changed your life? For instance, do you avoid certain situations now because you fear having a panic attack? Which situations?

*Generalized Anxiety Disorder:* Do you think of yourself as a nervous person? How long has this been so? Do you worry a lot? About what kinds of things? When you're feeling anxious, do you ever have physical symptoms, such as trembling or having sweaty palms? Do you feel dizzy? Does your heart pound? Do unexpected noises make you jump?

*Social Phobia:* Do you get very nervous when you have to do things in front of other people, such as writing or eating or speaking? Is it bad enough to make you avoid the situations? If you cannot avoid the situation, how nervous do you get?

*Obsessive Compulsive Disorder:* Do you ever have thoughts that you can't seem to get rid of, thoughts that occur over and over in your mind like a tape that is stuck? What thoughts are these? Are there certain behaviors that you feel compelled to do over and over? Do you have to do them a certain number of times? What would happen or what are you afraid would happen if you resisted doing these rituals? How much time do you spend on a daily basis with these activities?

---

## NATURAL HISTORY, EPIDEMIOLOGY, AND GENETICS

Because our diagnostic categories for anxiety disorders have changed dramatically over the last two decades, important clinical questions relating to the natural course, prevalence, and amount of genetic loading of these disorders are difficult to answer. Therefore, this section relies primarily on the more recent studies which, unfortunately, are limited to the information they yield on topics such as long-term outcome.

Panic disorder, occurring in 1 to 2 percent of the population, tends to arise in the mid-twenties and is twice as common in women as in men (Reich, 1986). It is unusual for it to arise after age 40. The natural course of panic disorder is variable. Most commonly, it waxes and wanes, with total remission uncommon. Often, patients describe months to a few years in which panic attacks are frequent, followed by a period of time with few attacks, although mild panic or agoraphobic symptoms may persist (Katon, Vitaliano, Anderson, Jones, and Russo, 1987). Later, often after years, the attacks recur in full force. Another group of patients seem to have chronic unremitting symptoms of panic with or without agoraphobia.

The consistent finding that there is an increased rate of panic in the families of panic patients indicates the familial nature of the disorder (Crowe, Noyes, Pauls, and Slymen, 1983). Furthermore, the increased concordance seen in monozygotic (genetically identical) as opposed to dizygotic (genetically related but not identical) twins indicates that at least part of the risk is genetically determined (Torgersen, 1983).

Panic patients frequently have other psychiatric disorders, the most common of which is generalized anxiety disorder. Major depressive episodes, which may occur before, coincident with, or following the panic disorder, are also common, seen in 50 to 70 percent of panic patients (Breier et al., 1984). The likelihood of a depression which occurs after the onset of the panic disorder is related to the length of time the patient has had panic disorder (Lesser et al., 1988). Additionally, both childhood separation anxiety disorder and alcoholism may also be seen more frequently in panic patients.

Although reliable information on its age of onset, sex ratio, and its natural history is not available, best estimates are that between 2 and 6 percent of the population, more women than men, have generalized anxiety (Weissman and

Merikangas, 1986). There is conflicting evidence for the familial nature of generalized anxiety disorder.

Simple phobias, which occur more in women by a 2:1 ratio, are common, although many of these patients never seek treatment. They have a relatively early age of onset, frequently in childhood. Compared to other anxiety disorders, simple phobias tend to have a more benign course. Genetic influences probably play a role in the development of some simple phobias, especially blood-injury phobias (Marks, 1986).

Social phobia typically arises in the teenage years and seems to be a chronic unremitting condition when not treated (Liebowitz, Gorman, Fyer, and Klein, 1985). It affects less than 1.5 percent of the population and may be slightly more common in men than women. There are no good genetic studies of social phobia, although there seems to be some heritable component to aspects of social anxiety such as discomfort when eating with strangers or when being watched working (Torgersen, 1979). Patients with social phobias may be at higher risk for depression and alcohol abuse.

Obsessive compulsive disorder (OCD) begins at an average age of 20 (Rasmussen and Tsuang, 1984). Recent studies indicate that it is far more common than had been previously thought, with a lifetime prevalence of 2.5 percent and women slightly outnumbering men (Robins et al., 1984). A common pattern of the disorder is chronic mild symptoms interspersed with acute episodes. However, approximately 10 percent of patients have a progressive downhill course in which the symptoms gradually take over more and more of their lives. There are few good genetic studies, but twin studies give some evidence of a genetic vulnerability.

Between 50 and 70 percent of OCD patients have obsessional personalities, implying a link between the two disorders. However, this also indicates that they are not the same disorder, since a significant number of patients with obsessions and compulsions do not have obsessional personalities. Common secondary diagnoses in these patients are depression, seen in up to 50 percent of patients, simple and social phobias, and separation anxiety disorders. A small number of OCD patients have Tourette's syndrome, a disorder arising in childhood and characterized by multiple tics (see chapter 8). In these cases, it is likely that the tics, obsessions, and compulsions are manifestations of the same disorder.

The prevalence of PTSD has been estimated as 1 percent (Helzer, Robins, and McEvoy, 1987). Little information is available on the natural history of the disorder. Some of the symptoms—such as the intrusive and numbing ones—may wax and wane over time, whereas the alienation from others may be more constant (Green, Lindy, and Grace, 1985). These patients may be at risk to have higher rates of alcoholism, depression, and anxiety while their families show high rates of alcohol abuse (Davidson, Swartz, Storck, Krishnan, and Hammett, 1985).

## MEDICAL DIFFERENTIAL DIAGNOSIS

Because so many anxiety symptoms, especially those of panic, are physical, patients with anxiety disorders often see a variety of medical specialists before seeking mental health consultation. In one study, 70 percent of a group of panic patients had seen more than ten physicians (Sheehan, Ballenger, and Jacobsen, 1980). Even after extensive medical evaluation has uncovered no medical disorder, and after many months of psychiatric education and treatment, some panic patients still need reassurance that they are not having heart attacks, impending strokes, or other catastrophes.

As with depression, a host of medical disorders can cause anxiety symptoms simulating generalized anxiety, panic, or both (see Table 4–2). The most

TABLE 4–2

*Medical Disorders and Drugs That May Cause Anxiety Disorders*

| | |
|---|---|
| Cardiovascular: | Drug withdrawal: |
| Mitral valve prolapse | Alcohol |
| Cardiac arrhythmia | Opiates/narcotics |
| Congestive heart failure | Sedatives/hypnotics |
| Hypertension (high blood pressure) | Endocrine: |
| Myocardial infarction (heart attack) | Carcinoid syndrome |
| Pulmonary embolus (blood clot) | Cushing's syndrome |
| Respiratory: | Hypoglycemia |
| Asthma | Hypoparathyroidism (low calcium) |
| Emphysema | Hyperthyroidism |
| Hyperventilation | Pheochromocytoma (adrenal tumor—see |
| Hypoxia (low oxygen) | text) |
| Drugs: | Premenstrual syndrome |
| Anticholinergic medications | Neurological: |
| Aspirin | Epilepsy |
| Caffeine | Huntington's disease |
| Cocaine | Migraine headaches |
| Decongestants | Multiple sclerosis |
| Hallucinogens | Pain |
| Steroids | Vertigo |
| Stimulants (including diet pills) | Wilson's disease |

commonly considered disorders, which are discussed below, are acute myocardial infarction (heart attack), hyperthyroidism, hypoglycemia, mitral valve prolapse, pheochromocytoma, and drug-related syndromes.

A look at the classic symptoms of a panic attack makes the common fear among panic patients of having a heart attack understandable. It would be difficult for anyone to experience a sudden episode characterized by shortness of breath, dizziness, palpitations, chest pain, and fear of dying without at least considering that a heart attack is in progress. The patient's age, a normal electrocardiogram, and a lack of signs of cardiac dysfunction help clarify the diagnosis.

Hyperthyroidism, characterized by anxiety, weight loss, sweatiness, tremor, heat intolerance, and tachycardia (fast heartbeat) can be confused with generalized anxiety. The prominence of the physical symptoms compared to the anxiety and easily obtained blood tests of thyroid function will distinguish between the two disorders.

Patients often ask about hypoglycemia as a cause of panic disorder. Although the symptoms of the two conditions are indeed similar, panic attacks rarely occur in a characteristic relation to meals—three to five hours after eating—as would be true with hypoglycemia. When panic patients are tested for hypoglycemia by glucose tolerance tests, they are virtually never found to have low blood sugar. Additionally, when hypoglycemia is induced in panic patients, the symptoms are experienced as different from panic attacks (Uhde, Vittone, and Post, 1984).

Mitral valve prolapse (MVP) may be associated with panic disorder. The miral valve connects the left atrium of the heart with the left ventricle. In MVP, when the heart contracts, the valve is abnormally pushed back into the atrium. This may be heard with a stethoscope as a click or seen in an echocardiogram (a test that uses sound waves to "visualize" the heart). MVP is found in 5 to 10 percent of the population, often undiagnosed and typically asymptomatic. In some patients, however, it is associated with palpitations or fatigue. Although the evidence is far from definitive, patients with MVP may be at higher risk for panic disorder while patients with panic disorder may be at higher risk for mitral valve prolapse (Schuckit, 1983a). At present, no hypothesis adequately explains the link between these two conditions. Does mitral valve prolapse cause panic symptoms? Do panic attacks somehow predispose patients to mitral valve prolapse? Are the two linked genetically? Regardless of the association, the presence of the prolapse does not change either the treatment or prognosis of panic disorder.

Pheochromocytomas are rare tumors of the adrenal glands that can cause discrete episodes of hypertension and anxiety symptoms by releasing excessive amounts of catecholamines such as adrenaline. Physical anxiety symptoms in these episodes are similar to those seen in panic disorder. The psychological symptoms, however, are less common in pheochromocytomas. For instance, feelings of terror, fears of losing control, anticipatory anxiety, and agoraphobia are unusual with adrenal tumors (Starkman, Zelnick, Tesse, and Cameron, 1985). Also, pheochromocytomas are rare compared to panic disorder. If a pheochromocytoma is clinically suspected, blood and urine tests can help make the diagnosis.

Drug use or withdrawal may be a sole cause of the symptoms or can exacerbate an ongoing anxiety disorder. Caffeine, which may cause symptoms of generalized anxiety or panic, is the most commonly used anxiety-producing drug, in part because it is often not regarded as strong enough to cause problems by the same people who consciously use it as a stimulant! Those who consume large amounts of caffeine to stay awake, such as students at exam times or shift workers who have a disruption of normal sleep-wake cycles, may complain of anxiety unaware that they are drinking five to ten cups of caffeinated beverages, including coffee and soft drinks. Patients with panic disorder are also more sensitive to caffeine (Charney, Heninger, and Jatlow, 1985). Many, but not all, have already stopped drinking coffee before seeking care. For those who haven't, however, tapering and ultimately discontinuing caffeine intake is mandatory. Although caffeine only rarely actually causes panic disorder, it may certainly make it worse.

Other stimulants, such as cocaine, amphetamines, diet pills, and nasal decongestants (which typically contain pseudoephedrine or other stimulants), can also cause or exacerbate anxiety. Blood tests and/or asking the patient directly are the only ways to ascertain whether drugs are causing the anxiety symptoms. In the case of cocaine abuse, characteristic signs such as coming late to appointments, missing appointments, and inconsistent money spending patterns will be present.

Drug withdrawal, primarily from sedatives or tranquilizers, can also cause anxiety symptoms. Alcohol is the classic substance that causes withdrawal anxiety, but benzodiazepine withdrawal, especially from the short-acting drugs such as alprazolam (Xanax) and triazolam (Halcion) is increasingly common (see chapter 11 for more details). A good history is the key to the diagnosis.

## MEDICAL AND LABORATORY EVALUATION

As noted above, many patients with anxiety disorders and most panic patients will already have had an extensive medical evaluation before seeking mental health care. For those who have not, it is appropriate that they consult an internist to exclude an undiagnosed medical disorder as a cause of the anxiety. Medical evaluations also help reassure those patients who are most frightened by the physical nature of their symptoms.

Basic laboratory tests to rule out obvious medical problems include many of the same tests recommended for evaluating depression. These include the general screening blood tests, thyroid function tests, and an electrocardiogram. If a specific diagnosis is being considered, further tests will be obtained.

## PSYCHIATRIC DIFFERENTIAL DIAGNOSIS

Because it is seen in so many psychiatric disorders, anxiety as a symptom can be easily confused with an anxiety disorder. Even more difficult is detecting an anxiety disorder in patients who have more than one source of anxiety. As an example, a patient with a mixed personality disorder characterized by feelings of inadequacy and fearfulness may also develop a panic disorder which may then be complicated by the anticipatory anxiety of another attack. Further confusing the diagnostic problem is the common occurrence of a patient with more than one anxiety disorder—for instance, panic disorder and generalized anxiety. Unfortunately, some of the clues that are helpful in distinguishing depression as a symptom from depressive disorders—genetic histories, the cyclical or episodic nature of the disorders—are not as useful for anxiety. With the exception of panic disorder and possibly obsessive compulsive disorder, strong genetic links for anxiety disorders either do not exist or have not yet been adequately demonstrated. Furthermore, the natural history of many anxiety disorders are simply not as clear as they are for depression. Therefore, until our knowledge about anxiety disorders increases substantially and our diagnostic system has more validity, distinguishing these disorders from others in which anxiety is a symptom will continue to be difficult. At present, the most distinctive symptoms that are helpful in diagnosing anxiety disorders are patterns of avoidance, discrete episodes of anxiety symptoms, and ritualistic behaviors.

In distinguishing panic disorder from other disorders in which anxiety is a major feature, the important clues are the crescendo nature of panic, the discrete nature of the attacks, the occurrence of some attacks that are spontaneous, and the agoraphobia that typically ensues. Panic disorder often coexists with other disorders, especially generalized anxiety and depression. Both social and simple phobias can be distinguished from panic by the specific situations that provoke the anxiety in the former. This distinction, however, may be difficult to draw for patients whose panic attacks are sometimes triggered by certain situations (such as being in a supermarket or driving). Hypochondriacal patients and panic patients share an exquisite body sensitivity and fears of catastrophic physical events. Hypochondriacs, however, do not describe clear panic attacks and do not become agoraphobic; they dwell exclusively on their physical symptoms, not on their anxiety as do panic patients.

For clinical reasons, distinguishing between generalized anxiety disorder (GAD) and similar syndromes such as adjustment disorder with anxious mood is not very important since the treatment options are identical. Thus, a disorder characterized by generalized anxiety symptoms but lasting less than six months (which is the time cutoff for GAD) may be called anxiety disorder NOS by DSM-III-R, but should be conceptualized and treated the same as GAD.

Agoraphobia and social phobia differ in that patients with the latter disorder fear doing something humiliating or embarrassing as opposed to fear of having a panic attack itself. In reality, this differentiation is not always easy to make, since in some socially phobic patients a fear of the anxiety symptoms themselves may gradually evolve, thereby blurring the distinction. Avoidant personalities (see chapter 7) resemble social phobics in that both are anxious about social situations. Social phobic patients, however, avoid very specific public situations and not intimate situations in general. The two disorders frequently coexist.

Obsessive compulsive disorder may be confused with major depression since ruminative thinking occurs frequently in the latter. Patients with depressive ruminations, though, do not generally perceive their thoughts as ego-dystonic or senseless as do those with OCD. Depressed patients will also have the other characteristic signs of their disorder such as sleep and appetite disturbances or diurnal variation, symptoms that are not present in uncomplicated obsessive compulsive disorder. The two disorders often coexist. Some schizophrenics will present with true compulsions. The presence of the typical features of schizophrenia other than delusional thinking will help distinguish it from obsessive compulsive disorder. However, a subgroup of obsessive compulsive patients may become overtly psychotic, with the psychosis focused exclusively on the obsessions and compulsions. These patients lose insight into the senselessness of their compulsions, and their obsessive thoughts become so intrusive that they are experienced as hallucinations (Insel and Akiskal, 1986).

## PSYCHOPHARMACOLOGICAL TREATMENT

Using psychopharmacological agents to treat anxiety is an ancient concept. Since the dawn of history, chemicals such as alcohol and opiates have been used to deaden feelings, diminish arousal, and induce calm. What is new, though, is the range of options available for treatment as well as the beginning of a more targeted approach to anxiety that links a specific medical treatment to the distinct anxiety disorder being treated. Certainly, as noted in the beginning of the chapter, our current diagnostic distinctions are neither as clear-cut nor as useful for predicting specific treatment responses as we would hope. One type of medication may be effective for three or four of the anxiety disorders we have discussed. For instance, the MAO inhibitor class of antidepressants is effective in treating panic disorder, social phobias, and post-traumatic stress disorder. Yet other diagnostic distinctions are important in predicting medication response. Cyclic antidepressants are fine first treatments for panic disorder but not for generalized anxiety or social phobia. Furthermore, if the first medications are ineffective, alternative treatments for the different disorders are not identical. For instance, benzodiazepines are fine alternatives to cyclic antidepressants for panic but not for social phobias. If the cyclic antidepressants are not an appropriate treatment for an individual—because of side effects or medical problems, for example—the diagnosis will help decide what other treatment should be considered.

As in the first half of this chapter, therefore, psychopharmacological strategies will be described by specific diagnostic categories. Simple phobias will not be discussed further since there is no evidence that medications are useful in their treatment.

## Acute Treatment of Panic Disorder

The notion that panic patients differ from those with other anxiety disorders in their treatment responses was first suggested in 1964, when Klein reported that antidepressants were effective for patients with discrete episodes of panic and subsequent constriction of activities (Klein, 1964). Since then, the treatment options have expanded, and three separate classes of medications—cyclic antidepressants, MAO inhibitors, and the benzodiazepines, especially alprazolam— have been demonstrated effective in treating panic. In no other psychiatric disorder is there such a wide range of equally effective treatments. Table 4–3 shows the advantages and disadvantages of these three medication groups. Because 60 to 90 percent of patients will show a significant response to any one of the three types of medications, the focus in developing a psychopharmacological treatment plan is therefore based on the needs of the individual patient (Ballenger, 1986).

Among the three major medication groups commonly prescribed for panic disorder, the cyclic antidepressants, especially imipramine, are the most well documented to have significant antipanic properties. Despite convincing proof, most of the cyclic antidepressants are likely to be effective in treating panic

TABLE 4–3

*Advantages and Disadvantages of Antipanic Medications*

| Medication | Advantages | Disadvantages |
|---|---|---|
| Cyclic antidepressants | Well established<br>Once-daily dosage | Delayed onset of action<br>Stimulant side effects<br>(with some)<br>Other side effects |
| Monoamine oxidase inhibitors | Possible increased antiphobic effects | Delayed onset of action<br>Dietary restriction, risk of hypertensive reaction<br>Other side effects |
| Benzodiazepines | Rapid onset of action<br><br>Effective against anticipatory anxiety<br>Few side effects | Drug dependence, withdrawal problems<br>Sedation, cognitive side effects |

disorder with the exception of bupropion. Reports on both trazodone and amoxapine are somewhat inconsistent, although some patients will respond to them.

Advantages of using the cyclic antidepressants for treating panic are their long history of successful use, once-daily dosing, usually at night, and their lack of addiction or withdrawal potential. Unfortunately, since panic patients tend to be exquisitely sensitive to side effects of any medications, they frequently have problems with the cyclic antidepressants, especially in the beginning of treatment prior to a therapeutic response and before accommodation to the side effects has occurred. Panic patients are also far more likely than are depressive patients to have an unwanted and uncomfortable stimulant response to the more noradrenergic cyclic antidepressants, such as desipramine and imipramine (Pohl, Yeragani, Balon, and Lycaki, 1988). This stimulant response, which can occur even at very low dose, is characterized by insomnia, agitation, and restless discomfort which is perceived, understandably, as the medication exacerbating the original problem. Lowering the medication dose temporarily, waiting, switching to a less stimulating antidepressant, or adding a beta-blocker which blocks many of these side effects are all useful strategies for decreasing the stimulant effect. Adding a benzodiazepine tranquilizer early in treatment along with a cyclic antidepressant can also be useful by decreasing the stimulant response and because of its own capacity to decrease panic.

Despite clear evidence of their effectiveness, MAO inhibitors are almost never used as first-line treatments for panic disorders. Assuredly, this is due to the cumbersomeness of the dietary restrictions necessary when they are prescribed (see chapter 9). In my experience, compared to depressed patients, those with panic also become more frightened about the diet and the possible consequences if the wrong food is ingested. Additionally, the common side effects seen with MAO inhibitors, such as postural dizziness or insomnia, seem to be more disturbing to panic patients than to depressed patients. Nevertheless, MAO inhibitors can be exceedingly effective antipanic medications. In the best study comparing a cyclic antidepressant to an MAO inhibitor, the two treatments were equally effective, although the MAO inhibitors were slightly better in diminishing phobic symptoms (Sheehan et al., 1980). Although phenelzine (Nardil) is the most well studied of the MAO inhibitors, the other two medications in this class, tranylcypromine and isocarboxazid, are also likely to be effective.

Benzodiazepines are the most recent of the major treatments for panic disorder. Alprazolam (Xanax) is the most well documented, although clonazepam (Klonopin), lorazepam (Ativan), and diazepam (Valium) have also shown clear antipanic effects. It is likely, but not yet demonstrated, that all medications of this class have antipanic effects (Charney and Woods, 1989). As a treatment for panic, benzodiazepines have a number of advantages. They are as effective as the antidepressants; their antipanic effects are evident quickly, often within the first week, and faster than the effects usually seen with antidepressants; they effectively diminish the anticipatory anxiety that accompanies panic since they are tranquilizers; they cause none of the typical antidepressant side effects such as dry mouth, stimulant effects, blood pressure changes, and the like; and tolerance to their antipanic effects does not seem to occur.

Over the last few years, however, the drawbacks of the benzodiazepines have become more apparent. The most important of these is their capacity to create both pharmacological and psychological dependence. Also, withdrawal symptoms may be extremely troublesome, especially with the shorter-acting medications such as alprazolam (see chapter 11 for a detailed discussion of this). These withdrawal symptoms can be manifested either by rebound anxiety upon discontinuing the medication or by interdose breakthrough symptoms or "mini-withdrawals" that occur just before the next scheduled dose, typically four hours after the last dose. Withdrawal difficulties are minimized by the use of the longer-acting agents such as clonazepam. The other major drawback of benzodiazepines is the common side effect of sedation.

When patients with panic disorder combined with agoraphobia and anticipatory anxiety are treated by any of these medications, not all the symptoms improve together. By definition, the universal effect of all antipanic medication is to decrease or abolish the panic attacks themselves. Medication effects on the phobic and anticipatory anxiety symptoms are more variable. Once the panic attacks cease, many patients will gradually re-expand their activities by them-selves, thereby creating their own "naturalistic" behavioral desensitization pro-gram over weeks and months, which then treats both their phobic and anxiety symptoms. Other patients need more structured intervention with at least some formal behavioral therapy following the successful treatment of the panic at-tacks.

As noted above, many patients with panic disorder suffer from a simulta-neous depression. When the panic disorder is successfully treated, the depres-sion usually remits too (Lesser et al., 1988). Occasionally, benzodiazepines seem to be the cause of a depressive syndrome when used in the treatment of panic. For most patients, however, treating the primary panic eliminates the secondary depression.

Given these considerations, on what basis does a psychopharmacologist de-cide whether to prescribe a cyclic antidepressant, an MAO inhibitor, or a benzodiazepine as a first treatment for a panic patient? Because all three are equally effective in groups of patients, most physicians will choose a medication based on their own individual experiences and biases. Many psychopharmacol-ogists will eschew benzodiazepines as a first treatment because of their potential for dependence; others think the risk is exaggerated. My own treatment strategy is to start with a cyclic antidepressant—usually desipramine because it has fewer side effects than most other antidepressants (see chapter 9). If stimulant side effects are a significant problem, I then switch to nortriptyline or imipramine which cause less stimulation but are more sedating. If one of these two cannot be tolerated or is ineffective, I then prescribe alprazolam. Its efficacy is unques-tionable; unfortunately so are its difficulties. I use MAO inhibitors as a third choice because of the dietary restrictions and side effects.

With good reason, Mark considered himself a mentally and physically healthy person. Now in graduate school, he had always done well academically, socially, and athletically. It was therefore especially dis-turbing to him when, at a time of school stress, he had a terrifying experience while sitting in a restaurant. Seemingly out of nowhere, he began to feel a pressure in his chest, difficulty in breathing, and dizzi-ness. He was absolutely sure that he was dying. After being taken to the emergency room, where he was told he had been hyperventilating (which he vigorously denied), he went to his family doctor who found no abnormalities on a variety of blood and heart tests. The doctor gave Mark alprazolam and told him to take it as needed if he started to ex-perience those feelings again. Over the next month, Mark had six or seven similar episodes in his car, in restaurants, and once in a movie theater. None of the subsequent episodes was nearly as bad as the first.

Yet, his fear of the episodes increased to the point that Mark avoided restaurants and became frightened of driving. He took the tranquilizer during each of these episodes and then on a daily basis to calm his growing anticipatory anxiety, yet the episodes continued.

Feeling ashamed of these symptoms and his reactions to them, Mark sought psychiatric help. He accepted the psychopharmacologist's diagnosis of panic disorder with some skepticism but agreed to be treated. In the beginning he was allowed to continue the alprazolam as needed. The first medication prescribed, desipramine 10 mg at night, seemed to make him worse, causing insomnia and heightened anxiety. Within one week of switching to nortriptyline (with the dose gradually increased over two weeks), Mark noticed both a decrease in his anxiety and fewer panic attacks. Within a month, the panic attacks stopped completely. Once the attacks ceased, Mark was quickly able to taper and then stop the alprazolam. Over a two-month period, his mild agoraphobic symptoms disappeared as he gradually and consistently pushed himself to expand his activities.

Although three quarters of panic patients obtain significant relief from one of the above medications, in some patients, residual symptoms remain. When this occurs, a first strategy is to rethink the diagnosis, focusing on coexistent disorders that may be complicating the panic (Fyer and Sandberg, 1988). Patients who suffer from a combination of anticipatory anxiety, generalized anxiety, and panic may not always (understandably) accurately distinguish between the sources of their discomfort. They may complain about continued symptoms, thinking these are "prepanic" feelings when they are due to anticipatory anxiety—worrying about panic. Since higher doses of antidepressants will not necessarily help this type of anxiety, the distinction is clinically vital. Another condition that may complicate the evaluation and treatment of panic patients is depression. Those patients whose depression does not remit along with the panic may describe social withdrawal and not wanting to leave the house; thus what looks like agoraphobia may actually be a manifestation of untreated depression. The third disorder that may coexist with panic and be associated with treatment failure is social phobia. These patients may show a greater response to MAO inhibitors (see below).

Alternative medication treatments for panic disorder include combining any two of the above drugs, or adding propranolol or buspirone to any one of the first-line medications. No study has systematically explored combining two of the standard treatments. Clinically, though, psychopharmacologists use this strategy frequently, especially the combination of a cyclic antidepressant plus alprazolam. Propranolol, a beta-blocker (see chapter 11), is occasionally prescribed for treating panic, but with limited success (Munjack et al., 1989). It should be reserved for use in treatment-resistant cases, typically prescribed in combination with more effective medications. Although buspirone is probably ineffective in treating panic when prescribed alone, it is occasionally helpful when used in combination with more standard agents.

### Continuation and Maintenance Treatment for Panic Disorder

Since the natural history of panic disorder is exceedingly variable and relatively unstudied, current recommendations for continuation and/or maintenance treatment can only be considered best clinical guesses. For most patients, a course of antipanic medication should be continued for six months to one year following clinical remission of symptoms before a slow tapering of the medication is attempted. If symptoms emerge during the tapering period, the dose is generally increased to the lowest effective level and continued for another six months when a second tapering should be attempted. Because discontinuation of alprazolam is particularly difficult with panic patients, the schedule for tapering the dose is usually very slow (Fyer, Liebowitz, et al., 1987). Antipanic medications should not be tapered at a time of significant psychological stress, such as moving to a new house, starting a new job, separation and divorce.

Similarly, the role of maintenance treatment for panic disorder—that is, the ongoing use of medication for years to prevent recurrent clusters of panic attacks—is an unexplored area in psychopharmacology. The most reasonable candidates for maintenance, though, would be patients who have a history of unremitting panic disorder for many years or decades and who have had at least two attempts at tapering their medication that have been unsuccessful because of the re-emergence of panic attacks.

### Generalized Anxiety Disorder

Because it is a poorly delineated syndrome with its borders rather blurred, treatment for generalized anxiety focuses on decreasing the symptom of anxiety, rather than on manifestations of a specific disorder. Therefore, in this section, we will discuss the pharmacological treatment of generalized anxiety, adjustment disorder with anxiety, and situational anxiety together. Currently, two types of medications are rational first choices—the benzodiazepines and buspirone. Six other medication classes are occasionally prescribed, but only as second-line treatments. Table 4–4 shows these medication groups.

By far, the benzodiazepines are the most commonly prescribed and most effective antianxiety medications currently available. As with their use in panic

TABLE 4–4

*Medications for Generalized Anxiety*

First-line agents:
 Benzodiazepines
 Buspirone
Others:
 Cyclic antidepressants
 Monoamine oxidase inhibitors
 Barbiturates
 Nonbarbiturate tranquilizers
 Antipsychotics
 Antihistamines

disorder, their advantages in treating generalized anxiety are impressive: they are effective when taken on an as-needed basis or when taken regularly; when taken chronically, they generally do not lose their effectiveness; they have no long-term adverse effects on any organ; and, when taken in overdose by themselves, they are extremely safe.

Unfortunately, all these positive points lulled a great many people, physicians included, into considering benzodiazepines as perfect medications rather than excellent ones. Thus, five to ten years ago, when it was the most popular antianxiety drug prescribed, diazepam (Valium) received a great deal of negative publicity for its capacity to cause withdrawal symptoms. More recently, both alprazolam (Xanax) and triazolam (Halcion) have been criticized in the popular press for withdrawal phenomena in the case of the former and cognitive side effects and adverse mood symptoms with the latter. All the criticisms have some basis in fact. Nonetheless, overall, benzodiazepines are still the best medications available to treat anxiety—when prescribed for the right people in the right doses for an appropriate length of time.

All benzodiazepines are equally effective as antianxiety agents. They are all somewhat sedating (as opposed to tranquilizing—see chapter 11), with clonazepam slightly more sedating than the others. In picking a specific benzodiazepine, the most important factor is the goal of the medication treatment. (Chapter 11 provides a detailed discussion of this topic.) If the purpose is to decrease anxiety during a period of extreme stress lasting for weeks and months, a long-acting medication, the effects of which will continue throughout the day, is best. Diazepam and clonazepam are examples of this type. If patients who need ongoing relief from anxiety are given a short-acting medication, they will need multiple doses throughout the day and will usually suffer from anxiety between doses as the effects of the medication wear off. On the other hand, patients who need treatment on a more intermittent basis—for example, during a particularly stressful day—will generally do better with a shorter-acting tranquilizer, such as alprazolam or lorazepam. Those who need only intermittent relief and take a long-acting benzodiazepine often complain of feeling drugged for many hours after the anxiety-provoking situation has passed. Frequently, however, patients will tell a psychopharmacologist at their first meeting that they took diazepam in the past for as-needed relief and did well with no hangover or untoward lingering effects. In these circumstances, it makes more sense to yield to patients' own individual experience than to treat them "according to the numbers."

Just as when they are prescribed for panic, the most important drawback to the benzodiazepines as antianxiety agents is their capacity to produce dependency and withdrawal symptoms when they are stopped (Noyes, Garvey, Cook, and Perry, 1988). Here too, the short-acting medications are more likely to be a problem, although generalized anxiety patients may have an easier time withdrawing from benzodiazepines than do panic patients. Because of their potential for dependency, patients with a history of drug problems, especially with sedating drugs, such as alcoholics, should be treated with benzodiazepines only with extreme caution.

The other disadvantages of the benzodiazepines are their capacity to cause sedation and decrease cognitive capacity (see chapter 11 for details). With patients who operate heavy machinery or drive cars for a living, sedation may be a potential hazard, especially in the beginning of treatment before tolerance to the sedating effects of the benzodiazepines has occurred. Cognitive deficits are manifested primarily by a diminished ability to learn and recall new information. These effects are probably maximal in the initial stages of treatment.

Buspirone (Buspar), the newest of the antianxiety medications, is chemically unrelated to the benzodiazepines. It is completely nonsedating and shows no additive effects when combined with alcohol, thereby making it safe in many circumstances in which the benzodiazepines might pose a hazard. It is nonlethal when taken in overdose, holds no addictive potential whatsoever, and no withdrawal effects are seen at any dose when it is stopped abruptly.

As a corollary to its nonsedating nature, however, buspirone is not effective in inducing sleep. Furthermore, it cannot be used on an as-needed basis; it is only effective if it is taken on a regular basis for at least one week. In this way it resembles antidepressants more than the benzodiazepines. The major concern with buspirone is its efficacy. Although the early studies comparing it to a variety of benzodiazepines demonstrated that the two classes of medications were equally effective, recent studies, as well as my experience and those of many colleagues, indicate that patients do not respond nearly as well to buspirone. Additionally, patients who have taken benzodiazepines in the past respond less well to buspirone (Olajide and Lader, 1987). Thus, the decreased recent response to buspirone may, in part, be due to its increasing use in patients with previous exposure to benzodiazepines. Whatever the cause, clinical experience casts some doubt on its efficacy. It may be an excellent choice, however, for sober alcoholics who complain of anxiety.

Cyclic antidepressants are effective for some patients with generalized anxiety (Hoehn-Saric, McLeod, and Zimmerli, 1988). However, their side effects and the two- to six-week delay in clinical improvement limit their usefulness for short-term anxiety relief. Another approach often used by internists and general practitioners is to prescribe low doses of sedating antidepressants such as doxepin (Sinequan) or trazodone (Desyrel) to anxious patients in order to improve sleep and cause mild daytime sedation. When used in this way, the side effect of the medication (sedation) is being used for a therapeutic purpose. Few psychopharmacologists use sedating antidepressants as a sole treatment for anxiety.

MAO inhibitors have never been systematically studied as a treatment for generalized anxiety disorder without depression. This is especially unfortunate given the substantial evidence of their efficacy in treating panic disorder. My own clinical experience has been positive in a few treatment-refractory cases.

Barbiturates have been used to treat anxiety for over eighty years. Like the benzodiazepines, they are available in both short- and long-acting forms, thereby providing flexibility. Unfortunately, they are extremely addictive medications and can cause a serious withdrawal syndrome which includes grand mal seizures. In contrast to the benzodiazepines, they are also easily lethal when taken in overdose. For all these reasons, barbiturates are rarely prescribed for anxiety. Occasionally, a patient may experience some benefit beyond what might be seen with benzodiazepines when given an occasional dose of one of the shorter-acting barbiturates.

During the 1950s and early 1960s, a group of tranquilizers were released that formed a bridge between the barbiturates and the benzodiazepines. The most commonly prescribed of these was meprobamate (Miltown); the most notorious was methaqualone (Quaalude) which is no longer available in the United States. These medications, initially thought to be much safer and less addicting than the barbiturates, turned out to be neither. As with the barbiturates, there are few reasons to prescribe them at this time except for the occasional benzodiazepine-intolerant patient.

Beta-blockers are also occasionally used for generalized anxiety (Noyes, 1985). They may be most effective with those patients whose anxiety symptoms are predominantly physiological—tremor, sweating, and fast heartbeat—with fewer psychological symptoms. At medium to high dose, they can cause depressive symptoms or significant fatigue.

The other two classes of medications occasionally prescribed for anxiety symptoms are antipsychotics and antihistamines. The antipsychotics may successfully tranquilize and/or sedate some patients. However, the risk of significant side effects, including tardive dyskinesia, should make their use unusual. If they are used for otherwise unmanageable anxiety, the more sedating antipsychotics such as chlorpromazine are generally prescribed. Antihistamines are sedating medications that are occasionally taken by patients whose potential for addiction precludes the use of benzodiazepines.

## Continuation and Maintenance Treatment of Generalized Anxiety

When antianxiety medications are prescribed briefly, as with adjustment disorders or for situational anxiety, continuation treatment is not a relevant issue. When the need for the medication no longer exists, it should be discontinued. Except when they have been taken intermittently, medications should virtually always be tapered since rebound symptoms, albeit short-lived, can be seen even after a few weeks of treatment with a short-acting benzodiazepine (Rickels, Fox, Greenblatt, Sandler, and Schless, 1988).

Many patients who suffer from chronic anxiety (typically more than one year) need not take tranquilizers continually. In a number of studies, when placebo is substituted for diazepam in a double-blind manner with anxious patients who have been successfully treated (as defined by a marked decrease in anxiety), approximately half of them will not become anxious for the first month following drug discontinuation (Rickels, Case, Downing, and Winokur, 1983). Unfortunately, a majority of these patients will have a gradual return of symptoms within one year (Rickels, Case, Downing, and Friedman, 1986). The implication of these two findings is that even chronic anxiety waxes and wanes in intensity over months and years and that most patients can be managed by the intermittent use of benzodiazepines with good chance of benefit.

There is, however, a subgroup of chronically anxious patients who derive consistent relief from a stable dose of benzodiazepines taken over many years and who quickly become more anxious upon medication withdrawal, even if it is correctly tapered to avoid withdrawal effects. If there is no evidence of tolerance (the need for progressively larger doses), it is appropriate to continue these patients on their stable and safe dose of medication.

## Social Phobia

Distinguishing between the limited and the more generalized types of social phobia is vital since the two subtypes differ in their medication responsiveness.

For patients with the performance anxiety subtype of social phobia, beta-blockers are the most well documented treatment (Liebowitz et al., 1985). Either propranolol or atenolol (which causes less sedation and fatigue) is likely to be effective. Typically, the medication is taken on an as-needed basis, usually a half hour or an hour before a public performance. MAO inhibitors may also be effective for performance anxiety, although the evidence is less clear, in part because many studies have not distinguished between performance and generalized types of social phobia. If MAO inhibitors are used for performance anxiety, they must be taken as a maintenance medication. Benzodiazepines are also sometimes prescribed on an as-needed basis with anecdotal success.

Within the last few years, MAO inhibitors have been shown to be effective in treating the more generalized form of social phobia (Liebowitz, Gorman, et al., 1988). Both phenelzine and tranylcypromine have been used successfully, although the evidence is strongest for the former. When treatment is successful, patients will describe a marked increase in the sheer number of social situations they will allow themselves to enter. One person may now accept dates, another may accept a position of leadership previously avoided because of the necessity of interacting more with others. The level of improvement is independent of any baseline depression. In my experience, even when the MAO inhibitors are helpful, other interventions—social skills training, psychodynamic therapy, confronting associated use of alcohol—are usually necessary for the best clinical response.

> Bob, now 22, had always been shy. In school, he was unable to participate in class discussions because of overwhelming anxiety when called upon to speak. This interfered with his grades, which, given his intelligence, were lower than expected. He felt like a failure in comparison with his siblings and was convinced he was a disappointment to his high-achieving parents. Throughout school, he was able to make a few friends with whom he could play sports, but he had no girlfriends. He described how he would be attracted to a girl from afar, yet when he approached her to start a conversation, he would become paralyzed with fear, turn bright red, and say no more than a few words before walking away in anguish. While in high school, he was seen in psychotherapy by a therapist who focused on self-esteem issues and helped Bob improve his social skills. Although Bob liked the therapist and felt better about himself and less criticized by his parents, he was still unable to approach girls or participate in class discussions. By the end of his freshman year of college, Bob was drinking a half bottle of wine a night, insisting that it was the only way he could relax and be less than profoundly self-conscious with others. His growing dependence on

alcohol frightened him and he re-entered therapy. His therapist suggested a psychopharmacological consultation, in which social phobia was diagnosed and tranylcypromine (Parnate) was recommended. After reaching a dose of 40 mg daily, which took six weeks to accomplish because of significant postural hypotension, Bob noted a marked increase in his ability to be with others without feeling overwhelmed with anxiety. He was able to talk to girls and feel only moderately nervous. In class, although still hesitant to speak up, he was able to do so at times. Despite his clear improvement, however, he did not diminish his alcohol use for many months because of his fear of being without it. Moreover, Bob found that he still focused on his feelings of failure. Because of this, he continued in psychotherapy, which benefited him greatly. One year after starting the medication, he felt far more confident and stopped psychotherapy, but continued on the tranylcypromine, still feeling unready to try going without it.

Whether beta-blockers are effective in treating generalized social phobia is uncertain. As in the case of MAO inhibitors and performance anxiety, many studies have not distinguished between the two types of social phobia. Neither cyclic antidepressants nor benzodiazepines have been investigated in any systematic manner for treating generalized social phobia.

Not enough is known about the natural history of social phobia to make any concrete suggestions regarding continuation and maintenance treatment. My own experience is mixed. When medication is effective, some patients seem to be able to develop social skills and social confidence. They can then stop taking the medication without the return of unmanageable symptoms in social situations. Others experience the return of the same paralyzing symptoms after discontinuing the medication, necessitating its resumption. In the absence of any studies, the same guidelines used with panic disorder are reasonable: six months to one year after a good clinical response, a tapering of the medication is indicated.

## Obsessive Compulsive Disorder

First suggested from an open clinical trial twenty years ago, the efficacy of antidepressants in treating obsessions and compulsions has now been confirmed by a number of double-blind studies. Clomipramine, just released in this country in early 1990, is the best documented effective medication, helping 60 to 70 percent of patients with obsessions and compulsions. Baseline depression is probably unimportant as a predictor of the response, suggesting a direct effect on the symptoms. Patients show increasing improvement over the first twelve weeks of treatment, although significant effect will usually be seen within the first four weeks (Insel and Zohar, 1987).

Other medications may also be effective in treating obsessive compulsive disorder, although none of them compare to clomipramine in the sheer documentation of their efficacy. The most promising of these other medications are the antidepressants that most closely resemble clomipramine in its specific effect on serotonin. Of these, fluoxetine is the most likely to be effective. It has the advantage of being virtually nonsedating in contrast to clomipramine which can be significantly sedating. Trazodone (Desyrel) may also have some beneficial effect. Most other cyclic antidepressants have been tried with only occasional success. When MAO inhibitors are prescribed, the best responders may be those patients who suffer from obsessive compulsive disorder and concomitant panic disorder (Jenike, Surman, Cassem, Zusky, and Anderson, 1983). Antipsychotics may be helpful for those patients whose disorder has become psychotic. The risk of tardive dyskinesia with prolonged use, however, must always be considered (see chapter 12).

Joseph had always been anxious and somewhat fastidious. Recently, though, his need for order seemed to increase to extraordinary proportions. Instead of just turning the water off after watering his lawn, he tightened the knob and then returned to check it at least five times in the course of the evening. He was concerned, he said, that if the water leaked, the ground would become flooded, which might result in a weakening of his house's foundations. His habit of checking on his children while they were asleep, which had always consisted of glancing into their rooms, had now escalated into taking their pulse, examining their breathing, and rearranging their blankets to make sure they would not suffocate. Not surprisingly, they awakened during these checks. Before leaving the house, Joseph was now compelled to check and recheck the oven, the windows, and the doors so many times that it took him thirty minutes or more to go from his house to his car. He was aware of the irrational nature of his rituals yet felt powerless to resist them.

Initially seen in psychodynamically oriented psychotherapy, Joseph explored his catastrophic fears and his difficulty in being soothed. The rituals, however, continued unabated and even worsened somewhat. A psychopharmacological consultant recommended fluoxetine in doses increasing to 80 mg daily. Eight weeks after starting the medication, Joseph felt a slight decrease in the compulsion to repeat these rituals. Over the next month, the time spent on his rituals decreased by more than half. On the recommendation of the consultant, Joseph sought further help from a behavior therapist who constructed a program of response prevention. Within three months, the compulsions were virtually gone.

Because only some obsessive compulsive patients have chronic symptoms, the recommendations for continuation treatment are identical to those given for panic disorder and social phobia: tapering the medication after six months to one year of use.

Finally, there is a small but consistent series of reports on the use of psychosurgery as a treatment for treatment-resistant paralyzing obsessions and compulsions. The surgery is limited to cutting neuronal tracts between part of the frontal lobe and the cingulate gyrus (in the limbic system). Although I have no personal experience with this treatment, studies suggest a good effect occurring gradually over many months after surgery in the majority of patients treated (Perse, 1988). Clearly, this is a treatment of last resort. Yet intense, severe obsessive compulsive disorder can make life unliveable, as anyone who has treated these patients can attest. Occasionally, extraordinary measures need to be considered.

## Post-traumatic Stress Disorder

Of all the anxiety disorders for which medications may be helpful, post-traumatic stress disorder (PTSD) has been the least investigated. In part, this stems from our belated attempts at defining the syndrome. Even more, though, it reflects the conceptualization of PTSD as etiologically related to a profound life event and diagnosed only in relation to that event. It is a counterintuitive notion (although not necessarily correct) to consider using medications to treat a reactive disorder. However, over the last five years, preliminary studies using pharmacological approaches have been encouraging. The cyclic antidepressants, MAO inhibitors, and carbamazepine have shown the most promise. For all three types of medications, the therapeutic effects are greater for decreasing the intrusion and hyperarousal symptoms than for the emotional numbing and avoidance (Friedman, 1988). If the avoidance symptoms are seen as secondary protective mechanisms that stem from the primary hyperarousal and intrusive symptoms, medication effects in PTSD are analogous to those seen in panic disorder in which the panic (hyperarousal) responds to medication but the phobic avoidance (like the numbing and avoidance aspects of PTSD) must often be treated separately. Continuing the analogy, successful pharmacotherapy of PTSD may make psychotherapy (which is mandatory in all cases) more productive as feelings become less overwhelming and reconnecting with the emotional world less threatening.

Several factors should be considered in deciding among the three medication choices: (1) the presence of associated depression would suggest the choice of an antidepressant; (2) a history of cocaine or alcohol abuse dictates against prescribing an MAO inhibitor (because of the dietary restrictions); (3) the prominence of explosive outbursts and/or head trauma might suggest prescribing carbamazepine because of its effect on neurological or episodic syndromes.

Benzodiazepines have been used to treat PTSD for many years. With the growing awareness of their potential for addiction and the observation that a substantial proportion of PTSD patients have concomitant alcohol abuse, prescribing benzodiazepines, especially the shorter-acting ones, must be considered with caution. The use of neuroleptics is best limited to the unusual patient with psychotic symptoms or extremely destructive behavior.

## INSOMNIA

Sleeping problems affect one third of the population, most of whom never seek treatment (Byerley and Gillin, 1984). Since many psychiatric disorders are associated with insomnia, the proportion of sleeping problems in psychiatric outpatients is even higher and may exceed 50 percent. Insomnia, however, is a symptom and not a disorder. Therefore, reasonable treatments, pharmacological or otherwise, cannot be discussed before noting the most common causes of insomnia.

### Diagnosis

Since there are no agreed-upon definitions of insomnia, it makes the most sense to describe it as a subjective sensation of sleeping poorly (Nino-Murcia and Keenan, 1988). Most patients will complain that they do not sleep enough hours, although others report sufficient sleep that does not feel restful or refreshing. Often, there is an extraordinary disparity between subjective complaints and the findings of a sleep electroencephalogram (EEG), which documents with precision how long it takes patients to fall asleep, how many times they awaken, and how long they sleep (Roffwarg and Erman, 1984). Nonetheless, the great majority of people complaining of insomnia have genuine difficulties sleeping.

When patients complain of poor sleep, they describe one or a combination of three patterns: difficulty falling asleep; disrupted sleep during the night, which is usually described as awakening multiple times and taking variable amounts of time to go back to sleep; or early morning awakening—getting up one or more hours before it is necessary or usual and being unable to go back to sleep. Although there are some stereotyped links between certain psychiatric disorders and patterns of insomnia, such as depression with early morning awakening or anxiety with difficulty falling asleep, there is enough variability to view this scheme with skepticism. It is more useful simply to describe all insomnia as disorders of initiating and maintaining sleep—called DIMS in the sleep nomenclature. Table 4–5 lists the common causes of insomnia.

The most common of these sleep disorders are those related to transient, short-term, or situational stresses. These might be due to interpersonal conflicts, job stresses, moving from one house to another, changing jobs, or anxieties about health. Jet lag is also a common cause of transient insomnia.

Insomnia that persists beyond a few weeks may also be due to stress (interpersonal difficulties are certainly known to extend beyond a few weeks!) but is more likely to reflect some underlying disorder. A patient who complains of persistent insomnia should be questioned about other depressive or anxiety symptoms (see chapter 3 and above for appropriate questions). Both unipolar and bipolar depression, mania or hypomania, generalized anxiety, panic disorder, obsessive compulsive disorder, and post-traumatic stress as well as other psychiatric disorders can present with insomnia. Psychotic disorders such as schizophrenia virtually always present with insomnia, although these disorders are less common in outpatient practices.

The use of drugs and alcohol is another important cause of insomnia. Alcohol itself has powerful effects on sleep. Everyone is aware of how drinking helps induce sleep onset. Fewer people know that the same alcohol that helps them

TABLE 4–5

*Common Causes of Insomnia*

Transient:
    Situational stress
    Jet lag
Persistent:
    Many psychiatric disorders: major depression, generalized anxiety, mania, etc.
    Drug and alcohol use
    Psychiatric medications, e.g., some antidepressants
    Medications for medical disorders
    Pain syndromes
    Primary sleep disorders
    Sleep apnea
    Nocturnal myoclonus
    Restless legs syndrome
    Psychophysiological insomnia (of unknown cause)

get to sleep will increase the likelihood of their awakening a few hours later due to alcohol's capacity to fragment and disrupt normal sleep patterns. When patients who have been drinking regularly stop, rebound insomnia will likely ensue, frequently setting up a desire to resume drinking in order to sleep—a strategy that exacerbates the problem. Similarly, if sleeping pills are stopped suddenly, rebound insomnia as well as nightmarish dreams are extremely common (see chapter 11 for details). It may seem that these situations would be easy to ascertain: patients would tell their therapists that they stopped drinking or taking sleeping pills and then had insomnia. More commonly, though, patients either hide the use of alcohol or hypnotics from the therapist or seem to have blocked this knowledge from themselves as well.

Stimulants, both illicit like cocaine and amphetamines and licit like caffeine drinks, can also cause insomnia. As with the use of sedatives, tranquilizers, and alcohol, patients may not be forthcoming about these substances unless asked.

Many medications appropriately prescribed for psychiatric purposes can also cause insomnia. Because they are often prescribed for disorders that are also associated with sleep disruption, the role of the medications can be obscured. Most common among these are antidepressants, especially MAO inhibitors and the more stimulating cyclic antidepressants such as bupropion (Wellbutrin) or fluoxetine (Prozac). Similarly, a number of medications prescribed for a variety of medical disorders, notably those used to treat asthma and hypertension, are associated with insomnia.

Many medical conditions can also cause insomnia. Aside from the obvious disorders associated with pain or discomfort, three specific medical sleep disorders are sometimes found in patients with insomnia (Byerley and Gillin, 1984). Sleep apnea is characterized by multiple periods of stopping breathing for more than ten seconds while asleep. The resumption of breathing often causes patients to awaken with a start. Complaints of daytime sleepiness are common, and patients' bed partners will describe loud snoring and irregular breathing. Nocturnal myoclonus, characterized by multiple episodes of "jerking" of the legs, may awaken either patients or their bed partners, who may complain of being kicked by these jerks. Restless legs syndrome is the third of the specific sleep disorders. Patients with this disorder describe peculiar feelings in their legs that cause an irresistible need to move around. This often diminishes the sensation. In some ways, it is subjectively similar to akathisia caused by the antipsychotics (see chapter 12).

A minority of patients with persistent insomnia have no obvious psychiatric or medical disorders, nor do they use substances or medications in a way that explains the sleep problem. In other words, they have insomnia as a disorder. The cause of this condition is unknown, although a frequent explanation is that a transient stress-related insomnia becomes persistent when patients focus on the problem and "try" to sleep. At that point, the heightened anxiety about the inability to sleep begins to be associated with typical sleep cues such as nighttime or being in bed and these become conditioned stimuli for insomnia. Despite relatively normal functioning in other areas of their lives, these patients become absorbed in the nightly struggle to sleep. It is likely that certain stable personality, temperamental, or psychophysiological traits such as being tense and easily aroused, tending to somatize distress, and possibly being a biologically light sleeper are also more common in this population (Roffwarg and Erman, 1985).

Certainly, therapists do not need to be able to distinguish among these various disorders. It would be helpful, though, to briefly evaluate a patient for some of the causes of insomnia if complaints of sleep difficulties arise. Are other symptoms of depression, mania, or anxiety present? Is the patient drinking or using drugs or has he recently changed his consumption of these substances? Spending a few minutes probing these few areas may yield a great deal of useful information.

## Treatment

Hypnotics, defined as medications causing sleep, are a common treatment for insomnia. Yet their use has declined significantly over the last decade. Only half as many prescriptions for hypnotics were written in 1982 compared to the peak use in 1971 (Mendelson, 1985). Furthermore, the majority of these sleeping pills—75 percent—were taken for less than two weeks. Still, the fact that over 4 percent of the entire population each year have been prescribed sleeping pills indicates the magnitude of our societal use of these medications. If one peruses any textbook or review article on the treatment of insomnia, it is clear that hypnotics are recommended only as a small part of the overall treatment. Why then do so many people take them in real life? The answer is twofold. First, it is likely that patients are given the pills quickly without a thorough evaluation of the insomnia. Second, since the benzodiazepines, the most common hypnotics prescribed, are so effective, it is simple for physicians to prescribe and patients to take a sleeping pill as opposed to using any other method of treatment. The hypnotics are also frequently refilled on a routine basis without a reevaluation of the ongoing need for them.

In general, the decision to prescribe hypnotics should depend on the cause of the insomnia. When short-term use is needed—for example, for jet lag or transient stress—benzodiazepines are safe and effective. If the insomnia is due to another psychiatric disorder, such as depression or an anxiety disorder, sleeping pills may be used transiently in the beginning of treatment, but it is even more important that the underlying disorder is treated. Insomnia due to the use of stimulants or alcohol, or to the withdrawal of sedatives/tranquilizers should be treated by addressing the underlying condition. If sleep apnea, nocturnal myoclonus, or restless legs syndrome are suspected, patients should be referred to a sleep expert for evaluation and treatment. Patients with sleep apnea should not take hypnotics because of the risk of increasing the time of not breathing.

The thorniest problem arises with patients who have chronic insomnia of no known cause. Without question, nonpharmacological approaches are best. The most important of these is described as good sleep hygiene, characterized by such habits as maintaining regular arousal times, exercising regularly, avoiding hunger at night, and the like (Hauri and Sateia, 1985). Other treatments include relaxation techniques, biofeedback, and other behavioral strategies. For those who do not cooperate with these techniques or for whom these approaches are unsuccessful, hypnotics are inevitably considered. When used in conjunction with nonpharmacological techniques, they can be extremely useful. What is less clear is whether their efficacy continues if taken over months and years (Mendelson, 1987). My own clinical experience is that some patients with chronic insomnia do maintain a good response to hypnotics over long periods of time.

With a few exceptions, the list of effective hypnotic medications overlaps greatly with those used to treat generalized anxiety disorder. (The four medications occasionally used to treat anxiety that are not effective as hypnotics are buspirone, monoamine oxidase inhibitors, clonidine, and beta-blockers.) Benzodiazepines are unquestionably the most commonly prescribed and most effective sleeping pills available. As with treating generalized anxiety, it is likely that all benzodiazepines are helpful as hypnotics. For treating insomnia, the primary consideration is how long the medication lasts. Short to intermediate acting benzodiazepines such as triazolam (Halcion) and temazepam (Restoril) will cause little hangover in the morning and, in the case of triazolam, may possibly cause early morning awakening as it wears off. The major disadvantage to the short-acting medications is the increased risk of causing dependence and precipitating withdrawal symptoms, including rebound insomnia, when they are stopped. The more long-acting benzodiazepines, such as flurazepam (Dalmane), cause more morning hangover but less dependence and fewer withdrawal symptoms when stopped. (See chapter 11 for more details on the different benzodiazepines and withdrawal symptoms.)

As noted earlier in the chapter, although both the barbiturates and the nonbarbiturate sedatives are effective as hypnotics and tranquilizers, they have been appropriately supplanted by the benzodiazepines. Because of its reputation (probably undeserved) as a safe drug, chloral hydrate has survived and is still used occasionally.

Sedating cyclic antidepressants such as amitriptyline (Elavil) and trazodone (Desyrel) are sometimes prescribed as hypnotics. Although they are safe medications, their potential for other side effects should make their use, especially amitriptyline, infrequent in treating insomnia. Similarly, antihistamines are also used to treat insomnia because they are sedating and nonaddictive.

The two types of medications used as hypnotics that are never used as daytime antianxiety agents are l-tryptophan and the over-the-counter sleeping pills. L-tryptophan is nonaddictive, and probably effective although less so than the benzodiazepines. Because it is a natural substance and available without a prescription, it has been favored by many. Unfortunately, l-tryptophan is currently unavailable because of recent toxic reactions (see chapter 11). It is not yet clear whether these reactions are due to the l-tryptophan itself or to impurities found in some preparations. Over-the-counter hypnotics generally contain a combination of an antihistamine and a sedating anticholinergic agent. They are only minimally effective and can cause a variety of side effects if taken in large quantities.

# 5

# Schizophrenia and Related Disorders

## DIAGNOSIS

Of all psychiatric disorders, schizophrenia is the one most synonymous with "mental illness," a term connoting a severe and disabling disorder that makes other people uncomfortable and fearful. Also, it is the disorder with which the term "craziness" is most frequently linked. As stated, these two statements are true: Schizophrenia *is* the most severe of all psychiatric disorders, usually characterized by a chronic course with frequent and sometimes prolonged hospitalizations. Approximately 25 percent of *all*, not just psychiatric, hospital beds in the United States are occupied by schizophrenic patients. The hallmark of schizophrenia *is* the prominence of psychotic or crazy thinking. Psychosis is defined in DSM-III-R as "gross impairment in reality testing and the creation of a new reality" (APA, 1987, p. 404). And DSM-III-R requires a phase of prominent psychotic symptoms to satisfy the criteria for schizophrenia.

In its classic, "textbook" form, therefore, schizophrenia is easy to diagnose: We would reserve the term for those patients who talk about their phone's being tapped by extraterrestrial beings or of the television's giving them messages about a new religion, who mutter to themselves as they walk on the street, have no friends, and are hopelessly disheveled. These patients pose no problem in diagnosis and, I presume, we would all think these patients deserve some type of treatment if they are to have any chance of a meaningful life in our society. The three difficult questions for diagnosis, however, are: (1) Are all schizophrenics as crazy as the description above indicates? (2) Do they all get worse over time? and (3) Are all patients with crazy, psychotic thinking schizophrenic? The answer to all these questions is assuredly no.

112

The link between psychosis and schizophrenia—the assumption that all psychotic patients are schizophrenic until proven otherwise—has been one of the most prominent, destructive, and incorrect principles in American psychiatry during the last fifty years. As recently as the early 1970s, medical students (including me) at good medical schools were being taught that "a touch of schizophrenia is schizophrenia"; that any bizarre or psychotic symptom that wasn't absolutely mood congruent and classic for mania or depression should be taken as evidence of schizophrenia regardless of whatever other clinical signs, symptoms, or family history features were also present. Additionally, American psychiatry was swayed by Bleuler's concept of schizophrenia with its emphasis on the "four As": autistic thinking, ambivalence, abnormalities in affect, and disturbed associations. Because this definition de-emphasized overt psychotic thought (such as delusions and hallucinations), it allowed patients to be diagnosed as schizophrenic because of inferred "schizophrenic" thought processes. By blurring the diagnostic boundaries of schizophrenia in these two ways—equating any psychotic thinking with schizophrenia and inferring schizophrenic thinking—American psychiatry broadened the boundaries of the schizophrenic diagnosis to unmanageable proportions. The most telling demonstration of this occurred twenty years ago with a study in which diagnostic principles in the United States and Great Britain were compared (Cooper, Kendall, & Kurland, 1972). Using a set of consistent diagnostic criteria and examining a series of consecutive admissions to hospital, the investigators found approximately equal numbers of schizophrenics and manic-depressive patients in Brooklyn and London. In reviewing the local diagnoses of these same patients, the investigators found that London psychiatrists had approximately the same diagnosis as did the study, whereas the Brooklyn psychiatrists had diagnosed schizophrenia *eight* times as often as manic-depressive illness! For mania specifically, of the twenty-two patients diagnosed as manic by the study criteria, twenty-one of them were diagnosed schizophrenic by the local psychiatrists.

The impact of these inaccurate diagnoses became magnified beginning in the 1950s when medication treatment for different disorders became available. Since a diagnosis of schizophrenia suggested the use of antipsychotics while manic-depressives were more appropriately treated with lithium, inaccurate diagnoses led to inaccurate treatment, with a real and potentially tragic impact on prognosis.

Since that time, the pendulum has swung in the opposite direction. Currently, DSM-III-R's definition of schizophrenia is the narrowest that exists (and narrower than that of its predecessor, DSM-III). As with the other psychiatric disorders in this book, our diagnostic criteria for schizophrenia are an amalgam of accumulated wisdom, data-based knowledge, and historical trends. As these change, so will our criteria. The current criteria should be considered a guide to diagnosis and *not* the revealed truth.

Unlike mood disorders, in which all patients, by definition, must have a disturbance in mood, schizophrenia has no core identifying characteristic. Whether this stems from the disorder's heterogeneity—is schizophrenia a group of disorders?—or from the varied expression of one central pathological process is unknown. What is clear is that there is no symptom that is diagnostic of schizophrenia. The "Schneiderian" symptoms, which are a group of psychotic symptoms thought to be pathognomonic of schizophrenia, have been demonstrated to be present in a variety of other disorders, including mood disorders (Pope and Lipinski, 1978). Similarly, Bleuler's "split" in schizophrenia, which the lay public misidentifies as multiple or split personalities, but which refers to the splitting of "the associative threads that tied together the fabric of thought" (Pfohl and Andreasen, 1986), is too unreliable a description to be used as a diagnostic key.

The core features of the DSM-III-R's definition of schizophrenia are a prolonged episode (lasting at least six months) in which (1) prominent psychotic symptoms are present for at least one week, (2) psychosocial functioning is markedly impaired, and (3) a major mood syndrome, if it exists, is relatively brief compared to the schizophrenic symptoms. Typically, there is a prodromal phase and a residual phase during the six-month minimum length of a schizophrenic episode. Table 5–1 shows the DSM-III-R criteria for schizophrenia.

The clinical symptoms that may be seen and are consistent with the diagnosis of schizophrenia are varied and include a veritable laundry list of delusions, hallucinations, and fractured cognitions. DSM-III-R has a particularly succinct and excellent description of these features (APA, 1987, pp. 188–190). Any clinician seeing a patient in the active phase of a schizophrenic episode will have no trouble recognizing the profound disturbance of thought. Making the diagnosis during the prodromal phase is much more difficult, especially for those patients who simply withdraw. An 18-year-old who presents with marked social isolation, dropping out of school, and lack of initiative meets three of the nine prodromal symptoms, yet it would be exceedingly difficult to know whether this is prodromal schizophrenia, atypical depression (assuming the classic sleep, appetite, or other symptoms were not present), or some version of adolescent regression secondary to an adjustment disorder or personality disorder. Frequently, it is only in retrospect that the symptoms are recognized as prodromal signs of schizophrenia. Of course, if a patient has had at least one previous episode, it is important to know his prodromal signs in order to diagnose more accurately the prodromal phase of an episode as early as possible.

Table 5–1

*Diagnostic Criteria for Schizophrenia*

A. Presence of characteristic psychotic symptoms in the active phase: either (1), (2), or (3) for at least one week (unless the symptoms are successfully treated):

(1) two of the following:

(a) delusions

(b) prominent hallucinations (throughout the day for several days or several times a week for several weeks, each hallucinatory experience not being limited to a few brief moments)

(c) incoherence or marked loosening of associations

(d) catatonic behavior

(e) flat or grossly inappropriate affect

(2) bizarre delusions (i.e., involving a phenomenon that the person's culture would regard as totally implausible, e.g., thought broadcasting, being controlled by a dead person)

(3) prominent hallucinations [as defined in (1)(b) above] of a voice with content having no apparent relation to depression or elation, or a voice keeping up a running commentary on the person's behavior or thoughts, or two or more voices conversing with each other.

B. During the course of the disturbance, functioning in such areas as work, social relations, and self-care is markedly below the highest level achieved before onset of the disturbance (or, when the onset is in childhood or adolescence, failure to achieve expected level of social development).

C. Schizoaffective disorder and mood disorder with psychotic features have been ruled out, i.e., if a major depressive or manic syndrome has ever been present during an active phase of the disturbance, the total duration of all episodes of a mood syndrome has been brief relative to the total duration of the active and residual phases of the disturbance.

D. Continuous signs of the disturbance for at least six months. The six-month period must include an active phase (of at least one week, or less if symptoms have been successfully treated) during which there were psychotic symptoms characteristic of schizophrenia (symptoms in A), with or without a prodromal or residual phase, as defined below.

*Prodromal phase:* A clear deterioration in functioning before the active phase of the disturbance that is not due to a disturbance in mood or to a psychoactive substance use disorder and that involves at least two of the symptoms listed below.

*Residual phase:* Following the active phase of the disturbance, persistence of at least two of the symptoms noted below, these not being due to a disturbance in mood or to a psychoactive substance use disorder.

(Continues)

TABLE 5–1 (Continued)

*Diagnostic Criteria for Schizophrenia*

*Prodromal or residual symptoms:*

(1) marked social isolation or withdrawal

(2) marked impairment in role functioning as wage-earner, student, or homemaker

(3) markedly peculiar behavior (e.g., collecting garbage, talking to self in public, hoarding food)

(4) marked impairment in personal hygiene and grooming

(5) blunted or inappropriate affect

(6) digressive, vague, overelaborate, or circumstantial speech, or poverty of speech, or poverty of content of speech

(7) odd beliefs or magical thinking, influencing behavior and inconsistent with cultural norms, e.g., superstitiousness, belief in clairvoyance, telepathy, "sixth sense," "others can feel my feelings," overvalued ideas, ideas of reference

(8) unusual perceptual experiences, e.g., recurrent illusions, sensing the presence of a force or person not actually present

(9) marked lack of initiative, interests, or energy

*Examples:* Six months of prodromal symptoms with one week of symptoms from A; no prodromal symptoms with six months of symptoms from A; no prodromal symptoms with one week of symptoms from A and six months of residual symptoms.

Reprinted with permission from the *Diagnostic and Statistical Manual of Mental Disorders, Third Edition, Revised.* Copyright 1987 American Psychiatric Association.

Recently, there has been an attempt to characterize the core symptoms of schizophrenia as either positive or negative. Positive symptoms are cognitive difficulties and unusual experiences, sensations, or beliefs present in schizophrenia and generally absent in normal functioning. These include hallucinations, delusions, bizarre behavior, and formal thought disorder (including loose associations). Negative symptoms are those capacities present in normal behavior that are absent or diminished in schizophrenia. These symptoms include lack of motivation, lack of social interest and skills, anhedonia, and poverty of speech. The distinction between positive and negative symptoms has been used in a proposed scheme for subtyping schizophrenic syndromes (see below).

Although not specifically noted in the DSM-III-R criteria, the presence of depressive symptoms (although not of a full major depressive episode) is common in schizophrenia, even in the midst of a florid psychotic episode (Knights and Hirsch, 1981). These depressive symptoms are expressed not only in social withdrawal but also in self-reported sadness, depressed mood, and suicidal ideation. A true depressive syndrome, with or without the vegetative signs of depression, occurs in up to 25 percent of patients, frequently manifesting itself soon after the resolution of an acute psychotic episode (McGlashan and Carpenter, 1976). The meaning or etiology of this postpsychotic depression has long been debated. It is likely that it represents a number of different clinical phenomena. Each patient's depression must be evaluated separately. The therapeutic plan then follows from the conceptualization of the depression. For instance, if the postpsychotic depression is thought of as a continuation of the natural history of a schizophrenic episode, the appropriate therapeutic strategy would be support and reassurance that the depression will lift after many months. If the postpsychotic depression is conceptualized psychodynamically as the loss of psychotic grandiosity or as representing the mourning of a cohesive self, gently exploratory psychotherapy is in order. The depressive state may also represent side effects from antipsychotic medication (Van Putten and May, 1978a) for which anticholinergic medication would be the appropriate intervention (see below). Another possibility is that the postpsychotic depression is actually a bipolar depression in a patient who has been misdiagnosed as schizophrenic, when the appropriate diagnosis was a psychotic manic episode, followed by a typical postmanic depressive episode. Using this formulation, the appropriate maneuver would be to stop the antipsychotic medication, consider lithium, and treat the patient as having a bipolar depression. If accompanied by typical vegetative signs of depression such as sleep and appetite disturbance, the possibility of the depressive state representing a true major depressive episode superimposed on schizophrenia (called depressive disorder not otherwise specified in DSM-III-R) must also be considered, since there is sufficient evidence that these states can be successfully treated with antidepressants. Finally, the depressive symptoms, if mild and characterized predominantly by anhedonia and poor motivation, may simply represent the negative symptoms of schizophrenia.

Regardless of the way in which depressive symptoms in schizophrenia are conceptualized, it is clear that suicide is a significant risk for patients with the disorder. Approximately 10 percent of schizophrenic patients will ultimately commit suicide (Miles, 1977), and the majority of those who do will have suffered from a depressive syndrome (Roy, 1986). In general, most schizophrenic suicides are not made during a florid psychotic relapse but during a less active phase of the illness. The usual clinical clues—hopelessness, depressive symptoms, communication of suicidal ideation and intent—are somewhat predictive, although schizophrenic suicide may also occur without warning.

Some symptoms, predominantly those described as evidence of a thought disorder or blunted or inappropriate affect, will be apparent in the clinical interview. Other symptoms must be elicited by specific questions. However, patients who have had these symptoms will often deny them because of paranoia or fear of the consequences of admitting to them, or because they hear voices instructing them not to tell anyone about these experiences. Therefore, as with so many other major psychiatric disorders, the use of outside informants, such as husbands, wives, or parents, is sometimes vital in gathering the appropriate information. For instance, despite the patients' denial of hallucinations, their families may describe them as having conversations when no one is present or as seeming to respond to voices not heard by others.

Therapists who do not frequently work with patients who experience the overtly psychotic symptoms seen in schizophrenia may find it difficult to ask specific questions about psychotic thoughts. Sample questions are listed here.

---

Have you ever felt as if people were trying to harm you? Do you have any idea why they wanted to harm you? (Frequently, probing for the rationale for the paranoia will elicit other psychotic thoughts.)

Does it seem that people are talking about you or making comments about you when you are in public? (A yes answer could indicate either ideas of reference or auditory hallucinations that are being attributed to passersby.)

Do you ever get the feeling that the radio or television is giving you special or specific messages? When you drive, do you ever think that the numbers or letters of the license plates of cars near you have special meaning?

Have you ever heard voices that other people couldn't hear? How often does this occur? What do the voices say? Were they telling you to do things? What were they telling you to do? (If yes, ask specifically whether the command hallucinations suggested potentially violent acts, such as suicide or homicide. Although they are an infrequent precipitant of suicide in schizophrenics, command hallucinations about suicide/homicide, when present, need to be taken seriously.) Did you hear more than one voice? Did they talk to each other about you?

(NOTE: Sometimes, patients will draw a distinction between voices heard inside and outside the head. The meaning of this distinction is unknown. The most important distinction would be between a thought and actually hearing a voice regardless of location. Also, people sometimes describe hearing whispers or hearing someone call their name as they go to sleep. If it only occurs at that time, it does not have major pathological significance.

Visual, tactile [feeling, tingling or crawling], or olfactory [smell] hallucinations also occur in schizophrenia but are less common than auditory hallucinations. The presence of these other types of hallucinations in the absence of auditory hallucinations suggest other diagnoses, such as drug-induced psychoses or some neurological disorders.)

Has it ever seemed that your thoughts were being broadcast out loud so that others could hear them?

Does it ever seem that your thoughts are not your own? Does it ever seem that someone is putting thoughts into your head, or taking them out of your head?

Does it seem as if your body is not your own or that someone else is in control of your body?

(NOTE: My experience of asking these questions is that patients who have never had the symptom in question, especially any of the last few listed above, will frequently not understand the question, since these experiences are somewhat bizarre, and will look at you blankly.)

---

## SUBTYPES OF SCHIZOPHRENIA

Traditionally, schizophrenia is divided into subtypes. In DSM-III-R, these subtypes are catatonic, disorganized (formerly hebephrenic), paranoid, undifferentiated, and residual. The first three subtypes are characterized by symptom patterns that exist during an acute exacerbation of the disorder. The undifferentiated type refers to any patient who is schizophrenic but who does not meet criteria for any of the other subtypes. Residual schizophrenia describes patients who have had at least one schizophrenic episode and are currently mildly symptomatic.

Whether subtyping schizophrenia according to these traditional categories is useful remains unclear. It is true that, compared to those with other types, patients with paranoid schizophrenia seem to have a later age of onset and may, in general, have fewer schizophrenics in their families (Pfohl and Andreasen, 1986). Unfortunately, a patient with one type may, over time, evolve into another type. Moreover, there is little evidence that treatment considerations differ among the types. Until more is known, the practice of subtyping is not clinically useful.

The most recent attempt at subtyping makes use of the positive/negative symptom dichotomy. As originally described by Crow (1980), Type 1 and Type 2 schizophrenia are different syndromes, or "dimensions of pathology," which might reflect different underlying pathologies. These were not meant to define two distinct subtypes of the disorder. Some patients may have both types of syndrome, while others may shift from predominantly positive to negative symptoms over time (Crow, Ferrier, and Johnstone, 1986). Type 1 syndrome of schizophrenia is characterized by a good premorbid course, predominantly positive symptoms, acute episodes with good response to antipsychotics, and complete remissions in which a chronic downhill course is not seen. Biologically, Type 1 schizophrenia is thought to reflect normal brain structure and evidence of excessive dopamine activity (explaining these patients' response to antipsychotics/dopamine blockers). Type 2 schizophrenia, on the other hand, is characterized by poor premorbid course, insidious onset, relatively poor response to antipsychotics, and a progressive downhill course with intellectual impairment. It is hypothesized that patients with Type 2 syndrome have a decrease in brain dopamine and would show evidence of brain cell loss (usually described as enlarged ventricles) on brain scans, such as the CAT scan.

Substantial evidence supporting the Type 1/Type 2 distinction exists. There does seem to be some clustering among abnormal CAT scans, poor intellectual function, and poor response to medication (Weinberger, 1986). Nonetheless, it would be premature to endorse the model unreservedly. Not only may a patient shift from Type 1 to Type 2 over time, but negative symptoms may also appear or diminish (Johnstone, Owens, Frith, and Crow, 1986). Furthermore, there may be multiple causes for negative symptoms in chronic patients, such as the effects of institutionalization, medication side effects, or depression.

In the United States, there has been a somewhat belated awareness of a later-onset subtype of schizophrenia arising during the forties, fifties, and sixties that is clinically difficult to distinguish from schizophrenia. These late-onset disorders have been called paraphrenias; DSM-III labeled them atypical psychoses; DSM-III-R calls them schizophrenia. In comparison to the early-onset disorder, late-onset schizophrenia affects predominantly females and is characterized by increased paranoid symptoms and a greater tendency towards chronicity. The psychotic symptoms do respond to antipsychotics (Harris and Jeste, 1988). Clinically, the implication is that although a nonmood psychosis (i.e., one that does not occur in the context of a full mood syndrome) arising in early adulthood is still the most common form of schizophrenia, the diagnosis cannot be ruled out because of a late age of onset.

## NATURAL HISTORY, EPIDEMIOLOGY, AND GENETICS

Schizophrenia is a disorder that typically first appears in early adult life. It tends to arise a few years later in women than men with an average age of first psychotic episode in the early twenties for men and the mid-twenties for women (Loranger, 1984). Schizophrenia affects 1 percent of people over a lifetime. Most, but not all, studies find the rate of schizophrenia to be slightly higher among men than women (Lewine, 1988).

The long-term outcome of schizophrenia is a topic that has been investigated repeatedly over the last hundred years. In fact, Kraepelin used a long-term poor prognosis as one of his key diagnostic features to distinguish schizophrenia from manic-depressive illness. As a generalization, chronic illness is the likely outcome in schizophrenia (Tsuang, Woolson, and Fleming, 1979). Yet a number of studies, using a variety of criteria to define schizophrenia, find a substantial subset of patients with the disorder who have a relatively good outcome as defined by lack of symptoms, work productivity, and social functioning. This good prognosis subset comprises approximately 20 percent of all schizophrenics (Pfohl and Andreasen, 1986). It has been surprisingly difficult to predict early in the course of the disorder who these good prognosis patients will be. In general, the best predictor in any sphere of functioning is a history of good premorbid functioning in that area (Strauss and Carpenter, 1974). Thus, a good work history prior to the first schizophrenic episode will predict a good capacity to work after illness onset, but not necessarily a good prognosis for socializing. However, given the diversity of outcome and our limited ability to predict it with any accuracy, in the initial years of the disorder *no* schizophrenic should be treated as an untreatable hopeless case.

Of all the psychiatric disorders, the familial and genetic roots of schizophrenia have been studied the most intensively. There is little doubt that schizophrenia is a familial disorder—that is, there is a significantly higher risk of schizophrenia in the relatives of schizophrenics than in the general population or in the families of patients with other major psychiatric disorders. This increased risk ranges between five and fifteen times the risk for the general population (Kendler, 1986). Demonstrating that a disorder is familial, however, does not help distinguish between environmental and genetic factors. Studies comparing monozygotic (identical) and dizygotic (fraternal) twins and studies of adopted-away children of schizophrenic parents *do* help make this distinction. The results of these studies give strong evidence that schizophrenia is not only familial but a genetic disorder as well.

Among the schizophrenia spectrum disorders, the evidence is strongest that schizotypal disorder and schizoaffective disorder, depressed type, are genetically linked to schizophrenia, while the evidence for paranoid disorder and atypical psychosis is far weaker.

## DISORDERS RELATED TO SCHIZOPHRENIA

### Schizophreniform Disorder

DSM-III-R uses six months as the minimum time criterion for diagnosing schizophrenia. An episode of schizophrenic-like symptoms that lasts less than six months—including prodromal and residual periods—is called a schizophreniform disorder. Thus, this disorder is simply a short episode of schizophrenia. The question, of course, is whether the six-month cutoff is meaningful. The results of studies done over the last decade are not consistent enough to answer this question definitively. It is likely that a substantial proportion of schizophreniform patients are otherwise typical schizophrenics with a short first episode while others may have another psychotic disorder with an atypical presentation. For clinical purposes, the only implication of a longer episode is that, in general, it predicts a poorer outcome (Pfohl and Andreasen, 1986). The length of the acute episode, however, should not alter the treatment plan.

### Schizoaffective Disorder

It is difficult to discuss schizoaffective disorder without first noting that the number of different sets of criteria used to define the disorder, even within the last ten years, makes generalizations precarious. As an example, DSM-III gave no specific criteria for schizoaffective disorder, in part because of the lack of consensus in the committee studying it. DSM-III-R does give defining characteristics, however, and they comprise a reasonable middle ground among the varying definitions. DSM-III-R schizoaffective disorder is characterized by an episode in which (1) a full manic or depressive syndrome coexists with the psychotic symptoms (the "A" criterion in Table 5–1) of schizophrenia, and (2) there has been a period of at least two weeks of hallucinations or delusions but no prominent mood symptoms. If the mood syndrome has been manic, the disorder is called schizoaffective disorder, bipolar type (schizomanic); if depressive, schizoaffective disorder, depressive type (schizodepressive). Thus, a patient with schizoaffective disorder will have an affectively colored psychotic period and another period of psychosis without mood symptoms.

> Barney, now 31 years old, has had psychiatric problems since he was 18. At that time, during his senior year in high school, he started using street drugs. Even when not using drugs, however, he became progressively more emotionally labile and had poor concentration, in marked contrast to his previously excellent school performance. At age 19, he had his first overt psychotic episode, characterized by grandiose, expansive thinking and delusions of grandeur (believing he was the reincarnation of God and was sent here to save the world), along with poor sleep and hyperactivity. Barney was soon hospitalized, during which time he lapsed into a severe depression sleeping fourteen hours nightly, staying in bed, and gaining twenty pounds. He recovered from this episode with medications. From age 21 through 24, Barney had

three episodes similar to the first one, except that the psychotic symptoms now occurred during the depressive phases as well as the hyperactive ones. The psychosis also became progressively more bizarre, including somatic delusions and prominent hallucinations. Between episodes, Barney was able to function and showed no evidence of psychosis. He enrolled in college and passed his courses. Yet his capacities seemed less than they had been before his first psychotic episode.

When he was 26, Barney had another psychotic episode, similar to earlier ones. However, after recovery from the depression, he noted that as he drove through the city, license plates held symbolic meanings for him—a license plate with more than one three meant that the holy trinity was watching over him, while the presence of sixes indicated that the devil was after him. He also had frequent feelings that people were commenting on his behavior as he walked through the streets. In class, he sometimes would feel that when his classmates shifted in their chairs, their body postures indicated their approval or disapproval of him. Despite vigorous treatment with psychotherapy and medications, which diminished the number of severe psychotic episodes, the subtler psychotic thoughts persisted.

But what is schizoaffective disorder? Is it a subset of schizophrenia? An unusual looking mood disorder? A separate psychotic disorder? Not surprisingly, the evidence is mixed (Levinson and Levitt, 1987; Levitt and Tsuang, 1988). As a group, schizoaffective patients have family histories with increased genetic loading for both schizophrenia *and* mood disorders. The prognosis for schizoaffective disorder tends to be better than that for schizophrenia and worse than that for mood disorders. Schizoaffective patients respond better to lithium than do schizophrenics, but not as well as bipolar patients. Currently, it is most helpful to view schizoaffective disorder as being composed of both schizophrenic and mood-disordered patients, all of whom show atypical symptoms and symptom combinations.

In trying to make the most accurate treatment plans and prognoses, it is helpful to distinguish between those with schizomania and schizodepression. In general, schizomania seems closer to bipolar disorder than to classic schizophrenia. The family histories of schizomanic patients are generally loaded with mood disorders and not with schizophrenia. They frequently respond to lithium. Their prognosis is reasonably good—similar to that of bipolar patients and not to schizophrenics. Schizodepression, on the other hand, is probably closer to classic schizophrenia. Families of patients with schizodepression show significant loading for schizophrenia and not as much for bipolar disorder; generally, these patients respond better to antipsychotics than to lithium; their prognosis is not as good as that of mood disordered patients and is much closer to that of schizophrenics.

## Delusional Disorder

Delusional disorder is DSM-III-R's term for what was previously called paranoid disorder. It is characterized by a persistent delusion that is relatively unchanging and not associated with the fragmented thinking or the psychosocial and occupational dysfunction of schizophrenia. There has been astonishingly little research published on the disorder. It seems to have some genetic link to schizophrenia, but not enough to describe it as an unusual variant of the disorder. Antipsychotics are generally prescribed since, like delusions of any cause, the delusions in this disorder tend to be refractory to psychotherapeutic intervention. Unfortunately, it is not known how helpful antipsychotics are in treating delusional disorder, because virtually no treatment studies exist and patients with this disorder are rare enough that there is little accumulated clinical wisdom (Kendler, 1980).

> For Erica, the evidence that her husband was having an affair was overwhelming. There was the time he came home with a wrinkle in his pants in a place usually unwrinkled; or the night when he arrived home fifteen minutes later than usual and slightly out of breath. The fact that he had just walked up the two flights of stairs to their apartment was irrelevant to her. She had even hired a detective to follow her husband, but he had found no evidence of an extramarital affair. Her conclusion was that her husband had discovered her plan to hire a private detective, had found this one first, and paid him to lie to her. Occasionally, she would threaten to expose her husband's philandering at his place of work, or to kill him and herself together, but she never made any moves toward carrying out these threats. Divorce was not an option, she said.
>
> Erica's certainty that her husband was having an affair had gradually intensified over the last few years of their ten-year marriage. Yet despite the energy she invested in her belief, Erica held a full-time job at a flower store and kept the house running well. She did not tell her few friends of her belief about her husband. During the one visit she and her husband had with me, she denied hallucinations or more global fears of persecution. At the end of the visit, she made it clear that she had no desire for individual treatment, nor was couples' therapy needed—only that her husband confess his affair and stop. Not surprisingly, they never returned for a second visit.

## Schizotypal Personality Disorder

It is likely that schizotypal personality disorder should be viewed as a schizophrenia spectrum disorder. Because it is classified as a personality disorder in DSM-III-R, however, it will be discussed in chapter 7 with the other personality disorders.

## MEDICAL DIFFERENTIAL DIAGNOSIS

If we ignore the brief psychoses frequently seen on medical wards due to acute illness, postoperative metabolic imbalance, and so forth (which, presumably, nonmedical psychotherapists almost never see), the list of medical diagnoses that resemble schizophrenia is not very long. This stems not from a lack of possibilities but from the dilemma that what we call schizophrenia is probably composed of a variety of neuropsychiatric diseases that, at present, are indistinguishable from each other. The major medical/neuropsychiatric disorder that can present with the psychotic symptom cluster seen in schizophrenia is organic mental disorder. Occasionally, temporal lobe epilepsy and brain tumors may present with schizophrenia-like states. Usually, though, signs of the primary neurological disorder, such as a documented history of seizures or asymmetric weakness, will simultaneously exist. In general, the presence of marked disorientation, confusion, memory impairment, possibly older age of onset (i.e., after age 30), and nonauditory hallucinations as the prominent perceptual symptom are helpful clues that point towards organic disorders and away from schizophrenia. These signs and symptoms should make the therapist and/or psychiatrist consider a neurological evaluation.

Organic mental disorder due to drug use is probably the most important etiology to rule out. Ongoing use of stimulants, especially amphetamines, can be indistinguishable from acute paranoid schizophrenia. Acute or chronic use of PCP (phencyclidine) or LSD can also precipitate a schizophrenic-like psychosis. Of course, schizophrenics may also use street drugs with regularity. The superimposition of a drug-induced psychosis on schizophrenia will simply present as a very disorganized psychosis, making differentiation of the two conditions virtually impossible. Urine or blood tests are mandatory if drug use is suspected. Obtaining information from the patient's family members or friends can also be helpful.

## LABORATORY EVALUATION

There are no tests routinely used in the evaluation of schizophrenia. Typically, the general screening battery of blood tests is obtained more for the sake of completeness than to look for a specific abnormality. If drug use is suspected, blood or urine tests are indicated. Most psychopharmacologists do not routinely order CAT scans or MRI (magnetic resonance imaging) scans in the evaluation of schizophrenia. Similarly, EEGs (electroencephalograms—brain wave tests) are not ordinarily indicated. However, if there is a suspicion of epilepsy or epilepsy-like symptoms, or if the course of the disorder or response to treatment is unusual, these tests are obtained.


## PSYCHIATRIC DIFFERENTIAL DIAGNOSIS


The distinction between schizophrenia and other psychiatric disorders in which psychotic thinking can occur is vital since the treatment may differ among the disorders. This is especially true in distinguishing between a psychotic mood disorder and schizophrenia. Since the presence of overt psychotic thinking should precipitate a psychiatric consult regardless of diagnosis, it is not vital that psychotherapists know all the nuances of how to distinguish among similar looking psychotic disorders. Nonetheless, a review of DSM-III-R's definitions of schizophrenia, schizoaffective disorder, and psychotic forms of mania and depression may be helpful. Table 5–2 summarizes the diagnostic distinctions.

Manias and depressions with mood-congruent psychotic features are relatively easy to diagnose. The full mood syndrome is present and the psychotic symptoms are all mood congruent and typical of the classic symptoms that have been described for decades. For depression, these might include depressive themes of poverty or psychotic guilt, of death or sin. For psychotic mania, the themes generally focus on grandiose themes—of special power, achievements, or identity.

Mood syndromes with mood-incongruent psychotic features are more confusing. Patients with this diagnosis will exhibit a full mood syndrome—mania with all its requisite features, or depression with the five of nine criteria listed in Table 3–1. In addition, such patients will exhibit psychotic symptoms that do *not* relate to mood themes but exist coincident with the mood syndrome; that is, the psychotic symptoms are present only when the full syndrome exists. The psychotic symptoms of mood-incongruent syndromes are the schizophrenia-like symptoms such as thought broadcasting, delusions of control, hearing two or more voices talk about the person, and so on.

If the mood-congruent psychotic features are present for two weeks or more in the absence of a full manic or depressive syndrome, then schizoaffective disorder or schizophrenia should be diagnosed. The distinction between these two disorders is based on the relative length of the mood syndrome in com-

TABLE 5–2

*Diagnostic Distinctions Among Disorders with Both Mood and Psychotic Symptoms*

| | *Mania or Depression with Mood-Congruent Psychotic Features* | *Mania or Depression with Mood-Incongruent Psychotic Features* | *Schizoaffective Disorder* | *Schizophrenia* |
|---|---|---|---|---|
| Full mood syndrome | Yes | Yes | Yes | Can be present but brief compared to psychotic symptoms |
| Timing of psychotic symptoms | Only when manic or depressed | Only when manic or depressed | During mood syndrome plus at least 2 other weeks, but brief compared to length of mood syndrome | Dominates clinical picture |
| Types of psychotic symptoms | Mood-congruent only. Themes of elation, poverty | Not related to mood themes | Not specified | Schizophrenic, not mood related |

parison to the period of time of psychotic thinking *without* prominent mood symptoms. If the mood syndrome with psychotic symptoms has been brief in comparison to the psychotic syndrome without the mood syndrome, then schizophrenia is diagnosed. If the mood syndrome is present for a significant amount of the total psychotic time, then schizoaffective disorder is the approprite DSM-III-R diagnosis.

Do these distinctions seem somewhat arbitrary, confusing, and not as easy to make with live patients as on paper? Absolutely. Are these distinctions transient way stations in history, likely to change with every new DSM editions? Without question. Unfortunately, though, we need some way to make diagnoses using current "best guesses" to distinguish among these conditions that look so much alike because these diagnoses have important treatment implications. As an example, a diagnosis of schizoaffective disorder, bipolar type, would help direct the psychopharmacologist towards lithium early on in treatment, whereas a diagnosis of schizophrenia would not.

Another important clue that helps most clinicians distinguish among similar diagnoses (although it is not used as a diagnostic clue in DSM-III-R) is family history. Most psychopharmacologists evaluating a patient with both prominent psychotic thinking and major mood symptoms who did not fit into our neat diagnostic boxes would use the psychiatric family history as an important variable in deciding which medication to prescribe. If the patient had a number of relatives who were chronically psychotic or dysfunctional, a diagnosis of schizophrenia would be likely. A family history with a manic-depressive parent who then stabilized on lithium would tip the diagnosis towards an unusual psychotic mood disorder and the treatment towards lithium.

Among the schizophrenia spectrum disorders, schizophreniform disorder is distinguished from schizophrenia by the length of the disorder. If it is less than six months in duration, then schizophreniform disorder is the diagnosis, although, as noted above, the clinical meaning of this distinction is dubious. Patients with delusional disorder do not exhibit the other signs of schizophrenia aside from the psychotic thinking; they remain more functional and generally show more fixed delusions than are seen in schizophrenia. Patients with schizotypal disorder (see chapter 7) are distinguished from schizophrenics primarily by never having an episode of acute dysfunctional psychosis. When viewed cross-sectionally—that is, without examining the lifetime course of disorder—schizotypal disorder is indistinguishable from residual schizophrenia.

Among the other personality disorders, borderline patients may present with psychotic symptoms. However, their psychotic episodes are far briefer than schizophrenic episodes. Additionally, the characteristic behavior of borderline personalities when the patient is not psychotic helps make the personality diagnosis. Schizoid patients show the interpersonal withdrawal characteristic of schizophrenia, but not the psychosis. Similarly, patients with paranoid personality disorder do not show the overt delusions of paranoid schizophrenia. Occasionally, it may be difficult to make this distinction because these patients are guarded and may not discuss all their symptoms.

Occasionally, obsessions and compulsions may be present as part of the symptom complex of schizophrenia. If the symptoms are first noted after the schizophrenic diagnosis is made, there is little diagnostic confusion. There is a small group of schizophrenic patients, however, during whose prodromal course obsessions and compulsions are prominent (Rasmussen and Tsuang, 1984). In these patients, one would look for increasing psychotic belief in the meaning of the rituals and, over time, for the more pervasive psychotic thinking and more global dysfunction seen with schizophrenic patients compared to obsessive compulsive patients.


## PSYCHOPHARMACOLOGICAL TREATMENT


It is unimaginable for a schizophrenic patient to be diagnosed correctly and to be seen by a mental health professional without the question of utilizing medications as part of the treatment arising. Antipsychotic medications have revolutionalized the treatment of this most severe disorder, helping to turn what was a hospital-based disorder into an outpatient disorder for which, in most cases, the hospital is utilized only intermittently. Yet the use of medications to treat schizophrenia, both acutely and in the maintenance phase of treatment, is not as simple as psychiatrists once thought. The initial dramatic effect of the medication, markedly reducing or eliminating profound psychosis in many individuals, hid a number of the serious limitations of treatment. It soon became apparent that not all the symptoms of schizophrenia responded equally to the medication. Also, a substantial proportion of patients did not respond at all. Furthermore, even though antipsychotics are extraordinarily safe— extremely high doses can be taken without fatal or profoundly dangerous consequences—their potential side effects when prescribed either acutely or chronically can have a negative impact on the patient's well-being. It must also be admitted that although many refinements in the use of medications have taken place recently, no major breakthroughs have occurred in the psychopharmacological treatment of schizophrenia in the last twenty-five years (although the release in early 1990 of a new antipsychotic, clozapine, may change this; see below). Thus, for this most severe of psychiatric disorders the medications that are virtually always tried and are frequently indispensable do not provide as much benefit as we had hoped thirty years ago.

Unlike other disorders such as depression or panic disorder, in which a number of different medication classes can be beneficial (discussed in chapters 3 and 4 respectively), psychopharmacological treatment of schizophrenia virtually begins and ends with the antipsychotics. Although other biological treatments (discussed later in this chapter) may be considered if the disorder is refractory to antipsychotics, significant evidence of efficacy for these other medications in treating the typical schizophrenic patient is lacking. This is equally true for acute and maintenance treatment. Therefore, this section will focus primarily on the use of antipsychotics in the various phases of treatment.

Before the role of antipsychotics in treating schizophrenia is discussed in detail, a definition of this medication class is necessary. The antipsychotics are medications that have potent effects in decreasing psychotic thinking, regardless of the diagnosis in which the psychosis occurs. Thus, these medications are used in a variety of disorders in which psychotic thinking is seen. Antipsychotics are also sometimes called neuroleptics or dopamine blockers (all currently available antipsychotics block the effect of the neurotransmitter dopamine). Further information on antipsychotics, including their use in disorders other than schizophrenia as well as the names, doses, and side effects of the individual medications, is found in chapter 12.

## Psychopharmacological Treatment of Acute Schizophrenia

Since 1952, when chlorpromazine (Thorazine) was first noted to have an extraordinary capacity to reduce psychosis, no new antipsychotic (with the possible exception of clozapine; see below) has been shown to be more effective. All currently available antipsychotics are equally effective in groups of patients. As with the role of cyclic antidepressants in treating depression, this is both bad news and good news. On one hand, there is no "best" antipsychotic. On the other hand, there is a good chance that if a patient cannot tolerate one antipsychotic, a different one may have fewer or different side effects with just as much chance of being clinically effective. In fact, the initial subjective response to an antipsychotic may be very important since an initial dysphoric response to a specific antipsychotic ("I hate this medication. It makes me feel terrible") may predict a poor response to the medication at the end of hospitalization (Van Putten and May, 1978b). Whether this dysphoric response reflects side effects or other factors is unknown. Therefore, the decision to pick a specific antipsychotic should rest on two considerations—past response and side effects. If there is a history of past hospitalizations, or past medication treatment, it is important for the psychopharmacologist to obtain any available information from the patient or, if possible, from family members or past therapists. If no past medication history exists, then side effect considerations are paramount.

Antipsychotics can be crudely divided into two groups: the low-potency antipsychotics (low potency does not imply low efficacy, just that a greater number of milligrams are needed for a therapeutic dose) are more sedating, cause more anticholinergic side effects such as dry mouth and constipation, and more postural hypotension (dizziness upon standing up) but fewer neurological side effects, called extrapyramidal symptoms (EPS). (See chapter 12 for details on side effects.) Medications such as chlorpromazine (Thorazine) and thioridazine (Mellaril) are representative of this group. The high-potency antipsychotics cause less sedation, anticholinergic, and postural hypotensive effects but cause far more EPS. Haloperidol (Haldol) and fluphenazine (Prolixin) are the prototypical high-potency antipsychotics. Of course, some antipsychotics are midway between these two extremes, causing some sedation and some EPS. Trifluoperazine (Stelazine) and thiothixene (Navane) are examples. The recent trend in treating schizophrenia is to prescribe the less sedating antipsychotics whenever possible, since sedation can be a significant problem with the low-potency medications, especially after the patient begins to improve. There is no evidence for the myth that sedating antipsychotics are better for agitated schizophrenics while nonsedating medications are more helpful for withdrawn patients.

The drug/placebo difference in treating acute schizophrenia is so clear and well established that it would be unethical to conduct further experiments with any of the standard antipsychotics. In the classic study published twenty-five years ago (Cole, Goldberg, and Klerman, 1964; Goldberg, Klerman, and Cole, 1965), 75 percent of patients on antipsychotics improved markedly with no patients deteriorating compared to 25 percent of patients on placebo who improved while 50 percent of patients got worse.

Given the variety of symptoms in schizophrenia, it is relevant to ask whether all psychopathology improves en masse with treatment or whether different symptoms show a differential response to antipsychotics. It is generally thought that negative symptoms are less responsive to antipsychotic medications than are positive symptoms such as delusions and hallucinations (Lydiard and Laird, 1988). This question is more important for maintenance treatment since it is difficult and probably irrelevant to evaluate negative symptoms during an acute frenzied psychosis. For acute schizophrenia, it is reasonable to assume that the more disruptive aspects of the disorder, however classified, are equally responsive to treatment.

Although some improvement is often seen quickly after antipsychotic medications are begun, the full therapeutic effects of antipsychotics in acute schizophrenia occur gradually over many weeks. There is some evidence that for many patients the response takes place in two phases—activity symptoms such as agitation or catatonic withdrawal respond first to medication, while the major effect on psychotic thinking occurs more slowly over many weeks (Kane, 1986). Whether this is so or not, the important issue clinically is to be aware that a patient who is still symptomatic after four weeks but has been gradually improving may not need higher doses of medication but rather a longer time on the same dose.

Among the various choices to be made during the treatment of acute schizophrenia is whether the medication should be administered as a pill, a liquid, or an injection. Without question, oral medication is preferable to injectable *if* the patient complies with treatment. This sounds reasonably straightforward but, as any clinician who has worked on an inpatient unit knows, some patients are astonishingly creative in finding ways of surreptitiously not taking their medications. The most common way is "cheeking" the medication: keeping the pill between the teeth and the inside of the cheek, swallowing the water, walking away from the nurses' station, and spitting the pill out. The use of liquid medication obviates this possibility. Short-acting injectable antipsychotics are generally reserved for involuntary patients who refuse oral medication.

Another important choice is how to manage acutely fragmented, agitated, paranoid, psychotic patients soon after they are admitted to hospital. Patients like this are extremely frightening to themselves, to other patients, and to the staff, and all concerns are focused on how to decrease the risk of violence. A common choice is to use repeated doses—perhaps every hour—of high-potency neuroleptics until the patient is calmed. Because of the inherent safety of the antipsychotics, extraordinarily high doses are sometimes used in this approach. Unfortunately, there is little evidence that this high-dose treatment, called "rapid neuroleptization," is more effective than giving moderate doses (Baldessarini, Cohen, and Teicher, 1988). It is probably used as much to treat the psychiatrist's and the staff's need to do *something*—and quickly—as it is for the patient. Another strategy, one that may be preferable, is to give a short- to intermediate-acting benzodiazepine in addition to the antipsychotic (Salzman, 1988). The advantage of this approach is that the medication will wear off relatively quickly and that the only possible side effect is sedation. The third possible strategy is physical restraint of the patient. Although this may sound primitive and even cruel to those without experience on inpatient wards, it can be effective and safe when done on modern wards with frequent observation. In fact, when treating an acutely frenzied, psychotic patient, all three of the above approaches are variations of restraint. The difference is simply that two are chemical and one is physical.

The trial of an antipsychotic to treat acute schizophrenia should last from four to six weeks. If no response is seen after three or four weeks of adequate doses, it is reasonable to switch to another antipsychotic. Of course, if a patient cannot tolerate a reasonable dose of one particular antipsychotic, another one that causes less of the offending side effect should be substituted. Since four weeks can be a very long time when a patient is overtly psychotic, it is common to switch after two to three weeks if absolutely no improvement, as opposed to partial improvement, is seen.

Clozapine (Clozaril) is the only antipsychotic that may offer some unique advantages (and unique risks) compared to the other medications in its class. In a recent careful study, clozapine was superior to chlorpromazine in clearly defined treatment-resistant patients (Kane, Honigfeld, Singer, Meltzer, and the Clozaril Collaborative Study Group, 1988). Also, it differs from other antipsychotics in that it causes virtually no extrapyramidal side effects and may be the only antipsychotic that does not cause tardive dyskinesia, the potentially irreversible movement disorder seen with long-term use of neuroleptics (see chapter 12 for details). These two side effect advantages are due to clozapine's weakness as a classic dopamine blocker. Its mechanism of action is not well understood. The major difficulty with clozapine is its capacity to cause agranulocytosis, a condition in which the bone marrow stops making white blood cells, thereby making the person vulnerable to overwhelming infection. Agranulocytosis is seen in 1 to 2 percent of patients treated with clozapine over one year. Weekly blood tests are therefore required during its use. Because of the risk of this potentially fatal side effect, clozapine's major use is in the treatment of patients who either have not responded to or cannot tolerate conventional antipsychotic medications.

## Alternative Treatments of Acute Schizophrenia

In considering alternative treatments for schizophrenia, three points are evident. One is that neuroleptics seem to be either ineffective or inadequately effective in 25 percent of patients. Second, the use of antipsychotics confers a risk of distressing, truly uncomfortable, and even dangerous side effects (discussed in detail in chapter 12). Third, despite decades of exploration, no alternative treatment has arisen to rival antipsychotics in efficacy or safety in treating schizophrenia. Nonetheless, a variety of secondary approaches do exist for use in conjunction with antipsychotics, or as single agents when patients are unresponsive to more conventional therapy. Table 5–3 lists these alternative psychopharmacological treatments.

Because of its pronounced effect in treating manic states and because of the difficulty in distinguishing between psychotic mood disorders and schizophrenia, it is not surprising that lithium has been explored as an alternative treatment for schizophrenia. Lithium is likely to be effective in only a minority of schizophrenic patients when prescribed alone or, as is more common, when given in combination with an antipsychotic (Delva and Letemendia, 1982). The extent of the improvement, when seen, is variable. Lithium should be tried

TABLE 5–3

### Alternative Treatments of Acute Schizophrenia

Lithium
Propranolol
Benzodiazepines
Electroconvulsive therapy (ECT)

in treatment-resistant schizophrenia, but the likelihood of a marked clinical effect is small.

Another alternative treatment is high-dose propranolol (Inderal), a beta-adrenergic blocker, commonly used to treat angina, high blood pressure, tremors, migraine headaches, and other medical conditions. Over the last decade, a number of studies have demonstrated that high-dose propranolol can be helpful to some patients when added to a neuroleptic but is less likely to be helpful when used alone (Rifkin and Siris, 1987). However, getting to a high dose of the medication can take one to two months. Furthermore, its side effects at high dose, especially on the cardiovascular system, are significant and possibly dangerous, thereby making propranolol a medication to be used for schizophrenia only after most other strategies have failed.

Benzodiazepines, the most common class of tranquilizers (see chapter 11), have also been used to treat schizophrenia. When prescribed alone (i.e., not in conjunction with antipsychotics) in extraordinarily high doses, these medications are occasionally effective. What seems more promising is the use of low- to medium-dose benzodiazepines in conjunction with neuroleptics (Wolkowitz, Rapaport, and Pickar, in press). This strategy may result in an improvement of clinical symptoms and may make it possible to minimize the dose of antipsychotics needed, thereby diminishing the risk of side effects.

Although electroconvulsive therapy has been used rarely in the last decade within the United States, there is a substantial literature from Great Britain on its use in treating schizophrenia. It does seem that ECT can be effective in treating acute schizophrenia, especially in those cases where catatonic symptoms are prominent (Weiner and Coffey, 1988). This raises the question of whether catatonic patients are simply misdiagnosed psychotic manic and depressed patients, since these disorders are known to be ECT responsive. A number of British studies have also demonstrated that ECT plus antipsychotics may speed the improvement of acute schizophrenia compared to use of antipsychotics alone. ECT is not effective in chronic psychotic states.

## Acute Treatment of Schizoaffective Disorder

In discussing the treatment of schizoaffective disorder, it is helpful to distinguish between schizomanic and schizodepressive subtypes. Even using this distinction, it is very difficult to make reasonable generalizations because of the heterogeneity of patients treated in different studies (Levitt and Tsuang, 1988). For treating schizomania, the three most common treatments are lithium alone, lithium plus antipsychotics, and antipsychotics alone. The results of treatment studies when taken together are mixed. Currently, antipsychotics alone or lithium plus antipsychotics are appropriate first-line treatments; lithium alone is helpful in a smaller subset of patients.

Schizodepressive patients, probably because their disorder is closer to pure schizophrenia, seem to do best with antipsychotics alone. If an inadequate response is obtained and depressive features are still prominent, adding an antidepressant at that point is reasonable.

## Continuation Treatment of Acute Schizophrenia

Once remission of the acute psychotic symptoms occurs, how long should the patient continue on medication if maintenance treatment is deemed inappropriate? The figures in the psychiatric literature vary enormously, from a low of a few months to three to five years. The wide range is partly due to the different purposes of the continuation period. Should it be used for simple symptom stabilization? Should a deeper exploration of family interactions or vocational rehabilitation occur then? Is this the time for social skills training? Clearly, the more ambitious the goals of the stabilization period, the longer continuation treatment will need to be.

## Maintenance Treatment of Schizophrenia

Since in most cases schizophrenia is a chronic disorder characterized by intermittent relapses, the question of prescribing maintenance medication treatment as a means of preventing or forestalling relapse inevitably arises. It is clear that, compared to placebo, maintenance treatment is more effective in preventing relapses. The rates of relapse on active medication in contrast to placebo in different studies are extremely varied, presumably because of patient selection. As a generalization, though, the relapse rate is twice as high in the placebo-treated patients as in the medication-treated patients. Once the actual relapse rates are examined, however, the limits of medication treatment become apparent. A reasonable guess is that approximately two thirds of patients on placebo relapse within one year compared to one third in drug-treated patients (Kane and Lieberman, 1987). So, even with active medication treatment, one of three patients will relapse within one year. The frustration, then, is that even though the medication is unquestionably effective compared to placebo, its effects are far from complete. Additionally, if patients who have done well on antipsychotics and have shown no relapses for three to five years are withdrawn from the medication, two thirds of them will relapse over the next eighteen months, indicating that the risk for relapse continues over years and that the medication confers no protection except when it is taken (Cheung, 1981).

Not only is the effect of preventing relapse less than perfect, but antipsychotics do not seem to alter some of the most fundamental psychopathology of the disorder. Although some schizophrenic patients behave, function, and feel normal when they are not in an overt psychotic state, more of them will exhibit clear signs of the disorder even when not in acute relapse. The negative symptoms—the lack of motivation, the relative social isolation, the poor social skills, the nonintegration with the world—continue even with optimum medication treatment. What this implies is the inadequacy of defining clinical outcome only by symptoms or rehospitalization rates for a disorder that affects so many different aspects of functioning. Patients on medication who are not psychotic or hospitalized over one year will be classified as "successes" in a research study. Yet they may spend their time in a board and care facility, smoking cigarettes, doing little of meaning or satisfaction for weeks, months, or years. Antipsychotics may be mandatory to keep schizophrenics from being frequently or chronically hospitalized—but too often they are not enough.

It is also relevant and important to examine the potential cost of maintenance medication, especially in terms of side effects. Through a series of elegant studies over the last few years, it has become clear that medium doses of antipsychotics are more effective than low doses in preventing psychotic symptoms. However, the cost of the higher dose is increased side effects that are frequently unrecognizable, subjectively distressing, and affect psychosocial functioning (Marder et al., 1984; Marder et al., 1987; Hogarty et al., 1988). In these studies, low-dose patients had psychotic exacerbations more frequently (as defined by an increase in psychotic symptoms) but these were well handled by simply increasing the medication dose without need for hospitalization. However, the low-dose patients were less physically slowed down, less tense, and exhibited less emotional withdrawal, implying that these symptoms were unrecognized subtle side effects of higher-dose antipsychotics.

These studies bring up the complex question of risk versus benefit of different doses of antipsychotics in schizophrenia. Is it worth some mild sluggishness in order to avoid times of mild auditory hallucinations or mild ideas of reference? How bad are the psychotic symptoms? How quickly do they evolve from mild to severe? How much do they affect the person's job or relationships? How sluggish is the patient on medication? Frequently, these questions can take years to answer fully for any individual, assuming different doses and a period off medication are tried. Other important variables include the amount of insight the patient has into his own prodromal symptoms, the patient's capacity to cooperate when prodromal symptoms arise, and the potential presence of friends, family, or counselors available to help monitor him during these times.

The most well-known complication of long-term use of antipsychotics is tardive dyskinesia (TD). Although details on tardive dyskinesia will be presented in chapter 12, no discussion on the risks and benefits of maintenance antipsychotics would be complete without addressing the concern about using a medication that can cause an irreversible side effect. It is clear that TD is a potential risk in any patient treated with any currently available antipsychotic (with the possible exception of clozapine) over an extended period of time. Furthermore, the risk for developing TD probably increases over the first five years of antipsychotic treatment, but not necessarily after that (Casey, 1987). Surprisingly, the long-term course of TD is variable; some patients show stabilization or worsening of the involuntary movements, while in others the movements may even diminish.

There is little doubt that the safest strategy if a patient has already developed tardive dyskinesia is to stop the antipsychotic, for this maximizes the chance that the movements will diminish or disappear entirely (Gardos et al., 1988). But what should be recommended if, after medication is discontinued, the patient relapses and is hospitalized? Is the decreased risk of TD worth the possibility of increased psychotic episodes and hospitalizations, with their attendant life disruption? The answer to these questions depends on individual factors with each patient: How prominent is the TD? How destructive are the relapses? How quickly do the relapses respond to treatment?

It would be extremely helpful to have well-documented predictors of those who are most likely to respond to medication or, even more, those who will do well off medication. Unfortunately, no such predictors are currently available.

Another possible strategy of maintenance treatment is intermittent pharmacotherapy in which the patient remains medication free except when prodromal psychotic signs are present (Herz, Szymanski, and Simon, 1982). The advantage to this approach is obvious: the patient is on medication for the shortest period of time necessary, thereby minimizing both acute side effects and possibly tardive dyskinesia. Intermittent pharmacotherapy, however, depends heavily on patient/family/therapist insight, support, and cooperation as well as an appreciation of the nature of the patient's prodromal signs.

Probably the most difficult decision for psychopharmacologists working with schizophrenic patients is how to treat a patient who exhibits chronic or frequently profound psychotic symptoms while on medications with little or no evidence of antipsychotic efficacy. Typically, this type of patient will be treated with higher and higher doses of antipsychotics each time an exacerbation or relapse occurs, despite the evidence that higher doses have not been effective and may even make the patient worse. If the psychopharmacologist then begins to lower the dose, the patient is likely to relapse—since relapse is probable in any case. This will be incorrectly interpreted by psychiatrist, therapist, patient, and/or family as evidence that the dose is too low and the escalation to higher doses then resumes. Those schizophrenic patients who show no evidence of a better response to high doses should be treated with a low to medium maintenance dose. For patients whose episodes are not prevented at all by a maintenance treatment of antipsychotics, the intermittent pharmacotherapy approach outlined above should be considered.

An important technical consideration in maintenance treatment of schizophrenia is whether to use oral or long-acting injectable antipsychotics. Currently, two injectable antipsychotics are available which last two to four weeks. The medication is mixed with an oil-based preparation such that after the injection into either fat or muscle (typically into the buttocks or the arm), it is released gradually over many days. The obvious advantage is that the daily struggle for compliance is avoided. Since relapses rarely occur soon after medication withdrawal, patients on oral medication who miss one day's dose or two may find they feel, if anything, slightly better. They then stop the medication entirely, convinced that they no longer need it, only to relapse months later since the effect of maintenance treatment is primarily preventive. With the use of long-acting injectable antipsychotics, the patient must comply only once every two to four weeks. Also, if the patient becomes more symptomatic, the always present problem of ascertaining whether noncompliance with medication helped precipitate the relapse is avoided. There is no evidence that long-acting injectable antipsychotics are more effective, only that compliance is better controlled. The primary consideration in the decision to use injectable antipsychotics, therefore, should be the individual patient's capacity to comply with medication treatment.

### Maintenance Treatment of Schizoaffective Disorder

The maintenance treatment of schizoaffective disorder, either bipolar or depressed type, is decided on purely empirical grounds. For schizomania, the most common maintenance treatment is probably a combination of a mood stabilizer, typically lithium, along with an antipsychotic. Schizodepressive patients are frequently treated with a maintenance regimen of either antipsychotics alone (reflecting their closeness to pure schizophrenia) or a combination of antidepressants plus antipsychotics. Occasionally, a schizodepressive patient will do best on lithium, an antidepressant, and an antipsychotic.

### Treatment of Depressed Schizophrenics

The use of antidepressants in the treatment of schizophrenia has had a rather checkered history with studies showing either a worsening of psychotic symptoms, no effect, or clinical improvement (Siris, Van Kammen, and Docherty,

1978). The confusion of results is, in part, related to (1) the difficulty in distinguishing between a true depressive syndrome and other dysphoric states, and (2) the possibility of differing effects if antidepressants are added during an acute psychotic phase of illness instead of a more stable and less psychotic outpatient phase. In general, it is prudent to avoid antidepressants during an active phase of schizophrenia, both because antipsychotics may improve depressive symptoms, but also because of the possibility that antidepressants will exacerbate the psychosis (Kramer et al., 1989). Antidepressants are more likely to be helpful when prescribed for stable nonpsychotic schizophrenic patients on maintenance antipsychotics, who have a depressive syndrome characterized by at least some of the classic symptoms of major depression and whose side effects are well controlled (Siris, Morgan, Fagerstrom, Rifkin, and Cooper, 1987). Although this group would comprise a minority of all schizophrenic patients who complain of depressive symptoms, antidepressants should be considered since some of them will respond.

# 6

# Disorders of Impulse Control: Eating Disorders, Drug and Alcohol Abuse, and Adult Attention Deficit Disorder (ADD)

Difficulties in impulse control are seen in a variety of psychiatric and psychological disorders. In a few of these, such as eating disorders and drug and alcohol abuse, these problems are central aspects of the pathology. In others, such as attention deficit disorder, the problems surrounding impulse control may not be as central but nonetheless are common and are frequently the clinical features that bring the patient to the attention of mental health professionals. Compared with previous chapters, less detail will be provided here on the disorders themselves, because medication is generally not a primary treatment for some eating disorders (specifically, anorexia nervosa) and drug abuse, and because less is known about adult attention deficit disorder.

## EATING DISORDERS

Both anorexia nervosa and bulimia nervosa, as they are called in DSM-III-R, are characterized by a preoccupation with food. Although separated into two disorders, there is overlap between the two as evidenced by the number of patients who meet criteria for both as well as by the evolution of some patients with anorexia nervosa into normal-weight bulimics over time (Hsu, 1988). Currently, the use of pharmacotherapy in treating these two disorders differs.

Medications are not frequently prescribed for anorexia nervosa but are utilized more often and with more documentation of success with bulimics.

### Anorexia Nervosa

In anorexia nervosa, there is an obsession with and a distortion of body image. Abnormal behaviors seen in anorexia nervosa are related to regulating this image. Patients with either of the major subtypes of anorexia nervosa—the restrictor or the bulimic—evidence fears of losing control. Restrictors utilize a variety of ritualistic behaviors to ward off loss of control, including exercise, obsessive calorie counting, and food rituals such as hoarding. Bulimic anorexics, despite similar preoccupations with body image, manifest cycles of losing control—by binge eating—and regaining control by purging.

At best, medications have a limited role in the current treatment of anorexia nervosa. Although many anecdotal reports have demonstrated the success of one treatment or another, there is no consistent body of evidence suggesting that any one particular type of medication is helpful. Furthermore, the studies that do exist have focused on short-term treatment during which time the goal is, above all, weight gain. There is no evidence whatsoever that medications alter the long-term outcome of anorexia nervosa. At the same time, however, it must be acknowledged that, in contrast to bulimia, few well-controlled studies have even examined the role of pharmacotherapy in treating anorexia nervosa. The reasons for this are as follows: First, anorexic patients, especially in the early stages of treatment when their weight is very low, are at high risk to have a variety of metabolic and other biological disturbances from the self-induced starvation. Because of this, there is an increased danger in using any medication. Second, patients with anorexia nervosa are exceedingly sensitive to and intolerant of nondangerous medication side effects, both from the starvation effects and from their own sensitivity to unwanted feelings or changes in their bodies. Third, these patients often equate taking medication with losing control, further increasing the resistance to taking them.

Conceptually, medications might be helpful in the treatment of anorexia nervosa in a number of ways: by stimulating appetite and/or promoting weight gain, by decreasing depression, by decreasing anxiety, and by diminishing obsessional thinking. All medications occasionally used for anorexia nervosa have one or more of these effects. However, since some of these symptoms—most notably, the obsessionality and the depression—are likely to be effects of starvation and not the cause, bringing about weight gain and better nutrition by any means will effectively treat these symptoms too.

One of the more promising of the medications sometimes prescribed for treating anorexia nervosa is cyproheptadine (Periactin), which blocks the effect of serotonin. Because serotonin increases feelings of satiety (being full) through an effect in the hypothalamus, cyproheptadine stimulates appetite. At least one study has demonstrated that restrictor anorexics gain weight more quickly when treated with cyproheptadine in an inpatient program (Halmi, Eckert, LaDu, and Cohen, 1986). Its efficacy in patients with milder anorexia nervosa is unknown. Cyproheptadine's major side effect is sedation.

Despite the lack of controlled studies demonstrating any consistent positive effect, antipsychotics have been among the more common medications used in treating anorexia nervosa (VanderEycken, 1987). Antipsychotics diminish anxiety and decrease the hypervigilance seen in these patients. They also promote weight gain in those with anorexia nervosa as they do in any patients who take them. The mechanism of this effect is unknown. Yet, as described in chapter 12, antipsychotics can cause a variety of side effects that are both uncomfortable and potentially dangerous in patients with anorexia nervosa (such as lowering blood pressure and exacerbating constipation).

Antidepressants are also prescribed in the treatment of anorexia nervosa. Initially, a part of this rationale stemmed from the prominence of depressive symptoms in patients with anorexia nervosa. However, depression in these patients is difficult to interpret because of the effects of starvation in causing dysphoric mood, apathy, and irritability, symptoms that then remit upon weight gain (Strober and Katz, 1986). Although well-controlled trials have not shown positive results, the antidepressants used in those studies were the most sedating and hypotensive ones which probably contributed to their poor outcome. Less sedating antidepressants are more easily tolerated and might be more helpful. Fluoxetine (Prozac) may emerge as particularly helpful since it has antiobsessional effects and will not cause the potentially rapid—and therefore psychologically threatening—weight gain seen with other antidepressants (Gwirtsman, Guze, Yager, and Gainsley, submitted). Often, the time to evaluate for treating an associated depression in patients with anorexia nervosa is after weight has been restored and the starvation effects on mood are less.

Other medications that have been prescribed for treating anorexia nervosa are lithium, opiate antagonists, and benzodiazepines. Only one small study (Gross et al., 1981) has shown lithium to be helpful in acute anorexia nervosa as demonstrated by greater weight gain over the first few weeks of treatment. Unfortunately, lithium is potentially dangerous with anorexic patients because of the risk of lithium toxicity in times of significant shifts in salt and water balance, situations that commonly occur in these patients. Because the endogenous opiates seem to contribute to regulation of appetite (Kaye, 1987), opiate antagonists such as naltrexone (Trexan) have also been used to treat anorexia nervosa. It is too soon to know if this approach will be helpful in a significant number of patients. Low doses of benzodiazepines may be useful in decreasing the anticipatory anxiety that accompanies mealtime for these patients (Andersen, 1987).

## Bulimia Nervosa

Those with bulimia share with anorexic patients the overconcern with body shape and size. The hallmark of bulimia, however, is the repetitive cycle of out-of-control binge eating alternating with a variety of behaviors that attempt to undo the effects of the binging, such as self-induced vomiting, laxative abuse, fasting, or vigorous exercising. Patients can simultaneously have anorexia and bulimia. The majority of patients who present for treatment, however, have normal-weight bulimia.

In contrast to anorexia nervosa, medications—specifically antidepressants—have documented efficacy in decreasing the binge-purge cycle in short-term treatment studies. Compared to those treated with placebo, bulimic patients on antidepressants will show a greater decrease in binge frequency, with that decrease averaging 75 percent across studies (Walsh, 1987). A variety of antidepressants have been utilized with the majority showing positive results. These have included the tricyclic antidepressants, such as imipramine and desipramine, the newer antidepressants, trazodone and fluoxetine, as well as the monoamine oxidase inhibitors (Pope and Hudson, 1989). There is no substantive evidence that one antidepressant has significantly greater efficacy than the others. Often, when one antidepressant is ineffective, a different one will work, so that several trials are warranted in the patient who fails to respond to the first antidepressant prescribed (Mitchell et al., 1989). Antidepressant doses in treating bulimia are the same as those for depression (see chapter 9 for details), and the time course to response—up to six weeks for a maximum response—is also similar. The other major class of medications that have been used in treating bulimia are the anticonvulsants such as phenytoin (Dilantin) and carbamazepine (Tegretol). Significant evidence for their efficacy, however, is lacking (Kaplan, 1987).

How can we best understand the mechanism of action of antidepressants in bulimia? A number of possible explanations should be considered, no one of which is definitive. The most popular is that bulimia is an unusual variant of depression. Bulimic patients tend to show increased rates of depression both while binge eating and over a lifetime (Levy, Dixon, and Stern, 1989). There is also some evidence, although not entirely consistent, that the families of bulimic patients show a high prevalence of depression, implying some sort of familial and possibly genetic link (Kassett et al., 1989). That antidepressants are so helpful in decreasing core bulimic symptoms could also be interpreted as evidence for bulimia being a "masked depression." Yet on further investigation, this hypothesis—that bulimia and depression are equivalent—is shaky. Sources of dysphoria in bulimic patients are multiple: depression is mixed with dysphoric mood stemming from poor self-esteem and shame due to the bulimia along with other characterological sources of depressed mood. The marked shifts in weight seen in normal-weight bulimia may also cause some of the biological characteristics of starvation, thereby causing depressive symptoms analogous to those seen in anorexia nervosa (Pirke, Pahl, Schweiger, and Warnhoff, 1985). Furthermore, the presence of depression in bulimic patients does not predict a better response to antidepressants in controlling binge frequency. Depression and bulimia, when they coexist, do not necessarily remit together; at times the binging may respond to treatment while the depression continues, while at other times the reverse sequence is seen. Overall, then, conceptualizing bulimia and depression as a single disorder with multiple manifestations seems inaccurate. What is more likely is that the two disorders are commonly occurring comorbid conditions, that is, that the presence of one condition (bulimia) makes the presence of the other (depression) more likely, analogous to the frequent co-occurrence of depression and borderline personality disorder (Strober and Katz, 1986). (The reverse sequence—that depressed patients are generally at higher risk to develop bulimia—is probably not true.) Conceptualizing bulimia and depression as separate conditions that are seen together with regularity has important implications in deciding when to introduce antidepressants in treating bulimic patients.

Another possible explanation for the effect of antidepressants in treating bulimia is related to the antianxiety properties of these medications. Bulimic patients often describe an increasing tension that culminates in a binge-purge cycle. Any treatment—including medications—that can diminish this tension may be associated with decreased binge frequency. No evidence supporting or negating this hypothesis currently exists.

Finally, since antidepressants have effects on those neurotransmitters that are involved with regulation of appetite, it is possible that the decrease in binging is due to the effects of medications on brain regulatory systems. Here too, this hypothesis has no significant experimental support.

Regardless of the mechanism of action of antidepressants in treating bulimia, they are effective agents, at least for short-term treatment and in many instances for up to several years. Some studies indicate a significant rate of relapse when medication is withdrawn (Mitchell, 1988); others find no evidence of a medication effect in long-term outcome. Additionally, side effects often become an increased problem following the initial treatment, especially with MAO inhibitors; consequently many patients stop the medication after months of treatment (Walsh et al., 1988).

Given the information just reviewed, what guidelines should a therapist use in considering the referral of a bulimic patient for possible antidepressant treatment? The first important point is to acknowledge that medications are far from being the only well-documented treatment for bulimia. A variety of psychological approaches utilizing cognitive, behavioral, educational, psychodynamic, and supportive techniques in both individual and group formats have shown clear evidence of efficacy (Yager, 1988). Second, studies comparing antidepressants to educational/cognitive/behavioral approaches are rare. Third, medications are sometimes difficult to use in bulimic patients: side effects are often problematic, affecting compliance; vomiting can cause erratic medication blood levels, making pharmacotherapy inconsistent; and the necessary dietary restrictions with the MAO inhibitors make these particular medications acceptable for only a subset of those with bulimia. Finally, there are no established predictors for antidepressant responses with bulimic patients.

Before suggesting the exploration of possible medication approaches with the patient, a clinician must first pay attention to the possible fears and resistances involved. Since issues of control are so central to bulimia, patients often are frightened of being addicted to medications and are concerned that taking medication is an indication of lack of self-control. Bulimics also fear that the medications will make them fat (Edelstein, 1989). Once the implications of using medications as a part of the treatment have been explored, therapists should consider a psychopharmacological consultation using the guidelines presented in Table 6–1.

Although the presence of depression does not predict a better antibulimic response to antidepressants, the medications may nonetheless successfully treat an associated depression, if present. The alleviation of the depression is likely to help the patient work more productively in any other treatment modality by increasing concentration and energy and by combating pessimism, negative expectation, and helplessness while promoting a general sense of well-being.

TABLE 6–1

*Guidelines for Considering Medications in Treating Bulimia*

Patient has moderate to severe current major depressive disorder
History of recurrent depression when *not* bulimic
Strong family history of primary depression
Patient has not improved from a well designed treatment program not involving pharmacotherapy

Since, as mentioned above, the multiple sources of depressive symptoms in bulimic patients sometimes blur the distinctions among these overlapping diagnoses, a history of depressions when the patient was *not* bulimic suggests that she is at high risk for a difficult-to-recognize major depressive episode which may then complicate the treatment of the bulimia. A strong family history of depression has similar implications. Finally, since there are no established predictors for response to any treatment for bulimia, the last guideline stresses the empirical nature of treatment planning. If the patient continues to binge and purge despite active participation in a multimodal treatment program, the addition of antidepressants may be very helpful.

## ADULT ATTENTION DEFICIT DISORDER

Clinical work, follow-up studies of children with attention deficit disorder (ADD), and the few investigations of those adults who complain of an ADD-like syndrome indicate that an adult form of this well-described childhood disorder exists. Unfortunately, DSM-III-R provides neither a meaningful name nor criteria for these patients. Adults with ADD would be given the diagnosis of attention-deficit hyperactivity syndrome or undifferentiated attention-deficit disorder (if hyperactivity is not present), the same as children. However, since ADD criteria include items such as "has difficulty playing quietly," they are not appropriate for adults, and there are no other generally accepted methods of making the diagnosis.

The best descriptors currently available are known as the Utah criteria (Wender, Wood, and Reimherr, 1985). Patients diagnosed as adult ADD must have demonstrated symptoms consistent with attention-deficit hyperactivity disorder when they were children, but as adults also exhibit two core symptoms and other associated ones. The core adult symptoms are persistent motor activity—characterized by restlessness and difficulty settling down—and attention deficits such as distractability, wandering off while doing tasks, and forgetting or misplacing things. Additionally, these patients must exhibit two of the five following characteristics: (1) affective lability—a lifetime of moodiness, sometimes in response to life events and other times spontaneously, with both dysphoria and periods of exictement that last from hours to days; (2) inability to complete tasks, disorganized ways of approaching a series of tasks, and leaving things unfinished while switching to another task; (3) a hot temper, with short-lived outbursts that may be frightening to both patients and others; (4) impulsivity in decisions involving both work and relationships with potential inappropriate risk-taking behavior; and (5) stress intolerance, as manifested by excessive emotional reactions to everyday life stresses. These are the patients who are described by others as moody, restless, unpredictable, and "all over the place," who just can't ever seem to stick to anything for very long and who tend to be underachievers. The impaired concentration, although chronic, is typically not global; the adult with ADD may be able to focus well on certain interests or tasks of particular interest, in contrast to the attentional problems of depression in which the concentrating deficit is more global (Wender, 1988). If adult ADD is suspected, it is usually helpful to meet with a significant other, especially the patient's parents, if possible, to obtain descriptions of childhood behavior.

Often, patients will present for treatment who may not meet the criteria as listed above—they may have no significant history of hyperactivity as children or as adults, for instance, yet still have a number of the traits described above. This might be especially true for adult women, since boys significantly outnumber girls in childhood ADD syndromes whereas the sex ratio among adults seems to be 1:1. Conceivably, girls with ADD are less likely to be hyperactive and therefore less likely to be behavioral problems despite similar attentional difficulties. Whether this group of patients with a "partial ADD syndrome" have a milder version of the disorder and whether they should be treated similarly is unclear since research on these moody, restless adults is in its infancy.

Over half of the children with ADD will continue to have significant symptoms of the syndrome as young adults (Cantwell, 1985a). Those who continue to show ADD symptoms are at high risk to have antisocial behavior, drug and alcohol abuse, or both (Gittelman, Mannuzza, Shenker, and Bonagura, 1985). This triad—adult ADD, antisocial behavior, and drug/alcohol abuse—is commonly seen among this population. If, instead of following ADD children into adulthood, one simply examines a group of adults with ADD and looks for evidence of other adult psychiatric disorders, the same increases in alcohol and drug abuse and antisocial personality are seen. High rates of generalized anxiety are also seen, as well as minor mood disorders such as dysthymic disorder and cyclothymic disorder (probably reflecting the varied expressions of these patients' moodiness) (Wender, Reimherr, and Wood, 1981). What has not been examined systematically are the personality characteristics of adult ADD patients, other than antisocial behaviors. Clinically, it seems that many would fit into the narcissistic/borderline group of disorders. This may reflect, however, the overlap in our definitions of the disorders: impulsiveness, affective instability, and temper outbursts are described as core symptoms of both types of syndromes. In my clinical experience as well as that of others, adults with ADD have chronic poor self-esteem and, not surprisingly given the moodiness and impulsivity seen in these patients, unstable relationships. The self-esteem difficulties seem related to the poor academic and vocational achievements that are far below what would be expected from their intelligence. This sense of failure may be especially poignant in those who have grown up thinking they were simply rotten kids who wasted their potential and became failures because of personality defects and not because of a disorder of attention and mood.

### Psychopharmacological Treatment

Medications with stimulant properties are the mainstay of treatment for adult ADD. These include those that cause heightened arousal as their primary effect—called stimulants (see chapter 13)—as well as certain antidepressants with analogous stimulating properties. Table 6–2 lists the medications that have been reported as effective in adolescents or adults with ADD.

Often, it is difficult to accurately gauge response to treatment for adult ADD. One reason for this is that stimulants have nonspecific effects on most people who take them, not just those with ADD. A single dose of oral d-amphetamine will cause surprisingly similar effects in normal adults and chiladren compared to children with ADD, with all three groups describing increased vigilance, increased learning, and decreased motor activity (Rapoport, et al., 1980). Another reason is that the ego-syntonic nature of the ADD may make it difficult for patients to self-evaluate accurately. Since so many of the manifestations of the disorder are behavioral, they are frequently easier to observe by others than by patients themselves. Therefore, as with making the diagnosis, it is vital to involve significant others in treatment evaluation.

Stimulants—primarily methylphenidate (Ritalin) and d-amphetamine (Dexedrine)—are the most commonly used treatments for adult ADD, as they are for childhood ADD. However, the documentation of their efficacy with adults in well-controlled studies is far smaller than that for children. Part of the reason for this is the lack of consensus on how to select the appropriate patients to be

TABLE 6–2

*Medications for Attention Deficit Disorder in Adults*

Stimulants:
    Methylphenidate (Ritalin)
    d-Amphetamine (Dexedrine)
    Pemoline (Cylert)
Monoamine oxidase inhibitors:
    Tranylcypromine (Parnate)
Cyclic antidepressants:
    Desipramine (Norpramin)

treated. Because many patients with impulsivity, irritability, and self-reported concentration problems have diagnoses other than ADD, treating a group of patients with a variety of disorders will predictably yield mixed results. Nonetheless, there is clear evidence that stimulants are helpful for some ADD adults: Patients show improvement in global functioning, increased attention, decreased motor activity, more mood stability and diminished impulsivity (Wender, Reimherr, Wood, and Ward, 1985). As with ADD children, stimulants are thought to work with adult ADD patients by increasing their level of alertness and capacity to attend, correcting a postulated poor attentional capacity with secondary hyperactivity and distractability. The positive effects of both methylphenidate and d-amphetamine begin quickly, within hours to days of reaching the correct dose. As with children, tolerance to the medication effects generally does not occur.

Stimulants do have drawbacks, though. First, their clinical effects last only two to five hours, necessitating three to four doses daily. Sustained release preparations of both methylphenidate and d-amphetamine exist but they are not always absorbed as gradually as one would want. Second, since a significant percentage of adult ADD patients have a history of drug abuse, it is tricky at best to give them an abusable drug. Furthermore, because some of these patients also engage in criminal behavior and stimulants have potential street value, the possibility that these medications will ultimately be ingested by persons other than those for whom they were prescribed is significant. Side effects seen with stimulants include irritability, anxiety, and insomnia in some patients, while others complain of excessive sedation or feeling like a zombie.

Pemoline (Cylert) is another stimulant whose advantages and disadvantages differ from those of methylphenidate and d-amphetamine. Overall, it is probably not as effective in treating ADD, although some patients respond extremely well (see the case presented below). However, in marked contrast to the other stimulants, it is virtually nonabusable, producing little or no euphoria and having no street value. The corollary to this is that, as opposed to the rapid effect of methylphenidate and d-amphetamine, pemoline's effects are seen gradually over many weeks. It is also long lasting so that it needs to be taken only once daily. Unfortunately, this makes pemoline more likely than the other stimulants to cause insomnia. Finally, because it causes liver inflammation in a small percentage of those treated, patients taking pemoline need to have regular blood tests, a procedure to which many patients object.

Although evidence for their efficacy is purely anecdotal and is probably less than for methylphenidate, both cyclic antidepressants and the monoamine oxidase inhibitors may also be helpful in treating adult ADD. Not surprisingly, those that may be most useful have the strongest effects on norepinephrine and dopamine, similar to the effects of stimulants. The cyclic antidepressant desipramine and the monoamine oxidase inhibitor tranylcypromine have both been reported as effective. Like pemoline, antidepressants are not abusable although their positive effects in ADD may be seen very quickly in contrast to their longer latency of action in treating depression. The use of the MAO inhibitors, however, is complicated by two clinical problems. First, tolerance to their effects in treating ADD is common. Second, because of the dietary restrictions inherent in their use (see chapter 9), these are not medications ideally suited to treat a population of impulsive patients with tendencies toward drug abuse.

On what basis, then, might a psychopharmacologist choose a specific medication to treat adult ADD? Without question, if the patient is cooperative and has no history of either drug abuse or significant criminal behavior, methylphenidate or d-amphetamine are the treatments of choice. If these medications are ineffective or cause intolerable side effects, or if either drug abuse or criminal behavior is present, then desipramine is usually prescribed with tranylcypromine a second choice, assuming the patient can adhere to the dietary and medication proscriptions. Pemoline would be another possibility for those with drug abuse tendencies.

Madeline was 26 years old and had lived a chaotic life since childhood. As a child, she had always been a behavior problem—demanding, moody, and angry at home and rebellious if disciplined at school, complaining of feeling constantly bored there. She would talk continuously in class and would not stop for more than short periods of time when disciplined. Sitting down and doing homework seemed impossible for her despite a remarkable variety of enticements, rewards, and punishments by her parents. If she was very interested in something, such as certain television shows, Madeline was able to sit for hours and watch them. Although no one thought of her as a "bad kid," Madeline seemed unwilling—or unable—to deal with her age-appropriate tasks. Her moods fluctuated enormously; she was mostly irritable and dysphoric, especially when pushed, but could also be playful, charming, and filled with grand and even grandiose plans at times. Because of her superior intelligence, Madeline was able to graduate from high school despite her behavioral problems. Following graduation, she lived in five cities in the next eight years. In each city, she would get low-paying jobs easily which would never last more than four months, because of poor attendance (explained by boredom according to her), fighting with her boss, and sullen behavior. After each move, Madeline quickly made friends and created good social supports. However, after a few months to years, she would feel increasingly restless and move somewhere else where the cycle would repeat. She had tried every possible street drug

but used only marijuana on a regular basis and intermittently drank
alcohol to excess.

Madeline came from a middle-class family in which there were two
paternal uncles and a first cousin with alcoholism. Her father was a
businessman who had had learning difficulties as a child but had never
been evaluated or treated psychiatrically.

Surprisingly, Madeline had had little contact with the mental health
field. She had seen a few therapists for no more than one or two visits
each in high school. At age 14, she was given methylphenidate (Ritalin) for a number of weeks. She remembered no response at all and
had discontinued the medication quickly.

Because of a growing frustration with her inability to create a successful career—which, being ambitious, she very much wanted—
Madeline sought therapy. After eliciting the above history, her
therapist recommended a psychopharmacological consultation, suspect-
ing ADD. When Madeline's parents confirmed the history, she was
given methylphenidate which caused marked dysphoria, even at low
dose. It was discontinued and pemoline (Cylert) was begun. After a few
weeks, she became more settled. Her moodiness, irritability, and occasional impulsive behavior were still present but in greatly diminished
proportion. More important, she was able to stay in her psychotherapy
for the next two years, dealing with her issues of self-esteem and incon-
sistency in relationships. She eventually stopped using marijuana regularly. Recently, she has been training as an assistant in film production,
a field she has now worked in for over one year. She continues in psychotherapy, making steady progress.

Systematic long-term studies of adult ADD—following these patients into
their thirties, forties, and fifties—do not exist. We know that a substantial
number of patients with childhood ADD seem to "outgrow" the disorder by the
time they are young adults. Would a similar proportion of young adults with
adult ADD show similar natural improvement by the time they are in their
thirties? Without this information, it is impossible to make recommendations
regarding long-term medication treatment for adult ADD. For now, then, the
best recommendation might be to taper and withdraw the medication period-
ically in order to reassess the continuing need for it. When this is done, it
should ideally be with the knowledge of significant others, since ADD patients
do not always recognize the changes in mood and behavior that might ensue
following medication discontinuation.

Additionally, my own clinical experience is that those patients with adult
ADD who seek treatment virtually always need psychotherapy. Even if they

have avoided substance abuse and are not particularly antisocial, they have grown up labeled as bad kids, underachievers, unable to accomplish as much as peers with similar intelligence. The effects on self-esteem (as exemplified by Madeline) are pervasive, appropriate social skills are often lacking, and patients frequently gravitate towards inappropriate peer groups. Once a good effect from medication has been achieved, long-term psychological work can be both productive and rewarding.

## ALCOHOL AND DRUG ABUSE

It may seem paradoxical, at best, to consider prescribing medications in the treatment of patients who have problems modulating their use of drugs since medications, after all, are simply prescribed drugs. Because of this paradox, of all the disorders discussed in this book, drug and alcohol abuse present the most difficult challanges. Psychopharmacologists treating substance abusers should therefore have intensive experience in prescribing medications *for these specific disorders*. In fact, there are some situations in which medications are mandated by law to be administered only by those facilities and practitioners specifically set up to treat the drug abuse—methadone treatment for heroin users, for instance. Even in other situations, however, the problems of drug and alcohol abuse require a unique combination of individual and group treatments without which any medication treatment will be worthless.

For both therapist and psychopharmacologist, the difficulties inherent in treating these patients are heightened by the potential consequences of inappropriate management. For instance, some substances such as cocaine can be stopped suddenly without significant risk to the patient; but abruptly stopping short-acting benzodiazepines that have been taken for a long time at high dose can cause grand mal seizures, and stopping high-dose barbiturates after prolonged use can be life-threatening.

Moreover, accurately diagnosing other psychiatric disorders in the presence of significant drug and alcohol abuse hovers between difficult and impossible. To thoughtfully evaluate an alcohol-abusing patient for a major depression, for instance, almost always requires weeks to months of sobriety, which the patient usually resists, insisting the alcohol is being used to treat an underlying depression (see below). It is in these types of clinical dilemmas that programs designed to work with alcoholics who may have other disorders (so-called "dual diagnosis" programs) can be extremely helpful.

Nonetheless, although they never play more than an adjunctive or transient role in overall treatment, medications can be helpful in four possible situations in treating drug and alcohol abuse: (1) in making detoxification safer, simpler, and less painful; (2) in diminishing craving for the abused substance; (3) in diminishing relapse; and (4) by treating coexisting disorders. In this section, I will review the use of medications for all four purposes, with a focus on outpatient treatment of drug and alcohol abuse rather than issues such as inpatient detoxification protocols.

## Alcohol Abuse

Since alcohol abuse is the most common substance abuse disorder, affecting over 13 percent of the American population over a lifetime (with even higher rates among those who have other types of psychopathology), the issue of recognizing and treating it is vital—and difficult (Regier et al., 1988). The problem is complicated by the availability of alcohol and its sanctioned status as a legal and acceptable drug in our society. In my experience, alcoholism is the most commonly missed diagnosis by mental health professionals, including myself.

In general, medications do not play a significant role in treating alcoholism. A variety of medications, especially the benzodiazepine tranquilizers, are frequently used in the detoxification process, more commonly in inpatient settings. Since there is a significant risk of medical problems when patients stop drinking after long periods of alcohol use, especially if they consumed significant quantities, it is often helpful to obtain a consultation from someone expert in this particular area before the detoxification occurs. This is especially true with those patients who have had major problems during previous withdrawals, those with serious medical illnesses, or those with multiple substance abuses who are likely to have a more complicated withdrawal.

No medication has yet been shown to be effective in decreasing alcohol craving. There are occasional reports suggesting that lithium will decrease the likelihood of relapse to drinking in nondepressed alcoholics, but it would be very premature to recommend this on a routine basis (Fawcett, Clark, et al., 1987). Preliminary evidence has also suggested that medications that block the reuptake of serotonin, thereby enhancing its availability in the brain, such as fluoxetine, may diminish alcohol craving (Meyer, 1989). Systematic studies using currently available medications, however, have not yet been carried out.

The most common use of medication in the maintenance/prevention phase of alcoholism is to cause an unpleasant reaction if the person does drink, thereby promoting a negative consequence to alcohol use. Disulfiram (Antabuse) is prescribed for this purpose. It works by blocking an intermediate step in the metabolism of alcohol, causing a marked increase in the blood level of acetaldehyde. Usually occurring from one-half hour to a few hours after ingesting alcohol, common symptoms from drinking while talking disulfiram are flushing, sweating, a throbbing headache, nausea, vomiting, chest pain, palpitations, and extraordinary malaise. In unusual circumstances, the reaction may be life-threatening. Disulfiram may serve primarily as a test of motivation or as a mild reinforcer for already motivated patients. Studies documenting its efficacy are few (Kranzler and Orrok, 1989). Patients taking disulfiram who want to drink will simply stop it for a number of days and then drink. Unfortunately, the amount of time needed off disulfiram to avoid a negative reaction with alcohol varies a great deal, thereby putting the patient at risk to have a reaction if he drinks. Reactions may also occasionally occur with disguised forms of alcohol such as cough syrup or aftershave lotion that is absorbed through the skin. Even without alcohol, disulfiram can cause side effects such as fatigue, restlessness, and an unpleasant taste. Overall, then, disulfiram cannot be considered a useful treatment for the majority of alcoholics. Its best use is in aiding those patients who are reasonably motivated but need help resisting the impulse to drink. By itself, disulfiram will *not* keep patients from drinking.

The trickiest and most common clinical dilemma regarding medications in treating alcoholics focuses on diagnosing and treating other coexistent psychiatric disorders or, as it is often framed, finding the underlying problem that "causes" the patient to drink. (It must be understood that little evidence supports such "causative" hypotheses.) A remarkable number of alcoholics also have other psychiatric disorders with estimates ranging up to 75 percent (Ross, Glaser, and Germanson, 1988). With the exception of other substance abuse disorders, the most common coexistent psychiatric disorders among alcoholics are major depression, anxiety disorders, and antisocial personality (Rounsaville and Kranzler, 1989). Compounding the problem even further is the fact that persistent drinking can cause a great number of the symptoms—such as depression, anxiety, confusion, or psychosis—that are seen in these other disorders (Schuckit, 1983b).

Distinguishing between alcoholism and depression is the most common of these diagnostic dilemmas since alcohol is a depressant, causing a variety of symptoms also seen in primary depression. Furthermore, many of the secondary effects of alcoholism, including the use of other drugs, psychological responses to life havoc induced by alcohol, and loss of social supports, may exacerbate the depressed mood. Therefore, depending on when the patient is interviewed and how the diagnosis of depression is made, estimates of depression in alcoholics have ranged from 3 and 98 percent! (Keeler, Taylor, and Miller, 1979). Depressive symptoms in alcoholics who are still drinking, however, rarely have the episodic course seen in primary depression. Instead, alcoholic depression tends to wax and wane in intensity within hours to days to weeks. Furthermore, if the patient stops drinking, depressive symptoms typically remit. Alcoholics who remain sober for years generally show no evidence of significant depressive symptoms. The best estimate is that for 90 percent of those with both alcoholism and depression together, the primary diagnosis is alcoholism, not depression (Schuckit, 1986). An additional point in this regard concerns the use of genetic histories. Contrary to findings of some older studies, it is now clear that patients with depression do not have greater numbers of alcoholics in their families, and alcoholics probably have no increased risk of depression in their families. In other words, the two disorders are genetically independent (Schuckit, 1986). Only in the families of patients with both alcoholism and depression in which the depression clearly preceded the substance abuse is there an increased incidence of both disorders (Merikangas, Leckman, Prusoff, Pauls, and Weissman, 1985).

Given the information just presented, how does a therapist—or psycho-pharmacologist—decide when a depressive syndrome in a heavy drinker should be evaluated for treatment with antidepressants? The answer is that the decision cannot and should not be made until the patient has stopped drinking. A minimum time of sobriety after which an evaluation for depression can be made is two weeks; many experts suggest that waiting a number of months is better since continued mood swings are often seen in abstinent drinkers for months following sobriety. Whatever the appropriate time frame, it is clear that prescribing antidepressants to heavy drinkers or to those who have been sober for only a few days is neither clinically warranted nor wise.

Similar considerations apply in evaluating anxiety symptoms in alcoholics, although less research has been done in this area. Here too, only in sober alcoholics can a reasonable evaluation for a concurrent anxiety disorder be made (Weiss and Mirin, 1989). Another important consideration in evaluating anxiety disorders is that antidepressants have virtually no addiction potential whereas benzodiazepines, the most common class of antianxiety medications, are capable of causing addiction. Abstinent alcoholics may experience more euphoria from benzodiazepines than do nonalcoholics, further enhancing the risk of excessive use (Ciraulo, et al., 1989). Because of this, buspirone (Buspar) (see chapter 11), which is completely nonaddictive and does not produce euphoria, may be particularly useful in treating anxiety symptoms in abstinent alcoholics.

Finally, when both alcoholism and another primary Axis I disorder coexist, there is a tendency, usually reinforced by the patient, to assume that treatment of the nonalcohol disorder will, by itself, treat the alcoholism. In general, this simply is not true. When two disorders coexist, they must both be treated independently and vigorously.

## Cocaine Abuse

As the use of cocaine has increased over the last fifteen years, and more dangerous and self-reinforcing preparations such as free-base and crack have proliferated in our society, greater attention has been paid to therapeutic interventions in the binge cycles of serious users. In conjunction with an increased understanding of the biology of cocaine, this has spawned an effort to find pharmacological aids to stop cocaine craving and/or to block the effects of the drug. By far, using medications to diminish craving in the immediate post-withdrawal period is the most promising current approach, with substantial supporting evidence already available. As in the treatment of alcohol abuse, however, medications cannot and should not be considered as other than an aid in the overall treatment program of these patients, strengthening and not substituting for the other more important nonbiological aspects of treatment.

Strategies for decreasing cocaine craving have been developed using our knowledge of two aspects of cocaine abuse—the biology of the drug and the time course of the withdrawal symptoms. Although it has effects on multiple neurotransmitters, cocaine's capacity to cause stimulation and euphoria is due principally to its ability to enhance dopamine activity in the brain, primarily, but not exclusively, by blocking the reuptake of dopamine, thereby allowing more of the dopamine to activate the postsynaptic receptors (Kleber and Gawin, 1986) (see chapter 2). Enhancing dopamine activity causes both acute stimulation and euphoria. It also causes paranoia, analogous to the hypothesized dopamine overactivity seen in other paranoid states such as schizophrenia (which is treated by dopamine blockers). Chronic use of cocaine, however, ultimately depletes the amount of dopamine available, producing both withdrawal and craving (Wyatt, Karoum, Suddath, and Hitri, 1988).

The cocaine withdrawal syndrome (crash) is characterized by predominantly depressive symptoms (Gawin and Kleber, 1986). Initially, in the first hours or days after the cocaine supply is depleted, users will describe a state of depression, anhedonia, insomnia, irritability, and some suicidal ideation. In short, patients look as if they are in the middle of a melancholic depression. They then typically become hypersomnolent and crave food. During this time, cocaine craving is low. Gradually, over days, patients' energy improves although anhedonia, mild dysphoria, and apathy persist. It is during this period when users feel flat and depleted that cocaine craving increases markedly, frequently culminating in obtaining a new supply of drug and a repetition of the cycle.

Because of these two observations, strategies for treating cocaine users have focused on increasing brain dopamine in this post-withdrawal period in an attempt to diminish the dopamine depletion and the cocaine craving. The cyclic antidepressant desipramine, bromocriptine (Parlodel), and amantadine (Symmetrel) are three medications for which some efficacy has been demonstrated. Currently, the evidence is strongest for desipramine. Compared to placebo in a double-blind trial, it will increase time of abstinence and decrease self-reported craving if taken daily in the post-withdrawal period (Gawin et al., 1989). Effects are seen within one to two weeks, although the positive effects seem to increase over the first four to five weeks. Doses prescribed are comparable to those used to treat depression.

Although the evidence for their efficacy is still small, bromocriptine and amantadine may also decrease cocaine craving with anticraving effects seen immediately in some patients (Extein and Gold, 1988). Bromocriptine's effects are limited by the frequent occurrence of significant headaches and nausea. There is no evidence that either medication has the potential to be addictive in humans, although animals do self-administer bromocriptine. Other medications that have been utilized without significant success in decreasing cocaine craving are lithium and methylphenidate (Ritalin). Finally, dopamine blockers, usually used as antipsychotics (see chapter 12), have just begun to be prescribed for cocaine abusers. Early reports demonstrated, not surprisingly, that, although dopamine blockers might diminish the effects of cocaine, they exacerbated the cocaine withdrawal-induced anhedonia, thereby promoting patient resistance to their use. However, preliminary results using low-dose flupenthixol, an experimental dopamine blocker with both antidepressant and antipsychotic properties, suggested that it might decrease cocaine cravings, possibly diminish cocaine effects, and be acceptable to patients (Gawin, Allen, and Humblestone, 1989).

Barry had attempted to stop his cocaine use many times before without success. Following binges, he would attend Cocaine Anonymous (CA) meetings for days to a few weeks but always ended up using again and dropping out of treatment. With his girlfriend threatening to break up with him and fearing being fired because of his increasingly erratic attendance at work, Barry sought help from a psychiatrist specializing in cocaine addiction. It was suggested to Barry that desipramine might increase the possibility of abstinence, but *only* in the context of a twelve-step program. When Barry agreed to attend CA meetings regularly, desipramine in doses increasing to 175 mg daily was prescribed. Barry used cocaine once soon after beginning treatment but then stayed clean for three weeks (a long time for him), following which he had another binge. He continued the desipramine, however, and over the next month felt a gradual decrease in his cocaine craving. Three months after starting desipramine, the medication was tapered and stopped without incident. Barry continued to work in the CA program and has now been clean for seven months.

Just as in evaluating alcoholics for other psychiatric disorders, it is useless to attempt to diagnose an underlying depression or manic-depressive illness while a patient is either using cocaine or in the first few weeks of abstinence, since the symptoms seen at that time are more likely secondary to the drug's effects than to a coexisting disorder. Cocaine abusers, however, are at high risk to abuse other substances, typically alcohol or tranquilizers, in order to modulate the cocaine-induced stimulation. This is especially relevant since those patients who abruptly stop benzodiazepines along with cocaine may have simultaneous withdrawal syndromes, one producing depression and the other, irritability and anxiety.

### Opiate Abuse (Heroin and Narcotic Analgesics)

Opiates are the most effective and most powerful painkillers available. Heroin is not legal in the United States, while morphine, meperidine (Demerol), hydromorphone (Dilaudid), oxycodone (Percodan), codeine, and propoxyphene (Darvon) are prescribed medications. Since the treatment of opiate abuse virtually always takes place in specialized facilities, the most important recommendation that can be made is that neither therapists nor general psychiatrists should treat serious opiate abuse in a solo practice setting.

Aside from the treatment of acute opiate overdose, for which naloxone (a narcotic antagonist which reverses the effects of the drug) is very effective, medications are used to aid opiate detoxification and prevent relapse. Detoxification can be aided by the use of methadone, a long-acting, oral medication which will, in part, substitute for the abused drug. Once a stable dose of methadone is achieved, it can then be withdrawn gradually over many days. A second approach is to use the antihypertensive medication clonidine, which is effective in blocking both the objective and, to a lesser extent, subjective effects of opiate withdrawal (Charney, Sternberg, Kleber, Heninger, and Redmond, 1981). Although side effects such as sedation and dizziness often complicate its use, clonidine is completely nonaddictive and may therefore be preferable to methadone.

During the ongoing maintenance program of opiate addiction, for those patients who seem to be unable to remain drug-free, either methadone or naltrexone (Trexan) can be prescribed. Methadone can be used as a long-term substitution drug that is prescribed under careful supervision or can be thought of as a transitional treatment with the long-term goal of complete abstinence.

Naltrexone is an opiate antagonist similar, in some ways, to naloxone (see above). It therefore blocks the effect if illegal narcotics are taken. As might be expected, its acceptance among addicts has not been high. It may be most helpful as an aid to those who have good social supports and are already well motivated.

## Other Drugs

In the treatment of drug abuse involving other drugs, medications play very little to no role, except in treating acute toxic reactions, a situation that is generally confined to emergency rooms. The only other use of medications is in detoxifying patients who take high doses of short-acting sedatives (such as barbiturates). In these cases, a common strategy is to substitute a long-acting barbiturate, such as phenobarbital in equivalent doses, and then gradually taper it over seven to ten days. Since blood levels of long-acting medications decrease gradually when tapered, withdrawal symptoms are minimized. A similar approach is sometimes used to withdraw a patient from short-acting benzodiazepines, in which a longer-acting tranquilizer, such as clonazepam, is substituted and then tapered.

# 7

## Personality Disorders

Compared to all other clinical entities described in this book, personality disorders are least characterized by symptoms that are easily elicited by a series of simple questions. The enduring and broad-based qualities and traits inherent in personality (and personality disorders) are inseparable from self and fit poorly into the medical-model, syndrome-based framework of DSM-III-R. An additional distinction is that of all the disorders described here, personality disorders are the ones with diagnostic criteria that are universally acknowledged as primitive: The individual personality disorders overlap enormously; the various methods of making the diagnoses almost never agree with each other; and the distinctions between personality traits and disorder are arbitrary at best. Yet I would be remiss if this book didn't cover the little that *is* known about the psychopharmacological treatment of personality disorders since this area is among the most exciting in psychiatry. Currently, most patients with personality disorders alone (i.e., without an additional Axis I disorder) would probably not benefit from medications (a statement I acknowledge is made without a shred of scientific evidence). Some do, however, in ways that may change the course of therapy that was previously mired in a therapeutic impasse.

### DIAGNOSIS

The notion of describing or diagnosing personality types or disorders is not new. From the ancient Greeks who suggested that the balance of the bodily humors determined personality types to the nineteenth-century term "constitutional psychopathic insanity" describing what we now call antisocial personality, there has always been interest in categorizing the patterns of behavior subsumed under the current use of the word personality. An unresolved issue is the method of classification: Should we use a dimensional approach, describing people along a continuum of traits, analogous to the measurement of intelligence, or a categorical approach in which disorders can be judged to be present or not and in which there is a defined demarcation between having the disorder and not having it? DSM-III-R uses a categorical scheme. Unfortunately, because there is so little empirical basis for the current categories, DSM-III-R seems—and to a large degree is—arbitrary.

The method of classification, although important in its own right, has important implications for treatment—in this case, prescribing medications. For we must consider what the goal of treatment is when a psychopharmacologist prescribes, for example, antipsychotics for a patient with borderline personality disorder. Is the medication supposed to treat a specific disorder which we call borderline personality? Or will it treat one or a few of the traits/feelings/behaviors that are typically found in these patients such as affective instability, traits that are really dimensional in quality? (A nonborderline patient can also exhibit marked affective instability. Would the same medication be effective for that patient? Are we treating specific symptoms seen in a personality disorder or are we treating the disorder itself?)

Even if we accept the categorical approach of DSM-III-R in defining personality disorders, the problem of overlap among the disorders makes diagnosis and treatment planning confusing. The personality disorder criteria in DSM-III described "pure cultures" of personality types—that is, the personality disorders were sharply defined but were so narrow in scope that many patients could only be defined as mixed or atypical personality disorder, a result that defeated the purpose of defining specific personality types in the first place. Because of this, DSM-III-R expanded the range of specific personality disorders, hoping to decrease the number of mixed disorders. Unfortunately, the cost of this change was a marked increase in the number of patients who met criteria for more than one personality disorder. Most patients with one personality disorder will meet criteria for at least one other (and frequently more) (Widiger and Rogers, 1989). The shift of diagnostic criteria also resulted in potentially marked changes in the frequency of individual personality disorders. In a recent study, the number of patients with schizoid personality disorder increased by 800 percent simply by changing the criteria from DSM-III to DSM-III-R! (Morey, 1988).

Because of the degree of overlap between specific disorders, it is difficult, for example, to describe MAO inhibitors as a treatment for the specific disorder of avoidant personality since those same patients will frequently be additionally diagnosed as borderline, paranoid, and dependent personalities. Are MAO inhibitors helpful for those disorders too? Does the presence of an additional personality disorder change the likelihood of response to the medication? These questions have yet to be explored.

In order to solve the problem of most personality-disordered patients meeting the criteria for more than one disorder, DSM-III-R describes personality disorder clusters in which a group of disorders that overlap the most in their diagnostic criteria can be considered as related entities. Cluster A comprises the odd or eccentric personality disorders. Within this group are the paranoid, schizoid, and schizotypal disorders. Cluster B, characterized by intense, chaotic emotionality, includes antisocial, borderline, histrionic, and narcissistic disorders. Cluster C, consisting of those disorders primarily manifested by anxiety or fear, is composed of avoidant, dependent, obsessive compulsive, and passive aggressive disorders.

Another important diagnostic issue in evaluating personality disorders and formulating coherent treatment plans, especially if medications are considered, is that of evaluating patients who have both Axis I, symptom-based, *and* Axis II personality disorders simultaneously, a clinical situation that is extremely common. (See chapter 1 for a discussion of DSM-III-R and the multiaxial diagnostic scheme.) The most common of these comorbidities is that of major depression and borderline personality disorder. Forty to sixty percent of borderline patients have a concomitant major depression (Gunderson and Elliott, 1985; Kroll and Ogata, 1987). The other common combination is that of schizotypal personality with schizophrenia (Docherty, Fiester, and Shea, 1986).

How can we understand the relationship between symptom-based, Axis I disorders and personality disorders? There are many possible models (Docherty et al., 1986). The classical psychodynamic model is that the personality disorder predisposes the individual to the Axis I disorder, typically depression. Thus, a narcissistic or dependent patient who relies on external objects to achieve a stable sense of self will be greatly affected by the loss of a relationship such that a depression might ensue. Another possibility is that the personality disorder is simply an attenuated version of the Axis I disorder. Using this model, the Cluster B personality disorders that are characterized by intense and erratic emotions would be thought of as unusual-looking bipolar disorders; dependent personalities would be considered mild chronic depressions. A third possibility is that the personality disorder is a result—or complication—of the syndromal disorder. Patients with panic disorder who are also dependent and avoidant would be conceptualized as first having had the panic disorder which then led to the personality disorder because of the fearfulness and helplessness that is a characteristic result of panic attacks. The fourth model postulates that the two coexisting disorders stem from the same causative factors. A combination of genetic predisposition and poor early environment would then result, for instance, in both depression and narcissistic personality disorder.

Of course, the models just presented are simplifications that allow us to begin to consider these complex relationships among disorders. For any individual patient, one model (or more than one) will fit the clinical picture better than others. Sometimes, a combination of models fits best. In the case of John (described in chapter 3), his narcissistic personality (a predisposing cause) may have contributed to his cocaine abuse which then precipitated his bipolar disorder which, in combination with his personality disorder, culminated in a demoralization state (as a complication).

The similarity of the diagnostic criteria for the two types of disorders is another cause for diagnostic confusion. For example, the use of diagnostic criteria for a personality disorder that include affective symptoms such as impulsivity, affective instability, intense anger, and suicidality immediately increases the likelihood of diagnosing both a mood disorder and a simultaneous personality disorder, in this case, borderline. The Axis I/Axis II distinction gives the appearance that each axis describes separate aspects of human behavior and functioning. To some degree they do. However, because we still use a variety of subjective feelings to define Axis I disorders (e.g., hedonic feelings in evaluating depression), and symptoms to describe Axis II disorders, there is still significant overlap in our criteria for symptom-based and personality disorders.

The last point to be made about the interaction between personality and Axis I disorders is that the presence of a disorder on either axis will make the evaluation of the other more difficult. The more obvious of these two situations occurs in the midst of an Axis I active episode during which time accurate personality assessment is fraught with difficulties (Hirschfeld et al., 1983). As an example, depression frequently provokes dependent, helpless feelings and behavior which may or may not reflect a person's characteristic personality style. To infer a dependent personality disorder during a time when a patient is fatigued, incapable of concentrating, having difficulty getting out of bed, and ruminating on themes of worthlessness is simply not valid. Similarly, manic patients will typically appear manipulative, hostile, and passive aggressive, behaviors that are inherent in the manic state and do not necessarily reflect the patient's enduring personality traits. Certainly, not all manifestations of personality will change during an episode of mania, depression, or schizophrenia, but enough do to suggest caution. It makes more sense simply to wait until the patient has emerged from the acute episode before making a personality diagnosis.

Conversely, the presence of a severe personality disorder may mask the onset of an incipient Axis I disorder. Two of the more common situations of this type are: (1) when a patient who is chronically dysphoric as part of a personality disorder has the new onset of a major depression, and (2) during the ongoing treatment of a borderline or narcissistic patient whose life is filled with constant crises and who begins to have bipolar/cyclothymic mood swings that are superimposed upon the person's life-event-driven chaos ( as shown in the case of Donna in chapter 14). In these cases, the key to accurate diagnosis is to ask the right questions. If a patient with a personality disorder appears to get worse during ongoing treatment, asking the questions needed to make the diagnoses of mania and/or depression (see chapter 3) will often help clarify the clinical situation.


## SUBTYPES


Because the DSM-III-R criteria for the individual personality disorders are, in general, neither particularly reliable nor valid as descriptions of discrete clinical entities (with the possible exception of antisocial personality disorder), this section will review the individual disorders by cluster. Of the individual disorders, only borderline personality disorder will be discussed in greater detail because it is the most prevalent personality disorder seen in clinical populations (Widiger and Rogers, 1989), and because of all the personality disorders, there is the most research and clinical experience in using medications to treat borderlines. Furthermore, since these are the most difficult patients in clinical practice, the issue of using medications with them arises frequently.


### Cluster A: The Odd or Eccentric Personality Disorders

Cluster A disorders encompass paranoid, schizoid, and schizotypal types. Patients with these personality disorders have the core characteristics of being interpersonally distant, emotionally constricted, and, in paranoid and schizotypal disorders, interpreting events in unusual ways. Historically, these disorders have generally been linked with schizophrenia, despite a lack of consistent evidence justifying this link for other than schizotypal disorder.

Paranoid patients are characterized simply by pervasive paranoid feelings and behaviors—expectations of being slighted, hypervigilance for subtle negative cues, excessive suspiciousness and mistrust without cause and so on. Virtually no research exists on paranoid personalities. Aside from the other disorders in this cluster, these characteristics are frequently seen in borderline or antisocial personalities.

Schizoid personalities are distant, removed people, having few (or no) friends, experiencing few (or no) intense emotions, and seeming indifferent to praise or criticism. Many of these patients could also be diagnosed as avoidant personalities because of the overlap in the diagnostic criteria. However, the hallmark of schizoid patients is that they do not miss having emotions and relationships, whereas avoidant patients are (allegedly) too pained to be with others but would like to be.

Schizotypal patients show the interpersonal constriction and emotional flatness of schizoid and paranoid patients but also exhibit a variety of odd cognitive and perceptual behavioral symptoms such as talking to themselves, speech that is difficult to understand, a tendency toward peculiar beliefs (such as telepathy), and experiencing illusions. It is likely that many of these patients are misclassified as personality disorders and should be more correctly thought of as having a schizophrenia spectrum disorder (Siever and Klar, 1986). Other schizotypal patients will also be diagnosed as borderline.

> Denise came to the clinic to be evaluated because of an inner sense that something was wrong, although she couldn't quite describe what it was. Talking about her feelings in a disjointed, hard-to-follow manner, she described how she lived by herself in a small house in a canyon outside Los Angeles with her six cats, three dogs, and many rabbits. Denise had no friends, explaining that she felt pressure when she was with people and a sense that they disliked her and were mocking her. Her communication with her animals was more satisfying. Furthermore, when people had visited her in the past, it annoyed her that they always commented on her collection of used aluminum foil which she kept in piles in the living room. At times, during smoggy days, she was sure she could feel an evil spirit pervading the atmosphere which promised the destruction of the city, an experience she related without any particular concern. She denied true hallucinations or well-formed delusions. When the interviewer expressed interest in Denise's sense of "something wrong" and offered to see her again, she compliantly agreed but didn't keep the appointment. Since Denise had no telephone in her house, the therapist wrote a letter to which there was no response.

## Cluster B: The Emotional, Chaotic Personality Disorders

Antisocial, borderline, histrionic, and narcissistic types are included in this group. These patients are characterized by their chaotic lives and, with the possible exception of antisocial personality, chaotic emotions and relationships. The presence of intense emotionality in these patients has led some recent observers to postulate a primary link between the Cluster B disorders and mood disorders. Regardless of how this link is conceptualized, these patients are at high risk to have an associated mood disorder. Most common is the dual diagnosis of borderline personality and major depression. Hysteroid dysphoria (see chapter 3), the proposed subtype of atypical depression characterized by narcissistic personality features and rejection-precipitated depressions, further highlights the clinical connection between Cluster B disorders and depression. Antisocial personalities are also at high risk for depressive disorders (Perry, 1985).

Antisocial personality disorder is currently defined more by pure behavioral characteristics, especially those related to aberrations from expected social behavior, than by more typical psychiatric symptoms or behaviors. It is common for these patients to be also diagnosed as borderline and/or passive aggressive personality.

Borderline personality disorder is characterized by emotional, intrapersonal, and interpersonal chaos. The choice of the term "borderline" is unfortunate since it implies that these patients are on the edge of another disorder. Historically, the term originally referred to borderline schizophrenia, but it is clear that using our current definitions, the majority of borderline patients have a disorder that is unrelated to schizophrenia. A small subgroup of patients who are diagnosed as both borderline and schizotypal, however, may have a disorder that is genetically related to schizophrenia (Docherty et al., 1986).

The use of the term borderline in this section refers to the definition set forth in DSM-III-R, not its use in the psychoanalytic literature in which borderline personality organization refers to a related but not identical concept. Table 7–1 shows the DSM-III-R criteria for this disorder. The eight criteria can be divided into three conceptual groups: affective dyscontrol (criteria 3 and 4), behavioral dyscontrol (criteria 2 and 5), and intrapsychic and interpersonal problems (criteria 1, 6, 7, and 8) (Cowdry, 1987). The division of borderline psychopathology in this way may be helpful in determining which of these patients are likely to improve with medications and which symptoms are the most likely to respond.

Histrionic personalities are primarily characterized by excessive emotionality and attention-seeking behavior. Dramatic and exaggerated responses to everyday situations are typical, as are unusually sexually seductive qualities. Many of these patients are also borderline.

Narcissistic personality is defined by behaviors and feelings that are midway between the profound chaos of borderline personalities and the less destructive features of histrionic patients. Narcissistic patients are characterized by preoccupation with self-aggrandizement and grandiosity with a striking lack of empathy for others.

### Cluster C: The Anxious and Fearful Personality Disorders

This group comprises avoidant, dependent, obsessive compulsive, and passive aggressive types. Patients with these disorders are characterized by constricting

TABLE 7-1

### Diagnostic Criteria for Borderline Personality Disorder

A pervasive pattern of instability of mood, interpersonal relationships, and self-image, beginning by early adulthood and present in a variety of contexts, as indicated by at least *five* of the following:

(1) a pattern of unstable and intense interpersonal relationships characterized by alternating between extremes of overidealization and devaluation

(2) impulsiveness in at least two areas that are potentially self-damaging, e.g., spending, sex, substance use, shoplifting, reckless driving, binge eating (Do not include suicidal or self-mutilating behavior covered in [5].)

(3) affective instability: marked shifts from baseline mood to depression, irritability, or anxiety, usually lasting a few hours and only rarely more than a few days

(4) inappropriate, intense anger or lack of control of anger, e.g., frequent displays of temper, constant anger, recurrent physical fights

(5) recurrent suicidal threats, gestures, or behavior, or self-mutilating behavior

(6) marked and persistent identity disturbance manifested by uncertainty about at least *two* of the following: self-image, sexual orientation, long-term goals or career choice, type of friends desired, preferred values

(7) chronic feelings of emptiness or boredom

(8) frantic efforts to avoid real or imagined abandonment (Do not include suicidal or self-mutilating behavior covered in [5].)

Reprinted with permission from the *Diagnostic and Statistical Manual of Mental Disorders, Third Edition, Revised.* Copyright 1987 American Psychiatric Association.

behaviors (similar to agoraphobia) that seem designed to limit risks. Thus, avoidant patients simply avoid interpersonal situations, dependent personalities avoid being personally responsible for decisions, obsessive compulsive patients use overly rigid rules that preclude new behaviors or situations, and passive aggressive patients avoid the consequences of open expression of feelings and create failure-producing situations, thereby limiting the risk of genuinely trying—and possibly failing. Compared to the other two clusters, patients in Cluster C have less in common. This is especially true for those with obsessive compulsive personalities who seem not to overlap with the other patients in this group (Kass, Skodol, Charles, Spitzer, and Williams, 1985).

Cluster C patients are thought to be at risk for a number of different Axis I disorders, although the evidence is still slim. Depression is thought to be common in patients with avoidant and dependent personalities, and social phobia may be common with avoidant personalities. Not surprisingly, obsessive personalities are generally considered to be at risk for developing obsessive compulsive disorder, despite a lack of documentation supporting this notion.

## NATURAL HISTORY, EPIDEMIOLOGY, AND GENETICS

By definition, personality disorders are chronic and enduring. However, the natural history of personality disorders has rarely been studied empirically. There is some evidence that antisocial personalities tend to improve spontaneously during middle age (Robins, 1987). Some borderline patients will show gradual improvement over decades, although as a group they are characterized by continued difficulties (McGlashan, 1986).

Epidemiological rates for most personality disorders are currently not possible to estimate because of the difficulties in making reliable diagnoses and the recency of our definitions. Only antisocial personality, found in 3 percent of the population with a male:female sex ratio of 6:1, has been studied (Robins et al., 1984).

The genetic links between personality disorders and a variety of Axis I disorders have been studied for only some specific personalities. Among the Cluster A disorders, high rates of schizotypal and paranoid personalities are seen in the families of schizophrenic patients (Kendler, 1986). For Cluster B disorders, antisocial patients have increased rates of alcoholism and somatization disorders in their families as well as high rates of other family members with antisocial personalities (Guze, 1976). The familial increase in rates of antisocial personalities is seen even in adopted-away offspring, implying that the link is at least partially genetic (Crowe, 1974). High rates of mood disorders are found in the families of borderline personality patients. It is not clear, however, whether the increased rate is found only in those patients with both borderline personality and mood disorders or whether all borderline patients have higher rates of mood disorders in their relatives (Gunderson and Elliott, 1985). Borderline patients may also have an increased rate of other borderline and antisocial personalities in their families (Pope, Jones, Hudson, Cohen, and Gunderson, 1983; Zanarini and Gunderson, 1988).

## PSYCHOPHARMACOLOGICAL TREATMENT OF PERSONALITY DISORDERS

In the treatment of most patients with personality disorders, especially milder ones, the issue of using medications as an adjunct to psychotherapy will never arise—nor should it. However, patients with the more difficult personality disorders, especially those with borderline personality, are at best difficult to treat and at times unmanageable. Behavioral outbursts, impulsive suicide attempts and gestures, intense overwhelming affects, occasional odd perceptual and cognitive experiences such as depersonalized states often leave both therapist and patient wondering whether medication might be of any help. As a generalization, the more severe the personality disorder, the more reasonable it is to pursue psychopharmacological consultation. This usually means borderline, schizotypal, and severe narcissistic personalities. Not coincidentally, the description of a personality disorder as more severe often refers to the presence of associated symptoms, such as those seen in Axis I disorders. As an example, a passive aggressive patient may have a clear pattern of maladaptive behaviors but a paucity of clearly describable psychiatric symptoms. A schizotypal patient, on the other hand, will have both abnormal interpersonal relationships along with clear symptoms such as paranoid ideation or magical thinking. The more a patient's difficulties can be described in symptom terms—as opposed to intrapsychic or interpersonal pattern terms—the more likely it is that medication may be somewhat helpful.

When pharmacotherapy is utilized to treat personality-disordered patients, what does the medication treat? There are three possibilities: First, medications may be treating the disorder itself, improving most or all of its manifestations. Second, medications may treat only associated Axis I disorders. In this model, medications do not really treat the personality disorder at all, but will improve the symptoms of concomitant Axis I disorders. Successfully treating an associated mood disorder in patients with borderline personality, for instance, will have a positive effect on their functioning and capacity to work in psychotherapy. Conceptually, alleviating the Axis I symptoms might relieve pressure on the personality, so that concurrent behaviors would be less pathological. The core personality disorder, however, would be untouched. Third, medications might treat specific symptoms. As mentioned above, the symptoms of borderline personality disorder can be divided into groups. Hypothetically, affective and behavioral dyscontrol symptoms may be more amenable to pharmacotherapy than are identity and interpersonal problems. In this model, *some* of the manifestations of personality disorders are best conceptualized as due to underlying biological instability—in mood (in borderlines), in thinking (in borderlines and schizotypals), or in anxiety (in avoidant personalities).

From my own clinical experience as well as from the few studies that are available, the evidence seems most convincing for the second and third mechanisms—that medications are likely to be most effective in treating associated Axis I disorders and/or some specific target symptoms of the personality disorder in question. However, note also that the presence of a personality disorder generally makes the Axis I disorder less responsive to medication. As an example, patients with both personality disorder and depression respond less well to antidepressants compared to those with uncomplicated depression (Joyce and Paykel, 1989). Occasionally, anecdotes are published in the psychiatric literature that describe supposedly successful treatment of patients with personality disorders by medication alone. The patient is usually described as a very emotionally unstable, chaotic borderline who is treated with lithium. At that point, the patient begins to settle down, gets married, becomes an accountant (or enters a similar stable profession), and lives happily ever after. Often, however, the last line of the case discussion quietly notes that after the introduction of the lithium, the patient stayed in psychotherapy to work on problems of self-esteem and relationships for the next few years. Although a number of Bipolar II patients who appear borderline will respond to lithium with a marked diminution of their personality chaos, I have yet to see such a patient respond *completely* to medication alone. A more likely scenario is that when medication is effective, it gives patients relief from intolerable affects, anxieties, or fragmented thinking, thereby allowing the psychotherapy to proceed more consistently. If pharmacotherapy is successful, instead of cutting their wrists, borderline patients will only *think* of cutting—but will not, or will call their therapist *before* actually being self-destructive. Although this may seem like a rather limited effect, it allows the therapy to deal with feelings and mastery instead of always mopping up after the damage has been done.

If we work on the assumption, then, that medication can only treat some of the psychopathology of personality disorders, it is vital that therapist, psychopharmacologist, and patient all have clear expectations for the treatment. Otherwise, the magical hopes and dichotomous thinking that these patients are prone to (either a treatment is completely effective or it is worthless) will ensure a preception of the medication as worthless, regardless of its actual effect.

Even with well-delineated expectations of what a medication will do, it is not always easy to evaluate the efficacy of treatment. Treating a concomitant major depression in a narcissistic personality will not alleviate the underlying dysphoria inherent in the patients' intrapsychic and interpersonal difficulties. If these patients are asked whether they are less depressed, they may vigorously deny it because, from their point of view, they still have depressed mood. But they may be sleeping better, be more hedonic, have more energy, and be less suicidal, observations they may not be aware of. The finding noted above, that depression in personality-disordered patients responds less well to antidepressants, may reflect the multiple sources of depressive symptoms in these patients and the difficulty in teasing them apart. Therefore, in evaluating the effect of medications in patients with personality disorders, information regarding the target symptoms must be specifically elicited and all possible sources of information must be utilized. Sometimes, this will mean more contact between therapist and psychopharmacologist; at other times, it may be helpful to obtain information from family members. Because of the potential transference difficulties with the therapist, it is sometimes easier to have the prescribing physician make contact with the patient's family.

Finally, psychodynamic aspects of using medications in severe personality disorders must be thoughtfully explored since, for many of these patients, the implications of being given pills to help deal with feelings will provoke powerful reactions that have important transference meanings. This issue is discussed in greater detail in chapter 14.

## PSYCHOPHARMACOLOGICAL TREATMENT OF SPECIFIC PERSONALITY DISORDERS

Table 7–2 shows the medications most likely to help in treating patients with personality disorders. The table is organized in keeping with the idea set forth above—that medications can also be helpful by treating associated Axis I disorders; these are also listed in the table.

### Cluster A: Odd or Eccentric Personality Types

The antipsychotics are the medications most likely to help patients with these disorders. Unfortunately, because both paranoia and lack of insight are so common in these disorders, few of these patients, especially those with paranoid and schizoid personalities, will enter treatment and even fewer will take medication. No studies on treating either paranoid or schizoid patients with medication exist. Indeed, recent observers noted that with regard to paranoid personality disorder "not a single report of successful treatment has ever been recorded" (Freeman and Gunderson, 1989).

There is some evidence, on the other hand, for the efficacy of low-dose antipsychotics in the treatment of schizotypal personalities (Hymowitz, Frances, Jacobsberg, Sickles, and Hoyt, 1986). Many of the patients treated in these studies were both schizotypal and borderline, however, thereby making it more difficult to ascertain therapeutic effects for pure schizotypal patients. Nonetheless, some schizotypal patients show improvement on a variety of symptoms including ideas of reference and odd communication but also in social isolation and phobic anxiety. The magnitude of the therapeutic effect tends to be modest, suggesting that although the medications help, they rarely make a dramatic difference in patients' symptoms or psychological functioning (Soloff et al., 1986b). Generally, the higher-potency neuroleptics have been used and at lower doses than are typically prescribed for schizophrenic patients. At this point, it seems that antipsychotics have a limited role in the treatment of schizotypal

TABLE 7–2

*Medication Strategies for Personality Disorders*

| Disorder | Associated Axis I Disorder[a] | Medications |
|---|---|---|
| *Cluster A* | | |
| Paranoid | [b] | [b] |
| Schizoid | [b] | [b] |
| Schizotypal | [b] | Low-dose antipsychotics |
| *Cluster B* | | |
| Antisocial | Major depression, attention deficit disorder | Antidepressants, stimulants (with caution) |
| Borderline | Major depression Hysteroid dysphoria, attention deficit disorder | Low-dose antipsychotics, MAO inhibitors, carbamazepine, stimulants (with caution) |
| Histrionic | Hysteroid dysphoria | MAO inhibitors |
| Narcissistic | Hysteroid dysphoria, cyclothymia/bipolar II | MAO inhibitors, lithium |
| *Cluster C* | | |
| Avoidant | Social phobia | MAO inhibitors, benzodiazepines |
| Dependent | Major depression, panic disorder/agoraphobia | Antidepressants, benzodiazepines |
| Obsessive compulsive | Obsessive compulsive disorder | Clomipramine, fluoxetine |
| Passive aggressive | [b] | [b] |
| *Other types* | | |
| Dysthymia | Major depression | Antidepressants |
| Cyclothymia | [b] | Lithium |
| Explosive | [b] | Carbamazepine, lithium, stimulants (with caution) |

[a]The medications in column 3 relate to either the personality disorder in column 1 *or* the Axis I disorder in column 2. See text for details.

[b]Unknown.

patients, although when patients respond to the medications, it is likely to be in a broad-based manner.

## Cluster B: Emotional or Chaotic Personality Types

Concomitant depressive disorders in these patients occur frequently, making antidepressants the most commonly prescribed medications. However, there is also a significant role for low-dose antipsychotics in treating borderline patients and possibly stimulants for some antisocial personalities.

There is no evidence that antisocial personality responds in any way to medications. These patients, though, may have simultaneous Axis I disorders that are medication-responsive, the most common of which are depression and attention deficit disorder (ADD). Depressions can be treated with antidepressants at typical doses while the ADD can be treated by stimulants. However, because amphetamine-like stimulants have clear street value, they must be prescribed with extreme caution to antisocial patients who have ADD (see chapter 6). Prescribing stimulants for antisocial patients without substantial clinical evidence for associated ADD is an invitation to therapeutic disaster.

As befits a disorder that is broad in its manifestations and difficult in its treatment, borderline personality has been treated with virtually every type of medication prescribed by psychiatrists. Often, they are prescribed out of the therapeutic desperation engendered during the tumultuous treatment. Despite the "shotgun approach" frequently used, there are some reasonable guidelines that can be made in treating borderline patients with medications.

The most well-documented observation is that some borderline patients show a clear, albeit limited response to low-dose antipsychotics (Soloff, 1987). Most of the research studies on this topic have focused on the more severe borderline patients who are hospitalized. Whether the results can be generalized to less disturbed patients is unknown. The therapeutic effects may be broad-based with improvements seen in anxiety, depression, feelings of self-control, and paranoia. Less improvement tends to be seen with the more intrapsychic and interpersonal symptoms. Clinically, my experience with borderline patients who are not in hospital is that those who are in crisis and show fragmented thinking and overwhelming anxiety respond best to low-dose antipsychotics, frequently averting either hospitalization or significant acting out. Because of the risk of tardive dyskinesia with prolonged use (see chapter 12), antipsychotics should be prescribed for as short a period of time as is clinically appropriate.

The prominent mood symptoms of borderline patients—the dysphoria, mood lability, and intense anger—seem to respond best to antipsychotics and monoamine oxidase (MAO) inhibitor antidepressants. The evidence for the efficacy of the cyclic antidepressants in treating borderline patients is mixed (Soloff et al., 1986b). Results of an early study suggested that lithium might be helpful for those borderline patients with prominent mood lability (Rifkin, Quitkin, Carrillo, Blumberg, and Klein, 1972). Unfortunately, the use of lithium in treating these patients has not been pursued further.

A notorious group of symptoms commonly seen in these patients is the tendency towards acting out anger, toward both themselves and others. Self-destructive behavior may be seen as a tension-reducing act, a means of communication, or both. When used to communicate distress, these acts are probably not responsive to medications. However, if we hypothesize the tension-reducing quality of these acts as expressing profound anxiety, the use of medications as alternative ways of decreasing the tension makes theoretical sense. MAO inhibitors, antipsychotics, and carbamazepine, the anticonvulsant with mood stabilizing properties, are all effective with some patients (Cowdry and Gardner, 1988). Benzodiazepines, such as alprazolam (Xanax), and tricyclic antidepressants, such as amitriptyline (Elavil), can sometimes cause a paradoxical effect in borderline patients precipitating an increase in behavioral dyscontrol, suggesting extreme caution in their use (Soloff, George, Nathan, Schulz, and Perel, 1986a; Cowdry and Gardner, 1988).

> Ann, 32 years old, has been in a very unstable marriage and has a 4-year-old child. She has had a long history of short stormy relationships, frequently with inappropriate partners. During her past relationships as well as during her current marriage, intense verbal screaming matches were common. She has never made a suicide attempt, although when feeling trapped, she has fantasized about it often. Chronic feelings of life dissatisfaction without a sense of how to improve things have been prominent during her adult years, as have feelings of emptiness.
>
> Because of her commitment to her child, Ann has stayed in her poor marriage. Fights were becoming more frequent, during which she recently began throwing plates and dishes. After the fights, she would feel numb, spending up to days in a blank, depersonalized state in which she would be unable to care for her son or do household chores. Despite ongoing twice weekly psychotherapy, both individual and marital, these episodes continued and became more frequent. A trial of MAO inhibitors resulted in unacceptable postural hypotension. The antipsychotic thiothixene (Navane) was then prescribed, starting at 2 mg daily and then increasing to 4 mg at night, and has had the effect of markedly diminishing the rage and the subsequent withdrawal. Because of this, Ann and her husband have been better able to effectively discuss and resolve some issues without the constant threat of marital dissolution, an improvement that has also allowed her to feel more competent. Over the last few years, Ann has discovered that the best use of the thiothixene is on an intermittent basis, taking it for a few weeks or months at a time when her life is particularly stressful. Her core feelings of emptiness, though, are unchanged and are a continual focus of her therapy.

Borderline patients often have other psychiatric disorders as well which may be hidden by the chaos of the personality disorder. Treatment of these associated states often results in somewhat more manageable psychotherapy. Most common among these is major depression. However, as noted above, these depressions may not be as responsive to antidepressants as are depressions in the absence of severe personality pathology. My clinical impression is that MAO inhibitors are more effective than cyclic antidepressants for treating major depressions in borderline patients. Patients with hysteroid dysphoria (see chapter 3) often have borderline personalities and show a clear preferential response to MAO inhibitors (Liebowitz, Quitkin, et al., 1988b).

The other Axis I disorder that may coexist with borderline personality is attention deficit disorder which is characterized by fluctuating moodiness, irritability, and impulsive behavior, similar to some borderline symptoms. As noted above with antisocial personality, the use of stimulants, which are the treatment of choice for ADD, must be approached with caution for those with drug abuse histories (see chapter 6).

To summarize the psychopharmacological treatment of borderline personalities: (1) The affective and behavioral symptoms tend to respond better than the intra- and interpersonal behaviors. (2) Psychotic symptoms (which are not part of the DSM-III-R definition) are also responsive to treatment. (3) When medications are effective, their effects tend to be modest. (4) Antipsychotics are the most well-validated medications. (5) MAO inhibitors and carbamazepine (Tegretol) are also helpful; carbamazepine may be especially useful for patients with explosive outbursts directed to self or others. (6) Treatment of concomitant depressions should be attempted with the expectation that these states will be less responsive than depressions in non-borderline patients.

Treating either histrionic or narcissistic personality disorders with medications has not been systematically explored. However, since hysteroid dysphoric patients often exhibit histrionic or narcissistic traits in their personality styles (along with borderline traits), a pattern of rejection-precipitated nonautonomous depressions might suggest the use of MAO inhibitors.

Harry was a successful screenwriter who was known among his friends and family as the "moody artiste" type. He seemed absorbed in his own work and reputation, consistently angry at others who were more successful, and demanding to those around him. Even though he worked in a field in which emotional outbursts were relatively common, Harry was notorious for his intolerance of rejection. If a screenplay was not sold or if his work was severely criticized, Harry would respond in one of two ways—either by overwhelming rage, during which times he would scream and belittle everyone around him, get into physical fights, and be incredibly obnoxious, or by disappearing from sight for one day to two weeks. During these withdrawals, he would stay in his house, refuse to talk to anyone on the phone, feel apathetic, and sleep up to fourteen hours daily. He had been in psychotherapy for over ten years with two different therapists. During this time, his sense of entitlement, demandingness, and envy had diminished to manageable proportions, but his response to rejection was unchanged. Tranylcypromine (Parnate) was prescribed in increasing doses up to 40 mg daily. The effect was dramatic: He was able to stay in meetings in which his work was being criticized without exploding or leaving. When his work was rejected, he felt very upset but was able to function. Because of sexual side effects, he ultimately decreased the dose to 20 mg daily which was less effective but still afforded him some significant benefit.

When Bipolar II disorder (Bipolar disorder NOS) or cyclothymia coexist with narcissistic personality, lithium can be helpful. Distinguishing between "biological" and "psychological" mood swings is difficult, especially when they coexist. (The case history of Donna in chapter 14 exemplifies this difficulty.) The best clues to the presence of true bipolar mood swings in narcissistic patients are behavioral manifestations of the hypomanias: The person not only feels grandiose and euphoric but exhibits behavioral changes associated with these feelings such as sleeping less, talking more, spending more money, making more long distance phone calls, or other typical signs of mania (Akiskal, Khani, and Scott-Strauss, 1979).

## Cluster C: Anxious or Fearful Types

Because patients in this group are probably at increased risk for concomitant anxiety disorders such as social phobia, panic disorder with agoraphobia, as well as depression, benzodiazepines and antidepressants are the most likely medications to be prescribed.

Avoidant personalities often have social phobic symptoms. When the two disorders coexist, treatment of the social phobia—most commonly with MAO inhibitors or benzodiazepines—may result in amelioration of some of the avoidant traits as well (see the case of Bob in chapter 4) (Reich, Noyes, and Yates, 1989). Whether medications would be helpful for avoidant patients without social phobia is not known.

Treating dependent personalities or traits with medications seems unlikely to be of benefit. Dependent people, however, are at risk to become depressed if the objects of their dependency reject or leave them. In these situations, treating the coexistent depression may provide some relief acutely, although it is unlikely to cause significant change in the personality disorder itself. Among panic disorder patients, there is a link between the presence of phobic avoidance or agoraphobia and dependent personality traits (Reich, Noyes, and Troughton, 1987). In treating patients with both disorders, it is probably more helpful to treat the anxiety disorder first, since without the capacity to go out into the world without having a panic attack, trying to decrease dependency seems fruitless. Dependent patients who seem constricted in their activities may have a panic disorder or agoraphobia and may not be aware of it (or may simply not mention it). It is therefore important to ask about panic or phobic symptoms in dependent patients.

Obsessive compulsive personalities are probably at higher risk to have obsessive compulsive disorder. The latter condition is treatable by clomipramine, fluoxetine, and possibly other antidepressants (see chapter 4). The underlying personality disorder is probably not treatable by current pharmacotherapy.

Passive aggressive personalities have been ignored completely in the psychopharmacological literature. Medications are unlikely to be helpful with these patients.

The two major personality types not described in DSM-III-R for which medications may be helpful are those characterized by chronic depressive mood or explosive outbursts. Some patients with depressive personalities or dysthymic disorder are potentially treatable by antidepressants. This is covered in more detail in chapter 3. Although some patients with impulsive violent outbursts will be diagnosed as borderline or antisocial personalities, there may be others who do not fit neatly into our personality subtypes (Liebowitz, Stone, and Turkat, 1986). These patients are typically moody and will describe repeated outbursts, usually provoked by seemingly trivial stresses. A pattern of job and relationship instability is common, as are substance abuse and/or head injuries. Some of these patients will respond to anticonvulsants such as carbamazepine (Tegretol), or to lithium or stimulants (if there is significant evidence of attention deficit disorder).

# 8

## Treatment of Special Age-Groups

### *Childhood/Adolescence, the Elderly, and Pregnant Women*

The vast majority of the accumulated experience in psychopharmacology has been derived from treating patients in the middle of their lives, in the age range of 20 through 60. This is even more true with new treatments or experimental uses of already established medications. Certainly, it makes good sense to avoid unproven treatments in the young, the old, or pregnant women. Elderly patients, who are more likely to suffer from concomitant medical disorders, are at higher risk to develop potentially harmful side effects. In children and adolescents, biological and psychological development might be adversely affected by psychopharmacological agents at such a sensitive time. Yet both young and old suffer from psychiatric disorders, some of which are unique to their age groups while others are common to all age ranges. Even with disorders that are seen in all age groups, such as depression or anxiety, special considerations apply in using medications with younger and older patients. Pregnancy occurs at a time of life when major psychiatric disorders, such as mania, depression, schizophrenia, and panic disorder may already be present. In treating pregnant women, the issue of potential medication effects on the fetus adds a unique concern. In this chapter, we focus first on the use of medications in treating disorders of childhood and adolescence, then turn to some special concerns about elderly patients and pregnant women.

### CHILD AND ADOLESCENT DISORDERS

Aside from the potential for long-term effects noted above, there are good reasons why mental health professionals have traditionally been reluctant to

178

treat children with medications. First, good research on the validity and reliability of psychiatric diagnosis in childhood is a very recent phenomenon, even more recent than that of adult diagnosis. Without established ways of making diagnoses, medications could hardly be considered as appropriate for specific disorders or even specific behaviors within disorders, a situation that raised concerns about a "shotgun" approach to treatment. Moreover, the shifting nature of age-appropriate behavior in children and adolescents makes diagnosis more difficult. Fortunately, over the last decade, there has been a concerted effort to clarify the nature of childhood disorders. These studies have demonstrated that disorders such as depression can be reliably diagnosed in children and adolescents. Second, the dependent relationships that children have with adults, both parents and mental health professionals, make the cooperative venture that is characteristic of good psychopharmacology more difficult and allow for possible abuse of medications as a coercive form of behavioral control without clear guidelines. Third, studies documenting the efficacy of medications to treat child and adolescent disorders are remarkably few in number. Attention deficit disorder, which has been treated with medications for over fifty years, is the only childhood disorder with any significant history. Only in the last decade, as our ability to diagnose childhood disorders has improved, has pharmacotherapy been investigated in a more thoughtful manner than previously. Finally, there are concerns that taking medications, especially over an extended period of time, will leave a serious, potentially permanent scar on children's and adolescents' sense of themselves and may plant the seeds of chronic self-esteem problems.

Each of these concerns is individually valid. Yet we must remember that medications should be considered only to treat patients—both children and adults—who are suffering from psychiatric/psychological problems of sufficient severity to interfere significantly with their lives. It is appropriate to worry about the effect of lithium on a 14-year-old's cognitive function and school performance. This risk, though, must be weighed against the psychological effect of the manic episode for which the lithium is being prescribed and *its* effect on self-esteem, peer relations, and school performance. Just as with adults, decisions on using medications in children need to be examined using a risk/benefit approach. The individual issues may differ but the method of making good judgments in treating youngsters with medications is the same as with adults. And, of course, considering the use of medications never negates the use of other types of treatments. In virtually all cases, a child or adolescent for whom medications are prescribed will need other types of concomitant therapy.

Table 8–1 lists the childhood disorders for which medications are often prescribed. Overall, principles used for prescribing medications for children

TABLE 8–1

*Commonly Used Medications in Child and Adolescent Psychiatry*

| Disorder | Medication Class (or Medication) | Efficacy Rating |
|---|---|---|
| Major depression | Antidepressants | + to + + |
| Bipolar disorder | Lithium | + + |
| Autism | Antipsychotics | + |
| Schizophrenia | Antipsychotics | + to + + |
| School phobia (separation anxiety) | Imipramine | + + |
| Obsessive compulsive disorder | Clomipramine | + + |
| Attention deficit disorder | Stimulants, antidepressants | + + + + |
| Night terrors | Benzodiazepines, antidepressants | + + + + |
| Somnambulism (sleep-walking) | Benzodiazepines, antidepressants | + + + + |
| Enuresis | Antidepressants | + |
| Conduct disorder | Haloperidol, lithium | + + |
| Aggressive, destructive behavior | Antipsychotics, lithium, beta-blockers | + + + |
| Tourette's disorder | Haloperidol, pimozide, clonidine | + + + + |

+ + + = Definite efficacy
+ + = Probable efficacy
+ = Possible efficacy

and adolescents and deciding on doses are similar to those used for adults, with two exceptions: First, for smaller children, doses are sometimes recommended based on a ratio of milligrams of drug per kilogram (2.2 lbs) of the patient's weight, written as mg/kg. Thus, d-amphetamine might be prescribed in 0.5 mg/kg dosage. For a 65-pound child, which would translate to 30 kilograms, the daily dose would be $0.5 \times 30 = 15$ milligrams daily. Second, because children's livers are more efficient in metabolizing drugs than are adolescents' and adults', medication blood levels are lower than one might expect, given children's weight. Therefore, somewhat higher doses are sometimes used. This does not mean that the medications are started at high doses but that gradual increases of dose to higher levels in the case of nonresponse are common.

## Mood Disorders

### Diagnosis

Among the key findings of the last decade of research in child psychiatry has been the consistent documentation of clearly recognizable depressions and manias in children and adolescents. Prior to 1975, studies of mood disorders were hampered by a number of traditions: the notion that children did not possess the intrapsychic maturity to have states such as depression or mania, both of which theoretically required a well-developed superego; the idea that normal adolescence was filled with turmoil, a point of view that discouraged searching for specific psychopathological syndromes in this age group; the quick acceptance of "masked depression" or "depressive equivalents" as ways that a mood syndrome would present; and the problem in both adult and child psychiatry of distinguishing between a major depressive syndrome, characterized by a group of signs and symptoms as well as a mood component (see chapter 3 for details), and other types of depressive pathology. Especially notable among childhood depressive states that may resemble major depression is the chronic demoralization seen in children who live in chaotic or nonnurturing environments and which is characterized by apathy, anhedonia, and dysphoric mood, but without the other vegetative signs of depression.

Major depression, using virtually the same criteria as used for adults, is unquestionably diagnosable in both children and adolescents (Carlson and Cantwell, 1980). To do so, clinicians must elicit the appropriate information from *both* parents and child, asking the questions about depressive symptoms directly but using language tailored to the patient's age and linguistic maturity, especially with prepubescent children. Children do not generally spontaneously report symptoms but will respond if asked directly in language they understand. For instance, a 7-year-old may not complain about depressed mood, and may deny it when asked, but may respond positively using different words, such as "blue" or "feeling bad inside myself."

Some few age-specific differences do exist between adult and childhood mood disorders, more in children than adolescents. Depressed children are more likely to look depressed, complain of somatic symptoms, show separation anxiety, and experience hallucinations (but not delusions) (Ryan et al., 1987). Children may express weight loss by simply not gaining the expected weight. Suicidal ideation is common in the depressions of both children and adolescents, though the former are less likely to act on these feelings, presumably because of cognitive difficulty in formulating and acting out an attempt (Ryan, 1989).

Other psychiatric disorders are often seen concomitantly with depression. In children, separation anxiety, other anxiety disorders, and conduct disorder are common; in adolescents, drug and alcohol abuse are often seen.

Mania can also be diagnosed in children and adolescents. The unusual childhood form of mania may be somewhat atypical in nature, presenting with mixed manic/depressive features as well as more classical symptoms such as pressure of speech and hyperactivity. Some of these children have a constellation of hyperactivity, impulsivity, and poor social adjustment that may be associated with a particularly strong genetic loading for bipolar disorder (Strober et al., 1988). Bipolar adolescents, on the other hand, are far from rare and look similar to adult presentations with the possible exception of increased schizophrenic symptoms (Strober, 1989). Adolescents with classic melancholic features and depressive delusions are at high risk to become bipolar over the next few years (Strober and Carlson, 1982).

### Pharmacotherapy

Conclusive evidence of the efficacy of antidepressants and lithium in treating child and adolescent mood disorders is currently lacking. Anecdotes and open studies suggest that, like adults, many young patients respond to these medications. However, very few double-blind studies on the use of antidepressants in this population exist and these do not consistently demonstrate a difference between medication and placebo (Campbell and Spencer, 1988). There are no controlled studies on the use of lithium for treating manic youngsters.

The above statements imply that, until more evidence has been gathered, prescribing antidepressants for children or young adolescents with depression should not be considered as routinely as with adults. Antidepressants should be reserved primarily for those patients who are moderately or severely depressed for a significant period of time—many months, for example—and/or when other modalities have not been helpful. It should be understood that taking antidepressants can have a number of different psychological meanings for children and their parents. Therefore, the therapist must be available to explore these issues.

Since the monoamine oxidase (MAO) inhibitor antidepressants are virtually never prescribed for children, the following discussion pertains to the cyclic antidepressants only. As with adults, when antidepressants are prescribed for children and adolescents, the technique of gradually increasing doses over days to a few weeks is used. Because of concerns about the effects of antidepressants on heart rhythms, electrocardiograms (EKGs) are taken before treatment, after major dosage changes, and if higher-than-usual doses are prescribed (Puig-Antich et al., 1987). There is a tradition of giving antidepressants to children in divided doses, because they metabolize medications far more quickly than adults. It is not clear, however, that this technique enhances the medications' effectiveness. Imipramine at doses of 0.5 mg/kg and gradually increasing to an upper limit of 5 mg/kg and nortriptyline in somewhat lower doses have been the most commonly studied. There is some evidence that measuring the blood levels of these two antidepressants to adjust the dose most effectively is helpful (Geller, Cooper, Chestnut, Anker, and Schluchter, 1986).

Side effects with the cyclic antidepressants are similar to those seen in adults (see chapter 9). Most common among these are dry mouth, constipation, sedation, dizziness caused by low blood pressure, and fast heartbeat. Because children are in school, the more sedating antidepressants should be prescribed only with good rationale.

Mark, 8 years old, had been a "C" student until third grade when he began failing his classes. Educational testing suggested a reading disability. Just after the completion of this testing, a friend reported to his teacher that Mark had confided that he was going to steal pills and kill himself. Alarmed, the teacher contacted the school principal who referred Mark and his parents for a psychiatric evaluation.

In the interview, Mark appeared withdrawn, made poor eye contact with the interviewer, and showed few spontaneous movements. His mood appeared down. When asked "Do you feel depressed?" he answered "What?" but said yes when asked "Do you feel sad . . . like crying . . . bummed out?" He did not speak spontaneously and, when answering questions, his speech was slow and soft. There was no evidence of psychosis, such as hallucinations or delusions. He initially denied suicidal plans, but did respond positively to the question "Sometimes kids who feel down feel so bad that they think about dying. Do you ever think about these things?" and "Do you ever think of ways you might try to hurt or kill yourself?" Mark described a plan to take his mother's antidepressant "sleeping pills" to kill himself, or to take a butcher knife to school and end his life there.

Mark's parents revealed that Mark had stopped eating well during the summer before third grade, had begun to complain of tiredness during that fall (which they attributed to the flu), and then stopped seeing his friends and playing computer games just before the psychiatric evaluation. Both Mark's mother and a maternal uncle had a history of major depressive episodes with suicidal ideation and attempts. A maternal cousin and grandfather had killed themselves.

Mark was admitted to the children's psychiatric ward where further testing revealed a developmental reading disability. Following blood tests and an electrocardiogram, nortriptyline, at an initial dose of 10 mg and gradually increasing to 30 mg was started in conjunction with a program of individual psychotherapy, social skills classes, and a special education program. He gradually improved over four weeks and was discharged to outpatient treatment. Six months later, while still in psychotherapy and in special education classes, the medication was discontinued without difficulty.

Despite the lack of well-controlled studies, lithium is generally considered the treatment of choice for mania in both childhood and adolescence (Strober, 1989). This is in part because of the impressive number of open studies attesting to lithium's effectiveness, but also because of the imperviousness of mania to nonbiological intervention. The technique of lithium administration with children is identical to that for adults (see chapter 10), with blood levels guiding doses. Young manics often need and tolerate higher blood levels—as much as 1.5 to 1.8—than do older patients. Side effects with lithium are the same as seen with adults: polyuria (increased urination), thirst, tremor, weight gain, and possible cognitive effects. It is especially important to look for cognitive effects since they may affect school work and may be lessened by lowering the medication dose. Long-term consequences of lithium begun in childhood and adolescence are unknown.

## Psychotic Disorders

### Diagnosis

The childhood disorders most characterized by severe disturbances in thinking and interpersonal relationships are pervasive developmental disorders, of which the most well known are autistic disorder and childhood schizophrenia. Although some authors combine both groups of patients into one disorder, most of the evidence suggests that they are separate (Green, 1988). Autistic disorder has a very early onset, usually before age 3. It is characterized by global disturbances in human relations such as lack of responsiveness or interest in people, indifference to physical contact with others, difficulty being soothed, poor peer relations, along with communication impairment with severe speech delay or impairment including poor use of nonverbal communication. Additional features often seen in autistic children are stereotyped movements and an excessive need for sameness. Childhood schizophrenia, not recognized as a separate disorder by DSM-III-R, is very rare in early childhood and is generally characterized by the same symptoms as the adult form: hallucinations, delusions, fragmented thinking process and odd associations, and emotional blunting (Beitchman, 1985). Thus, although there is some overlap between the two disorders, autistic disorder has an earlier onset and affects more global aspects of functioning while childhood schizophrenia is characterized by more classical psychotic symptoms.

### Pharmacotherapy

Autistic disorder itself is not treatable by medications. However, some of the manifestations of the disorder can be ameliorated somewhat by antipsychotics which make the children more accessible to intensive behavioral programs. Those with hyperactivity, aggressiveness, and stereotypies are more likely to improve than are those with withdrawal and hypoactive presentations (Campbell, 1987). Haloperidol has been the most commonly used medication, in part because of its lack of sedating effects relative to other antipsychotics (see chapter 12 for details). Fenfluramine (Pondimin), a serotonin antagonist usually prescribed as an appetite suppressant and weight-loss aid has been of some benefit when given to autistic children, although more recent studies have been rather disappointing (Campbell et al., 1987).

In contrast to adult schizophrenia, there are still too few studies on the effects of antipsychotics in childhood schizophrenia to evaluate their efficacy. It is generally assumed that the medications are helpful in reducing the psychotic symptoms of the disorder, although there are some suggestions that the improvement seen may be less than in adults (Campbell and Spencer, 1988). As with their use in adult patients, picking one antipsychotic over another is based more on side effects than on differing efficacies. Sedating antipsychotics will help agitation but cause somnolence and may interfere more with learning processes. Conversely, the high-potency, nonsedating antipsychotics cause neurological side effects (discussed in detail in chapter 12), possibly with greater frequency than with adults. Youngsters treated with antipsychotics for extended periods of time are also at risk for tardive dyskinesia. Thus, antipsychotics, when used in children, should be constantly reevaluated to ensure that the lowest doses are used for the shortest periods of time.

## Anxiety Disorders

### Diagnosis

Systematic inquiry into the nature and treatment of anxiety syndromes in children is lacking. As with adults, it is common for a child to have more than one of these disorders. Some are easily recognizable as early onset of otherwise typical adult disorders. The evidence is clearest for simple phobias, obsessive compulsive disorder and post-traumatic stress disorder. Recent studies, however, have suggested that child and adolescent cases of panic disorder, social phobia, and generalized anxiety disorder may not be as rare as previously assumed (Leonard and Rapoport, 1989).

Three anxiety disorders specifically seen in childhood are delineated by DSM-III-R: separation anxiety disorder, avoidant disorder, and overanxious disorder. In separation anxiety, children are frightened to be away from parents or from home, often complaining of physical symptoms when separation (e.g., school) is anticipated. School phobia is a specific type of separation anxiety. A link between panic disorder and agoraphobia as seen in adults and separation anxiety has been postulated (Gittelman and Klein, 1984). Avoidant disorder is characterized by excessive avoidance of contact with unfamiliar people while having good relationships with family members or familiar people. By its definition, it seems linked to the adult syndromes of avoidant personality and social phobia. Overanxious disorder is the child and adolescent equivalent of generalized anxiety disorder with the diagnostic criteria focused more on cognitive symptoms such as worrying and less on the physical manifestations of anxiety.

### Pharmacotherapy

Because of the paucity of good studies, the use of medications for child and adolescent anxiety disorders is based mostly on individual clinical experience and unsupported recommendations. Studies comparing medications to other therapeutic approaches are virtually nonexistent. Their use is generally reserved for those disorders which have a significant negative impact on the child's life and development.

The only two disorders for which medications have been documented as effective are school phobia and obsessive compulsive disorder. Almost twenty years ago, imipramine was shown to decrease school phobia (Gittelman-Klein and Klein, 1971). For unclear reasons, there has been little interest in further evaluating this finding in research studies. This is especially surprising with the now well-documented finding of imipramine's efficacy in adult panic disorder which may be linked with school phobia. Two studies have now demonstrated the efficacy of clomipramine (Anafranil), the recently released antidepressant (see chapter 9) for the treatment of childhood obsessive compulsive disorder (Flament et al., 1985; Leonard, Swedo, Rapoport, Coffey, and Cheslow, 1988).

Anecdotally, benzodiazepines and antihistamines are prescribed for a variety of childhood anxiety syndromes. In contrast to adult treatment, antihistamines such as diphenhydramine (Benadryl) are often used as the first treatment, especially with young children. However, since antihistamines are significantly sedating, their use for daytime anxiety may be limited. Since tolerance to their effects is also common, they should be used intermittently. Clinical situations that are sometimes treated with benzodiazepines are overanxious disorder, anticipatory anxiety, and school refusal. Side effects with benzodiazepines are similar to those seen with adults except that disinhibition, a paradoxical reaction in which the patient becomes aggressive and irritable, may occur more commonly in children. Most child psychiatrists are therefore reluctant to prescribe these medications to children with problems of impulse control (Simeon and Ferguson, 1985). As with adults, if benzodiazepines are used for any significant period of time, tapering the dose as opposed to sudden withdrawal is appropriate.

## Attention Deficit Disorder

### Diagnosis

Previously called minimal brain dysfunction and the hyperactive child syndrome, attention deficit disorder (ADD) is the most extensively studied disorder in child psychiatry as well as the disorder for which medication is the best validated treatment. Its current official term in DSM-III-R is attention-deficit hyperactivity disorder. ADD is currently defined by the criteria listed in Table 8–2. Not all children show all symptoms, nor are the symptoms apparent in all settings. The disorder may be most obvious in a stimulating environment that offers many distractions, such as a schoolroom with many other children. In a different situation, such as focusing on a video game or engaging with one person, the child may not show any abnormalities. Because of this, ADD is typically diagnosed after the child has begun school, where there are increased distractions and a more inflexible routine compared to home. Although the diagnosis may be made at any time, the symptoms of ADD never appear for the first time in late childhood or adolescence. A syndrome characterized by distractibility, inattentiveness, and behavioral change that first occurs in fourth grade following three years of normal school behavior may be adjustment disorder, depression, or another disorder, but is not ADD.

Descriptively, these are restless children whose core features are inattentiveness, impulsivity, and hyperactivity. In school, they appear not to listen and often leave work unfinished or complete assignments sloppily. They impulsively blurt out answers and fail to wait their turn both in classroom situations and in games with peers. They interrupt teachers frequently and talk to other children excessively. At home, impulsivity is manifested by behaviors such as grabbing a hot pan or knocking things over when reaching for something in haste. Adolescents with ADD will impulsively leave a task for which there had been a previous commitment. Hyperactivity is expressed differently depending on the child's age. Young children tend to show gross motor overactivity while older children and adolescents are more fidgety and restless.

TABLE 8–2

*Diagnostic Criteria for Attention-deficit Hyperactivity Disorder*

**Note:** Consider a criterion met only if the behavior is considerably more frequent than that of most people of the same mental age.

A.  A disturbance of at least six months during which at least eight of the following are present:
    (1)  often fidgets with hands or feet or squirms in seat (in adolescents, may be limited to subjective feelings of restlessness)
    (2)  has difficulty remaining seated when required to do so
    (3)  is easily distracted by extraneous stimuli
    (4)  has difficulty awaiting turn in games or group situations
    (5)  often blurts out answers to questions before they have been completed
    (6)  has difficulty following through on instructions from others (not due to oppositional behavior or failure of comprehension), e.g., fails to finish chores
    (7)  has difficulty sustaining attention in tasks or play activities
    (8)  often shifts from one uncompleted activity to another
    (9)  has difficulty playing quietly
    (10) often talks excessively
    (11) often interrupts or intrudes on others, e.g., butts into other children's games
    (12) often does not seem to listen to what is being said to him or her
    (13) often loses things necessary for tasks or activities at school or at home (e.g., toys, pencils, books, assignments)
B.  Onset before the age of seven.
C.  Does not meet the criteria for a pervasive developmental disorder.

Reprinted with permission from the *Diagnostic and Statistical Manual of Mental Disorders, Third Edition, Revised.* Copyright 1987 American Psychiatric Association.

Although controversy about the issue exists, it is likely that a subset of children have a disorder manifested by attentional and cognitive impairments without hyperactivity. Previously this was more simply described as ADD without hyperactivity; DSM-III-R calls it undifferentiated attention-deficit disorder. Because the behavioral component of hyperactivity usually prompts the initial referral of ADD children, those without hyperactivity are more likely to go unrecognized. It may be that girls are overrepresented among these nonhyperactive ADD children as opposed to the hyperactive population which is predominantly male (Berry, Shaywitz, and Shaywitz, 1985).

ADD is commonly seen in association with other disorders, notably conduct and oppositional disorders (Cantwell and Hanna, 1989). Additionally, ADD children often have difficulties that are secondary to their disorder, such as poor self-esteem, disturbed peer relations, and poor school and work performance (Weiss, 1985). As ADD children grow up, the symptoms disappear in many of them but are present in over half during adolescence and in a significant minority during early adulthood (Cantwell, 1985b). Chapter 6 reviews adult ADD.

### Pharmacotherapy

Without question, stimulants are the treatment of choice for children with ADD. They have been amply documented as effective, with 75 percent of children showing a positive response (Cantwell and Hanna, 1989). Although stimulants' ability to slow down hyperactive children is often thought of as paradoxical, they probably work by diminishing the attentional symptoms with a secondary decrease in the hyperactivity. As mentioned in the discussion of adult ADD, the quieting effect of stimulants may also be observed in normal children. The magnitude and quality of the response to stimulants is variable. Improvements may be seen in attention, distractability, hyperactivity, and increased mood stability. Secondary effects may be seen in improved school performance. If the child has developed some of the complications of the disorder with disturbances in self-esteem, demoralization, and poor relationships, these are not likely to improve quickly because of an increased attention span. In these cases and with those children with concomitant conduct disorder, additional psychotherapeutic and behavioral interventions are mandatory.

The same three stimulants used in adult ADD are prescribed for children: methylphenidate (Ritalin), d-amphetamine (Dexedrine), and pemoline (Cylert). By far, methylphenidate has been utilized the most, both in research studies and in general clinical use, although d-amphetamine is as effective (Gittelman Klein, 1987). Some response is seen very quickly, typically within the first day or two, at any dose. Some children respond better to one stimulant or the other. Therefore, if the first stimulant tried is ineffective, the other is generally prescribed. Optimum dosing requires careful balancing to maximize the desired effects of diminished hyperactivity and improved functioning and avoid excessive side effects. As with adults, both methylphenidate and d-amphetamine are short-acting drugs, necessitating two or three doses daily. Sustained-release forms of both medications are not as helpful as the standard forms. Fortunately, there is little evidence that tolerance develops to the positive effects of stimulants when used for ADD, although some children will need a small dosage increase soon after the initial dose stabilization.

Pemoline may be somewhat less effective than either of the other two stimulants and takes longer to work, often up to many weeks. Its major advantage is that it needs to be taken only once daily because of its longer duration of action (Conners and Taylor, 1980). Since there is a small risk of liver inflammation when pemoline is used in ongoing treatment, intermittent blood tests are necessary.

An important issue in treating ADD children with stimulants is whether the medications should be discontinued on weekends (called drug holidays). An advantage of this approach would be to diminish some side effects and to continually reassess the need for ongoing treatment since, as mentioned, ADD diminishes in many patients over time. Drug holidays over weekends may, however, have adverse effects on the child's relationships with family and friends. To test for the need for ongoing medication, it makes more sense to discontinue the stimulant two or three times yearly with one of those times over the school summer holidays. However, a significant number of ADD patients will need to continue the medication into adolescence and beyond.

Antidepressants are occasionally prescribed for children with ADD with some positive results. Specifically, imipramine and desipramine, two of the more stimulating cyclic antidepressants, can be effective treatments (Biederman, 1988). Similarly, some of the monoamine oxidase (MAO) inhibitor antidepressants are effective. The dietary restrictions necessary with the latter group of medications, though, probably preclude their use in most children and adolescents. Antipsychotics may be helpful for the hyperactivity symptoms, but do not improve and may exacerbate the attentional problems. Finally, despite a great deal of press and individual testimonials, dietary approaches in treating ADD, including the Feingold Kaiser-Permanente diets, show no consistent evidence of efficacy in controlled studies (Kavale and Forness, 1983).

## Sleep Disorders

### Diagnosis

The two major sleep disorders seen primarily in childhood are night terrors (called sleep terror disorder in DSM-III-R) and sleepwalking, also called somnambulism. Night terrors are characterized by episodes of sudden arousal from sleep in which the child typically sits up in bed, screams in terror, sometimes gasps for air, breathes quickly, has a rapid heartbeat, sweats, and appears completely terrified. The child is typically unresponsive during the terror and confused if awakened during an episode. Amnesia for these episodes, which usually occur during the first third of the night, is common. Night terrors occur intermittently, generally at intervals of days or weeks, and are more likely when the child is stressed or fatigued. Night terrors are unrelated to the more common occurrence of nightmares.

Sleepwalking also tends to occur during the first third of the night and is characterized by sitting or standing from a sleeping position, walking in a clumsy way, occasionally bumping into obstacles, and mumbling or talking incomprehensibly. These episodes can lead to serious injury if the child trips or falls down stairs. As with night terrors, the child is difficult to awaken during sleepwalking. Amnesia for the episodes is virtually universal, and when informed of his behavior, the child is usually ashamed and perplexed. Sleepwalking is more likely to occur when the child's bladder is distended and can be precipitated by calling the child's name. Medications such as antipsychotics and lithium may trigger these episodes (Nino-Murcia and Dement, 1987). Sleepwalking tends to start around age five and typically disappears by early adolescence. It is not associated with significant psychopathology except in those patients whose disorders extend into adulthood (Kales et al., 1980).

### Pharmacotherapy

Both night terrors and somnambulism begin during deeper levels of sleep, called delta sleep. They are not associated with REM (rapid eye movement) periods when most dreaming occurs. Therefore, if the symptoms are worthy of pharmacological treatment, the medications prescribed are those that shorten or suppress delta sleep. Benzodiazepines and the cyclic antidepressants, such as imipramine, are most often used with generally very good results. Other treatment interventions, such as ensuring regular sleep hours, having the child empty his bladder before sleep, and, in some cases, using self-hypnosis are also effective. Medications tend to be prescribed intermittently at times of highest risk, such as when the child is physically ill or under stress.

For children with insomnia secondary to acute stress or anxiety, the antihistamines, such as diphenhydramine (Benadryl) in doses of 25 to 50 mg or promethazine (Phenergan), 12.5 to 50 mg, are often effective, especially when used intermittently.

## Behavioral Conditions

### Enuresis

Repeated episodes of urinating in the bed or clothes is a common problem of childhood, affecting 5 percent of 5-year-olds and 2 percent of 10-year-olds. Although primary treatments for enuresis are nonpharmacological, the antidepressant imipramine is occasionally used with some success. The mechanism by which imipramine diminishes enuresis is not well understood but is unlikely to be related to its antidepressant effect, since the antienuretic effect is seen within days of starting the medication, in contrast to the weeks needed for depression to remit. Doses used are relatively low—1 to 2 mg/kg. Tolerance to imipramine's antienuretic effects is often seen. Even when it continues to be effective, symptoms usually recur after the medication is stopped. Therefore, it is usually reserved for those children who have not responded to the more classical behavioral approaches such as the "pad and bell" technique.

### Conduct Disorder

As with antisocial personality in adults, which it resembles to a great degree, the defining characteristics of conduct disorder are purely behavioral. They describe an unruly child who consistently violates the usual norms of social behavior and commits a pattern of aggressive acts toward others over at least a six-month period. Isolated acts of aggressive behavior are therefore not considered conduct disorder. Typical conduct disorder behaviors include stealing, lying, fire-setting, cruelty to animals, physical fights, and forcing another person to engage in sex. Many diagnostic schemes, including DSM-III-R, divide conduct disorder into subtypes, depending on whether the aggressive acts are done alone (solitary aggressive type) or as part of a group (group type). Since the definitions of the subtypes have shifted with each diagnostic scheme, their validity is unknown. A significant proportion, but probably less than half, of conduct-disordered children grow up to be antisocial adults (Bailey and Egan, 1989). Their long-term prognosis is generally poor.

There are no established treatments, either behavioral, psychological, or biological, for conduct disorder. Analogous to adult personality disorders (see chapter 7), medications, when used to treat conduct disorder, should be considered to treat specific behaviors and concomitant disorders and *not* the primary condition. Therefore, they can never be thought of as more than adjuncts to other equally unproven treatment modalities.

Two comorbid conditions commonly seen with conduct disorders which may be amenable to psychopharmacological treatment are attention deficit disorder and major depressive disorder. Stimulants are therefore prescribed for those children with ADD and conduct disorder. If effective, the child might exhibit an improvement in his ability to focus and a decrease in impulsive behavior. Intentional aggressive activities are unlikely to improve. When used to treat conduct disorder in the absence of ADD, stimulants are ineffective. Antidepressants can be prescribed for depressed conduct-disordered children with some positive effect on mood. Those children with conduct disorder plus abnormal electroencephalograms (EEGs) or overt seizure disorders are often given anticonvulsants with possible benefit. Anticonvulsants have not been shown to be useful for conduct disorder in the absence of either of these two conditions (Bailey and Egan, 1989).

Both antipsychotics and lithium have been given to severely disturbed conduct-disordered children with some positive results. In the only well-controlled study on this topic, both lithium and haloperidol were more effective than placebo in decreasing aggressiveness, hyperactivity, and hostility in a group of severely disturbed, hospitalized prepubertal children (Campbell et al., 1984). Side effects were more of a problem with haloperidol than with lithium. Whether these findings apply to less disturbed nonhospitalized children is unknown.

### Aggressive, Destructive Behavior in Mentally Retarded Children

As currently used, the nonspecific term *mental retardation* comprises many different syndromes caused by a variety of etiologies, including genetic, viral, toxic, and traumatic. The essential features of mental retardation are subaverage intellectual functioning and deficits in adaptive functioning. Medications have no place in the treatment of the core deficits. However, since concomitant psychiatric disorders are more common in mentally retarded individuals, prescribing medications for these associated conditions should be considered as they would be for those of normal intelligence (Szymanski, Rubin, and Tarjan, 1989). Unfortunately, the most commonly used medications, antipsychotics, have often been prescribed in an abusive manner, in which the goals of the treatment have been to induce docility and enhance compliance. There is, however, a place for medications in treating the subset of mentally retarded individuals who exhibit repeated self-injurious and aggressive behavior. In these situations, the medications must be considered as adjunctive treatments as best, prescribed to diminish specific behaviors and not a disorder. Most commonly used are the high-potency, relatively nonsedating antipsychotics such as haloperidol. Constant attention must be paid to possible side effects, particularly those such as the motor restlessness of akathisia (discussed in detail in chapter 12) which can easily be mistaken as anxiety, especially in individuals with lesser verbal skills who may have difficulties describing physical feelings. Beta-blockers, used in other circumstances to treat anxiety and some medication-induced side effects (see chapter 11), are also prescribed to diminish aggressive behaviors. Compelling evidence of the beta-blockers' efficacy does not exist (Campbell and Spencer, 1988). Finally, as with conduct-disordered children, lithium is occasionally prescribed to decrease aggression.

## Tourette's Disorder

### Diagnosis

Among the group of childhood tic disorders, Tourette's is the most severe, characterized by a chronic array of motor and vocal tics. Vocally, the tics can be grunts, coughs, clicks, or sniffs while motor symptoms can be eye blinking, tongue protrusions, hopping, or twitches in the face or body. Tics can also be complex, involving activities such as squatting, deep-knee bends, posturing, and retracing steps. A rather well-known but less common tic occurring in less than a third of Tourette's patients is coprolalia, characterized by sudden verbal outbursts of obscenities. Patients may also describe mental coprolalia which is the sudden intrusive thought of obscene words or phrases experienced as ego-dystonic. Tourette's patients can also show typical obsessive or compulsive symptoms. Whether these should be considered as unusual examples of tics or as a true associated obsessive compulsive disorder is a matter of some debate. Some Tourette's patients also show significant attention deficit symptoms.

Tics can be voluntarily suppressed for brief periods of time. Anxiety and stress may make the tics worse, although a waxing, waning quality of the disorder is typical. Despite these observations, Tourette's is unquestionably a neuropsychiatric disorder with manifestations in both neurological and psychiatric realms. It does both a patient and his family an extreme disservice to consider the tics, coprolalia, or other symptoms of Tourette's as manifestations of conflicts about hostile impulses. This does not imply that psychological intervention with the child and/or with the family is not useful for these patients. Family interactions or psychological difficulties can certainly alter the course of Tourette's—but they are not the cause.

### Pharmacotherapy

With the discovery that antipsychotics dramatically decreased the tics of Tourette's disorder, medications became the core of effective treatment. The capacity of the medications to block the neurotransmitter dopamine, which is involved with the regulation of movement, is the most likely explanation for the positive effect. Haloperidol, in small doses such as 0.5 mg up to 5 mg daily, is the most commonly used. Pimozide, a more recently released antipsychotic, is also prescribed, with only slightly less efficacy (Shapiro et al., 1989). Clonidine, typically prescribed for hypertension, is the third of the commonly used medications for Tourette's. It may not be as effective as the antipsychotics in controlling the tics but may diminish behavioral problems caused by attentional difficulties or irritability (Erenberg, 1988).

Unfortunately, all three medications have significant side effects that limit their usefulness. Haloperidol can cause sedation, cognitive blunting, and weight gain as well as put these patients at risk for tardive dyskinesia (see chapter 12). Pimozide shares these side effects but may also cause cardiac problems (Leckman, Walkup, Riddle, Towbin, and Cohen, 1987). Clonidine does not produce weight gain or tardive dyskinesia but is very sedating and causes low blood pressure.

Because of these side effects, medications for Tourette's are typically prescribed on an intermittent basis if possible, reserved for the times when the tics and other symptoms flare up and compromise the patient's psychosocial functioning and self-esteem. This treatment strategy also keeps the total amount of medication to a minimum in order to reduce the chances of long-term side effects, such as tardive dyskinesia. There is no evidence that medication changes the long-term course of the disorder but it may improve psychosocial functioning with family and peers.

## GERIATRIC DISORDERS

With the exception of the dementias, psychiatric disorders in the elderly are the same as those affecting younger patients. Unique age-specific considerations, however, affect both diagnosis and treatment plans in the elderly, especially those involving medications. Table 8–3 lists these considerations. For therapists, the meaning of these differences is that a medical evaluation is a more urgent issue when older patients present for treatment because of the greater likelihood that an undiagnosed medical disorder or a medication side effect is causing or exacerbating psychological symptoms. A second implication is that if a referral for psychopharmacological consultation is appropriate, it should be made, if possible, to a practitioner who is knowledgeable about prescribing medications for the elderly.

TABLE 8–3

*Special Considerations in the Diagnosis and Psychopharmacological Treatment of the Elderly*

Diagnostic considerations:
  Presence of concomitant medical disorders, both diagnosed and undiagnosed, causing psychiatric symptoms
  Ongoing use of medications causing psychiatric symptoms
Therapeutic considerations:
  Possible decreased metabolism and excretion of medication leading to higher blood levels
  Greater sensitivity to having side effects
  More negative medical consequences to side effects
  Interaction of psychiatric medication side effects with ongoing medical disorders and ongoing medications
  Possible compliance difficulties, including forgetting pills, confusing pills of one type with another

Compared to younger patients, the elderly are far more likely to be taking ongoing medications. Thirty percent of all prescriptions are written for those age 65 and older even though they make up only 11 percent of the population (Thompson, Moran, and Nies, 1983). This makes for potential additive effects or negative interactions if a psychotropic medication is prescribed. The most important of these interactions, since it is often unrecognized, is the additive effect of medications in causing sedation and/or confusion. Not only do many medications prescribed for psychiatric disorders cause sedation, but so do some antihypertensives (blood pressure pills), all narcotic analgesics (pain killers), and, of course, sleeping pills and alcohol. The problem is often further compounded by the use of over-the-counter remedies, many of which can also cause sedation.

Another common problem in using psychotropic medications is the elderly patient's increased susceptibility to becoming grossly confused from medications with anticholinergic properties (see chapter 12). Those medications that block the effect of acetylcholine can cause decreased memory, confusion, and, occasionally, delirium. Most antidepressants, many antipsychotics, over-the-counter sleeping pills, and medications used to block antipsychotic side effects, as well as many medications used for diarrhea, have anticholinergic effects. Taking any one of these medications would be unlikely to cause significant problems, but in combination, additive toxicity becomes more probable.

Because the elderly tolerate high doses of medications less well and are subject to greater side effects at any dose, the most important guideline used by psychopharmacologists is to start at approximately half the usual adult dose of any medication and increase doses far more slowly than usual. Side effects should be elicited more aggressively since the consequences are potentially more serious. As an example, a 30-year-old with postural hypotension (low blood pressure upon change in position) from an antidepressant, who experiences dizziness when he stands up, will usually hold onto a rail or other support and typically does not fall—or if he does, he falls gracefully, avoiding harm. A 70-year-old with the same drop in blood pressure, even without other causes for postural unsteadiness, such as arthritic hips, is more likely to miss the rail, fall, and risk breaking a hip or ribs.

Although the issues in Table 8–3 are always relevant for a psychopharmacologist to consider, they do not apply to all patients. For instance, even though those over 65 are less likely to metabolize drugs well and therefore need smaller doses of medications, some elderly patients not only tolerate high doses, but need them for a clinical response. More than any other recommendation, the most important is that the doses of medications in the elderly should be prescribed using an individualized approach.

## Pharmacotherapy for Common Disorders

### Mood Disorders

The key issue in evaluating and treating depression in the elderly is recognizing it. Among the diagnostic dilemmas, distinguishing depression from dementia is the most common. Signs that help distinguish between these two disorders are presented in chapter 3. Another difficulty in evaluating a mood disorder in elderly patients is the tendency to perceive a depression as "understandable" given the patient's difficult life circumstances—and therefore not consider active treatment. For instance, a depression that arises following a major stroke can respond to antidepressants, even though it may be understandable (Robinson, 1987).

Increasing age does not change the range of antidepressant options for treating depression. Cyclic antidepressants, monoamine oxidase inhibitors, and electroconvulsive therapy are all appropriate treatments. Other than the general rule of starting with lower doses and increasing more slowly, the major differences are in the increased caution needed if highly sedating or highly anticholinergic medications are prescribed. Stimulants are also prescribed for the elderly apathetic depressed (see chapter 3).

For older bipolar patients, lithium is still the treatment of choice. However, because kidney function is always diminished in the elderly, doses are lower. Additionally, more elderly patients seem to respond to lithium blood levels—such as 0.4 mEq/l—that would typically be subtherapeutic for younger patients. Elderly patients may also become lithium toxic more easily and at lower blood levels, suggesting that more frequent lithium levels be obtained during dose adjustments.

### Psychotic Disorders

All the common side effects with antipsychotics are also seen when these medications are taken by the elderly. The hypotensive effects (lowering blood pressure) must be watched especially closely. Because the risk of tardive dyskinesia increases as patients age, maintenance treatment must be considered even more carefully than usual.

### Anxiety Disorders and Insomnia

The major danger in treating anxiety or insomnia is the potential accumulation of benzodiazepines because of the slower metabolism of medications in older patients. Especially with tranquilizers with long durations of action (see

Table 11–3), the amount of medication in the blood may build up, causing morning hangovers or even around-the-clock cognitive changes. However, many older patients have taken flurazepam (Dalmane) for years as a hypnotic with no evidence of sedation or other negative effects.

### Medications Used in Treating Dementias

As more people survive into old age, the group of disorders that present with dementia is an increasing problem for psychiatrists specifically, and society in general. Dementia is characterized by impairment of memory, abstract thinking and judgment, personality changes, and—ultimately—deficits in functioning. A number of different causes for dementia can be identified, the most common of which is Alzheimer's disease, called primary degenerative dementia of the Alzheimer type in DSM-III-R. The second most common cause is multi-infarct dementia, which is characterized by a series of small strokes in the brain. Currently, the most important treatment for dementia is diagnosing other less common but more reversible causes, such as hypothyroidism (low thyroid), vitamin deficiencies, or associated depressions that will exacerbate the dementia.

Neither Alzheimer's disease nor multi-infarct dementia is treatable in any reasonably effective manner by medications. Despite this, a number of medications are often prescribed for these patients. Most often prescribed is a group of drugs called ergoloid mesylates, the most common of which is marketed as Hydergine. Although Alzheimer's disease is not characterized by poor circulation or inadequate oxygen flow to the brain, Hydergine has some effects as a vasodilator (opening blood vessels) or as a metabolic enhancer. Regardless of its mechanism of action, Hydergine is, at best, weakly effective and does not change the clinical picture substantially (Hollister and Yesavage, 1984).

Medications, specifically antipsychotics, however, are commonly prescribed for demented patients who are severely agitated, especially at night when confusion characteristically increases or when the dementia is complicated by overt psychosis with paranoid delusions. As with the treatment of agitation in the mentally retarded, antipsychotics are sometimes prescribed abusively, in excessive doses, for unclear reasons, and for too long. When used at low doses, however, with care taken to recognize and minimize side effects, they can be of help. Improvements seen with antipsychotics are usually modest, not striking (Salzman, 1987). Side effects often limit the usefulness of antipsychotics. When antipsychotics are not helpful for agitation, a variety of other medications, such as beta-blockers (see chapter 11) or carbamazepine (see chapter 10) are tried, usually with limited success.

## MEDICATIONS DURING PREGNANCY

Any sensible physician would recommend that, if possible, women who are pregnant or are planning a pregnancy should avoid all medications, especially in the first trimester when the most important fetal development occurs. Any and all other therapeutic modalities are preferable to medications in these circumstances. Furthermore, if medications are secreted in breast milk—as are all agents used in psychiatry—they should be avoided in the postpartum period if the mother of a newborn plans to breastfeed. These statements are easy to make, and pure in their conclusions. In real clinical situations, however, the risk of any potential treatment must be weighed against other variables, such as the risk of not treating, or the possible benefits of treating. Therefore, as with so many situations regarding psychotropic medications, knowledge can only take us so far. After reviewing the little information that is available about medications in pregnancy, difficult judgments on risks versus benefits must be made by the woman, possibly her family, her therapist, and the psychopharmacologist involved.

Negative consequences of taking medications during pregnancy can be thought of in three ways: (1) Overt malformations of the fetus/infant may result, described as teratogenic effects; (2) Medications may have toxic effects on the fetus or newborn, such as causing more difficulty breathing at birth or decreased muscle tone; (3) The infant may be well formed but may show behavioral abnormalities later in life. Currently, there is no evidence for behavioral effects, although these would be the hardest to document.

Although further details are available in recent review articles (see Mortola, 1989, or Cohen, Heller, and Rosenbaum, 1989), the teratogenic risks can be summarized as follows: If taken during the first trimester, lithium is the only psychiatric medication that has been consistently documented to increase the risk of fetal abnormalities, specifically increasing the risk of a malformation of the heart and major blood vessels called Ebstein's anomaly. Unfortunately, carbamazepine, the most promising of the mood stabilizers other than lithium, has also recently been shown to be teratogenic (Jones, Lacro, Johnson, and Adams, 1989). There is no substantive evidence that cyclic antidepressants, monomine oxidase inhibitor antidepressants, or antipsychotics increase the risk of fetal abnormalities, although teratogenic effects of MAO inhibitors have been seen in animals. Benzodiazepine tranquilizers are thought by some to cause increased rates of cleft palates despite a lack of clear evidence supporting this.

Possible toxic effects to the fetus can occur from the use of medications during pregnancy, but the actual incidence and long-term significance of this is not known. Any medication that changes blood pressure, such as some antidepressants or antipsychotics, may decrease the blood supply to the uterus. Similarly, benzodiazepines or lithium may cause some infants to be born with decreased muscle tone. The ultimate consequences of these effects are unknown.

Given the possibilities of fetal malformation or ill effects, why would anyone even consider prescribing medications for a pregnant woman? As suggested above, the answer lies in the risk of not treating. For mild depressions or minimal to moderate anxiety, it makes sense to avoid all medications. But how does one proceed with a psychotically depressed woman who is significantly suicidal? Or a manic woman who sleeps only two hours a night, is hyperactive, drives dangerously, and takes drugs and alcohol? Or a schizophrenic woman who is delusional about her unborn child and is not eating because of her psychosis? Even with the best nonbiological treatments available, these states may still exist and be dangerous to the developing fetus. How dangerous is the mania compared to lithium for the fetus's health? An assessment of the relative risks of different medications may also be helpful. If a manic woman needs medication during the first trimester, for instance, antipsychotics might be safer than lithium. Electroconvulsive therapy (ECT) should also be considered an important treatment option with possibly fewer risks for the fetus than medication for pregnant women who are severely depressed or manic (Sitland-Marken, Rickman, Wells, and Mabie, 1989). For each situation, the risks and benefits of all possible options must be thoughtfully reviewed.

Reasonable guidelines for breastfeeding seem easier, since the health of new-borns is not affected by *not* breastfeeding. All psychiatric medications are se-creted in breast milk in variable amounts. Therefore, if a mother of a newborn needs to take medication—when, for instance, a severe postpartum depression exists (see chapter 3)—breastfeeding should be stopped even where no clear evidence of abnormalities to the newborn have been documented. In these situations, psychotherapeutic intervention may aid in helping the woman deal with possible feelings of failure or the loss of her own maternal needs because of the inability to breastfeed.

# SECTION
# FOUR

# 9

## Antidepressants

It is now thirty years since the initial reports on the effects of the first tricyclic and monoamine oxidase (MAO) inhibitor antidepressants were published almost simultaneously. During this time, the number of antidepressants with documented efficacy has expanded dramatically; there are now sixteen cyclic and MAO inhibitor antidepressants available, and more are likely to be released over the next few years. In addition, the use of the antidepressants has expanded. Cyclic antidepressants are now used for panic disorder, chronic pain syndromes, bulimia, peptic ulcer disease, and migraine headaches. Similarly, the use of MAO inhibitors has increased over the last decade, especially in the treatment of atypical depression, after a period of relative disuse in the 1970s. The antidepressants are a mainstay of treatment in modern psychopharmacology.

### HISTORY

Prior to the late 1950s, the somatic treatment of depression consisted of three options. The first was stimulants resembling amphetamine which had the effect of increasing energy and activity. Their capacity in treating severe depression, however, was limited. Electroconvulsive therapy (ECT), the second option, had been first used in the late 1930s. Although ECT was unquestionably effective as a treatment for depression, it was a frightening and dangerous treatment at that time. (See chapter 13 for modern and safe use of ECT). The third option was time. One of the most important "treatments" for depression prior to the modern era was waiting. Since the great majority of depressions were, and are, time limited in nature (albeit lasting many months), simply keeping the patient from committing suicide during that time would allow spontaneous recovery to take place.

As with so many other discoveries in medicine, imipramine, the first tricyclic antidepressant, was discovered serendipitously through the careful observations of a researcher/clinician. In the early 1950s, soon after the discovery of the antipsychotic properties of chlorpromazine, a European investigator, R. Kuhn, was testing a similar compound, hoping to find another effective antipsychotic. The drug he tested, imipramine, was ineffective as an antipsychotic but improved the mood of some of the depressed schizophrenics. Further testing showed imipramine to be effective with depressed patients. The tricyclic antidepressant era had begun.

At the same time, iproniazid, an antitubercular drug known to inhibit monoamine oxidase (MAO), an important intraneuronal enzyme (see chapter 2), was noted to elevate the mood of tuberculosis patients, even causing euphoria and overactivity in some. By 1958, the same year that Kuhn's research on imipramine was published, two independent studies reported that iproniazid was effective in treating depressed patients. Thus, within one year, the two most important discoveries in the pharmacological treatment of depression were reported (Ayd and Blackwell, 1970).

In the twenty years following those first discoveries, the clinical and research gains consisted of elucidating some of the biological abnormalities in depression, finding uses for antidepressants in treating other disorders, and developing other but very similar tricyclic and MAO inhibitor drugs. Clinically, however, these new medications did not translate as major breakthroughs since the antidepressants released were so similar to imipramine and the first MAO inhibitors. In the last decade, a new class of cyclic antidepressants has emerged. These new antidepressants do not necessarily contain a three-ringed structure (tri[3]-cyclics) as do imipramine and similar medications, but they do show clear antidepressant efficacy. This has been helpful in understanding the mechanism of effect of all antidepressants since now dissimilar chemicals can be seen to cause similar clinical effects. It is hoped that further investigation of the common effects or "the final common pathway" of all effective antidepressants will shed light on the core biological abnormalities of depression. The new antidepressants also show different side effect profiles (not surprising since their chemical structures are so different). Clinically, however, these new agents are not more effective than the older ones. Imipramine is still the "reference" drug in antidepressant trials; new antidepressants are tested to see if they are *as* effective as imipramine, not more effective.

The near future promises the release of newer antidepressants which, if the current pattern continues, will have even fewer side effects, be utilized effectively in a wider group of disorders, and be more expensive than the older antidepressants. What seems to be years away is an antidepressant that is truly superior—one that is consistently more effective than any cyclic antidepressant released since 1958.

The evolution of the MAO inhibitor class of antidepressants has followed a similar path. The early MAO inhibitors were toxic to the liver and were ultimately withdrawn from clinical use. The currently available MAO inhibitors are not significantly toxic but all share the same side effects (although in slightly different proportions) and the same problem with dietary restrictions because of the attendant risks of hypertensive (high blood pressure) reactions if the wrong foods are eaten (see below). In these ways, as with the cyclic antidepressants, the MAO inhibitors have not progressed much as a class of medications in thirty years. The next important breakthrough for MAO inhibitors will be the availability of a medication as effective as the current agents but devoid of dietary restrictions—or at least less dangerous in this regard. Preliminary research on investigational MAO inhibitors is proceeding toward this goal.

## CYCLIC ANTIDEPRESSANTS

### Clinical Uses

The cyclic antidepressants (ADs) are used to treat a variety of disorders, both psychiatric and medical, listed in Table 9–1. Not all cyclic ADs have been tested in all the disorders listed.

Certainly, all the cyclic ADs are effective in treating depression, both unipolar and bipolar. There is no substantive evidence that any one is better than

TABLE 9–1

*Disorders for Which Cyclic Antidepressants Are Useful*

| Disorder | Efficacy Rating |
|---|---|
| Depression, both unipolar and bipolar | + + + |
| Panic disorder | + + + |
| Generalized anxiety | + |
| Obsessive compulsive disorder | + + |
| Cocaine abuse | + + |
| Bulimia nervosa | + + |
| Post-traumatic stress disorder | + |
| Chronic pain syndromes | + + |
| Attention deficit disorder | + |

+ + + = Definite efficacy
+ + = Probable efficacy
+ = Possible efficacy

any other in treating either of these depressive subtypes. Among the other depressive subtypes, only psychotic depression has been demonstrated to be poorly responsive to the cyclic ADs. (The use of antidepressants for depression is discussed extensively in chapter 3.)

Cyclic ADs are well documented as effective treatments for panic disorder with or without significant agoraphobic symptoms. (Lydiard and Ballenger, 1987). The primary therapeutic effect of the medications is thought to be the blocking of spontaneous panic attacks. The medications are probably not as effective in treating the phobic or behavioral symptoms in panic disorder. Rather, the blocking of the panic attacks allows patients to decrease and eliminate phobic behavior, either by themselves or with the help of a behavioral program.

By far, the most well documented of the available cyclic ADs in treating panic disorder is imipramine. It is likely that most medications in this class with the exception of bupropion are effective in treating panic, although recent evidence for the efficacy of trazodone and amoxapine is mixed.

There is some controversy as to the appropriate doses of cyclic ADs in treating panic disorder. Most controlled studies indicate that the doses should be comparable to those used in treating depression. Numbers of clinicians, however, myself included, have seen excellent results with low doses of antidepressants in treating panic disorder, far lower than is generally effective for depression. It may be, of course, that since panic patients are unusually sensitive to certain side effects, we tend to increase the doses more slowly than when treating depressed patients, thereby allowing more patients to respond in this low-dose range. Conceivably, if the dose were increased more slowly with depressed patients, we might see a similar proportion of low-dose responders.

The effectiveness of cyclic ADs in treating generalized anxiety has been examined surprisingly infrequently. Numerous studies from pre-DSM-III days used cyclic ADs for patients with mixed anxiety-depression syndromes. Unfortunately, the change in classification systems since then precludes knowing the nature of the patients treated in these earlier studies. Recently, however, imipramine was found to be superior to the tranquilizer chlordiazepoxide (Librium) in patients with generalized anxiety (Kahn et al., 1986). More evidence is needed before any general comments regarding the effectiveness of cyclic ADs in generalized anxiety can be made.

Of all the cyclic ADs, clomipramine is unquestionably the most well documented as effective in treating obsessive compulsive disorder (DeVeaugh-Geiss, Landau, and Katz, 1989). It is effective in reducing both obsessions and compulsions, regardless of whether depression is present (Insel and Zohar, 1987). Among the other cyclic ADs, fluoxetine and to a lesser extent trazodone, which are the most similar to clomipramine in their biological effects, are the most likely to be effective, with the evidence far stronger for the former (Levine, Hoffman, Knepple, and Kenim, 1989). Doses of cyclic ADs used for obsessive compulsive disorder approximate those used for depression, except for fluoxetine which is prescribed at higher doses. Significant clinical effects are typically seen within the first four weeks of treatment although gradual continuing improvement may occur over the first twelve weeks.

Convincing evidence now exists that desipramine, and possibly imipramine, can be helpful in decreasing self-reported craving as well as increasing the time of abstinence in cocaine abusers (Gawin, Kleber, et al., 1989). Positive effects are seen after one to two weeks of treatment with gradually increasing effects over six weeks. Doses are similar to those used for treating depression.

Without question, the cyclic ADs are effective in decreasing binges and purges in a substantial number of bulimics (Pope and Hudson, 1986). It is likely, although not proven, that all cyclic ADs are effective in bulimia with imipramine and desipramine being the most well-documented medications. Bupropion, however, should not be prescribed for bulimic patients because of a significant risk of grand mal seizures (Davidson, 1989). Fluoxetine, at slightly higher doses than are used for depression, may offer a particular advantage with bulimic patients because of its low incidence of side effects and its lack of weight gain. The effect of cyclic ADs on binging is independent of the presence of depression. (See chapter 6 for further discussion.)

Cyclic antidepressants are also occasionally prescribed in the treatment of post-traumatic stress disorder. In a number of open trials and recently in the first double-blind study, they have demonstrated efficacy in decreasing nightmares, flashbacks, and intrusive recollections (Frank, Kosten, Giller, and Dan, 1988).

Chronic pain syndromes from a variety of causes including diabetes, back pain, and facial pain have been effectively treated with antidepressants for over twenty five years (France, Houpt, and Ellinwood, 1984). Most studies have used the more serotonergic cyclic ADs, such as amitriptyline (Elavil) and doxepin (Sinequan). This reflects both the longstanding clinical tradition in which sedating ADs were preferentially used (the serotonergic ADs tend to be more sedating than noradrenergic ADs) as well as the evidence that serotonin is centrally involved in the neurotransmission of pain sensation and relief. (See chapter 2 for discussion on neurotransmitters). It is conceivable, however, that the noradrenergic ADs, such as desipramine, would be equally effective. As with other noneffective syndromes, the presence of depression does not consistently correlate with clinical response to antidepressants in chronic pain patients. Most studies have used smaller doses of ADs to treat pain than to treat depression. Whether this reflects the more conservative use of antidepressants by nonpsychiatric physicians or a true response at lower doses is not known.

Cyclic antidepressants are occasionally prescribed for adult patients with attention deficit disorder (now labeled either attention-deficit hyperactivity disorder or undifferentiated attention-deficit disorder in DSM-III-R). Because of the hypothesis that attention deficit disorder may, in part, be related to abnormalities in norepinephrine regulation, and because of its specific effect on blocking norepinephrine reuptake, desipramine has been the most commonly prescribed. Controlled studies evaluating cyclic ADs for adult patients with ADD do not exist, but some anecdotes suggest a positive effect.

### Biologic Effects

The effectiveness of cyclic ADs in treating as wide a variety of disorders as those listed in Table 9–1 is both exciting and confusing. How can we understand all these actions in concert? Are chronic pain syndromes "masked" depressions, or masked obsessive compulsive disorders? In what way is bulimia related to panic disorder? Assuming that all disorders that respond to the same treatment are the *same* disorder is inconsistent with clinical experience. Both medicine and psychiatry/psychology are filled with examples of diverse disorders responding to one treatment. (As just two of many possible examples, calcium channel blockers are used to treat migraine headaches and angina; hypnosis can be effective both in treating chronic pain syndromes and in recovering repressed memories). The multiple clinical capacities of one class of treatment can be best understood by the diverse biological properties of the medications. As noted in chapter 2, all medications used in psychiatry (and probably all medications used in any field) are impure; that is, they do not have a single biological effect—that being the one we want—and no others. Side effects, as an example (as opposed to symptoms from a toxic overdose), are due to the unwanted diverse biological effects of the drug. Thus, antidepressants cause dry mouth by blocking cholinergic receptors (anticholinergic property). Yet there is no evidence that blocking that particular receptor is in any way related to the capacity of the medication to alleviate depression. The perfect antidepressant, therefore, would be devoid of cholinergic blocking properties, and of dry mouth. The perfect medication—one that affected only the parts of the brain that we wanted, and had only the specific clinical effect that we wanted—would have no side effects.

Returning to the cyclical ADs, it is clear that this class of medications has a variety of biological and clinical effects. Table 9–2 shows the known effects of an individual ADs on a few neurotransmitter systems. Which of these proper-

TABLE 9–2

**Effects of Cyclic Antidepressants on Neurotransmitter Systems**

| Antidepressant Name | Norepinephrine Reuptake Blocking | Serotonin Reuptake Blocking | Acetylcholine Blocking |
|---|---|---|---|
| Amitriptyline | + | + + + | + + + |
| Amoxapine | + + | + | + |
| Bupropion | 0 | 0 | + |
| Clomipramine | + + | + + + | + + + |
| Desipramine | + + + | 0 | + |
| Doxepin | + | + + | + + |
| Fluoxetine | 0 | + + + | 0 |
| Imipramine | + + | + | + + |
| Maprotiline | + + + | 0 | + |
| Nortriptyline | + + | + | + |
| Protriptyline | + + | + | + + |
| Trazodone | 0 | + + | 0 |
| Trimipramine | + | + + | + + |

0 = None
+ = Minimal
+ + = Moderate
+ + + = Strong

ties are important in treating depression, which in treating panic? Until more is known of the biological abnormalities in the disorders for which cyclic ADs are helpful, these questions cannot be answered. (Chapter 2 reviews the current hypotheses of depression and panic disorder).

With the exception of bupropion, all the cyclic ADs currently available block the reuptake of norepinephrine, serotonin, or both into the presynaptic neuron (see chapter 2 for background). Figure 9–1 shows this schematically; Table 9–2 shows the effect of each cyclic AD on both of these neurotransmitters. This blockade has the initial biologic result of increasing the amount of neurotransmitter available to the postsynaptic neuron. As discussed in more detail in chapter 2, according to the original monamine hypothesis of depression, increasing the amount of norepinephrine (NE), serotonin (5-HT), or both would correct the presumed deficit in these chemicals and cause a clinical remission. This hypothesis ignored the fact that reuptake blocking is immediate (within hours of the first dose of an antidepressant) yet clinical response is delayed for weeks. Therefore, an additional biologic effect beyond reuptake blocking was needed to explain the antidepressant capacity of the medications. Ultimately, what became apparent was that cyclic antidepressants shared the capacity not

**Figure 9–1** Cyclic Antidepressants as Reuptake Blockers

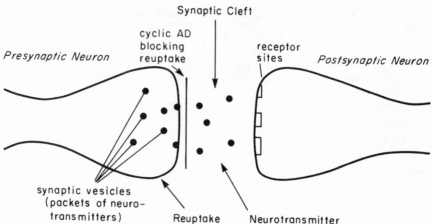

only to block the reuptake of neurotransmitters but also to alter the sensitivity of the receptors that regulate the system. Since the sensitivity of the receptors in large part determines the cells' response to the neurotransmitters, these changes are likely to be central to the effect of the antidepressants. What is still unclear is which of the receptor changes are most central to the clinical properties of the cyclic ADs.

Moreover, there may be more than one mechanism to alter the receptors of the system—it is likely that altering NE *or* 5-HT receptors may each be effective and that each may set in motion a series of changes that results in a more normally functioning system and, ultimately, a clinical response. Probably the best way to summarize our current understanding of antidepressants' effect in treating depression is that they reregulate a very complex system such that the right neurotransmitters are present in the right balance at the right time. In this way, the effect of cyclic ADs can be thought of as analogous to resetting an improperly functioning thermostat. Of course, understanding the mechanism by which ADs work implies nothing about the "cause" of depression, nor does it preclude the effectiveness of other treatments for depression, such as psychotherapy.

Research on the mechanism of action of cyclic ADs in treating panic disorder has focused on the medications' effect in decreasing adrenergic function in the locus ceruleus, the part of the brain that contains the major nucleus of norepinephrine-containing cells (see chapter 2). As with the research in depression, the present hypotheses suggest that cyclic ADs work by affecting the adrenergic receptors, by altering their sensitivities and thus reregulating the system (Charney and Heninger, 1985).

Since the cyclic ADs most effective in treating obsessive compulsive disorder have predominantly serotonin reuptake blocking properties, the mechanism of therapeutic effect is generally thought to be related to alterations in serotonergic function. Further research, including more conclusive evidence that nonserotonergic ADs are ineffective, is necessary before any further statements on this topic can be made.

Since there is little research that suggests a coherent biologic explanation for bulimia, the mechanism of action of cyclic ADs in this disorder is equally obscure. Common hypotheses discussed in more detail in chapter 6 are: (1) bulimia is a "depressive equivalent"; therefore, the mechanism of action of the medications is the same as for depression; (2) antidepressants decrease bulimic symptoms by diminishing the anxiety that builds before a binge; (3) since food intake is controlled in the brain by a complex system that includes norepinephrine and serotonin, cyclic ADs may reduce bulimic symptoms by altering the activity of these two neurotransmitters.

The two major hypotheses for the efficacy of antidepressants in chronic pain syndromes are that (1) antidepressants work via their mood enhancing effect, and (2) since both norepinephrine and serotonin, especially the latter, play an important part in the neurological pathways that mediate pain and its inhibition, the effect of cyclic ADs is due to direct action on pain mechanisms. The fact that antidepressants decrease pain even in the absence of depression is supportive of this hypothesis.

## Choosing a Cyclic Antidepressant

Table 9–3 shows the currently available cyclic ADs, their classification (tricyclic or other), trade names, usual beginning doses, and usual dosage range. The choice of a specific antidepressant depends on the disorder being treated and the individual medication's efficacy for that disorder, as well as side effect considerations. These topics are covered in the chapters on individual disorders and earlier in this chapter.

As shown in Table 9–3, cyclic antidepressants are often classified as either tricyclic or heterocyclic. Tricyclics are all distinguished by their chemical structure—they all have three rings, hence tri-cyclics (see Figure 9–2). The newer medications, all of which have been released since 1980, have variable chemical structures. With the exception of amoxapine and clomipramine, they do not have the classic three rings of a tricyclic (see Figure 9–3). However, the number of rings in a compound's chemical structure is clinically irrelevant. It may make for impressive advertising (e.g., "a truly unique structure," implying that this is a new kind of medication), but the mech-

TABLE 9–3

*Cyclic Antidepressants*

| Name (Trade Name) | Beginning Dose (mg daily) | Usual Dosage Range (mg daily) |
|---|---|---|
| *Tricyclics* | | |
| Amitriptyline (Elavil, Endep) | 25–50 | 100–300 |
| Amoxapine (Asendin) | 50–100 | 150–400 |
| Clomipramine (Anafranil) | 25–50 | 100–250 |
| Desipramine (Norpramine, Pertofrane) | 25–50 | 100–300 |
| Doxepin (Sinequan, Adapin) | 25–50 | 100–300 |
| Imipramine (Tofranil) | 25–50 | 100–300 |
| Nortriptyline (Aventyl, Pamelor) | 10–25 | 50–150 |
| Protriptyline (Vivactil) | 10 | 15–60 |
| Trimipramine (Surmontil) | 25–50 | 100–300 |
| *Heterocyclics* | | |
| Bupropion (Wellbutrin) | 100 | 300–450 |
| Fluoxetine (Prozac) | 20 | 20–40 |
| Maprotiline (Ludiomil) | 25–50 | 100–225 |
| Trazodone (Desyrel) | 50 | 150–400 |

*Note:* These doses are general guidelines only.

anism of action of all the cyclic antidepressants is likely to be the same, and their effects on various neurotransmitters—norepinephrine (NE), serotonin (5-HT), or both—are not correlated with the number of rings. The newer antidepressants primarily differ from the more established tricyclics by their side effects—and their cost—but there is *no* consistent evidence that they differ in antidepressant efficacy.

**Figure 9–2** Typical Tricyclic Structure

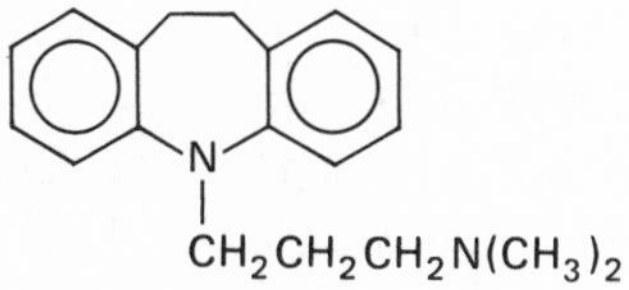
N
$CH_2CH_2CH_2N(CH_3)_2$

IMIPRAMINE

## Techniques for Prescribing

The techniques of prescribing to be discussed here will assume that the treatment is for depression. Variations in prescribing for the other disorders will be addressed later. The method of starting a cyclic AD is similar for all medications, with the exception of fluoxetine. The initial starting dose is low and is gradually increased over seven to fourteen days to the lower end of the therapeutic range. Using imipramine as a prototype for those antidepressants with the same dosage range, this would translate to starting at 25 or 50 mg (milligrams) daily for one to three days, then increasing by 25 mg every day or two or by 50 mg every three days up to 150 mg daily. The analogous starting dose for nortriptyline is 10 to 20 mg, increasing to 75 mg over the first one to two weeks. Typical doses of amoxapine, trazodone, and bupropion are higher than those for imipramine. Fluoxetine is unique in that its starting dose, 20 mg, is likely to be the appropriate final dose for many patients.

Since most antidepressants are somewhat sedating (although some are more sedating than others), most psychopharmacologists tend to prescribe them all at bedtime, no matter what the daily dose. The major exceptions to this are bupropion and fluoxetine. The advantage to taking the entire dose at night is

**Figure 9–3** New Heterocyclic Antidepressant Structure

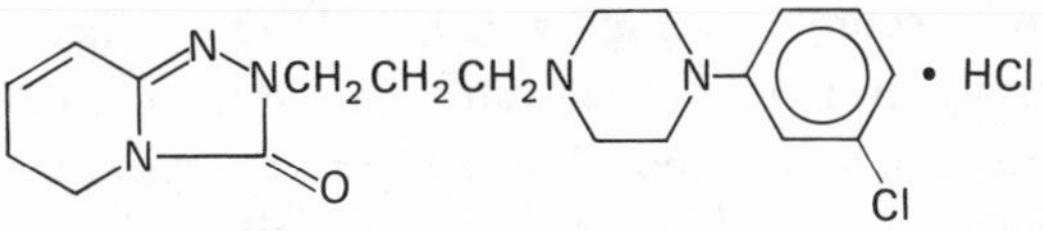
N
$NCH_2CH_2CH_2N$
N
N
O
• HCl
Cl

TRAZODONE

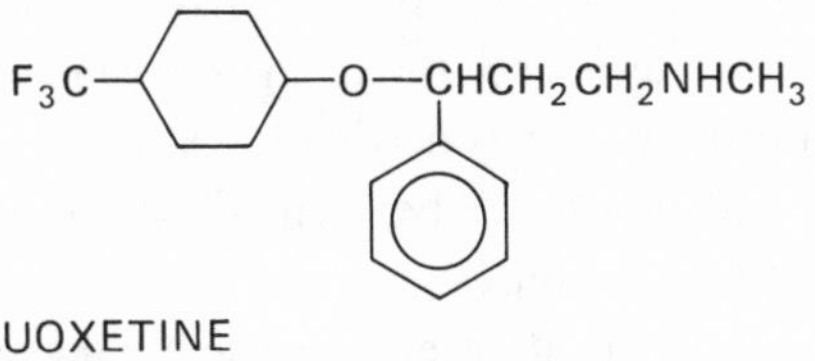
$F_3C$
$O—CHCH_2CH_2NHCH_3$

FLUOXETINE

that whatever sedation exists is maximum during sleep (a fine time to be sedated). There is no evidence that dividing the daily dose increases efficacy. Also, since all cyclic ADs with the exception of trazodone have long half-lives (i.e., they stay in the body for a long time before getting metabolized or excreted), the level of the antidepressant in the blood does not vary dramatically over a twenty-four-hour period even when taken once daily. Finally, since compliance is a major problem with all medications, the more times during the day patients have to remember to take their pills, the more likely they are to forget at least one dose.

There are times when the rule of prescribing cyclic ADs all at night is not appropriate. Trazodone, with its short half-life, theoretically may be more effective if prescribed in divided doses. Clinically, though, this does not seem to be true (Wheatley, 1980). Unfortunately, since it is one of the most sedating medications, it is sometimes difficult for patients to take it during the day. My own clinical experience is that taking trazodone all at night works well, although the manufacturer cautions that giving more than 300 mg at any one time may be unsafe. The elderly may also have problems taking an entire daily dose at night, especially since they more frequently arise during the night to urinate—at a time that they may be maximally sedated from the antidepressant.

Bupropion must be taken on a divided-dose regimen with no more than 150 mg at any one time because of the risk of grand mal seizures if the entire daily dose is ingested at once. Since bupropion is also stimulating, the doses are given in the early part of the day.

The other situation in which taking the entire daily dose at night is unhelpful is when the patient becomes stimulated by the antidepressant. This is expected with fluoxetine, which, like bupropion, is among the least sedating of the antidepressants and is typically taken in the morning. Stimulation can also occur with any of the less sedating ADs, such as desipramine, imipramine, nortriptyline, proptriptyline, or amoxapine. If the patient experiences insomnia, jitteriness, or a feeling of being "wired," taking the medications earlier in the day and possibly in divided doses can alleviate the problem.

Antidepressants generally do not show a significant clinical effect during the first week or even two weeks of treatment. A possible exception is amoxapine which may work somewhat faster. Amoxapine, however, has other problems that limit its usefulness (discussed later in this chapter). Many studies examining the question of "time to response" for antidepressants have concluded that four weeks is the very minimum that is needed for an adequate trial. Six weeks is frequently needed for full benefit to be seen (Quitkin, Rabkin, Ross, and McGrath, 1984). Many early responses may be placebo responses or a therapeutic response to side effects; if an agitated patient takes a sedating antidepressant, he will feel somewhat better within the first week simply because of the antiagitation property of the medication. This effect, however, is separate from the true antidepressant effect which has nothing to do with sedation or activation. Similarly, a patient with psychomotor retardation taking fluoxetine may feel more energetic within days; the major effect of the medication on his depression will generally not be evident for three to six weeks.

Typically, if no response is seen after two or three weeks and side effects are minimal, the antidepressant is gradually raised to the maximum dose shown in Table 9–3. If no response is seen after six weeks of gradually increasing doses, a number of different strategies can be employed. The simplest is to obtain a plasma level of the antidepressant to evaluate the adequacy of the medication dose. (Plasma is the liquid portion of blood, as opposed to the cells. All chemicals in the blood are actually in the portion of blood that is plasma. Most psychopharmacologists use the terms plasma level and blood level interchangeably). Technically, this involves drawing a small amount of blood (only one tube is needed) and measuring the amount of the antidepressant in the circulation. This is reported as a concentration—for example, $X$ ng/ml (where ng is a nanogram, or 1 millionth of a mg, and ml is a milliliter, or 1 thousandth of a liter). For some—but not all—antidepressants, a blood level within a certain range will correlate with maximum improvement. Table 9–4 shows the three cyclic ADs for which blood levels correlate best with therapeutic response (Task Force on the Use of Laboratory Tests in Psychiatry, 1985). For all the other cyclic ADs, one can measure the blood level, but the "correct amount" needed for maximum effect is unknown.

As an example, if a patient is taking imipramine 300 mg daily and, after five weeks, has shown no response, it would be appropriate to measure the imipramine blood level. If the level is 68 ng/ml, it would be both safe and

TABLE 9–4

*Antidepressants for Which Therapeutic Blood Levels Are Established*

| Drug | Therapeutic Blood Level in ng/ml (Approximate) | Comment |
|---|---|---|
| Imipramine | 180–300 | Blood level = combination of imipramine and desipramine (its major metabolite) levels |
| Desipramine | 125–300 | Least well established of the three ADs listed |
| Nortriptyline | 50–150 | Therapeutic window (see text) |

reasonable to increase the dose above 300 mg daily with a good chance of seeing a better response. The body "sees" the blood level, not the dose. True toxicity occurs when the blood level is too high, no matter what the dose. With careful monitoring of the blood level, the dose can be increased until the level is in the therapeutic range. If that same patient on imipramine 300 mg daily had a blood level of 261 ng/ml, raising the dose would be unlikely to be helpful.

For cyclic ADs for which a therapeutic blood level range has not been established, measuring the level when the patient has not responded to a high dose is less helpful. It can reassure both patient and psychopharmacologist, though, that raising the dose would be safe. For instance, a trimipramine level of 24 ng/ml is assuredly low. Therefore, the dose can be raised. The relative value of a trimipramine level of 81 instead of 141, however, is unknown.

Nortriptyline is interesting in that it has a "therapeutic window"—a range above which or below which clinical response diminishes. Figure 9–4 shows this graphically. Side effects play no part in the poor response above the window. If a poor response is seen with nortriptyline and the blood level is 192, the correct change would be to *lower* the dose, with a good chance of seeing a better response. Although other cyclic ADs may also show a therapeutic window, the current evidence is convincing only for nortriptyline.

If a patient does not respond to a full trial of a cyclic AD, many psychopharmacologists would prescribe a second cyclic AD, usually with a different neurotransmitter effect. (For instance, a nonresponse to trazodone, which is serotonergic, might be appropriately followed by a trial of desipramine, which is noradrenergic). However, after two cyclic ADs have been given, each for an adequate trial (enough dose for six weeks), it is rarely if ever worth the effort to prescribe a third cyclic AD. Although virtually no studies exist on this point, it is generally thought that either a patient is a cyclic AD responder or not. Trying every medication in the same class is an unwise therapeutic strategy.

**Figure 9–4** Therapeutic "Window" for Nortriptyline Plasma Levels. Response is maximum between 50 and 150 ng/ml.

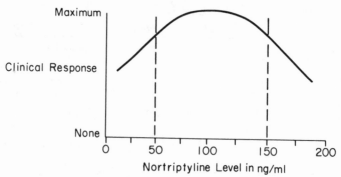

Many psychopharmacologists, however, will not try even a second cyclic AD if the patient has not responded to a full trial of the first one. At that point, switching to a different class of treatment, such as MAO inhibitors or lithium, would be the next appropriate therapeutic tack.

Nonresponse to an adequate trial of a cyclic AD must be distinguished from a trial that is cut short by side effects. For instance, a patient who takes doxepin and cannot tolerate more than 75 mg daily because of sedation should be switched to a less sedating cyclic AD. At this point, the patient is not a cyclic AD nonresponder; he should be correctly conceptualized (and treated) as receiving an inadequate trial because of side effects. In this kind of situation, trying three, four, or five medications of the same class *would* be appropriate to find one medication that the patient can tolerate. He may still not respond to that medication, but it is important to distinguish between a nonresponder and someone whose medication trial was cut short because of side effects.

To summarize general rules of prescribing a cyclic AD for depression, the three major mistakes frequently made are (1) starting too fast (increasing the dose too quickly), (2) stopping too low (not increasing the dose high enough), and (3) stopping too soon (not giving the antidepressant the four to six weeks it may need to show an effect).

Increasing the dose too quickly ignores the body's ability to accommodate to side effects (see Side Effects section below). A dose of medication that causes significant sedation initially may be completely nonsedating after a few weeks, but the body needs those days and weeks to accommodate. If the dose is raised too quickly, the unpleasant side effects that may result will scare the patient away from taking the medication again. It's generally not worth saving a few days at the cost of such negative physical and psychological reactions to the medication.

When first seen in consultation, Marilyn had been depressed for two months. Her internist had already tried her on two different antidepressants, neither of which she tolerated. Understandably, Marilyn felt pessimistic about the possibility of benefiting from medication. In reviewing her prior history, I learned that her internist had prescribed doxepin (Sinequan) and amitriptyline (Elavil), two of the most sedating antidepressants, at starting doses of 50 mg the first night. Although these were average initial doses, for Marilyn, they were excessive. Both times, she became sedated to the point of being dysfunctional and refused to take a second dose of either medication. Because of this, I gave her desipramine, a relatively nonsedating antidepressant, starting at 10 mg daily. Over the next fifteen days, the dose was slowly raised to 75 mg. Initially, Marilyn complained of feeling spacy but not to a degree that necessitated discontinuing the medication. Over the next two weeks, despite an increase in the dose to 125 mg, the spaciness diminished. Five weeks after beginning desipramine, Marilyn's mood began to improve. One week later, she felt substantially improved with only minimal medication side effects.

The second error in prescribing cyclic ADs is to assume that patients who have not responded to a higher dose (e.g., imipramine 200 mg daily) will not respond to a higher dose. This is simply not true in many cases. It is in these situations that blood levels can be very helpful.

It is often very difficult for patient, therapist, and psychiatrist to wait four to six weeks for an antidepressant response to occur. Time is slowed down during depression, the patient may be suffering greatly and asking for relief daily, and suicidal ideation may be present, worrying everyone. There is a great temptation to switch medications if no response is evident after three weeks. I have often prescribed an adjunctive medication (such as $T_3$—see chapter 3) during the fourth or fifth week simply to do *something* to alleviate the seemingly interminable wait. Still a significant number of patients will respond during the fifth and sixth weeks of treatment. Be patient; try to help your patient be patient.

Another important general rule in prescribing cyclic ADs concerns their use in treating elderly patients. Geriatric patients get depressed as do younger ones; and they respond as well or nearly as well to antidepressants as do younger ones (Gerson, Plotkin, and Jarvik, 1988). At the same time, the elderly are more likely to have medical problems and/or be on medications that interact with antidepressants. They are also more likely to be bothered by significant side effects. All of these observations point to the need for greater caution in prescribing cyclic ADs for the elderly. In general, doses should be half to two-thirds of those used in younger patients. However, some elderly patients need doses comparable to those used in treating younger patients. Measuring the blood level of the antidepressant can be extremely helpful in finding the most effective and least dangerous dose in treating the elderly depressed. The trick is to be conscious of avoiding the two poles of too aggressive, potentially dangerous treatment and undertreatment that will limit the usefulness of the medications and allow the depression to continue.

For the majority of the disorders listed other than depression, with the exception of panic disorder and obsessive compulsive disorder, the cyclic ADs are prescribed in the same manner as in depression. As mentioned earlier, panic patients may respond at somewhat lower doses than is typical of depression. More importantly, however, they are also more sensitive to the stimulating effects of any antidepressant prescribed (Pohl et al., 1988). It is common, for instance, for a panic patient to respond to a small dose of imipramine (which has mildly stimulating properties) with a marked increase in anxiety and insomnia. This may necessitate either decreasing the dose (since accommodation to the stimulating effect is often seen within a few days to a week) or switching to a slightly less stimulating antidepressant. In contrast, when obsessive compulsive disorder is treated with fluoxetine, doses are increased more quickly to higher levels.

## Side Effects

Cyclic ADs cause side effects in the majority of patients who take them. It is important, though, not to think of side effects as a unitary phenomenon that is either present or absent. Some side effects may be common and only minimally bothersome. Others may be common early in treatment and then disappear over time. As with so many other treatment decisions, the possible use of an antidepressant must be evaluated using a risk/benefit ratio, with side effects being one of the risks. Thus, simply rattling off a list of side effects that are possible with an antidepressant to a patient who is considering taking that medication is unwise and unfair. (Unfortunately, this is the approach taken by the *Physicians' Desk Reference* [PDR], which should be considered more of a marketing and medico-legal document than a clinical guide.)

Depressed patients also commonly attribute depressive symptoms to side effects from the antidepressant. Therefore, it is sometimes helpful for the psychopharmacologist to ask about various complaints (such as constipation or anxiety) that are frequently seen as either symptoms or side effects before beginning medication treatment. In an interesting study that examined the emergence of side effects during treatment with desipramine, subjective complaints were associated with *pre*treatment symptoms and depression scores, and not desipramine blood levels, implying that much of what distresses the patient who is taking an antidepressant may be due to or subjectively magnified more by the disorder than by the medication (Nelson, Jatlow, and Quinlan, 1984).

When the topic of side effects is discussed with the patient before an antidepressant is prescribed, four points should be emphasized: (1) the difference between likely and unlikely side effects, (2) the need to distinguish between uncomfortable and dangerous side effects, (3) the accommodation to side effects that commonly occurs, and (4) ways to diminish side effects such that the patient's anxiety is contained rather than heightened. Different patients want and need different levels of detail. For some patients, anticipating the unwanted effects confers mastery; for others, it promotes anxiety. The exact presentation must therefore be tailored to the individual patient.

Table 9–5 presents the three most common types of side effects seen with the cyclic ADs and the likelihood of seeing them with any individual medication. Table 9–6 lists other side effects sometimes seen with these medications.

The most common side effects seen with the cyclic ADs are the anticholinergic side effects, so called because they are due to the blockade of cholinergic receptors. The anticholinergic effects are dry mouth (the most common), constipation, urinary hesitation, and blurry vision. Additionally, some patients, especially the elderly have decreased memory and poor concentration because of anticholinergic effects. (Of course, since depression itself is characterized by these two cognitive symptoms, caution must be used in interpreting these symptoms as side effects). Occasionally, a patient who is on multiple medications with anticholinergic effects can exhibit an anticholinergic delirium. This unusual and serious condition is a toxic psychosis characterized by confusion, visual hallucinations, and disorientation. Anticholinergic delirium must be distinguished from an exacerbation of the primary psychiatric problem since the treatments are, not surprisingly, very different.

Anticholinergic side effects that are extremely bothersome can be treated by reversing the cholinergic blockade at the various affected organs or by taking

TABLE 9–5

**Common Side Effects of Cyclic Antidepressants**

| Medication | Anticholinergic Effects | Sedation | Postural Hypotension |
|---|---|---|---|
| Amitriptyline | + + + | + + + | + + + |
| Amoxapine | + | + | + + |
| Bupropion | + | 0 | 0 |
| Clomipramine | + + + | + + + | + + + |
| Desipramine | + | + | + + |
| Doxepin | + + | + + + | + + |
| Fluoxetine | 0 | 0 | 0 |
| Imipramine | + + | + + | + + + |
| Maprotiline | + | + + | + |
| Nortriptyline | + | + + | + |
| Protriptyline | + + | + | + + |
| Trazodone | 0 | + + + | + + |
| Trimipramine | + + | + + | + + |

    0 = None
    + = Minimal
  + + = Moderate
+ + + = Severe

Note: Postural hypotensive effects have not been well documented for some cyclic ADs. Ratings shown are best guess estimates.

## TABLE 9–6

### *Other Side Effects of Cyclic Antidepressants*

Sexual dysfunction: anorgasmia, erectile dysfunction, priapism (with trazodone)

Stimulation: nervousness, irritability, palpitations, tachycardia (fast heartbeat), tremor, sweating

Weight gain

Indigestion

Edema (swelling)

Extrapyramidal symptoms: stiffness, slowness, restlessness (rare except with amoxapine)

Rash

Speech blockade (rare)

Seizures (rare but more common with maprotiline, clomipramine and bupropion)

bethanechol, a cholinergic medication. Thus, dry mouth can be treated by cholinergic mouth wash (along with cheaper and easier maneuvers, such as chewing sugarless gum) or bethanechol. Constipation can be a significant problem, especially with the elderly. It is best treated by the use of bulk, either in food such as bran, or bethanechol. If these remedies are ineffective, laxatives can be used cautiously. Urinary hesitation can be especially troublesome for elderly males who have enlarged prostates (which also obstruct urine flow). In general, the use of "antidotes" for side effects is recommended only when the patient has close to intolerable discomfort. Otherwise, the patient might end up taking five medications—one for the primary disorder and the others to treat various side effects!

Sedation is an extremely common side effect, seen with most of the cyclic ADs. Luckily, it is also a side effect to which patients often experience significant accommodation, such that at the end of a few weeks of treatment, a profoundly sedating medication may be only minimally sedating. Unfortunately, this is not always the case. As mentioned above, sedation is unnecessary for an antidepressant effect. If a patient has significant anxiety or insomnia, a possible strategy (other than prescribing a sedating antidepressant) is to prescribe a relatively nonsedating antidepressant plus a tranquilizer; the tranquilizer can then be withdrawn when the depression lifts. If sedating antidepressants are used, patients will still be taking a sedating medication even after they are no longer agitated. The best ways to manage medication-induced sedation are to give the antidepressant all at night, or to wait for sedation to diminish, as it will over time. Caffeine in the morning can help, but it can also cause anxiety.

Postural hypotension is a relatively common side effect that is manifested by a drop in blood pressure upon change of position, especially when standing up.

The subjective complaint associated with this blood pressure drop is a feeling of dizziness or lightheadedness when getting up or starting to walk. When severe, it can cause loss of balance or even fainting, potentially resulting in serious injury. This is a significant problem when treating elderly patients, who may have poor balance to begin with. As noted in Table 9–5, the cyclic ADs differ markedly in their capacity to produce postural hypotension. For patients with this problem, choosing a medication such as fluoxetine or nortriptyline may be very helpful. There are a number of potential treatments for postural hypotension, such as increasing salt intake, wearing support hose (to increase blood return from the legs), and a variety of medications.

Sexual side effects can be seen from cyclic ADs, the most common of which are decreased erection and/or anorgasmia. Since decreased sexual function is also extremely common in depression, the sexual symptoms may be caused by both the depression and the medication-induced side effect simultaneously. The most important strategy used for combating these side effects is waiting—for the depression to remit and/or accommodation to occur. Occasionally, switching to a different antidepressant can help. There are reports of antidote medications, notably bethanechol and cyproheptadine (a serotonin antagonist), to reverse antidepressant-induced sexual side effects. The reports are sparse, and my own experience has been only intermittently successful with these agents.

Trazodone, alone among the cyclic ADs, has caused priapism—a prolonged painful erection in the absence of sexual stimulation. Although this condition is rarely seen, it may cause permanent impotence by decreasing blood flow to the penis. If a patient reports this, have him stop taking the medication and go to the emergency room immediately.

Some patients will experience a variety of stimulation side effects from the cyclic ADs, especially those with marked noradrenergic effects (see Table 9–3). Fluoxetine and bupropion are the only non-noradrenergic cyclic ADs that cause these side effects with regularity. Stimulation effects are manifested by a fast heartbeat (tachycardia), insomnia, anxiety, and/or a tremor. The tachycardia may be frightening or uncomfortable but is not dangerous, except for some patients with preexisting heart disease. The insomnia can frequently be controlled by taking the antidepressant early in the day. The tremor (and the tachycardia) can be treated by low-dose propranolol.

The last of the major cyclic AD-induced side effects is sweet craving and weight gain. With some patients, this can be a problem of monstrous proportion, causing great anguish and precipitating noncompliance. The statement, "I would rather be depressed than get fat" is often heard during the discussions of medication-induced weight gain. In one study using imipramine, 15 percent of patients gained more than ten pounds within four months (Fernstrom, Krowinski, and Kupfer, 1986). The weight gain is real and does not just reflect regaining the weight frequently lost as a symptom of depression. There are no predictors of weight gain (Garland, Remick, and Zis, 1988). Among the individual cyclic ADs, fluoxetine and bupropion are least likely to cause weight gain, with fluoxetine promoting weight loss at higher doses. Desipramine and trazodone may also cause less weight gain than the others. The mechanism of the weight gain is unknown. Hypoglycemia is clearly *not* the cause. Proposed mechanisms include histaminic blocking properties of the antidepressants and changes in serotonin and norepinephrine function in the hypothalamus, the area of the brain that regulates appetite, feelings of satiety, and carbohydrate hunger.

The best treatment for the antidepressant-induced sweet craving and weight gain is prevention. Warning the patient *before* treatment can be very helpful. Drinking high-calorie drinks when thirsty from antidepressant-induced dry mouth is also preventable. Once the weight has been gained, dieting and exercising are always helpful, just as they are for losing weight from any cause. Patients frequently get discouraged, however, because they find that a vigorous program that would ordinarily allow them to lose two pounds weekly when not on an antidepressant causes only a half pound weight loss while on medications. Anorectic (decreasing appetite) medications are sometimes used but their ultimate effectiveness is unknown.

Finally, a significant drawback of the cyclic antidepressants concerns their lethality if taken in overdose. Paradoxically, the patients at highest risk for suicide are prescribed the most dangerous medications—ingestion of as little as one week's dose of antidepressants is potentially lethal. Some of the newer antidepressants, specifically trazodone, fluoxetine, and bupropion, are significantly less dangerous than the other ADs when taken in overdose. Patients who take more than one extra day's worth of medication should be taken to the emergency room immediately.

## Second-Generation Antidepressants

The more recently released cyclic ADs are often called second-generation ADs. With the exception of amoxapine and clomipramine, they have a different chemical structure than the older cyclic ADs, that is, they are not tricyclics. Despite my earlier comments that they are no more consistently effective than the older tricyclics, there is sufficient curiosity about them to warrant a brief review of these newer medications.

Amoxapine (Asendin) was released in 1980. Structurally, it is a tricyclic with mixed effects on norepinephrine and serotonin. It has low-moderate anticholinergic effects and is not very sedating. There is some evidence, albeit conflicting, that amoxapine works faster than the other cyclic ADs. Amoxapine's major problem is that it is metabolized in the liver into loxapine, an antipsychotic. Potential side effects with loxapine, and therefore from amoxapine, are the same as those seen with other antipsychotics, including the risk of developing tardive dyskinesia with prolonged use. (See chapter 12 for more details on side effects of antipsychotics.)

Maprotiline (Ludiomil) has been available since 1981. It has a different chemical structure than the tricyclics, and is a pure norepinephrine reuptake blocker that causes moderate sedation and anticholinergic effects. It is more likely to cause epileptic seizures than the other cyclic ADs and should not be prescribed to patients with seizure disorders. Because of this problem, the doses used for maprotiline are lower than those recommended for imipramine and similar compounds. When taken in overdose, maprotiline is as dangerous as the tricyclic antidepressants.

Trazodone (Desyrel), released in 1982, has a unique chemical structure. It has selective serotonergic effects with virtually no effect on norepinephrine reuptake. Despite clear evidence of its efficacy, many clinicians have anecdotally noted that trazodone may be less effective in severe depression. Trazodone is very sedating and is effective in quickly diminishing both insomnia and anxiety. It has very few anticholinergic side effects but can produce dizziness and priapism (rarely). It is relatively safe if taken in overdose.

Fluoxetine (Prozac), released in 1987, is a potent and pure serotonin reuptake inhibitor. It has an extremely long half-life. Clinically, this means that its side effects may last for a longer time after fluoxetine is discontinued, although the onset of therapeutic effect is the same as with other cyclic ADs. Fluoxetine is unique in that its starting dose, 20 mg daily, is a sufficient dose for many patients. Thus, the usual time needed to gradually build up the dose may be avoided. Without question, it has the fewest side effects of any currently available antidepressant. It causes virtually no anticholinergic effect or postural hypotension and is minimally sedating. Although the relative lack of side effects is a major advantage, there is no evidence from clinical studies that fluoxetine is more effective—just easier to tolerate. Nonetheless, many clinicians, myself included, have treated a number of patients who describe a distinctly better response to fluoxetine compared with other antidepressants. Fluoxetine can cause nervousness, nausea, fatigue, and headaches. It does not cause weight gain and seems to promote weight loss, especially at higher doses. It is relatively safe when taken in overdose.

Bupropion (Wellbutrin), released in 1989, does not have significant effects on either norepinephrine or serotonin. Thus, it is not clear how it exerts its antidepressant effect. Its major side effects are related to its stimulating properties. It causes no significant blood pressure effects or sedation and is only minimally anticholinergic. Like most of the newer cyclic ADs, it is relatively safe in overdose.

Clomipramine (Anafranil) is a tricyclic antidepressant that has been used extensively in Europe for decades and was released in the United States in early 1990. It has strong serotonergic effects. There is significant evidence that clomipramine is not only an effective antidepressant but has clear antiobsessive compulsive effects (DeVeaugh-Geiss et al., 1989). Its side effect profile is similar to the other tricyclics, but with moderate to severe anticholinergic effects, sedation, and orthostatic effects. At higher doses, it is more likely than the other tricyclics to cause epileptic seizures.

## MONOAMINE OXIDASE (MAO) INHIBITORS

Even though MAO inhibitors were first shown to have antidepressant efficacy at the same time as the tricyclics, they have been used only a fraction as much since then. This stems from two separate but important early observations, one of which suggested a lack of efficacy in endogenous (melancholic) depressions, while the other focused on life-threatening side effects. In the last decade, both of these clinical observations have been shown to be gross overstatements. With the luxury of our vantage point twenty years later, MAO inhibitors should be considered effective in melancholic depressions (although maybe not equal to cyclic ADs), but with a broad spectrum of effect in more atypical depressive disorders. The dangerousness of the MAO inhibitors, due to the effect of ingesting tyramine-containing foods or stimulant-containing medications, can be minimized greatly with proper patient education and cooperation. Two recent reviews estimated the risk of serious hypertensive reactions as 1 to 3 percent (Robinson and Kurtz, 1987; Rabkin, Quitkin, McGrath, Harrison, and Tricamo, 1985). Nonetheless, MAO inhibitors are medications that still frighten many patients, physicians, and therapists who are unaware of the more recent clinical studies.

### Clinical Uses

Just as with the cyclic ADs, the MAO inhibitors show efficacy in a variety of different disorders. These disorders, listed in Table 9–7 overlap substantially with the cyclic AD list. The only disorders for which MAO inhibitors seem to be effective and the cyclic ADs ineffective are borderline personality disorder (*without* associated major depressive disorder) and social phobia. The compar-

TABLE 9–7

*Disorders for Which MAO Inhibitors Are Useful*

| Disorder | Efficacy Rating |
|---|:---:|
| Depression—unipolar, bipolar, and atypical | + + + |
| Panic disorder | + + + |
| Bulimia nervosa | + + |
| Social phobia | + + |
| Borderline personality disorder | + |
| Post-traumatic stress disorder | + |
| Obsessive compulsive disorder | + |
| Chronic pain syndromes | + |
| Attention deficit disorder | + |

+ + + = Definite efficacy
+ + = Probable efficacy
+ = Possible efficacy

ative efficacy of the antidepressant classes for each disorder, and the pros and cons of using each, are discussed in the chapters on each disorder.

As noted above, it was initially thought that the MAO inhibitors had their only significant effect in atypical depressions (defined in a variety of ways) and were relatively ineffective in the classical and more severe depressions. In retrospect, this was in large part due to the small, probably inadequate doses used in those early studies. Over the last decade, a number of studies have demonstrated that, when prescribed in higher doses, MAO inhibitors are clearly effective in melancholic depressions (Davidson, Giller, Zisook, and Overall, 1988). Although there is a paucity of studies on the topic, bipolar and unipolar depressions are probably equally likely to respond to MAO inhibitors. Because they are simpler to use (due to the dietary restrictions needed with all available MAO inhibitors) and the evidence for their efficacy is far greater, the cyclic ADs should still be considered the appropriate first treatment for most cases of major depression.

The situation is different with atypical depressions. Over the last twenty years, this category has encompassed a heterogeneous multitude of depressive syndromes, including those characterized by prominent anxiety, phobias, histrionic features, somatic complaints, interpersonal sensitivity, fatigue, and "reverse vegetative signs," such as hypersomnia, hyperphagia, and reversed diurnal variation (depression worse in the evening) (Davidson, Miller, Turnball, and Sullivan, 1982). For many of these patients, the MAO inhibitors may have a specific effect. Currently, therefore, some psychopharmacologists prescribe

MAO inhibitors first for patients with depression and panic attacks, and for those whose depressions have many atypical features, are nonautonomous (i.e., are responsive to the environment), and who are particularly sensitive to rejection (see chapter 3).

No study has systematically compared the antidepressant efficacy among the three MAO inhibitors. At this point, then, it seems warranted to consider them equal, with the choice of a specific medication decided by other criteria, such as side effect profile.

### Panic Disorder

MAO inhibitors are very effective in the treatment of panic disorder, with therapeutic effects seen irrespective of any depressive component (Pohl, Berchou, and Rainey, 1982). The MAO inhibitors may also be effective in diminishing the anticipatory anxiety and phobic avoidance seen in panic disorder (as opposed to the seemingly more pure effect of the cyclic ADs in blocking the panic attacks without changing other symptoms) (Sheehan, Ballenger, and Jacobsen, 1980). Among the MAO inhibitors, phenelzine is the most well studied in panic disorder, although it is likely that all are effective. Tranylcypromine, with its greater stimulant properties, will cause more unwanted stimulation/anxiety. Doses used for treating panic disorder and the time to response are the same as in depression (see Table 9–8).

MAO inhibitors have been used with increasing frequency over the last few years to treat normal-weight bulimia. Clinically, using these medications for bulimia is appealing for two reasons (Walsh, 1987): first, bulimic patients often present with a mixed anxiety/depression picture along with their eating symptoms in a manner reminiscent of the atypical depressions thought to be responsive to MAO inhibitors. Second, the anxiety/tension that seems to be a precipitant to many binges suggests the possible use of medications with

TABLE 9–8

*Monoamine Oxidase Inhibitors*

| Name (Trade Name) | Dosage Range (mg daily) | Comments |
|---|---|---|
| Phenelzine (Nardil) | 45–90 | Most well studied |
| Tranylcypromine (Parnate) | 30–60 | Most stimulating |
| Isocarboxazid (Marplan) | 30–60 | Least used but equally effective |

powerful antianxiety effects, such as the MAO inhibitors. Two controlled studies (Walsh et al., 1988; Kennedy et al., 1988) and many anecdotes using all the MAO inhibitors have demonstrated the success of these medications in diminishing both binges and purges. However, the strict requirement for dietary controls when using these medications makes their use with bulimic patients tricky at best. Interestingly, a recent study using phenelzine with bulimics noted no problems with hypertensive reactions (presumably because of careful patient selection), but found that the usual MAO inhibitor side effects such as postural hypotension and sedation severely limited their usefulness. Eighty-nine percent of the patients who *improved* in that study discontinued treatment during the follow-up phase, the majority due to side effects (Walsh et al., 1988).

Social phobia is another anxiety disorder for which MAO inhibitors are prescribed. They may be more effective in the generalized form of social phobia than in the performance anxiety type (see chapter 4 for details) (Liebowitz, Gorman, et al., 1988a). Of the three MAO inhibitors, evidence is strongest for phenelzine and tranylcypromine.

MAO inhibitors have been used to treat impulsive borderline personality disorder patients. In a recent double-blind study comparing many different psychopharmacological treatments in a group of borderlines with depressed mood, hysteroid dysphoria, (see chapter 3), extensive destructive behavioral outbursts (such as wrist cutting or physical violence), but without a current major depression, tranylcypromine was effective in improving mood, rejection sensitivity, and suicidality with some effects on decreasing behavioral outbursts (Cowdry and Gardner, 1988). Further studies are needed to confirm the generalizability of these results. Similar to treating those with bulimia or ADD, prescribing MAO inhibitors with their dietary restrictions for impulse-driven borderline patients can be dangerous. Patients must therefore be selected carefully.

Post-traumatic stress disorder (PTSD) has been successfully treated with MAO inhibitors in a few open trials and in one recent double-blind study (Frank et al., 1988). Theoretically, MAO inhibitors are attractive for treating PTSD because of their mixed antipanic/antidepressant properties. Phenelzine has been used the most in these reports, although all medications in this class are likely to be effective.

MAO inhibitors may be effective for occasional patients with obsessive compulsive disorder. Unfortunately, the evidence for efficacy rests primarily on anecdotes. One study suggested that those obsessive compulsive patients with associated anxiety and panic attacks may respond best (Jenike, Surman, Cassem, Zusky, and Anderson, 1983).

The use of MAO inhibitors with chronic pain syndromes has been infrequent despite the preliminary evidence that they may be helpful. This is probably because pain clinics tend to be directed by anesthesiologists who are wary of, and inexperienced with these medications. Chronic pain patients frequently exhibit atypical depression syndromes with anxiety, somatic preoccupation, and reversed vegetative symptoms, suggesting the use of MAO inhibitors on this basis alone (Dworkin and Caligor, 1988). Moreover, in one study, phenelzine was superior to the cyclic AD amitriptyline in patients with chronic pain and depression (Raft, Davidson, Mattox, Mueller, and Wasik, 1979).

Attention deficit disorder (ADD) in adults is another disorder for which MAO inhibitors have been prescribed recently. Since this literature is in its infancy, few generalizations are possible. Other than investigational MAO inhibitors, tranylcypromine has been used most. According to some experts, the major problem with the MAO inhibitors is that tolerance may develop during treatment, a phenomenon rarely seen with other agents used to treat ADD (Wender, 1988). Additionally, prescribing medications with dietary restrictions for patients with problems of impulse control is a real concern. If tranylcypromine's effects in adult ADD are similar to those seen when it is used to treat childhood ADD, results may be seen within the first few days of treatment, far sooner than is seen when MAO inhibitors are used in depression.

### Biologic Effects

As shown in Figure 2–3, MAO is an intraneuronal enzyme that metabolizes a variety of neurotransmitters. These neurotransmitters include norepinephrine, serotonin, dopamine, phenylethylamine, tyramine, and others. Given the number of different neurotransmitter systems affected by MAO, it is not surprising that, like the cyclic ADs, MAO inhibitors have such a broad range of effects, even broader than the cyclic ADs. Because MAO inhibitors decrease an enzyme that metabolizes neurotransmitters, their initial effect, like those of the cyclic ADs, is to increase the amount of norepinephrine, serotonin, and other neurotransmitters. However, as with cyclic ADs, it cannot be assumed that the increased availability of neurotransmitters soon after the MAO inhibitors are taken is the mechanism by which these medications cause a clinical effect. Just as the cyclic ADs cause a delayed (after two weeks) change in the regulation of the neurotransmitter receptors, so do the MAO inhibitors. Since the alteration in receptor sensitivities occurs at the same time as clinical response generally becomes evident, it may be that, as with the cyclic ADs, it is this alteration that mediates the antidepressant response.

It is also clear that MAO exists in two forms, MAO-A and MAO-B. MAO-A metabolizes norepinephrine and serotonin while MAO-B has a specific effect on dopamine and phenylethylamine. All currently available MAO inhibitors are nonselective; that is, they affect the A and B forms equally. Investigations with selective MAO inhibitors suggest that it is inhibition of the A form that is more important for antidepressant activity. This contrasts with the observation that in human brains (as compared with kidney, liver, and other organs in which MAO is found), 75 percent of the MAO is in the B form (Robinson and Kurtz, 1987). However, a statement about the brain as a whole tells us nothing of what is occurring in the specific parts of the brain that are relevant to antidepressant mechanisms. It is possible that MAO-A is preferentially utilized in the parts of the brain regulating mood, affect, and cognition, despite MAO-B being the more common form in the brain overall.

## Choosing a Medication and Techniques for Prescribing

The three commonly prescribed MAO inhibitors, along with their dosage ranges are listed in Table 9–8. It is likely that all three MAO inhibitors are equally effective in treating depression. However, they are not equally potent; just as with the cyclic ADs, the number of milligrams of medication needed to effect an equivalent response differs among the three drugs. Unfortunately, there is a discrepancy of opinion as to how best to evaluate their potencies. The dosage ranges in Table 9–8 are consensus values based on psychopharmacological studies, textbooks of psychopharmacology, and my own clinical experience. Because of the lack of agreement for these values, do not be surprised if you work with a psychopharmacologist whose "usual" doses of these medications differ from those listed in the table. As an example, a recent psychopharmacology textbook noted isocarboxazid, 20 to 30 mg/daily equivalent to 30 to 50 mg/daily of tranylcypromine while a recent British review article thoughtfully declared that isocarboxazid 60 mg was equivalent to 20 to 30 mg of tranylcypromine, a fourfold difference in the potency ratio (Schatzberg and Cole, 1986; Pare 1985). So much for the exactness of medicine!

The same guidelines presented above for prescribing cyclic ADs are also used with the MAO inhibitors: They are initially prescribed at low doses and then gradually raised. Since sedation is generally the most distressing early side effect with antidepressants in general, and because the MAO inhibitors are less sedating than the cyclic ADs, the doses may be raised slightly faster. An additional consequence of lesser sedation with the MAO inhibitors is that they are usually not taken at bedtime. Morning administration of MAO inhibitors is also helpful for decreasing the insomnia frequently seen with these medications.

MAO inhibitors are taken either in one daily dose or in divided doses. Although the half-lives of all three medications are short (measured in a few hours), their effects on MAO inhibition last far longer. Thus, taking the entire daily dose once daily should—and does—work just as well as divided doses. The major reason to divide the dose is to prevent intense side effects one to two hours after taking the entire daily dose. The most common symptom from ingesting a large amount of an MAO inhibitor is postural hypotension, manifested as dizziness or even fainting, especially upon changing position from lying or sitting to standing.

A reasonable beginning dose for each MAO inhibitor is two pills daily (20 mg for tranylcypromine and isocarboxazid and 30 mg for phenelzine). For a patient who may be particularly frightened by the medication, starting with one pill daily for a few days before increasing to two pills daily is often helpful. This can then be increased to three pills after three to seven days. Doses can then be increased by one pill every week to ten days depending on side effects and therapeutic response.

The MAO inhibitors are similar to the cyclic ADs in that from three to six weeks may be needed for a therapeutic response to occur. Certainly, earlier response are sometimes seen. Tranylcypromine frequently causes an early, usually helpful, stimulant response, with patients noting increased energy and mood. This is generally not the same as the later more global antidepressant response.

If a patient is taking a reasonably high dose of an MAO inhibitor, has few side effects, and shows no clinical response, strategies for evaluating the use of even higher doses are not the same as with the cyclic ADs. Accurately measuring the blood or plasma levels of an MAO inhibitor is, unfortunately, not possible, although some research and university laboratories can measure MAO inhibition. This test measures the medication's percentage of inhibition of the enzyme monoamine oxidase in the platelet. (The assumption is made that MAO inhibition in the platelet is a reasonable, albeit crude, marker of brain MAO inhibition). Maximum clinical response is generally seen when 80 percent or more of the platelet MAO is inhibited. Thus, if a patient on phenelzine 75 mg daily shows no response to treatment but shows 90 percent platelet MAO inhibition, raising the dose is unlikely to be helpful. On the other hand, if the MAO inhibition is 60 percent, then raising the dose may indeed cause an increased clinical effect.

The best approximation of evaluating the adequacy of the MAO inhibitor dose is by using a dose-by-weight ratio. An early study using phenelzine demonstrated that the best clinical responses were seen in patients who were taking at least 1 mg of phenelzine per kilogram (2.2 lbs) of body weight (Robinson, Nies, Ravaris, Ives, and Bartlett, 1978). For a 70-kilogram man (154 lbs), therefore, the threshold for an adequate dose would be 70 mg daily. Clearly, many patients will respond at lower doses than this; but for those who don't, the 1 mg/kg ratio is a good guide. The implication, of course, is that large patients, who may weigh over 200 lbs, probably need comparably larger doses of medications. Although the same ratios have not been studied for tranylcypromine or isocarboxazid, it is reasonable to use .67 mg/kg as the ratio, given the dosage ranges shown in Table 9–8. Whatever guidelines exist, the most important is still common sense. For patients who show no clinical response *and* have no side effects, it generally makes sense to increase the dose gradually until they have a positive response or until significant side effects ensue.

Among the three MAO inhibitors, the choice of a specific medication should be made by either history of past response or side effect profile. In general, tranylcypromine is the most stimulating of the three. Sometimes, this is a useful side effect—for example, in treating a depressed patient with psycho-motor retardation—while for others, it is a significant problem, requiring a switch to a different medication if the stimulation doesn't resolve over time. Phenelzine, conversely, is the most sedating, while isocarboxazid is in the middle.

Despite the warning in the *Physicians' Desk Reference* that "Parnate (tranyl-cypromine) should not be administered to any patient beyond 60 years of age . . ." (PDR, 1989, p. 2026), elderly depressed patients are clearly responsive to MAO inhibitors (Georgotas et al., 1986). In fact, theoretically, they may be more likely to respond, since monoamine oxidase increases as a normal con-comitant of aging (Plotkin, Gerson, and Jarvik, 1987). Increased MAO would decrease the amounts of neurotransmitters, which might then make certain elderly individuals more vulnerable to clinical depression. As with the cyclic ADs, side effects may be more of a problem in the elderly, especially the postural hypotensive effects.

### Food and Drug Interactions

The most salient aspects of treatment with MAO inhibitors are the dietary and medication restrictions (especially the former). Patients always remember if they have ever been treated with an MAO inhibitor if you simply ask "Did the doctor say you couldn't eat cheese while taking the medication?" Furthermore, the warnings about what might happen if dietary restrictions are ignored—a sudden increase in blood pressure (hypertensive reaction), stroke, or even death—are certainly enough to scare anyone, especially if the person is de-pressed, somatically preoccupied, or anxious. A great deal of the lore about MAO inhibitors is a residue of twenty-plus years ago, when neither patients nor doctors knew the cause of the hypertensive reactions. At that time, these medications *were* dangerous in unpredictable ways and their reputation was justified. Unfortunately, reputations are difficult to change. A quick perusal of the way the *Physicians' Desk Reference* describes the risks and side effects of these medications should be enough to convince anyone that terrifying warnings, albeit unjustified, still abound. It must be remembered that the MAO inhibitors can be dramatically effective with a great number of patients. The risks mentioned above are all real—but preventable in the vast majority of cases given our current knowledge. We must also remember that the potential morbidity and even mortality of depression or severe anxiety disorders is far from trivial itself. As always, potential risks and potential benefits must be weighed and compared in order to truly assess a treatment's dangerousness.

A review of tyramine, the most common amino acid in food that raises blood pressure, will help clarify the MAO inhibitor/food list. Tyramine is found in a variety of foods, the majority of which are aged foods. Anyone—on MAO inhibitors or not—will experience a rise in blood pressure if enough tyramine is absorbed into the bloodstream. Therefore, one important variable is how much tyramine gets absorbed. Ordinarily, when a person not on MAO inhibitors ingests a tyramine-containing food (such as aged cheese), the enzyme monoamine oxidase (MAO) which exists in the lining of the intestinal tract and in the liver (through which all absorbed foods pass first) metabolizes the tyramine so that very little gets into the bloodstream. Thus, anyone on an MAO inhibitor will absorb an increased amount of tyramine. Once tyramine is absorbed, it is taken up into the cells where it releases norepinephrine, and this in turn raises the blood pressure. Since MAO metabolizes norepinephrine within the cells, patients on an MAO inhibitor have greater stores of norepinephrine to be released, thereby raising the blood pressure even more. These two mechanisms—the increased absorption of tyramine and the increased release of norepinephrine—explain why patients on MAO inhibitors can have hypertensive reactions when they ingest tyramine-containing foods. Some foods capable of causing a hypertensive reaction do not contain tyramine but contain other amines with similar properties. With these other foods, the explanation is identical to that for tyramine.

There are many different lists that enumerate all the foods that have ever been reported to cause a hypertensive reaction in patients on MAO inhibitors. Most of these lists are absurdly long and do not distinguish between foods that may have caused a reaction in one individual on one occasion and those likely to cause reactions frequently. Unless the patient on MAO inhibitors also has an obsessional personality disorder, these long, overly inclusive lists are likely to result in random noncompliance. It is far better to have a shorter list with which a reasonably cooperative patient will be able to comply.

This seemingly simple task—that of giving an appropriate list of proscribed foods with MAO inhibitors—can demonstrate the difference between working with a knowledgeable psychopharmacologist and dealing with a competent psychiatrist who is inexperienced in psychopharmacology. Moreover, as with explaining side effects in general, how the information is presented is as important as what is presented. The MAO/food list can induce fear and dread, or a sense of realistic dangers that is mastered with minimal effort, depending on the person presenting it. Psychotherapists are not expected to know the nuances of these lists. It is extremely helpful, however, if you are knowledgeable enough to help your patient deal with the appropriate concerns, as well as allay inappropriate fears that surround the MAO inhibitors.

Table 9–9 lists the foods that are likely to provoke hypertensive reactions in patients on MAO inhibitors. As is clear, some foods must never be eaten, while others can be consumed in limited quantities. Even among lists that distinguish appropriately between likely and unlikely risks, there may be some differences. This stems from the lack of extensive chemical analysis for a great number of the foods listed. The major offenders, however, are almost always the same. With only rare exceptions (e.g., broad bean pods, which contain dopamine), these forbidden foods are aged. As food ages or ferments, tyramine is formed. Thus,

TABLE 9–9

*Food Restrictions for Patients on MAO Inhibitors*

*Foods and Beverages to Avoid Completely*
Cheese—all kinds—except cottage cheese and cream cheese
Smoked or pickled fish (canned tuna is OK)
Fermented meats, such as summer sausage, pepperoni, salami
Beef liver or chicken liver
Yeast/protein extracts—such as Marmite and Bovril spreads
Sherry, vermouth, brandy, red wines—especially Chianti (white wine and champagne are OK)
Fava or broad bean pods (Italian green beans). The beans themselves are OK. String beans are OK
Overripe figs or overripe bananas—young bananas (white pulp) are OK

*Foods and Beverages to Be Used in Moderation*
Beer
Yogurt
Sour cream
Canned or powdered soup
Avocados
Raspberries
Sauerkraut
Chocolate
Caffeine

*Note:* These instructions must be followed for two weeks after stopping the MAO inhibitor.

even a food that has little tyramine when absolutely fresh, such as liver, can contain a significant amount of tyramine when it is left out, even for a few hours.

There are two important reminders regarding this list. One, a food that causes no reaction the first ten times it is eaten can provoke a reaction the eleventh time. In the case of cheese, for example, this happens because each wheel of cheese contains a different amount of tyramine. Also, the amount of tyramine varies greatly depending on whether the particular slice comes from the rind or the center of the wheel. Thus, there is simply no way of knowing that any cheese (other than cottage cheese or cream cheese) is safe, no matter how many times the patient has eaten it without problems. If your patient describes a cavalier attitude towards an MAO diet, you should not only refer the patient back to the psychiatrist for clarification and education about the diet, but also consider exploring any possible psychodynamic roots of the dietary indiscretions. Is it a rebellion against parental authority as represented by the physician? Is there a flirtation with self-destructive behavior? Is limit testing in other situations part of the patient's character style? If the patient confides in the therapist that he is "cheating" on the MAO diet, encouraging the patient to deal with the psychiatrist directly would be best. If the patient refuses and continues to risk a major medical catastrophe through dietary indiscretions, informing the psychopharmacologist yourself is appropriate if a working relationship has previously been established with the patient's knowledge and consent.

The second reminder is that it is the amount of tyramine ingested (and absorbed) that is important in understanding the risk of hypertensive episodes. Four glasses of Chianti (a red wine), for instance, are more likely to provoke a hypertensive reaction than are two ounces. The foods listed under "consume in moderation" generally contain a small amount of tyramine; if a great deal of any of them is eaten, however (such as four ripe avocados in one sitting), a hypertensive reaction is possible.

There is also a group of medications listed in Table 9–10 that can provoke hypertensive episodes in patients taking MAO inhibitors. With the exception of the two opiates, meperidine (Demerol) and dextromethorphan (found in many cold/cough medicines and usually labeled as DM), these medications are all stimulants and provoke hypertension by the increased release of norepinephrine, as explained above for foods. Tyramine is not involved with the medication-induced reactions. The major dangers are with the cold medications, many of which are sold over the counter. There are a few safe cold tablets that are pure antihistamines, but most of them contain decongestants which can easily provoke a hypertensive episode. A good general rule is to have the patient call the psychiatrist about any new medication.

A hypertensive headache is described by most patients as a severe, pounding

TABLE 9–10

*MAO Inhibitors—Medications to Avoid*

*Medications with Stimulant Properties*

Virtually all cold, cough, or sinus medications (except pure antihistamines such as Benadryl, Chlortrimeton, or Seldane)

Weight reducing or pep pills

Asthma inhalants (except for steroid sprays or Intal)

Epinephrine in local anesthesia, such as is used in dental work (the local anesthesia itself is safe)

Cocaine

Amphetamines, speed

Other antidepressants (except in special circumstances)

*Certain Opiate Narcotics*

Demerol (meperidine)

Dextromethorphan—found in many cold and cough preparations usually labeled as DM)

*Note:* All antibiotics are safe, as are aspirin, plain Tylenol, Advil, or Motrin.
Patients should check with their psychiatrists before taking any other medicines. They must also tell their doctors or dentists that they are taking an MAO inhibitor.
These instructions must be followed for two weeks after stopping the MAO inhibitor.

headache, very unlike a typical tension headache and somewhat reminiscent of a severe migraine. It typically starts explosively, usually within minutes to an hour of ingesting the offending substance. Associated symptoms of a hypertensive reaction may be nausea, visual disturbances, sweating, and anxiety. Any blood pressure rise that is of medical concern is associated with a severe headache. Small rises of blood pressure may occur without any symptoms. These are not of concern since they are not dangerous.

Psychiatrists vary in the instructions they give patients to follow in the event of a sudden headache while taking an MAO inhibitor. My recommendations are to go to an emergency room where the patient's blood pressure can be measured. If it is high, a number of medications can be given that will lower the blood pressure promptly. Other psychopharmacologists give patients a small dose of a medication, nifedipine (Procardia) that will lower blood pressure so that they can treat their hypertension themselves. Except in situations in which patients are likely to be far away from any help (e.g., backpacking or traveling in exotic places), I am wary of this approach since not all headaches are hypertensive, and I would rather have them evaluated and treated under carefully monitored conditions. Certainly, if a patient calls you in a situation in which a hypertensive headache seems likely, have him go to the nearest emergency room.

All currently available MAO inhibitors are capable of causing hypertensive episodes, although tranylcypromine may be somewhat more likely to do so than the other two. It is difficult to accurately state the risk of hypertensive episodes from MAO inhibitors. As noted above, two recent studies estimated the probability of having a hypertensive episode that resulted in the patient going to the emergency room as 1 to 3 percent. Assuredly, the risk of actual harmful events, such as a stroke, is far less, and in the range of one per many thousands. Nonetheless, the food and medication list must be taken seriously or the MAO inhibitors should be stopped.

One of the most important messages about the MAO diet that is often accidentally omitted concerns methods of stopping the medication. In general, patients must stay on the diet and avoid potentially dangerous interacting medications for fourteen days after stopping an MAO inhibitor. (If a switch is made from one MAO inhibitor to another, fourteen days between the two medications is also required). It takes that long for the cells to resynthesize MAO in sufficient quantity to make a hypertensive episode unlikely after a pizza with anchovies and pepperoni, washed down by a Chianti.

## Other Side Effects

Beyond the hypertensive risks, the MAO inhibitors can cause side effects similar to those seen with the cyclic ADs. These are listed in Table 9–11. The previous discussion about how to present side effects with cyclic ADs, distinguishing between minor and major side effects, applies equally to the MAO inhibitors.

Paradoxically, for a class of medications for which the major danger is a hypertensive reaction, the most common side effect is postural hypotension. Only when certain foods or medications are ingested does hypertension occur; otherwise, the MAO inhibitors are decidedly hypotensive. The hypotension is clinically manifested by the same complaints as described when it is caused by

TABLE 9–11

*Common Side Effects of MAO Inhibitors*

Postural hypotension
Weight gain (less with tranylcypromine)
Sexual dysfunction—anorgasmia, erectile dysfunction, retarded ejaculation
Insomnia
Energy slumps
Stimulation (especially with tranylcypromine)—nervousness, irritability, tremor, sweating, tachycardia, palpitations
Edema (swelling)
Muscle twitching

a cyclic AD—a feeling of dizziness, especially upon standing up quickly or getting out of bed. It can occur with any of the MAO inhibitors, although tranylcypromine may cause it less frequently, presumably due to its stimulant-like effects. Clinically, the hypotensive effects with the MAO inhibitors are more troublesome than with the cyclic ADs. The treatments for postural hypotension are the same as when it is caused by the cyclic ADs—switching medications, increasing salt ingestion, wearing support hose, and taking various medications that increase blood pressure.

Weight gain can be a woeful problem with phenelzine and isocarboxazid, but generally not with tranylcypromine. Presumably, this reflects the amphetamine-like properties of the latter which help curb any appetite increase that might be seen. My own clinical experience is that the MAO inhibitor-induced weight gain more commonly reflects increased sweet craving and actual increases in caloric ingestion than with the cyclic ADs for which a variety of weight-gaining mechanisms may be operating. As with the cyclic ADs, the only real treatments are prevention, diet, and exercise.

Sexual side effects are relatively common with MAO inhibitors. Difficulty in sexual arousal, difficulty with erections, and/or anorgasmia have all been reported. Retarded ejaculation is also seen, a side effect that when mild is enjoyed by some. Sexual side effects are likely to be dose-related; one hopes that the threshold for the side effect is not at the same dose as the threshold for therapeutic effects. The sexual difficulties may also diminish over time. Switching to another MAO inhibitor if sexual side effects appear is sometimes helpful. As with the cyclic ADs, some "antidotes" exist, although, in my experience, they are successful in only a minority of cases.

Although most systematic studies do not mention it as a significant problem, I have found insomnia and "energy slumps" to be among the most disturbing and refractory of MAO inhibitor side effects. These seem to be separable from insomnia from overstimulation. Typically, patients describe being able to initiate sleep, but awaken during the night "wide awake." They can usually distinguish this from depressive insomnia—they don't feel anxious, just very awake. Simultaneously, they will describe a period of profound exhaustion in the late afternoon that lasts up to two hours and then remits either spontaneously or after a brief nap. These side effects occur with all three MAO inhibitors. Varying the time of taking the medications is generally not helpful, although it should be tried. The MAO inhibitor-induced insomnia is notably resistant to treatment. Typical remedies include benzodiazepine hypnotics, or trazodone, which should be started before the MAO inhibitor (see chapter 3).

A variety of stimulation side effects can be seen with MAO inhibitors, especially tranylcypromine. The most obvious of these is that of feeling "buzzed," as if one had taken amphetamines or drank too much coffee. A second stimulation effect is a mild hand tremor which can be socially embarrassing. An early cue to this is a subtle change in handwriting. Switching to taking the medication in the morning can be helpful with some of these side effects (such as the overstimulation), as can lowering the dose. Changing to a different MAO inhibitor should also be considered. Beta-blockers must be used with caution, but can decrease the tremor effectively.

Edema (swelling) is sometimes seen with MAO inhibitors. Diuretics can be helpful in diminishing it. The edema is usually not severe enough to warrant discontinuing treatment.

# 10

## Lithium and Other Mood Stabilizers

Since bipolar disorder is characterized by the seemingly opposite states of mania and depression, there has long been an emphasis on finding medications that would treat and/or prevent both states. These medications are generally thought of as mood stabilizers, although they have both discrete antimanic and antidepressant qualities as well as overall mood stabilizing properties. Lithium is the most well known, well studied, and most effective of these mood stabilizers. Following the initial glow of lithium's success, psychiatry became increasingly aware of the substantial number of patients who either did not respond or could not tolerate lithium. Over the last decade, therefore, a number of other medications have been studied that seem to have true lithium-like mood stabilizing qualities. At present, then, psychopharmacologists have a number of options for prescribing in order to diminish abnormal mood swings.

### LITHIUM

#### History

The first report of lithium's efficacy in treating acute mania was published in 1949, years before the discovery of the antidepressants or of the first antipsychotic. Yet lithium's widespread acceptance and use did not occur until years after these other agents were firmly ensconced as part of modern psychopharmacology. The primary reason for the delay was rooted in the disastrous results that occurred when lithium was used as a salt substitute for hypertensive patients in the 1940s and 1950s. At that time, it was hoped that by using lithium chloride instead of sodium chloride (table salt) in flavoring food, hypertensive patients would be able to cut down on salt intake, thereby lowering their blood pressure. Unfortunately, virtually nothing was known at that time of lithium toxicity or of the dangers of unrestricted lithium ingestion without monitoring. Not surprisingly, this uncontrolled use of lithium in soups, meats, french fries, and the like resulted in serious lithium toxicity and, tragically, some deaths. After this experience, the medical community was wary of using lithium in any dose for any reason. The United States was notably behind Central Europe and Scandinavia in recognizing lithium's efficacy. Indeed, in 1961, twelve years after the initial report of lithium's efficacy and more than five years after two other studies done in Europe documented lithium's positive effect in mania, an editorial in the *Journal of the American Medical Association* declared that there were no accepted medical uses for lithium in medicine (Wingard, 1961). A second reason for lithium's delayed acceptance was that the initial study in 1949, written by John Cade, was published in the *Medical Journal of Australia*, a journal that was not well circulated in Western Europe or the United States. Furthermore, Cade's original rationale for using lithium in mania was filled with incorrect assumptions. Despite this, however, he demonstrated that lithium did control manic symptoms (Cade, 1949). Cade's ultimate discovery of lithium's effect can be best ascribed to serendipity with a large dose of careful observation. With the past negative experiences of lithium still fresh in physicians' minds, Cade's observations and those of Schou after him were viewed with great skepticism. A final reason for the delay in lithium's acceptance by the medical community was the lack of interest on the part of pharmaceutical firms to investigate and promote lithium. Since lithium is a natural product (see below), it is unpatentable. It was, therefore, not profitable for drug companies to spend money investigating a compound that any other firm could then produce without the research costs.

Despite the delay in accepting the efficacy of lithium in treating acute mania and in the prophylaxis of mania, ongoing research continued to document the extent of lithium's effect in bipolar and unipolar mood disorders. By the mid 1970s, lithium was regarded as somewhat of a wonder drug in psychiatry with acute and prophylactic effects, able to dramatically ameliorate or abolish the symptoms of a most severe disease with only minimal side effects. Initial skepticism had evolved into the honeymoon period. The bubble was burst in 1977 when the first report of lithium's potential destructive effect on the kidney was published (Hestbech, Hansen, Amdisen, and Olsen, 1977). Now, over a decade later, both lithium's considerable therapeutic effects and its limitations and side effects are perceived more clearly. On balance, lithium should be considered an extremely effective treatment, lifesaving for some—but not all—affectively ill patients, the benefits of which far outweigh its risks in most cases.

## Clinical Uses

The appropriate uses for lithium, listed in Table 10–1, are predominantly in the treatment of mood disorders. Some other, less established indications do exist and will be discussed below.

Lithium is prescribed for a variety of clinical reasons in treating mood disorders. The two most common and well-documented uses are for the treatment of acute mania and in the maintenance (preventive) treatment of bipolar disorder. Its effect in treating acute mania and/or hypomania has been documented for over thirty years and is, at this point, an observation beyond question (Jefferson, Greist, Ackerman, and Carroll, 1987). Because it takes seven to ten days for its antimanic effect to be significant and because acute mania frequently requires a quicker behavioral effect, lithium is often combined with a neuroleptic initially (see chapter 3). Nonetheless, if prescribed alone, lithium would show the desired effect, although slightly delayed. Most patients describe the effect of lithium as normalizing a manic mood state as opposed to being tranquilized. Lithium blood levels generally needed for the treatment of acute mania are between 0.7 and 1.2 mEq/1 (milliequivalents per liter—see discussion of blood levels later in this chapter).

TABLE 10–1

*Disorders for Which Lithium Is Useful*

| Disorder | Efficacy Rating |
|---|:---:|
| Acute mania, hypomania | + + + |
| Bipolar disorder—maintenance | + + + |
| Bipolar II disorder—maintenance | + + |
| Cyclothymia—maintenance | + + |
| Mixed states | + + |
| Acute depression—bipolar | + + |
| —unipolar | + |
| Unipolar depression—maintenance | + + |
| Adjunct to antidepressants in treatment-resistant depression | + + |
| Schizoaffective disorder | + + |
| Schizophrenia | + |
| Aggressive outbursts | + |
| Alcoholism | + |
| Premenstrual syndrome | + |

+ + + = Definite efficacy
+ + = Probable efficacy
+ = Possible efficacy

Lithium's other well-documented effect is as a maintenance treatment in bipolar disorder. As with acute mania, this clinical effect is now firmly established (Jefferson et al., 1987). Preventive treatment with lithium is equally effective against both manias and depressions (Consensus Development Panel, 1985). It is also important to remember that a positive effect only *sometimes* means a complete eradication of episodes. In many patients, a positive effect means a diminution of frequency, intensity, or length of episodes that still occur. Thus, partial effects with lithium are common. Furthermore, the full preventive therapeutic effect from lithium may not occur until six to twelve months after beginning treatment (Schou, 1986).

In general, doses and lithium blood levels needed for maximum prophylactic effect are lower than for acute effects. Most studies suggest that levels of 0.6 to 0.8 mEq/1 are optimum, although many patients will do well on levels of 0.5 and others may need levels of 1.0 or greater (Consensus Development Panel, 1985).

Lithium's prophylactic effect in Bipolar II disorder (bipolar disorder NOS in DSM-III-R) is less well studied. At present, however, it should still be considered the best treatment available (Kane et al., 1982).

Cyclothymia is the third of the bipolar subtypes for which lithium is frequently prescribed. Although few controlled studies exist, a wealth of anecdotal material suggests the positive effect of lithium in diminishing the rapid and short-lived mood swings of cyclothymia (Akiskal, Djenderedjan, Rosenthal, and Khani, 1977).

Mixed states (those with simultaneous features of both mania and depression) may also respond to lithium, although possibly less well than classic mania (Secunda et al., 1985). The appropriate treatment of mixed states has not been studied systematically.

For acute depression, lithium is not the equal of antidepressants. There is a subpopulation of patients, however, more bipolars than unipolars, who do respond to lithium with an acute antidepressant effect (Fieve and Peselow, 1983). Because of the risks of precipitating a manic episode if an antidepressant alone (i.e., without lithium) is prescribed for a bipolar patient, lithium is often prescribed first for bipolar depression with an antidepressant prescribed later if needed. Since unipolar patients do not share the same risk of an antidepressant-precipitated manic episode, lithium is rarely prescribed first.

In contrast to its effect in treating acute unipolar depression, lithium is clearly effective in preventing unipolar depressions (Consensus Development Statement, 1985). Since most patients are not treated with lithium during their acute depressions, compared to antidepressants lithium is not as commonly used prophylactically with these patients.

Another use of lithium in mood disorders is as an adjunctive treatment to antidepressants in treatment-resistant unipolar depression (Heninger, Charney, and Sternberg, 1983). When used in this manner, lithium is added after the antidepressant has been prescribed without success for a number of weeks. Lithium blood levels seem to be irrelevant when it is used adjunctively, and positive responses are seen equally with levels ranging from 0.3 to 1.0 mEq/l.

Schizoaffective disorder is also treated with lithium. There is conflicting evidence whether patients with more prominent affective than schizophrenic features respond more favorably to lithium, although most clinicians and investigators think so (Maj, 1988). In addition, there is evidence, although not convincing, that some patients with excited schizoaffective disorders will show a better response to lithium plus an antipsychotic than to an antipsychotic alone (Biederman, Lerner, and Belmaker, 1979). Unfortunately, all treatment studies with schizoaffective patients are hampered by the different diagnostic criteria used across studies.

Lithium is occasionally prescribed in the treatment of pure schizophrenia (without schizoaffective features) (Delva and Letemendia, 1982). It is unusual, however, for lithium to be effective in schizophrenia when used alone (as opposed to a combination treatment with antipsychotics). In general, lithium is reserved for use with schizophrenic patients who are refractory to treatment with neuroleptics.

Lithium may also be used with some success in decreasing aggressive outbursts from a variety of causes in individuals, ranging from the mentally retarded to prisoners who are neither mentally retarded nor bipolar. Clinically, it is prescribed more for spontaneous outbursts in response to minor provocations, than for premeditated violence (Schou, 1986).

Alcoholism has been treated with lithium in a number of studies. Acutely, lithium may have some effect in decreasing alcohol-induced confusion and the desire to drink without altering the alcohol-induced high (Judd and Huey, 1986). In treating alcoholics with depression, lithium may decrease relapse rates. With pure alcoholics (without secondary depression), lithium may also decrease drinking somewhat, although the evidence is sparser (Fawcett, Clark, et al., 1987).

Lithium is often mentioned as a treatment for premenstrual syndrome (PMS) despite a paucity of evidence that it is helpful. In general, it is most likely to help with those women who show a subtle mood disorder throughout the menstrual cycle with premenstrual exacerbation (Steiner, Haskett, and Osmun, 1980).

## Biologic Effects

Unlike all other medications used in psychiatry, lithium is a naturally occurring compound, discovered in 1817 and found in rocks, water, plants, and animals.

Most of the lithium used for medicinal reasons in the United States is mined in North Carolina. (The word is derived from the Greek word *lithos* which means stone.) It is an element closely related to sodium and potassium. Lithium is commercially available in a variety of preparations, such as lithium carbonate or lithium chloride, commonly referred to as lithium salts. (This use of the term "salt" should not be confused with table salt, which is the colloquial term for the compound sodium chloride.) The specific lithium salt prescribed is irrelevant—it is the lithium ion that is effective. Currently, virtually all lithium prescribed in the United States is lithium carbonate, but lithium citrate is just as effective.

Nowadays, the idea of a medication being "natural" is assumed to be a good thing. It simply is not so. Lithium is natural, but, as we will see, is as toxic or more toxic than most other medications in psychiatry with clear negative effects on the thyroid and kidney that are not shared by the synthesized medicines.

Lithium's mechanism of action in treating mood disorders, either acutely or preventively, is currently unknown. Studies of lithium's effects on the neurotransmitters known to be involved in mood regulation indicate that its most consistent effect is in enhancing serotonergic activity. Because serotonin function seems to be altered in depression (see chapter 2), increasing serotonergic function may explain some of lithium's capacity to treat and prevent depression (Bunney and Garland-Bunney, 1987). Yet these effects cannot easily explain lithium's capacity to treat mania. Of more interest, lithium has also been shown to inhibit the second messenger systems, the systems that regulate the effects of all neurotransmitters (see chapter 2). By inhibiting second messenger function, lithium would cause a decrease in the effects of all neurotransmitters. If this is borne out by future research, it would potentially explain both lithium's antimanic capabilities as well as its overall mood-stabilizing prophylactic qualities (Baraban, Worley, and Snyder, 1989).

### Techniques for Prescribing

Table 10–2 lists the various brands of lithium currently available. All preparations of lithium are equally effective for any and all uses of the medication. The only important differences among the preparations are whether they are capsule or tablet, liquid or pill, slow release or regular release, and 300 mg or 450 mg pills. The standard and most commonly used preparations are the 300 mg capsules, marketed by a variety of pharmaceutical firms. There is no difference among these preparations, although patients can be frightened if the pharmacist gives them yellow and gray capsules when their last bottle contained pink capsules. The liquid form of lithium is rarely used except for those who

TABLE 10–2

*Lithium Preparations*

| Generic Name (Trade Names) | Strength | Types |
|---|---|---|
| Lithium carbonate (Eskalith, Lithane) | 300 mg | Capsules |
| Lithium carbonate (Lithotabs) | 300 mg | Tablets |
| Lithium carbonate (Lithobid) | 300 mg | Sustained-release tablets |
| Lithium carbonate (Eskalith-CR) | 450 mg | Sustained-release tablets |
| Lithium citrate (Cibalith-S) | 8 mEq/5cc = 1 teaspoon (equivalent to a 300 mg pill) | Liquid |

have significant problems swallowing pills or with manic inpatients who may be surreptitiously "cheeking" their lithium pills. The slow-release forms of lithium are indeed absorbed more gradually than regular lithium carbonate; however, it is not clear whether this is at all advantageous to patients. Initial side effects such as nausea may be slightly less if slow-release tablets are prescribed, especially in the beginning of treatment. Within a few weeks, though, the nausea usually disappears, leaving increased cost as the major difference between slow-release and generic lithium carbonate. Moreover, slow-release lithium preparations may increase the incidence of diarrhea (Jefferson, Greist, Ackerman, and Carroll, 1987).

Before starting lithium, it is mandatory to obtain measures of thyroid and kidney function since these organs are sometimes adversely affected by the drug (see below). Most psychopharmacologists obtain a panel of blood tests (including a test for kidney function—called creatinine) that measure a number of bodily functions and chemistries, and a thyroid test. Sometimes, especially with older patients, an electrocardiogram is ordered, although this is not mandatory with younger patients.

More than any other medication in psychiatry, lithium is regulated by blood levels, so much so that in communicating about lithium, doses are not relevant. Lithium is measured as a concentration in the blood (or serum, which, similarly to plasma, refers to the liquid part of blood) in units of milliequivalents per liter, or mEq/l. Lithium levels have achieved this importance for three reasons. First, because there is only a small difference between therapeutic and toxic lithium levels, there is a need for careful dosage regulation. Blood levels allow more "fine tuning" for dose adjustment than does following the daily dose. Second, the appropriate blood level range within which maximum response to lithium will be seen has been well established (in contrast to our ignorance about the appropriate blood levels for most antidepressants or carbamazepine). Third, also in contrast to blood levels of most other medications, lithium levels are both inexpensive and easy to do. Therefore, patients can afford them and the results from most laboratories can be trusted.

The proper way to measure a lithium level is to draw the blood approximately twelve hours (between ten and fourteen hours is acceptable) after the last lithium dose. Since lithium levels are typically drawn in the morning before the first medication dose, patients often accidentally take their morning pill(s) and then get their lithium level drawn. Since a lithium level of 0.6 mEq/l taken twelve hours after the last dose will be 1.3 or more two hours after the dose, the accidental ingestion of the morning pills will dramatically change the blood test result and render it useless.

Food does not interfere with lithium levels; therefore, patients can eat within the twelve hours. They do need to have taken their lithium without missing doses for four days prior to the blood test for accurate results. After initiating therapy, or following a dosage change, five to seven days should elapse before testing the new level. (In the elderly, waiting seven to ten days is needed, since they take longer to achieve a "steady state"—a constant level after a dosage change.)

As mentioned above, different patients will require different lithium levels for maximum response. In general, levels needed for an acute antimanic response are higher than those needed for a prophylactic response. Individual differences, however, are commonly seen. Thus, some patients may show a response at levels of 0.4 mEq/l but exhibit intolerable side effects at 0.7. Conversely, some individuals, albeit rare, may need levels of 1.3 or above to achieve a therapeutic response and may tolerate that level easily. As always, careful observation and common sense will ensure the most appropriate treatment. Patients who are doing well at a level of 0.5 mEq/l should not have their dosage increased, just as those with profound side effects at 0.7 must have their dose decreased.

There is no right way to start lithium. In general, inpatients, acutely manic patients, or younger patients are started at higher doses than are those who are either hypomanic, depressed, older, or need prophylactic treatment. The more urgent patients can be started at doses of three to four tablets daily (300 mg each) in at least two and preferably three divided doses, with lithium levels measured every two to three days until the desired blood level and clinical effect are achieved. In less urgent situations, starting at two tablets daily and waiting five days before the first level is reasonable. In this situation, adjustment to the correct blood level may take a number of weeks. Quicker and more aggressive methods of dose adjustment may make an early response more likely but also increase the risk of side effects which are not only unpleasant but may affect future compliance. When initially prescribed, lithium is taken after meals to decrease potential nausea. This nausea almost always disappears within weeks.

After doses are adjusted to the desired level and clinical effect, most psychopharmacologists will try to simplify the medication regimen as much as possible. For virtually all patients, this means taking the entire daily dose in no more than one or two divided doses. Moreover, there is some evidence that some of lithium's negative effects on the kidney may be lessened by taking a single daily dose (Plenge and Mellerup, 1986). Therefore, the only reasons to take lithium more than twice daily are if side effects are significantly less when the dose is taken three or four times daily or if the patient is more comfortable with more frequent doses and doesn't forget to take the medication.

Once the lithium level is established and is steady—that is, two consecutive blood levels do not vary by more than 10 to 15 percent at the same dose—levels may be checked far less frequently. Checking lithium levels every three to four months in a clinically stable outpatient is sufficient. There are a number of clinical situations, listed in Table 10–3, in which levels must be checked more frequently. In virtually all of these situations, changes in lithium levels occur in conjunction with alterations in kidney function, hydration, and/or salt intake. Unlike any other medication in psychiatry, lithium is not metabolized. (Lithium is therefore not dangerous in patients with liver disease.) Rather, it is filtered by the kidneys and excreted unchanged in the urine. Any situation in which kidney function or salt and/or water balance (which alters the way the kidney handles lithium) is changed will result in an increase or decrease in lithium levels. The most interesting of these is the way the kidneys excrete lithium during mood changes. It is clear that even with complete compliance, lithium excretion increases (with a decreased lithium level) in mania and decreases

TABLE 10–3

*Situations in Which Lithium Levels Should Generally Be Checked*

After a change in dose (5–7 days later for younger patients, 8–10 days later in the elderly)

During major changes in weight (e.g., diet)

During treatment with diuretics

During a change in mood (both to check compliance and because lithium levels decrease in mania and increase in depression)

During physical illness, including the flu. Occasionally, lithium is stopped until the illness remits

If lithium toxicity is suspected

(causing an increased level) in depression (Kukopulos, Minnai, and Muller-Oerlinghausen, 1985). The exact mechanism for this change is not known.

Other than the occasional lithium levels, the two other blood tests taken routinely during maintenance lithium treatment are thyroid and kidney tests since these two organs are the ones that are potentially adversely affected by long-term lithium treatment (see below). These simple blood tests are drawn less frequently, typically every six to twelve months. If subtle abnormalities are found, the frequency of the blood tests is increased.

## Side Effects

Lithium can cause a great number of side effects. Because patients may be on lithium for many years or even a lifetime, there is an understandable concern about both the distressing and potentially dangerous aspects of these side effects. Yet at the same time, a common side effect is not necessarily distressing, and a distressing side effect is not always dangerous. As an example, Table 10–4 shows the most common and most distressing side effects seen with lithium in a recent study (Gitlin, Cochran, and Jamison, 1989). Whereas thirst and increased urination are the most common side effects, cognitive effects and weight gain are the most distressing. And, as always, risks must be weighed against potential benefits. If lithium decreases the number of manic episodes by 70 percent, is that worth a mild tremor and increased urination? Is it worth a significant tremor and weight gain? The balance must be decided separately for each individual.

The most common side effects with lithium are increased urination (polyuria) and increased thirst (Vestegaard, 1983). (An associated side effect, dry mouth, is also commonly seen.) Almost always, these two side effects coexist, since the polyuria causes mild dehydration which then causes the thirst. These symptoms are due to lithium's effect on promoting the excretion of a more dilute urine in

TABLE 10–4

*Lithium Side Effects*

| Most Common | Most Distressing |
|---|---|
| 1. Thirst | 1. Weight gain |
| 2. Excessive urination | 2. Cognitive effects |
| 3. Weight gain | 3. Excessive urination |
| 4. Fatigue | 4. Nausea |
| 5. Dry mouth | 5. Fatigue |

Adapted from Gitlin et al., *Journal of Clinical Psychiatry,* 50 (1989), 127–131. Copyright 1989, Physicians Postgraduate Press. Reproduced with permission.

a manner similar to alcohol. The polyuria is somewhat progressive; that is, the longer someone has been on lithium, the greater the problem (Bendz, 1983). As long as the patient's thirst mechanism is intact (which it virtually always is) and the patient has access to fluids, these symptoms are not dangerous. And most importantly, the presence of polyuria is unrelated to the possibility of dangerous kidney damage (Schou, 1988). If the increased urination is profound, the careful use of certain diuretics can be helpful in decreasing the urine volume.

Tremor is another common side effect (although it was seen infrequently in the study from which Table 10–4 was taken). It is typically increased with effort of some sort, such as stretching out the arms, holding a coffee cup, or writing. Occasionally, the tremor is first noticed by a change in handwriting. It is worsened by any of the factors that worsen tremors, such as caffeine ingestion or anxiety. If the tremor is particularly distressing, propranolol, a beta-blocker, can be extremely effective in diminishing or abolishing it.

Although not as common as polyuria, weight gain is a potentially significant side effect, in large part because of how distressing it is to many patients and how difficult it can be to lose the weight. Weight gain can be substantial. One study found that 20 percent of lithium-treated patients gained more than 10 kilograms (22 lbs) (Vestergaard, Amdisen, and Schou, 1980). The cause of the weight gain is unknown, although a number of factors may all contribute. One of the most preventable and treatable causes of the weight gain is the ingestion of high-calorie drinks in response to lithium-induced thirst. Drinking noncaloric drinks would clearly help. A second possible cause is hypothyroidism, seen in a small percentage of lithium-treated patients. Accurate diagnosis is possible via a simple blood test, and appropriate treatment (with thyroid hormone) can then be instituted. Third, lithium sometimes causes edema, a retention of salt and water which can be treated with diuretics, if needed. Finally, however, it does seem that lithium has some unexplained direct effect on fat and/or carbohydrate metabolism such that patients can gain weight even in the absence of increased caloric intake. Treatment for the weight gain includes prevention, education about diet, exercise, treating associated medical side effects (such as hypothyroidism), and combating discouragement when the weight loss is slower than expected.

The most underappreciated side effects from lithium are those related to altered cognition. Patients frequently complain of a variety of thinking changes that they attribute to the medication, such as poor concentration, impaired memory, or a sense of dullness in their thinking. Among the many studies that have examined this topic, most, but not all, do not find demonstrable cognitive changes from lithium. Since these same cognitive changes can be symptoms of mild depression or may express the loss of heightened hypomanic creativity, many psychopharmacologists and researchers are skeptical that lithium causes cognitive problems. My own experience with patients, however, convinces me that these effects are real and that the tests of cognition used in these studies are, in general, too insensitive to delineate the cognitive changes.

An associated complaint about lithium is that creativity is diminished. Clearly, this is a very important issue given that a disproportionate number of artists are bipolar. The most interesting study on this topic recently demonstrated that the number of associations to target words as well as the number of "idiosyncratic associations" as a measure of creativity were diminished by lithium (Shaw, Mann, Stokes, and Manevitz, 1986). For most bipolar artists, though, the generally increased productivity on lithium (since the artist no longer spends significant periods of time hospitalized or psychotic or profoundly depressed) makes up for the potential loss of short-term creative bursts.

Since lithium's effects on both general cognition and creativity are probably correlated with the lithium level, a useful strategy for patients who complain of these side effects is to lower the lithium dose. If the cognitive problem continues on the lower dose, or if breakthrough episodes begin to occur, switching to another mood stabilizer may be necessary.

Subtle coordination problems may also be caused by lithium. The complaints usually relate to mild clumsiness or dropping things.

The last two commonly reported side effects from lithium are edema (swelling) and diarrhea. If severe, the edema can be treated with diuretics. It is unusual that the diarrhea is severe enough to warrant either adding an antidote or switching to another medication.


## Lithium's Effects on Thyroid and Kidneys

The two organ systems that are adversely affected by lithium are the thyroid gland and kidneys. Because this statement is sometimes incorrectly translated as "lithium causes kidney failure," or "lithium is an extremely dangerous drug," the topic is worth reviewing.

Lithium decreases both the synthesis and release of thyroid hormone in the thyroid gland. Subtle evidence of these changes, usually by blood tests, can be found in a substantial proportion of lithium-treated patients. In the majority of these patients, such changes do not cause any symptoms. However, between 3 and 10 percent of patients may show signs of hypothyroidism, such as fatigue, apathy, sluggishness, weight gain, hypersomnia, dry skin, and coarse dry hair. Since most of these symptoms are the same as those seen in depression, distinguishing between the two can be very difficult in the absence of thyroid blood tests. Women are at higher risk for lithium-induced hypothyroidism, just as they are for hypothyroidism from any cause. Luckily, a low thyroid state is among the easiest conditions in medicine to treat. A once-daily dose of thyroid hormone can easily supply the necessary thyroid hormone. Thus, although lithium does indeed cause thyroid dysfunction, a knowledgeable psychopharmacologist will be able to diagnose it if it occurs and treat it with ease. Typically, thyroid blood tests are obtained every six months to one year. This often allows the psychiatrist to discover an abnormality on the tests before the patient has any symptoms of hypothyroidism.

Lithium's effect on the kidney is more complicated. A brief digression on kidney function will help. The kidney has two major functions—filtering toxins, which takes place in the glomeruli, and regulating salt and water balance, which occurs in the tubules. When people are in renal failure, a condition that necessitates either dialysis (an artificial kidney machine) or a kidney transplant, it is because the filtering mechanism is lost. The tubular system can sustain significant damage, but as long as the brain is correctly regulating salt and water craving (thirst), and there is free access to salt and water, no significant problems should arise. Lithium has well-documented negative effects on the tubular system, as exemplified by the commonly observed increased urination in lithium-treated patients. Happily, though, lithium does *not* cause progressive destruction of the glomeruli with loss of filtering function. Thus, although lithium does adversely affect certain aspects of kidney function, there is no evidence that this damage is life threatening. In order to be careful, however, psychopharmacologists measure the serum creatinine, a measure of the kidneys' filtering capacity, every six months to one year.

## Lithium Toxicity

Because the difference between therapeutic and toxic doses of lithium is relatively small, it is important for anyone who treats patients on lithium to be aware of the signs of lithium toxicity. These are listed in Table 10–5. The earliest signs are usually a worsening tremor (often described as progressing from a fine to a coarse tremor), significant diarrhea, nausea, and ataxia (poor balance). If the toxicity is recognized at this stage, the lithium dose can be lowered and significant damage is rare. If the toxicity continues to the point of mental confusion or decreased consciousness (which can occur at levels of 1.8 or above), the possibility of significant neurological damage exists. Thus, early recognition is key. If a patient you are seeing shows any of these signs, tell him to not take any more lithium until he speaks to his psychiatrist, who should be called immediately.

TABLE 10–5

*Signs of Lithium Toxicity*

| Mild | Moderate | Severe |
|------|----------|--------|
| Mild apathy, lethargy | Increased lethargy | Somnolence |
| Weakness | Confusion, drowsiness | Gross confusion |
| Unsteady balance | Gross ataxia | Profound loss of balance |
| Nausea | Vomiting | Urinary incontinence |
| Decreased concentration | Slurred speech | Random muscle twitching |
| Worsening hand tremor | Muscle twitching | Coma |
| Diarrhea | | |

The causes of lithium toxicity are all related to changes in hydration or salt balance, as noted in the section on lithium levels. Thus, a new diet (especially if it involves decreasing salt intake), fasting, fever, a virus that causes significant vomiting, and/or diarrhea are all potential causes. Interestingly, exercise may cause a *decrease* in lithium levels, despite the relative dehydration involved, because lithium is excreted in sweat at greater than serum levels (Jefferson et al., 1982). Certain medications (including ibuprofen, which is now sold over the counter) can cause lithium toxicity, as can a kidney infection, although this is relatively rare.

## OTHER MOOD STABILIZERS

Aside from lithium, the two other medications with documented efficacy—both acutely and prophylactically—in the treatment of mood disorders are two anticonvulsants, carbamazepine (Tegretol) and sodium valproate, also known as valproic acid (marketed as Depakene or Depakote). Although these two medications are anticonvulsants, this does not imply that any evidence exists that mood disorders are unusual seizure disorders (such as grand mal seizures). The most reasonable theoretical assumption is that mood disorders are characterized by a heightened excitability in the areas of the brain that regulate emotion and that the anticonvulsants decrease that excitability (Post, 1986). Additionally, as was noted earlier when discussing the various uses of antidepressants, it is common for different disorders to respond to the same treatment. Neither medication has been investigated in either research studies or clinical practice to the extent that lithium has, but the relatively common occurrence of partial responses and nonresponses to lithium makes the use of these drugs increasingly common in treating mood disorders.

## Carbamazepine

### Clinical Uses

Prior to its use in treating mood disorders, carbamazepine (Tegretol) was typically prescribed for the treatment of seizures arising in the temporal lobes and limbic structures, the areas of the brain that are central in the regulation of mood, and for paroxysmal disorders such as trigeminal neuralgia, a disorder of the facial nerve, characterized by excruciating paroxysms of pain. It was first noted to have mood stabilizing properties twenty years ago, when investigators observed that the medication not only controlled seizures, but decreased the affective instability often seen in patients with temporal lobe seizures. Because of these observations, carbamazepine was prescribed to patients with mood disorders. The results of these trials demonstrated that carbamazepine can be an effective medication for some patients with mood disorders.

Clinically, the evidence that is most convincing is carbamazepine's efficacy in treating acute mania (Post, 1988). When used for this purpose, positive effects are seen by the second week, with improvement increasing for the first three weeks of treatment. There is also some evidence, although less than that for acute mania, that carbamazepine is effective in the prophylaxis of bipolar disorder, preventing both manias and depressions (Prien and Gelenberg, 1989). Its true long-term (over five years) efficacy as a maintenance treatment for bipolar mood disorders is unknown. Some investigations have suggested that patients with rapid cycling (having four or more episodes per year) are more likely to respond to carbamazepine (Post, 1988).

Carbamazepine's efficacy in treating acute depression is far weaker and less well established than its effects in acute mania or as a maintenance treatment for bipolar disorder. At this point, it can be recommended as an acute antidepressant treatment for treatment-resistant patients only. According to preliminary results, patients with bipolar depression may be more likely to respond than those with unipolar depression (Post, Rubinow, and Ballenger, 1986). Virtually no studies have examined carbamazepine as a prophylactic treatment for recurrent unipolar depression.

Carbamazepine has also been used recently in the treatment of patients with borderline personality disorder with behavioral outbursts, such as physical violence or self-mutilation (e.g., wrist cuts, cigarette burns, or multiple overdoses) (Cowdry and Gardner, 1988). When administered in a double-blind manner, carbamazepine significantly decreased behavioral outbursts in an objective measurable way. Its effects on decreasing dysphoric mood were present but weaker.

Anecdotal, uncontrolled evidence exists to support the use of carbamazepine in the treatment of post-traumatic stress disorder (PTSD) (Lipper et al., 1986). Because the symptoms of PTSD can be thought of as the reexperiencing of traumatic events and because carbamazepine may have a specific effect in decreasing responses to repeated triggered phenomena (see next section), it is likely that this line of clinical investigation will continue.

Among other uses for carbamazepine, there have been preliminary indications that it can decrease withdrawal symptoms from both alcohol and benzodiazepine tranquilizers (Ries, Roy-Byrne, Ward, Neppe, and Cullison, 1989; Malcolm, Ballenger, Sturgis, and Anton, 1989). There is also evidence, albeit primarily anecdotal, that carbamazepine is effective in decreasing "rage attacks" in patients who do not show evidence of a seizure disorder. As with other medications used to treat behavioral outbursts, it is thought that the medication is most effective in the more "eruptive violence" that occurs impulsively as an exaggerated response to a provocation and is less effective or ineffective in violence which is premeditated. Finally, there are a few reports of carbamazepine's effect in treating bulimia. It has, at best, a minor role in treating this disorder.

### Biologic Effects

The most common hypothesis that purports to explain carbamazepine's effect in treating mood disorders relates to its effects on decreasing kindling in the limbic area of the brain (Post, Uhde, Putnam, Ballenger, and Berrettini, 1982). Kindling can be thought of as the progressive increase in neural excitability with repeated stimulation. Experimentally, this would be demonstrated by needing less and less electrical stimulation to cause an overt behavioral effect (Post, Rubinow, and Ballenger, 1984). With repeated electrical stimulation, it is even possible to cause spontaneous electrical discharges in the absence of stimulation. Thus, a system that was initially barely responsive to a low-dose stimulus can ultimately spontaneously discharge.

Kindling is analogous to behavioral sensitization, a process in which repeated applications of unchanging doses of chemical substances result in increasing behavioral effects with subsequent doses. Both these processes—kindling and sensitization—can be thought of as the opposite of tolerance, in which it takes more and more of a stimulus to achieve the same response. Tolerance is common with many substances of abuse. After repeated use of barbiturates, for example, progressively higher doses are needed to achieve the same sedative effect that was initially achieved by a small dose.

Carbamazepine is extremely effective in inhibiting the development of kindling in the limbic area, compared to its effects in other parts of the brain. Thus, its prophylactic effect in mood disorders may be due to its ability to prevent the easily provoked electrical and biological changes seen when a particular stress, be it the time of year (for those patients whose episodes occur on a seasonal basis), sleep deprivation, or the loss of a relationship, causes a response in a susceptible patient.

It is also possible that the kindling model explains the recent finding that the first few manic episodes in a bipolar patient are more likely to be related to stressful life events than are later episodes (Ambelas, 1987). After a number of precipitated episodes, the system may become kindled, or more sensitive, requiring less and less of a provocation to be triggered. Ultimately, as is seen with individual neurons, the system may spontaneously discharge; that is, affective episodes may occur without a precipitating event. Instead, at this point, the patient would show the pattern of endogenously occurring episodes without relation to life events or stresses.

Although clearly speculative, the changing relationship over time between life events and affective episodes could have important psychotherapeutic implications (Post, Uhde, Roy-Byrne, and Joffe, 1986). Early psychotherapeutic intervention, either cognitive/behavioral or psychodynamic, might diminish the magnitude of the person's responses to certain stressors either by desensitization or, in psychodynamic therapy, by diminishing the power of an event by divorcing it from the affective intensity of the earlier childhood event. This diminished response to stressful events would then make precipitation of episodes less likely. The same intervention years later, after "spontaneous episodes" have arisen, might be less useful in altering the course of the disorder.

At this point, the explanation above, although theoretically satisfying, lacks documentation. There is no direct evidence linking the antikindling effect of carbamazepine with its effect in mood disorders. Nonetheless, the indirect evidence as well as the links of the hypothesis to what is known about the course of mood disorders suggest it as a useful model for further studies.

Carbamazepine has a variety of different effects on a number of the neurotransmitter systems (Post, 1987). Its effects on noradrenergic mechanisms and on the benzodiazepine receptor sites may be especially relevant to its clinical actions. It is not currently possible, though, to correlate the clinical and biochemical effects of carbamazepine with each other.

### Techniques for Prescribing

Carbamazepine is available in 100 mg and 200 mg tablets. For most patients, starting doses are either 100 or 200 mg twice daily. Average doses are generally 800 to 1000 mg daily, although therapeutic effects can be seen in daily doses as low as 400 mg or as high as 1200 to 1600 mg. As with other medications, when it is prescribed for an acute syndrome such as mania, carbamazepine is increased more rapidly than when it is being used prophylacti-cally. For acute mania, the dose can be raised by 200 mg every few days to 800 or 1000 mg by the end of seven or eight days. For maintenance treatment, raising the dose by 200 mg every three to four days is more common.

Because it has a short half-life, carbamazepine needs to be prescribed in divided doses. Optimally, it would be given three or four times daily to keep the level in the blood constant as well as to diminish side effects. Because it is often difficult to remember midday or late afternoon doses, many patients take it on a twice-daily regimen. There are no studies examining whether the phar-macologic regimen (i.e., the number of daily doses) has any relationship to carbamazepine's efficacy.

Obtaining carbamazepine blood levels to help regulate the dose is very com-mon. Most laboratories will declare that the therapeutic range for carbam-azepine blood levels is 4 to 12 mg/l. Unfortunately, no relationship between blood levels and therapeutic response has been established (Post et al., 1983). This range should therefore be used as an approximate guide only.

### Side Effects

Carbamazepine can cause a variety of side effects that are of potential concern. What is always remembered by patients and clinicians alike about this medi-cation, however, is the very rare possibility of a bone marrow reaction in which the production of white blood cells (which fight infection) and/or platelets (which promote blood clotting) is diminished or ceases. Reading the *Physicians' Desk Reference* warning about this possibility is a frightening experience. Cer-tainly this risk needs to be taken seriously, because the reaction is potentially fatal (as, of course, penicillin allergy is). It must be remembered, though, that the incidence of this bone marrow suppression is estimated to be between one in 40,000 and one in 125,000 patients (Post, 1988). As always, the risks and benefits must be weighed. Most psychiatrists who prescribe carbamazepine obtain blood counts before treatment and then every two to four weeks for six months and at variable intervals thereafter, since 85 percent of the cases re-ported (a total of 38 cases prior to 1982) have occurred within the first six months of treatment (Pisciotta, 1982). Yet it must be acknowledged that the frequent checking of blood counts is more reassuring psychologically and med-icolegally than it is clinically helpful since the idiosyncratic bone marrow suppression can occur explosively, without warning, making random tests un-likely to diagnose it early. It is best if patients know to call their doctor and to obtain a blood count immediately at the first sign of infection or unusual bleeding.

This rare but disastrous bone marrow suppression is sometimes confused with the very common but benign lowering of the white blood cell count (Joffe, Post, Roy-Byrne, and Uhde, 1985). Typically, carbamazepine lowers the white count by 25 to 35 percent, an amount that still leaves the number of white cells well within the normal range.

Aside from the risk of severe bone marrow depression, other less dangerous effects can also be seen with carbamazepine. The most common of these are dizziness, ataxia (poor or unsteady balance), diplopia (double vision), sedation, and nausea. These side effects are typically dose related. As with many other medications, side effects can be diminished by increasing doses more slowly. Occasionally, a patient who has shown only a partial response to lithium will be prescribed a combination of lithium plus carbamazepine. At times, this combination can cause a marked increase in the neurological side effects, such as ataxia and diplopia. In these cases, lowering the dose of one or both medications can be very helpful.

## Valproate

### Clinical Uses

Similar to carbamazepine, valproate's primary use is in the treatment of epilepsy. It has been used to treat psychiatric disorders only recently in the United States, despite its occasional use in Europe for this purpose for a longer time. All statements regarding its usefulness are based on less experience and less well controlled studies than with carbamazepine and must therefore be viewed as less definitive.

Nonetheless, using the preliminary information available, it would seem that, in the treatment of mood disorders, valproate has effects similar to those of carbamazepine: Its most well-documented effects are for treating acute mania and in the prophylaxis of bipolar disorder (Fawcett, 1989). Valproate's efficacy in treating acute depression seems to be weak, and it may be more effective in preventing manias than depressions. It has been combined with lithium with good effect in a number of studies.

Among the suggested predictors of response to valproate in treating mood disorders are (1) rapid cycling (four or more episodes per year) and (2) a mildly abnormal electroencephalogram (EEG—brain wave test) (McElroy, Keck, and Pope, 1987). Again, because the patients treated in these studies were not randomly assigned to different treatments, it is impossible to know whether the results seen can be generalized to the "garden variety" bipolar patient.

Valproate has also been utilized in the treatment of schizophrenia (McElroy, Keck, Pope, and Hudson, 1988). These results are more contradictory, with some patients improving while others worsened. At present, valproate should only be considered as a treatment for schizophrenic patients for whom standard treatment has been unsuccessful.

More recently, preliminary studies have suggested the possible efficacy of valproate in treating panic disorder and bulimia. More work is needed in these areas.

### Biologic Effects

Most explanations of valproate's effects in treating both neurological and psychiatric disorders have centered on its ability to potentiate the effects of GABA (gamma-aminobutyric acid), an important inhibitory neurotransmitter found throughout the central nervous system. Enhancing GABA effects would have the effect of potentially decreasing both electrical activity (explaining its effects in diminishing seizures) and biochemical activity, similar to the hypothesized explanation of lithium's effects by dampening second-messenger activity (discussed earlier in this chapter) (McElroy et al., 1988).

### Techniques for Prescribing

Valproate is available in two forms, Depakene and the enteric coated form, Depakote. (Enteric coating is used to decrease stomach irritation.) Except when prescribed as a liquid, Depakene is available only in 250 mg capsules. Depakote is available in 125, 250, and 500 mg tablets. As with carbamazepine, valproate doses can be increased more quickly when used acutely than prophylactically. In general, the starting dose is 250 mg twice daily with increases of 250 mg every three to five days. Average daily doses of valproate are 1000 to 1500 mg daily, although higher doses may be occasionally needed. Like carbamazepine, valproate has a short half-life; therefore, it is usually taken three to four time daily.

Valproate blood levels are available to help monitor the dose. Unfortunately, as with carbamazepine, there is no evidence that blood levels correlate with therapeutic efficacy (McElroy et al., 1987). Nonetheless, the recommended range for a therapeutic trial of valproate is 50 to 100 mg/l.

### Side Effects

Valproate has fewer and milder side effects than carbamazepine. The most common side effects are nausea, diarrhea, mild tremor, and hair loss. Depakote seems to be extremely effective in diminishing or avoiding the nausea completely. Sedation occurs, but uncommonly.

The rare bone marrow suppression seen with carbamazepine does not occur with valproate. The major concern is a rare idiosyncratic hepatotoxicity (liver toxicity) that has occurred with valproate use. A recent study showed that all cases of fatal hepatotoxicity occurred when the medication was prescribed for infants, in combination with other anticonvulsants such as phenytoin (Dilantin) or phenobarbital, or in patients with multiple neurological disorders (Dreifuss, Santilli, and Langer, 1987). When used by itself in adolescents or adults, valproate never causes serious hepatotoxicity. Therefore, the risk for psychiatric patients is nil.

# 11

## Antianxiety Medications and Hypnotics

Human beings have been using chemicals to relax and to induce sleep since prerecorded history. Currently, the public tends to distinguish between medications that decrease anxiety—tranquilizers, which are technically called anxiolytics (literally the loosening of anxiety)—and others used to induce sleep, called hypnotics. It is often assumed that since the two goals are different, the medications to treat them must be too. This is untrue. Most medications used to treat anxiety also treat insomnia, often in the same dose. The myth of two separate treatments has largely been due to patterns of individual consumption ("I take a Xanax to relax and Dalmane to sleep") and to the advertising patterns of pharmaceutical firms which want the public to think of a medication as a treatment for a specific condition and not as one of many that are broad in their effects. Thus, flurazepam (Dalmane) became a hypnotic while diazepam (Valium) became a tranquilizer, although they could easily have been reversed without sacrificing effectiveness. Of course, as we will see, all tranquilizers are not identical, even within the same medication class, but the similarities far outweigh the differences. In this chapter, therefore, we will consider both tranquilizers and hypnotics together. In keeping with modern prescribing practices, the focus will be on the use of benzodiazepines—the class of tranquilizers that includes Valuim, Xanax, and Halcion—and of buspirone (Buspar) with less attention given to the older less commonly used tranquilizers.

### HISTORY

From the beginning, when alcohol was recorded as the first tranquilizer, society has been aware of the double-edged nature of calming agents. On one hand,

261

they have the positive effects of helping people relax, loosening their inhibitions, and allowing for an easier time slipping into a peaceful sleep. On the other hand, when taken in too large a quantity, these same potions inhibit the capacity to work, make people clumsy, cause a sleepiness that is dangerous in some circumstances, and are potentially addictive with larger and larger doses being used to maintain a clinical effect. For some people, the goals of relaxation and sleep are replaced by the craving for the medication itself and all else fades into unimportance.

Over the last 120 years, the goal has been to discover a tranquilizer that would calm but not cause too much somnolence, that would be effective but not addictive, that would decrease physical tension but not cause clumsiness. From the discovery of chloral hydrate in 1869 to the barbiturates in 1903 to the nonbarbiturate sedatives such as meprobamate (Miltown) and finally to the benzodiazepines starting with chlordiazepoxide (Librium) in 1960 and diazepam (Valium) in 1963, each new class of medications was thought to achieve this goal of being the perfect tranquilizer. In general, although each new class of compounds (with the possible exception of the barbiturates) came closer to the ideal, they never came as close as initially hoped or touted. The nonbarbiturate sedatives are slightly less addictive and less lethal in overdose than the barbiturates but are far from the nonaddictive "safe" medications initially promised. Benzodiazepines are indeed safe when taken in overdose, but are potentially addictive (although much less than their predecessors), can be dangerous when taken in conjunction with alcohol, and can cause significant impairment in physical and cognitive performance. Only buspirone (Buspar), released in 1986, seems to be devoid of the ill effects of all other tranquilizers. Unfortunately, though, it is not useful for inducing sleep, is ineffective when taken intermittently, and its efficacy in treating severe anxiety symptoms is doubtful. Its discovery, however, promises that new classes of antianxiety medications are on the horizon. The search for the perfect tranquilizer continues.

## BENZODIAZEPINES

### Clinical Uses

The benzodiazepines are the medications most commonly prescribed for any psychiatric symptoms or disorders. Between 1 and 2 percent of adults use benzodiazepines regularly for one year or more while 9 to 10 percent of the population will use them at least occasionally over one year (Mellinger and Balter, 1981). Despite concerns about their ill effects, the widespread use of these medications accurately reflects their fundamental efficacy and safety when prescribed cautiously and knowledgeably. Unfortunately, because they are so easy to prescribe, benzodiazepines are often given to patients by internists and psychiatrists alike without sufficient appreciation of their potential problems. With the possible exception of depression, for which alprazolam (Xanax) is sometimes effective, the disorders for which the benzodiazepines are useful all involve heightened levels of arousal. Table 11–1 lists these disorders.

Insomnia—both primary (not due to any other disorder) and secondary—is frequently treated with benzodiazepines. These medications are most effective when taken on an occasional basis or for short periods of time (e.g., a week or less). To diminish jet lag they are also frequently used to induce sleep on flights that involve crossing several time zones. Although some studies suggest that the hypnotic effect diminishes after one week or more of continuous use, clinical experience and a number of other studies indicate that some patients continue to sleep better on a chronic stable dose of medication for months and years (Mitler, Seidel, Van den Hoed, Greenblatt, and Dement, 1984). Whether this reflects an intial medication effect followed by a behavioral conditioning to the act of ingesting the pill ("When I take this pill, I know I will fall asleep more easily") or a prolonged pharmacological effect of the medication is unknown. Although they are all effective, some benzodiazepines are more commonly prescribed for insomnia than others. As will be discussed more below, the individual agents differ primarily in how quickly they act and how long their effects last. Clinically, flurazepam (Dalmane), triazolam (Halcion), and temazepam (Restoril) are the ones used most for insomnia.

The second common use of benzodiazepines is in treating situational anxiety. Probably the most common—and least studied—of these uses occurs when

TABLE 11–1

*Disorders for Which Benzodiazepines Are Useful*

| Disorder | Efficacy Rating |
|---|---|
| Insomnia | + + + |
| Situational anxiety | + + + |
| Generalized anxiety disorder | + + + |
| Panic disorder | + + + |
| Major depression | + + |
| Mania | + + |
| Acute alcohol detoxification | + + + |

+ + + = Definite efficacy
+ + = Probably efficacy
+ = Possible efficacy

people keep one or two tranquilizer pills in their pocket to be used at a time of particular stress—at work, in a relationship crisis, or during a stressful day. Benzodiazepines are also often prescribed during the few weeks to months of a stressful situation, called adjustment disorder with anxious mood in DSM-III-R. When used in this way, all the benzodiazepines are likely to be effective, although alprazolam and diazepam are the most popular.

Generalized anxiety, a more prolonged (months to years) anxiety disorder, is also very responsive to benzodiazepines. Here too, all the benzodiazepines are likely to be effective, although triazolam is virtually never used for this purpose because its actions are so brief. Despite its rare use for generalized anxiety, flurazepam is likely to be as effective as the others. The long-term use (more than four months) of benzodiazepines for chronic anxiety is somewhat controversial (see below). However, many patients do indeed stay on low to moderate doses of tranquilizers for many years without developing tolerance to the effects of the medication (Rickels, Case, Downing, and Winokur, 1983). When used for chronic anxiety, optimal doses vary enormously.

Among the most well-documented effects of benzodiazepines is their ability to block panic attacks. The bulk of the studies have focused on alprazolam (Xanax). Its immense popularity is, in large part, due to the impressive scientific and popular publicity it garnered during a series of studies on its antipanic properties (Ballenger et al., 1988). In the last few years, solid evidence has appeared documenting antipanic effects of lorazepam (Ativan), clonazepam (Klonopin), and, to a lesser extent, diazepam. It is likely, but not proven, that all benzodiazepines have antipanic properties (Charney and Woods, 1989). Benzodiazepine doses for panic are typically higher than those for generalized or situational anxiety.

Alprazolam has been documented as an effective antidepressant in outpatient depression. Despite large-scale studies showing that alprazolam is equally likely to be effective in both severe and mild depressions (Rickels et al., 1987), my own clinical experience is that more severe depressions are refractory to alprazolam's antidepressant effect. Doses of alprazolam used to treat depression are the same as those prescribed for panic disorder. No other benzodiazepine has been shown to share alprazolam's antidepressant effect, although the majority have not been tested.

Many benzodiazepines are also prescribed as an adjunct to antidepressants in the treatment of acute depression. When used in this way, they should be thought of as simply helping to calm the anxiety and agitation of acute depression and not as medications with any primary antidepressant effect. Similarly, benzodiazepines are occasionally used adjunctively to antipsychotics in the treatment of acute schizophrenic episodes. This should not be confused with a primary antipsychotic effect which the benzodiazepines do not have.

Acute mania can be effectively controlled by benzodiazepines. Most of the research and clinical experience has centered on clonazepam, which is the most sedating medication of its type (Chouinard, 1988). Lorazepam has also been used with some success. Whether the antimanic efficacy of these two benzodiazepines extends to all medication of this class is unknown. There is no good evidence that benzodiazepines are effective by themselves as a preventive treatment in bipolar mood disorders.

Benzodiazepines are also prescribed in the acute detoxification from alcohol (Kranzler and Orrok, 1989). They will successfully diminish the acute withdrawal syndrome (including grand mal seizures) which can be severe at times and even, on rare occasions, life threatening. The two oldest medications of this class—chlordiazepoxide and diazepam—are the most commonly used for this purpose.

## Biologic Effects

As so often happens in pharmacology, the discovery of the benzodiazepines' clinical effects preceded the first clue as to their mechanism of action by many years—seventeen, to be exact. The modern understanding of these medications began in 1977 with the discovery of a specific receptor site on the surface of neurons to which all benzodiazepines seemed to specifically bind—in other words, a benzodiazepine receptor (Mohler and Okada, 1977; Squires and Braestrup, 1977). That a group of related medications all shared a clinical and biological effect—in this case, decreasing anxiety and binding to a specific type of receptor—does not necessarily indicate a causal link between these two findings. This is analogous to the link between dopamine blocking and antipsychotic effects (see chapter 12). Just as was demonstrated for antipsychotics, it was also discovered that the clinical potency of a benzodiazepine correlates highly with how tightly the medication binds to the receptor site. As an example, alprazolam, which is clinically effective in 1 mg doses, binds to the benzodiazepine receptor far more tightly than does diazepam, which is clinically effective in 10 mg doses. Furthermore, if the benzodiazepine receptor is blocked, benzodiazepines are no longer effective. Collectively, this was good evidence that the benzodiazepine receptor was the site mediating the medications' clinical effects.

The next link in the chain of understanding was the discovery that benzodiazepines enhanced the activity of GABA (gamma-aminobutyric acid), a widespread neurotransmitter in the brain that primarily exerts an inhibitory effect on neurotransmission (Tallman, Thomas, and Gallagher, 1978). Further research demonstrated that both benzodiazepine and GABA receptors are parts of the same structure, called a "supramolecular receptor complex" which is composed of the two receptor sites and a channel through which electrically charged particles flow, in this case, chloride (Paul, Marangos, and Skolnick 1981). Figure 11–1 shows this schematically. The effect of chloride flow is to change the electrical charge across the cell membrane, therby making it more refractory to excitatory impulses—in other words to decrease neurotransmission. Thus, any chemical that increases chloride flow into the cell inhibits neurotransmission and "slows things down." Benzodiazepines do not affect chloride flow directly; only through their effects on GABA can they significantly affect the cell's electrical activity. This indirect path through which the benzodiazepines affect chloride ion flow may explain why overdoses with these medications are never lethal. In contrast, barbiturates, which seem to affect chloride flow directly, even in the absence of GABA, are extremely lethal in overdose (Skolnick, Moncada, Barker, and Paul, 1981).

Benzodiazepines also have multiple effects beyond those seen in decreasing anxiety. These diverse actions are probably mediated at the different sites at which benzodiazepine receptors are found. For instance, the benzodiazepines decrease grand mal seizures by their effects on receptors in the cortex, the area controlling motor movements; their ability to cause muscle relaxation (they are commonly used for back spasms and are probably the best muscle relaxants

**Figure 11–1** Benzodiazepine Receptor

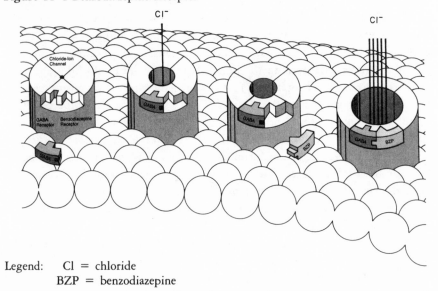

Legend:    Cl = chloride
           BZP = benzodiazepine

From S. Paul (1987), *The Biochemical Basis of Anxiety*, Upjohn, Kalamazoo, Mich. Reprinted with permission of The Upjohn Company.

available) is due to their effects on spinal cord neurons. Their capacity to decrease anxiety probably occurs in the limbic system, the part of the brain that is primarily involved with regulation of emotions (see chapter 2) (Paul, 1985).

Why would receptor sites exist that seem so specifically linked to a synthesized class of medications first released in the 1960s? It hardly seems likely that these receptors were the product of a thoughtful Creator who anticipated the synthesis of Valium! What is more plausible, of course, is that the benzodiazepine receptor site is the target of a naturally occurring antianxiety agent—an endogenous Valium, as it were. Thus far, this putative natural tranquilizer has yet to be discovered and synthesized. The search for this compound, however, is analogous to the recent discovery of the endorphins, the group of naturally occurring analgesics whose effects are mimicked by opiates, such as morphine.

The discovery of a number of compounds that affect anxiety and alter the effects of benzodiazepines has further clarified how these receptors work. Beta-carbolines are chemicals which, when given to animals (and, in a very few experiments, humans), cause agitation, fright, and anxiety. Administering these compounds, which also bind to benzodiazepine receptors, will block or reverse the effect of benzodiazepines. It is as if beta-carbolines produced the exact opposite effects of benzodiazepines. For this reason, they are called "inverse agonists" (although the term "active antagonists" might be more appropriate) (Insel et al., 1984).

Another group of compounds, called receptor antagonists, seem to bind to benzodiazepine receptors but have no intrinsic effect on anxiety or agitation at all. However, they will reverse both the antianxiety effects of benzodiazepines as well as the anxiety-producing effects of the beta-carbolines (Costa, 1985). The most likely explanation, as shown in Figure 11–2, is that these antagonists "fill" the receptor sites, thereby preventing the effect of any active compounds, but not causing any changes themselves.

Thus far, the types of anxiety models utilized in the research on benzodiazepine receptors are most analogous to situational or generalized anxiety. How benzodiazepines effectively treat panic disorder is not as well understood. They may work by increasing the effects of GABA, which inhibits activity at the locus ceruleus, the area thought to be centrally involved in panic attacks (see chapter 2 for details). Alternatively, since there are neural connections between the limbic system (in which benzodiazepine receptors are found in high concentrations) and the locus ceruleus, benzodiazepines' antipanic effects may be best explained as indirect (Gorman, Liebowitz, Fyer, and Stein, 1989).

Alprazolam's seemingly specific effect in treating depression is also not well understood. The slight difference in chemical structure between alprazolam and the other benzodiazepines may be one explanation. There is also some evidence that alprazolam has an effect on some aspects of brain adrenergic function

**Figure 11–2** Benzodiazepine Receptor Agonist and Antagonist

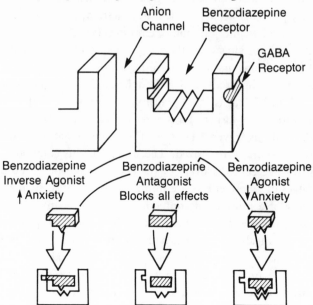

Adapted from T. R. Insel et al. (1984), *Archives of General Psychiatry*, 41, 741–750.
Reprinted with permission.

similar to that of the cyclic antidepressants (Fawcett, Edwards, Kravitz, and Jeffriess, 1987). Before this issue can be further clarified, however, we must await the evaluation of the other benzodiazepines as antidepressants.

## Choosing a Benzodiazepine

The twelve benzodiazepines available for oral use are all equally effective in decreasing arousal and anxiety and in helping to diminish insomnia. Table 11–2 lists the currently available benzodiazepines and their general dosage ranges. One additional benzodiazepine, midazolam (Versed), will not be considered further here since it is administered only intravenously as an anesthetic aid prior to surgery.

As with the antipsychotics, it is possible to classify the benzodiazepines into subgroups based on their chemical structure. In general clinical use, these subclassifications are not helpful. The important distinctions among the benzodiazepines that are well understood are how quickly they act and how long they last. Table 11–3 classifies the medications according to these criteria. Aside from these two known ways in which the benzodiazepines differ, a number of other factors are sometimes relevant in a psychopharmacologist's

TABLE 11–2

*Benzodiazepines*

| Generic Name | Trade Name | Usual Dosage Range (mg/day) |
|---|---|---|
| Alprazolam | Xanax | 0.5–4 |
| Chlordiazepoxide[a] | Librium | 10–100 |
| Clonazepam | Klonopin | 0.5–3 |
| Clorazepate | Tranxene | 7.5–60 |
| Diazepam[a] | Valium | 5–40 |
| Flurazepam | Dalmane | 15–30 |
| Halazepam | Paxipam | 40–160 |
| Lorazepam[a] | Ativan | 1–6 |
| Oxazepam | Serax | 15–90 |
| Prazepam | Centrax | 20–60 |
| Temazepam | Restoril | 15–30 |
| Triazolam | Halcion | 0.125–0.5 |

[a] Available in injectable form

choice of one agent over another. These are the patient's potential for addiction, the drug's rate of redistribution from the brain to the rest of the body (see below), and the individual patient's past experience with these medications.

Speed of onset of action is sometimes, but not always, an important consideration. For instance, if the medication is prescribed to treat insomnia, it is relevant whether the problem occurs nightly (and can therefore be anticipated and treated preventively) or intermittently and unpredictably. In treating a symptom occurring occasionally, such as difficulty falling asleep, a rapid-to-intermediate-acting medication like flurazepam is preferable so that after taking the sleeping pill, the patient doesn't stare at the ceiling for an hour or more, waiting for the medication to work. If the symptom is predictable, either slow- or fast-acting medications can be equally effective simply by taking the slower-acting pill earlier. Of course, in real life, it is easier for patients to take a sleeping pill a half hour before bedtime than one and a half hours before, at which time they may be away from home or unsure of when they will want to go to sleep.

An identical set of considerations applies in treating anxiety. The need for an occasional tranquilizer in times of particular stress suggests using a rapidly acting medication like diazepam. For the treatment of an ongoing anxiety state for a few weeks or longer in which the patient is taking a maintenance dose on a daily basis, speed of action is not important. In fact, more rapidly acting benzodiazepines may be at a disadvantage in these situations because they may produce more of the "rush" of sleepiness or spaciness that occurs at the peak of

TABLE 11–3

*Characteristics of Benzodiazepines*

| Generic Name (Trade Name) | Rapidity of Effect | Half-life (Rate of Elimination) |
|---|---|---|
| Alprazolam (Xanax) | Intermediate | Intermediate |
| Chlordiazepoxide (Librium) | Intermediate | Long |
| Clonazepam (Klonopin) | Intermediate | Intermediate–long |
| Clorazepate (Tranxene) | Rapid | Long |
| Diazepam (Valium) | Rapid | Long |
| Flurazepam (Dalmane) | Intermediate | Long |
| Halazepam (Paxipam) | Slow | Long |
| Lorazepam (Ativan) | Intermediate | Intermediate |
| Oxazepam (Serax) | Intermediate–slow | Intermediate |
| Prazepam (Centrax) | Slow | Long |
| Temazepam (Restoril) | Intermediate | Intermediate |
| Triazolam (Halcion) | Intermediate | Short |

the medication's effects. A slowly acting medication such as prazepam, therefore, might be preferable in treating ongoing anxiety, especially for those patients who are sensitive to the initial sedation of the benzodiazepines.

Rate of elimination from the body is the other major way in which the benzodiazepines differ. This property is commonly referred to as the half-life and is defined as the amount of time it takes for the blood level of the medication to decrease by half. The goal of the treatment will, in large part, determine the importance of the half-life. In treating insomnia, if the problem is in initiating sleep and the patient tends to be sensitive to side effects, a benzodiazepine that lasts a relatively short to intermediate length of time, such as triazolam or oxazepam might be preferable. Similarly, if the problem to be treated is anxiety around a short-lived situation such as a plane ride or in anticipation of an anxiety-provoking meeting, the use of short- or intermediate-acting benzodiazepines such as lorazepam or alprazolam would be preferable to longer-acting compounds such as clorazepate. But in treating ongoing anxiety lasting a few weeks or more, giving patients short-acting medications that may wear off within four to six hours will necessitate their taking a pill three or four times a day with the possibility of anxiety symptoms between doses. In these situations, the longer-acting benzodiazepines such as diazepam might be preferable. However, a potential disadvantage of using long-acting medication for an extended period of time—two weeks or longer—is that the blood levels of these medications gradually accumulate over time such that the level of diazepam in the bloodstream after three weeks of taking 20 mg daily is far higher than after three days on the same dose. For some patients, especially the elderly, this may predispose to greater somnolence and other side effects.

The half-life of the medication is also important in predicting possible withdrawal symptoms. (See below for an extended discussion of this topic.) By definition, the longer the half-life, the more gradually the drug will disappear from the body. With the long half-life benzodiazepines such as diazepam or clorazepate, this means a smaller chance of significant withdrawal symptoms because the medication "tapers itself" over many days. As will be discussed below, even with long-acting benzodiazepines, gradual tapering of the dose is frequently needed. With short or intermediate half-life drugs, such as alprazolam or triazolam, the quick drop in blood levels after a patient stops the medication is almost a guarantee of withdrawal symptoms unless the dose is decreased slowly. Since withdrawal symptoms reinforce the sense of needing medication both psychologically and biologically, their intensity is inherently linked with the addictive potential of any drug. Short half-life benzodiazepines, therefore, should be prescribed with greater caution to patients with potential addiction problems, especially to sedative-type drugs.

The considerations just noted, however, do not always fit with clinical experience. Other factors, some of which are still not well understood, also affect pharmacological activity. As an example, the effects of single doses of diazepam (Valium) do not necessarily continue for two to three days as one might expect from its half-life. The reason for this is that a major determinant of a benzodiazepine's clinical activity is not how much of the medication is in the body, but the amount of time it stays in the brain and available to the benzodiazepine receptors. A single dose of a medication that reaches the brain quickly—but leaves the brain quickly too—will have a clinically short duration of action even though it may stay in the fat and other body tissues for a long time thereafter (and be defined as having a long half-life). Diazepam, as an example of such a drug, is absorbed quickly and gets to the brain quickly, thus explaining its rapid onset of effect. But because it also then disappears from the brain rapidly, via distribution to other body tissues, its clinical effects diminish even though its tissue levels remain substantial (Greenblatt and Shader, 1987).

Another important clinical consideration is that of tolerance. As discussed above, all benzodiazepines are both sedating (making the person sleepy) and tranquilizing (decreasing anxiety). With ongoing use of a benzodiazepine, tolerance develops more to the sedation than to the tranquilizing effect (Lucki, Rickels, and Geller, 1985). Thus, a medication that is effective but too sedating initially can, after days to weeks, continue to be effective with virtually no side effects. The development of tolerance explains why benzodiazepines that are slowly eliminated don't always show increasing side effects as the blood levels gradually increase over weeks of continual use. Even as the amount of the drug in the body increases, tolerance develops simultaneously, generally causing a decrease in side effects.

Despite all these considerations—rate of absorption, half-life, the shifting from brain to the rest of the body, the development of tolerance—in the final analysis, the benzodiazepines are more similar than different. How then should physicians in general, or psychiatrists pick a specific benzodiazepine for a particular patient? As with so many other medication choices, a patient's past experience with a particular drug should still be the most important determinant. If a patient has no prior experience with benzodiazepines, most psychopharmacologists will prescribe any one of three to five specific medications—usually one or two short half-life drugs and two or three of the longer-acting variety. I generally prescribe alprazolam and lorazepam as the former and diazepam, flurazepam, and clonazepam as the latter, but one could easily substitute others with equal likelihood of a good effect.

### Techniques for Prescribing

In treating intermittent anxiety, doses such as diazepam 5 mg, lorazepam 1 mg, or alprazolam 0.5 mg are generally effective, although individual sensitivities may necessitate slightly higher or lower doses. For insomnia, typical doses are flurazepam 15 to 30 mg, temazepam 15 to 30 mg, or triazolam 0.125 to 0.25 mg. Rapidly acting benzodiazepines (see Table 11–3) such as diazepam should be taken approximately 15 to 20 minutes before the desired effect. For intermediate drugs, 30 to 40 minutes are appropriate, while an hour may be needed for slow-acting medications like prazepam.

If benzodiazepines are being prescribed to decrease anxiety around the clock for days to weeks, most psychopharmacologists will start with a low dose and gradually increase over a number of weeks if needed. Typical initial doses would be diazepam 5 to 10 mg, lorazepam 1 to 2 mg, or alprazolam 0.5 to 1 mg.

Doses should be increased by the equivalent of 5 mg of diazepam every four to five days if needed.

It makes sense to start all patients on a divided-dose regimen at the beginning of treatment, regardless of which benzodiazepine is being prescribed, in order to decrease the acute sedation that is typically seen one to two hours after taking the medication. When benzodiazepines with short or intermediate half-life are prescribed, they should always be given in divided doses. Alprazolam, as a typical example, is generally taken three or even four times daily. Even with such short intervals between doses, many patients experience symptoms just before the next pill as a type of miniwithdrawal symptom (see below). Long half-life medications may be given once or twice daily with good effect.

Average effective antianxiety doses are 20 to 25 mg of diazepam or its equivalent. A patient's response in the first week of treatment is a good predictor of ultimate response (Downing and Rickels, 1987). Maximum improvement from the medication is generally seen within the first six weeks of treatment (Rickels, Case, and Downing, 1982). As noted above, tolerance to the tranquilizing effects—as opposed to the sedating effects—of the benzodiazepines is not common.

When an anxious patient does not respond to reasonable doses of a benzodiazepine, should the psychopharmacologist raise the dose further? If no side effects are evident and the patient is likely to respond—for example, when the medication is being prescribed for a short-lived stress-precipitated anxiety state—the answer is yes. Increased responses above diazepam 40 mg or alprazolam 4 mg daily for treating generalized anxiety are, however, unusual. For refractory cases, it would be helpful if benzodiazepine blood levels were available, analogous to those used for the cyclic antidepressants. Unfortunately, they are not. If a therapeutic trial of one benzodiazepine is cut short by side effects, switching to another may be helpful. For instance, significant sedation soon after taking a dose of medication may be solved by switching to another benzodiazepine which is absorbed more slowly.

When treating panic disorder with benzodiazepines, the doses utilized tend to be higher than for anxiety. Since the bulk of the research experience has been with alprazolam, its antipanic dose is reasonably well established at 2 to 6 mg daily with initial doses generally 0.5 mg three times daily (Fyer and Sandberg, 1988). My own experience, though, is that many panic patients respond at 1 to 2 mg daily. At any dose, the medication must be given multiple times during the day. Occasionally, much higher doses—up to 10 mg daily or more—are prescribed to treat panic. Initial and usual doses when alprazolam is prescribed to treat depression are the same as those for panic.

When clonazepam is used to treat acute mania, the doses prescribed range from moderate to prodigious—2 to 6 mg daily are common and 10 mg or more are used with regularity. Whether these high doses are more effective than moderate doses or reflect the pressure to do something to diminish the manic symptoms is unknown.

### Benzodiazepine Withdrawal

The controversy surrounding the problem of withdrawing patients from benzodiazepines makes this an appropriate topic for discussion midway between techniques for prescribing and side effects since it encompasses both subjects. Therapist and psychopharmacologist alike must be aware of the realistic problems as well as the unwarranted publicity surrounding the discontinuation of benzodiazepines. Soon after the benzodiazepines were released, the first report of significant withdrawal symptoms appeared (Hollister, Motzenbecker, and Degan, 1961). Because that study utilized doses far in excess of what is usually prescribed, withdrawal symptoms from typical doses were initially thought to be unusual. Assuredly, the issue was underappreciated. Over the last decade, there has been increased attention on the problem because of publicity in the lay press, the increasing use of shorter-acting benzodiazepines (with the likelihood of more intense withdrawal symptoms), and a series of excellent studies that carefully examined the topic.

Many patients taking benzodiazepines for any significant period of time will suffer withdrawal symptoms soon after stopping the medication. Before the seriousness of the problem can be evaluated, however, there are four important issues to be considered. First, withdrawal symptoms and the return of the anxiety symptoms for which the medication was initially prescribed need to be distinguished—which is not always easy. Typically, it is thought that rapid-onset symptoms occurring within the first week after stopping the medication are due to withdrawal, whereas underlying anxiety emerges more gradually over a number of weeks. Not all patients (nor many physicians or therapists) necessarily know this, however, and overlap or confusion between the two conditions is common. Second, the effect of psychological dependence, especially given the high incidence of dependent personality in anxious patients, may magnify potential physical withdrawal symptoms. Third, it is important to distinguish mild withdrawal symptoms that may be no worse than one to three days of insomnia and irritability from more significant symptoms that are more disruptive. Finally, how the medication is withdrawn has an enormous impact on the difficulties the patient experiences. In most withdrawal studies, the benzodiazepine is stopped abruptly. Yet it is clear from everyday clinical experience (mine included) and the few studies that have examined the issue that tapering a benzodiazepine will eliminate or diminish much of the withdrawal syndrome, regardless of the original reasons for its use (Noyes, Garvey, Cook, and Perry, 1988). There is virtually no clinical reason to abruptly stop a benzodiazepine. Patients, though, sometimes feel that the best way to stop using a drug is simply to go cold turkey. The resulting discomfort is preventable if patient, therapist, and psychopharmacologist discuss these issues beforehand. In summary, to acknowledge that benzodiazepines can cause withdrawal symptoms is not tantamount to saying they are dangerous or that the psychopharmacologist, patient, or therapist is helpless if the medication should be stopped.

What common symptoms are seen when benzodiazepines are suddenly withdrawn? Table 11–4 lists them. As is obvious, the list comprises a group of typical anxiety symptoms, both psychological and somatic, and some atypical sensory phenomena such as depersonalization, heightened sensitivity to sound, touch, or light, and perceptual distortions. Since these symptoms are sometimes seen in anxious patients before treatment, it is still not clear whether any of these are specific to withdrawal. There are sporadic reports of depression, paranoia, or in the most extreme and unusual cases, seizures. Fortunately, these

TABLE 11–4

*Possible Symptoms of Benzodiazepine Withdrawal*

Psychological:
    Anxiety
    Agitation
    Irritability
    Depressed mood
    Poor concentration, forgetfulness
Physical:
    Tremor
    Insomnia
    Loss of appetite
    Nausea, vomiting
    Sweating
    Tachycardia (fast heart rate)
Sensory:
    Depersonalization, derealization
    Hypersensitivity to light and/or sound
    Paresthesias (tingling)
Rare:
    Paranoia
    Severe depression
    Delirium/psychosis
    Grand mal seizures

are exceedingly rare. When they do occur, they are more likely with the more short-acting benzodiazepines such as alprazolam.

The time course of the withdrawal symptoms reflects the half-life of the benzodiazepine used. With long half-life drugs, the symptoms begin after twenty-four hours, peak after four days, and disappear by the third week (Rickels, Schweizer, Csanalosi, Case, and Chung, 1988). Withdrawal from short half-life drugs, on the other hand, can cause symptoms by the end of the first day and peak on the second or third day (Busto et al, 1986). Triazolam, the shortest-acting of the benzodiazepines, may show rebound symptoms within twelve hours after drug discontinuation. There are even some reports of rebound insomnia towards early morning when triazolam is taken in the beginning of the night (Kales, Soldatos, Bixter, and Kales, 1983).

It is difficult to predict the likelihood of withdrawal reactions from benzodiazepines. Estimates from various studies have ranged from 0 to 100 percent (!), reflecting both the varied definitions of withdrawal and the presence of risk factors that will affect the likelihood of these symptoms (Noyes et al., 1988). Table 11–5 shows these risk factors. The most well-documented of these predictors are taking the medication for a longer time, short half-life of the drug, and abrupt discontinuation (as opposed to tapering).

Rebound insomnia can be seen as soon as after six nights of continuous use of relatively high dose (0.5 mg) triazolam which is then abruptly discontinued (Greenblatt, Harmatz, Zinny, and Shader, 1987). These quickly occurring withdrawal effects, however, consist of no more than one or two nights of difficulty falling asleep and can be prevented by tapering the dose even over four nights. For longer half-life drugs, rebound insomnia is typically seen three to four nights after the medication is withdrawn (Gillin, Spinweber, and Johnson, 1989).

The other risk factors listed in Table 11–5 are less well established. Those

TABLE 11–5

*Factors Predicting Benzodiazepine Withdrawal Symptoms*

Medication predictors:
    Longer time on drug[a]
    Short half-life[a]
    Abrupt withdrawal[a] (vs. tapering)
    High dose
Patient predictors:
    History of alcohol or drug (especially sedative) abuse
    Personality factors—dependency and passivity traits
    Panic disorder
    Past experience with benzodiazepines

[a] Most well established

with histories of drug or alcohol abuse may be at higher risk to abuse benzo-diazepines and therefore also to have difficulties withdrawing from them (Ciraulo et al., 1988). High doses are a logical risk factor although this has rarely been studied. Clinical observations, including my own, have noted marked difficulties in withdrawing patients with panic disorder from alprazolam (Fyer et al., 1987). Patients with dependent traits have been noted to experience more severe withdrawal symptoms (Rickels, Schweizer, Case, and Garcia-Espana, 1988). Of course, this may simply reflect the fact that these patients have fewer coping skills and are intolerant of and afraid of any change in the way they feel. Finally, patients' past experience with benzodiazepines may sensitize them in some way such that withdrawal symptoms after subsequent use are more likely (Rickels et al., 1988).

Although it may sound as if discontinuing benzodiazepines is fraught with difficulties, for the majority of patients who do it *correctly* and with appropriate support and advice, it is not a major life trauma. Most important, educating and reassuring patients will help make the withdrawal much easier. Patients must know that the therapist and psychopharmacologist will work with them during the withdrawal period. They should anticipate that some anxiety or insomnia may be transiently experienced. It must be made clear that the speed of the tapering of the medication (since the benzodiazepines should *always* be tapered after any significant period of use) can always be slowed down if significant symptoms arise. Occasional doses of as-needed medication during the course of withdrawal should be allowed and not seen as a failure of will or character. With some patients, four to six months is not an excessively long time to gradually taper benzodiazepines. Most importantly, the speed of the taper should be slow or slower.

Sometimes, no speed of tapering a short-acting benzodiazepine is effective in controlling withdrawal symptoms. In these cases, a few strategies available to the psychopharmacologist can be very helpful. The most common of these is switching to a long-acting benzodiazepine. The most popular of these switches is from alprazolam to clonazepam (Herman, Brotman, and Rosenbaum, 1987). This can be done over a few days to weeks since there is cross-tolerance between benzodiazepines (i.e., using one medication will prevent withdrawal symptoms of the other because they affect the same receptors in the brain). It is then much easier to taper the long-acting medication since the blood levels fluctuate much less within the course of a day and decrease so slowly over days. I have found this method helpful. However, because it is often difficult to ascertain the correct equivalent dose of the longer-acting medication for any individual, the cross-over time (typically no more than a few days) is often characterized by transient withdrawal or sedation symptoms. There is also preliminary evidence that, for unclear reasons, carbamazepine (Tegretol) can diminish benzodiazepine withdrawal symptoms (Ries, Roy-Byrne, Ward, Neppe, and Cullison, 1989). Because buspirone (see below) is not a benzodiazepine, it is not useful in diminishing withdrawal symptoms.

> Linda's panic disorder had been successfully treated with alprazolam 1 mg three times daily. She experienced mild anxiety symptoms five hours after each medication dose until she took her next pill, but was otherwise symptom-free. Seven months later, a slow tapering of the medication was begun. Initially, she did well with the lower dose, eventually decreasing to 0.5 mg three times daily. At that point, lowering the dose, even at a rate of 0.125 mg every week, seemed to cause withdrawal symptoms. After three unsuccessful attempts to decrease the dose below 1.5 mg daily, alprazolam was switched to clonazepam over one week. During that time, Linda was alternately anxious and slightly sedated as the dose of the new medication was adjusted while the alprazolam was discontinued. After one week, however, Linda was taking 1.5 mg of clonazepam twice daily and experiencing no anxiety symptoms between doses. Over the next three months, clonazepam was decreased at a rate of 0.25 mg weekly until it was discontinued without the return of anxiety.

## Other Side Effects

Table 11–6 lists the common side effects seen with the benzodiazepines. Almost all of these relate to aspects of central nervous system depression. The most frequently observed of these is sedation to which there is significant accommo-

TABLE 11–6

*Side Effects of Benzodiazepines*

| |
|---|
| Common: |
|   Sedation |
|   Fatigue |
|   Ataxia (poor balance) |
|   Slurred speech |
|   Memory disturbances |
|   Psychomotor impairment |
| Rare: |
|   Intoxication |
|   Aggressive behavior |
|   Mania (with alprazolam) |

dation over the first few days to weeks of treatment. Despite this, sedation is the side effect that most limits the use of higher doses of benzodiazepines. The extent of the cognitive and psychomotor effects with these medications is somewhat controversial.

Unquestionably, benzodiazepines can limit the ability to learn and recall new information, especially around the time of peak sedation, which is typically one to two hours after ingestion (Greenblatt, Harmatz, Engelhardt, and Shader, 1989). Yet patients who use benzodiazepines chronically (for many months or years) generally show no cognitive deficits except if tested during the one hour of peak sedation, implying that tolerance to the sedation may be linked to tolerance to cognitive side effects (Lucki and Rickels, 1986). Triazolam may cause greater memory impairment, including episodes of true amnesia, than other benzodiazepines (Scharf, Fletcher, and Graham, 1988). This may be due to a specific effect of triazolam beyond the sedation that is produced during its peak action.

Soon after starting benzodiazepines, most patients will show diminished psychomotor skills (Taylor and Tinklenberg, 1987). The clinical importance of these effects is difficult to gauge, but the usual warnings to patients about driving a car or operating dangerous machinery are entirely appropriate. The evidence that these deficits persist with chronic use is mixed. When benzodiazepines are taken along with alcohol, sedation, cognitive, and psychomotor side effects are enhanced in an additive manner. Thus, one drink may feel like two (or one Xanax may feel like two) but no explosive potentiating effects (such as one drink feeling like six) occur.

Intoxication, aggressive behavior, and mania are unusual side effects that occur, albeit infrequently, with benzodiazepines. Intoxication is dose-related and should be understood in a manner similar to alcohol intoxication: a little bit will sedate, a lot will intoxicate. The presence of intoxication is a clear indication that the dose is too high and must be lowered immediately. Aggressive behavior or disinhibition has long been described as an occasional side effect of benzodiazepines. It is far less common than is supposed, probably occurring in less than 1 percent of patients treated with benzodiazepines (Dietch and Jennings, 1988). The evidence that it occurs more with one medication than another is unconvincing. Alprazolam may specifically precipitate manic episodes (Noyes et al., 1988). It is unclear whether this is related to alprazolam's allegedly specific effect of alleviating depression. Finally, benzodiazepines can precipitate a depressive syndrome in a subset of treated patients.

Given these observations, how should the issue of benzodiazepine use be handled? More important for the readers of this book, how should therapists help counsel their patients on this issue? Because the majority of benzodiazepine prescriptions are written by primary care physicians, not psychiatrists, the therapist may be the only mental health professional involved. First, despite the potential withdrawal problems noted above, among all the psychotropic medications in current use, benzodiazepines are unquestionably the safest. Therefore, patients can be reassured that, especially with the older longer-acting brands, the evidence for safety and lack of tolerance, even over years, is impressive. Second, if the benzodiazepines should be discontinued, the recommendations above will aid enormously in making this a relatively benign experience for all involved. If the primary care physician who has prescribed the medication is not familiar with the issues of benzodiazepine withdrawal, obtaining consultation with a psychopharmacologist experienced in these matters may be helpful. Third, since both anxiety and insomnia wax and wane in intensity over time, a patient's need for a benzodiazepine will also vary. Thus, if someone can not stop the medication at one time, it is worth retrying at another time.

## BUSPIRONE

The newest antianxiety medication, buspirone (Buspar), is completely unrelated to all previous tranquilizers, including the benzodiazepines, and represents the first new type of antianxiety agent released in twenty-five years. Originally, it was investigated as a possible antipsychotic because of its effects on dopamine, but it proved ineffective in treating schizophrenia. Further investigation revealed its antianxiety properties.

Clinically, the only current use for buspirone is in treating generalized anxiety disorder. In most, but not all of the initial studies, buspirone was as effective as benzodiazepines in decreasing anxiety (Rickels and Schweizer, 1987). Anxious patients previously treated with benzodiazepines may be less likely to respond to buspirone (Olajide and Lader, 1987). Buspirone's onset of action is slightly slower than that of the benzodiazepines, although positive effects are often seen by the end of the first week.

In contrast to the benzodiazepines, buspirone is ineffective when taken on an occasional basis and is virtually nonsedating. The advantage to this, of course, is that patients taking buspirone rarely complain of feeling drugged or "spacy" in the way they often do with benzodiazepines. The drawback is that buspirone cannot be used to treat acute situational anxiety (no one carries a Buspar in his pocket in case of a stressful day!) or insomnia. There is no substantial evidence that it is helpful in other anxiety disorders, such as panic disorder, obsessive compulsive disorder, or social phobia.

Buspirone's mechanism of action is unknown. It does not significantly affect either GABA, the inhibitory neurotransmitter, or the benzodiazepine receptor site, implying that buspirone's ability to decrease anxiety is mediated through a unique action on neurotransmitters. Its major biologic effects are on dopamine and serotonin. Buspirone shows evidence of both increasing and decreasing dopamine activity while decreasing some aspects of serotonin function in certain parts of the central nervous system (Riblet et al., 1984). Whether these biological effects are central to the medication's capacity to decrease anxiety is unknown.

Starting doses of buspirone are 5 mg twice daily, with increases of 5 mg approximately every four days. Average daily doses are 20 to 25 mg, although some patients will do best on 60 mg daily. Buspirone should always be given in at least two or three divided doses, since it has a short half-life and because of increased side effects one to two hours after the ingestion of a large single dose.

As noted in chapter 4, however, there is increasing clinical evidence over the last few years, both from the ongoing experience of psychopharmacologists (including myself) and from some recent studies (Rickels, Schweizer, Csanalosi, et al., 1988), that patients do not find buspirone to be as effective in decreasing anxiety as the early studies suggested. Why then is there so much interest in this drug? The answer lies in its side effect profile: the problems it doesn't cause that benzodiazepines do. More than any other single factor, the key attraction of buspirone is that it has no potential for addiction or dependence. Because buspirone lacks an immediate clinical effect, it also has little or no intrinsic reinforcing properties and is therefore at very low risk for abuse. This suggests its use with anxious alcoholics for whom the risk of benzodiazepine dependence is high.

Buspirone also causes no withdrawal syndrome, even when discontinued abruptly after months of continual treatment (Rickels et al., 1988). Because it is not sedating to any significant degree, buspirone does not cause any decrease in either cognitive or psychomotor skills, which may translate clinically into fewer problems while learning new information and greater safety when driving a car. Moreover, in contrast to the benzodiazepines, it does not show additive sedating or discoordinating effects when taken with alcohol. Thus, one alcoholic drink with buspirone feels like one alcoholic drink.

The most common side effects of buspirone are nausea, dizziness, and occasional headaches. Side effects seem worst one to two hours after taking the medication and then generally subside. As a rule, though, buspirone is extremely well tolerated. There have been occasional reports of buspirone causing extrapyramidal symptoms akin to those caused by antipsychotics and explainable by its effects on dopamine (Patterson, 1988). It remains to be seen whether this will be a common problem. Because of the clinical similarity between akathisia (the motor restlessness associated with antipsychotics) as a side effect and anxiety as a symptom, therapists and psychopharmacologists should be alert for the occasional patient who may complain of buspirone increasing anxiety as an akathisia-like side effect.

## NONBARBITURATE SEDATIVES AND HYPNOTICS

Chronologically released midway between the barbiturates and the benzodiazepines were a group of diverse compounds that were commonly prescribed to treat anxiety and insomnia in the late 1950s and 1960s. These medications include meprobamate (Miltown), used primarily as a tranquilizer, and ethchlorvynol (Placidyl), glutethimide (Doriden), methyprylon (Noludar), ethinamate (Valmid), and methaqualone (Quaalude). The latter five were primarily considered hypnotics, although Quaaludes were frequently taken as a recreational drug in the late 1960s and 1970s. (Because of the widespread abuse with Quaaludes, it was withdrawn from the market and is now unavailable in the United States.) Initially, these drugs were thought to be a major advance over the barbiturates in both lack of addictive qualities and safety in overdose. Unfortunately, they were neither to any significant degree. They are addictive, with the capacity to cause severe withdrawal symptoms, and are lethal if taken in overdose. Because of this, once the benzodiazepines were released and became more widely used, the nonbarbiturate sedatives faded in popularity, as they should have. Currently, there is no good reason to prescribe any of these medications as a first-line drug for anxiety or insomnia unless the patient, usually older, has used it safely and effectively without problems in the past. Otherwise, these medications should be left to the history books.

The oldest hypnotic (other than alcohol), available since 1869 and still used with some regularity, is chloral hydrate (Noctec). Because its half-life is relatively short, it has some utility as a sleep-inducing agent in doses of 1 to 2 grams. It is not nearly as safe as many people assume, with the possibility of a lethal overdose if only 5 to 10 times the therapeutic dose is ingested. Chloral hydrate can also produce physical dependence as exemplified by the number of people addicted to it early in the century.

## BARBITURATES

The barbiturate sedatives and hypnotics dominated the treatment of anxiety and insomnia from the early part of this century until twenty-five years ago. There are still some medical and psychiatric uses for the barbiturates. Phenobarbital is commonly prescribed for the treatment of seizure disorders while some short-acting types, such as thiopental (Pentothal) are used as anesthetics. Amobarbital (Amytal) has long been used to help diagnose catatonic states. Patients in catatonic states who are given amobarbital intravenously will often "wake up," respond to questions appropriately, and give information on their thought processes (which often include psychotic experiences.) Once the drug wears off, the patient typically lapses back into catatonia. Thus, the technique is much more helpful diagnostically than therapeutically. Because catatonic states seem to be less common than in the past, this use of barbiturates is now unusual. Similarly, amobarbital is used, albeit rarely, as a "truth serum" to recover repressed memories after traumatic events. As with its use in catatonic states, the medication seems to decrease the frozen state of either repression or cata-tonia by causing short-lived relaxation. The last current use of barbiturates is to sedate an acutely agitated inpatient who is behaviorally dangerous. Even in this way, however, amobarbital has generally been replaced by lorazepam which is similarly effective but safer.

In the treatment of anxiety and insomnia, barbiturates have appropriately fallen into disfavor since the introduction of the benzodiazepines. A number of different barbiturate preparations—amobarbital, butabarbital (Butisol), me-phobarbital (Mebaral), pentobarbital (Nembutal), and secobarbital ( Seconal)—are still available. They are highly addictive, cause severe and potentially fatal withdrawal syndromes, and are easily fatal if taken in overdose. As with the nonbarbiturate sedatives, the only reason they are prescribed at present is for the rare patient who has used them in the past with success and does not need them on a regular basis.

## L-TRYPTOPHAN

Probably the safest sleep-inducing agent available is l-tryptophan, an essential amino acid that is ultimately converted to the neurotransmitter serotonin. Because of its nonprescription status, pharmaceutical firms have had no incen-tive to fund research on l-tryptophan and there are few good studies on its efficacy and safety. It does seem to be an effective hypnotic, generally in doses of 1 to 5 grams, although it may not be quite as effective as the benzodiazepines (Hartmann, 1977). If taken in excessive quantities, it is safe and causes neither physical dependence nor withdrawal symptoms. Its major drawbacks are high cost and large pill size. Unfortunately, l-tryptophan has recently been with-drawn from circulation because it may precipitate toxic reactions, possibly allergic in origin, some of which have resulted in fatalities. It is not yet clear whether these reactions are due to the l-tryptophan itself or to impurities found in some preparations.


## ANTIHISTAMINES


Medications such as hydroxyzine (Atarax or Vistaril) and diphenhydramine (Benadryl) are antihistamines that are primarily used in the treatment of allergic conditions. Because they are also sedating, they are occasionally used as hypnotics or, more rarely, as daytime antianxiety agents. They are more sedating than tranquilizing and not nearly as effective as benzodiazepines. However, they show no capacity to be addictive and are therefore occasionally prescribed for alcoholics for whom the risk of addiction to other tranquilizers is high. Other than drowsiness, the major side effects of the antihistamines are anticholinergic effects such as dry mouth, constipation, urinary hesitation, and possibly confusion if taken in too high a dose, especially by an elderly patient. Some of the over-the-counter sleeping aids contain antihistamines, often in combination with sedating anticholinergic compounds such as scopolamine (Byerley and Gillin, 1984).


## CLONIDINE


Clonidine (Catapres) is used primarily in the treatment of hypertension. However, because its mechanism of action is to decrease the activity of norepinephrine in the central nervous system, it has been investigated in the treatment of a variety of psychiatric conditions. Its most well-documented psychiatric use is in diminishing the withdrawal symptoms from opiates, such as heroin (Bond, 1986). A second established use for clonidine is in the treatment of Tourette's disorder, the childhood syndrome characterized by tics (see chapter 8). It has also been used in the treatment of panic disorder and generalized anxiety with less favorable results. Although it seems to be beneficial for some patients, its therapeutic effects are limited by sedation, hypotension (low blood pressure), fatigue, and the development of tolerance to its antianxiety effects (Uhde et al., 1989). When prescribed, it is started at a dose of 0.1 mg twice daily, increasing every two to four days up to 0.6 to 0.7 mg daily. Higher doses than these are unlikely to yield greater benefit.

## BETA-BLOCKERS

Beta-blockers are a group of medications used in general medicine for a variety of disorders, including angina, hypertension, and migraine headaches, that are also effective psychopharmacological agents. The most commonly prescribed beta-blockers in psychiatry are propranolol (Inderal) and atenolol (Tenormin). With the possible exception of their use in performance anxiety, they are not first-line drugs for psychiatric disorders. Nevertheless, they are often useful.

Three different anxiety disorders are sometimes treated with beta-blockers. For many years, either propranolol or atenolol has been prescribed for performance anxiety (Liebowitz, Gorman, Fyer, and Klein, 1985). Because performance anxiety is both intermittent and predictable, the medication is typically prescribed on an as-needed basis. When used for generalized anxiety, propranolol is less effective than the benzodiazepines and is therefore rarely used as a first-line agent. Propranolol may be more effective in diminishing the physical symptoms of anxiety, such as fast heartbeat and sweaty palms, than the psychological and subjective components. Similarly, propranolol is probably effective for only a small group of patients with panic disorder and far inferior to the other available treatments (Noyes, 1985).

More common is the use of beta-blockers to decrease medication side effects characterized by excessive movement. Tremors induced by lithium and by the more stimulating antidepressants are effectively treated by propranolol on either an as-needed basis or with continual use. Propanolol also successfully decreases akathisia, the motor restlessness caused by antipsychotic agents (Adler et al., 1987). It is prescribed either alone or in combination with anticholinergic medications.

Other less common uses for beta-blockers are in treatment-resistant schizophrenia (typically administered in extraordinarily high doses), aggression (especially in brain-damaged individuals) and, rarely, in alcoholism (Lader, 1988).

The presumed mechanism of action of beta-blockers is by decreasing some of the effects of the neurotransmitter norepinephrine, through blocking the beta-adrenergic receptor. (As noted in chapter 2, each neurotransmitter has a number of types of different receptor sites.) All conditions for which the beta-blockers are helpful are characterized by some degree of heightened arousal, either physical or psychological. What is not clear is whether these medications work in the central nervous system, at the nerve endings throughout the rest of the body, or both.

Doses of the beta-blockers depend on the disorder being treated. For performance anxiety, taking propranolol 20 to 40 mg or atenolol 50 mg one hour before the anxiety-producing event is sufficient. In treating panic or generalized anxiety, propranolol 40 mg is typically prescribed, given in two to four divided doses, gradually increasing by 40 mg every four days up to 160 mg. Doses for treating either lithium-induced tremor or akathisia tend to be lower, typically 20 to 60 mg daily, with half the dose given every twelve hours.

The most common side effects of the beta-blockers are lightheadedness, dizziness, and fatigue (Noyes, 1985). It is generally thought that the sluggishness/fatigue symptoms are more common with beta-blockers that cross into the brain more easily, such as propranolol. Depression has been reported to occur with propranolol, especially at doses over 100 mg daily.

# 12

## Antipsychotics

In 1952, the treatment of schizophrenia shifted course forever when chlorpromazine (Thorazine) was demonstrated to be effective in dramatically decreasing psychotic agitation. Within a few years, it became clear that this medication could significantly decrease psychotic thinking with or without agitation. With these discoveries, the road to transforming what had been a hospital-based disorder into an outpatient disorder with only intermittent hospitalizations was opened. Since then, over a dozen other antipsychotic drugs have been developed and released, all of which are as effective as chlorpromazine for treating psychotic states. Unfortunately, none, with the possible exception of clozapine, has demonstrated greater efficacy than chlorpromazine. Once the initial glow of the antipsychotics waned, it became obvious to clinicians and researchers alike that these medications were simultaneously invaluable and inadequate. Although psychotic symptoms were controlled in the majority of patients, other disabling symptoms of schizophrenia were less affected. In addition, psychotic relapses, although diminished by antipsychotics, still occurred with regularity in treated schizophrenic patients. Furthermore, the emergence of tardive dyskinesia, the potentially irreversible movement disorder caused by the long-term use of antipsychotics was first reported in the late 1950s and has become a source of increasing concern over the last twenty-five years. Now, over thirty-five years after the first antipsychotic was released, the treatment of psychotic states, especially schizophrenia, is difficult to imagine without the antipsychotics. But the limitations of these medications are all too apparent to patients and clinicians alike.

### HISTORY

Prior to 1952, no medications available in Western medicine had any major effect in treating either the profound agitation or the psychotic thinking of

288 THE PSYCHOTHERAPIST'S GUIDE TO PSYCHOPHARMACOLOGY

schizophrenia. (Interestingly, before this time, in India the rauwolfia plant had been successfully used to tranquilize patients suffering from mental disorders. In fact, the word tranquilizer was first used to describe the effect of the active ingredient of rauwolfia, reserpine, later marketed as the first antihypertensive and notable for causing depression in some patients) (Bein, 1970). Before then, insulin coma, cold packs, and electroconvulsive treatment (ECT) were the only treatments available.

Chlorpromazine was first investigated as a potentially sedating and hypothermic (decreasing temperature) medication for use in surgery (Deniker, 1970). Following the documentation of chlorpromazine's efficacy in schizophrenia, a number of similar compounds were released, all of which had similar antipsychotic properties. This was hardly surprising since the new compounds were first synthesized by altering the structure of chlorpromazine slightly and testing for similar effects. Other antipsychotics that were not structurally similar to chlorpromazine were tested because of their similar biological and behavioral effects in animals. Some of these antipsychotics, though, had notably different side effects. As an example, haloperidol, first released in Europe in 1958, was noted to be far less sedating than chlorpromazine but also caused far more Parkinson's disease-like side effects, such as stiffness and restlessness.

Unfortunately, the testing of new compounds based on similarity to older ones in either chemical or clinical effects frequently results in a generation of "me too" drugs that do not offer new approaches in pharmacotherapy. This has been the case in the field of schizophrenia research where the newer antipsychotics have been screened in animal models for their ability to cause dopamine-blocking effects similar to existing medications. The only new antipsychotic that may be genuinely different than all previous ones is clozapine, which was just released in 1990 in the United States. Clozapine represents the first antipsychotic in over thirty years that has truly different chemical and possibly clinical properties.

Other than the development of novel antipsychotics, most of the ongoing research in the pharmacotherapy of schizophrenia has focused on refining the use of current agents. For instance, there is a growing awareness that the doses used over the last decades may have been higher than needed for optimum response. Low-dose strategies and the need for only intermittent medication for some patients have therefore been important topics of investigation. Similarly, with the recognition and increasing concern about tardive dyskinesia as a long-term side effect of antipsychotic medication, another major thrust of research has been to understand the cause of this movement disorder, explore methods of minimizing the risk of its occurrence, and to pursue successful treatments. Unfortunately, no consistently successful treatment has yet been discovered. The search continues.

## CLINICAL USES

The use of the term *antipsychotics* and not *antischizophrenics* correctly suggests these medications' broad pattern of clinical efficacy. (These medications are also called neuroleptics, a word coined by the early French researchers meaning "that which takes the neuron.") They are at least somewhat helpful in treating any disorder in which psychotic thinking is prominent. For schizophrenia, in which the psychotic symptoms are central, neuroleptics are vital. For other disorders in which psychotic thinking plays a lesser role, these medications can be useful but generally in a more adjunctive role. Antipsychotics are also beneficial in some disorders in which overt psychotic thinking is not present. The best example of this is nonpsychotic mania. Presumably, dopamine blocking, as the likely mechanism of the antipsychotics' effectiveness, may be helpful in some nonpsychotic states, possibly by decreasing arousal. Table 12–1 lists the disorders for which antipsychotics are most appropriately prescribed.

Schizophrenia is unquestionably the most important and most common disorder for which antipsychotics are prescribed. In groups of patients, all antipsychotics except clozapine are equally effective in treating schizophrenia, although there are numerous anecdotes of one medication being more effective than the others in a particular individual (Kane, 1986). If preliminary studies are confirmed, however, clozapine may be the first antipsychotic with more efficacy in treating schizophrenia than all other medications (Kane, Honigfield, Singer, Meltzer, and the Clozaril Collaborative Study Group, 1988). The antipsychotics show clear efficacy in both treating an acute schizophrenic episode, causing a marked decrease in psychotic experiences such as delusions and hal-

TABLE 12–1

*Disorders for Which Antipsychotics Are Useful*

| Disorder | Efficacy Rating |
|---|:---:|
| Schizophrenia | + + + |
| Schizoaffective disorder | + + |
| Mania | + + + |
| Psychotic depression | + + |
| Borderline personality disorder | + + |
| Dementia, including Alzheimer's disease | + |
| Tourette's syndrome | + + |
| Drug-induced psychoses | + |

+ + + = Definitive efficacy
+ + = Probably efficacy
+ = Possible efficacy.

lucinations, as well as reducing diffuse and loose thought processes. They are also very effective in decreasing relapse rates of schizophrenia when they are prescribed as a maintenance treatment (Davis, Schaffer, Killian, Kinard, and Chan, 1980). Chapter 5 provides more details on these effects.

Schizoaffective disorder is also commonly treated with antipsychotics (Levitt and Tsuang, 1988). In acute schizoaffective disorder, bipolar type, the antipsychotics may be prescribed alone but frequently are combined with lithium. Schizoaffective disorder, depressed type, is typically treated with antipsychotics in conjunction with antidepressants, although antipsychotics are sometimes prescribed alone. Chlorpromazine (Thorazine) and haloperidol (Haldol) are the most well studied for this disorder although it is likely that all the antipsychotics would be effective.

Acute mania is another condition for which antipsychotics are frequently prescribed. As in treating other disorders, haloperidol and chlorpromazine are the most well studied (Goodwin and Zis, 1979). Haloperidol is probably the most commonly prescribed for mania, in part because of the research evidence, but more because its relative lack of sedation allows higher doses before somnolence becomes a problem. Because of this, acutely manic patients in hospital are frequently treated with astonishingly high doses of haloperidol. Since there is no evidence that very high doses are better than moderate doses, the high doses mostly reflect the need to do something—anything—to diminish the symptoms of an acute frenzied mania.

Warnings abound in the psychiatric literature about the risks of using antipsychotics in the maintenance treatment of bipolar disorder, primarily because of the possibility of tardive dyskinesia. Nonetheless, there are some patients who need maintenance neuroleptics along with a mood stabilizer like lithium for the optimum control of symptoms. Unfortunately, other patients are treated with maintenance antipsychotics without first being tried off the medications following the acute episode. Antipsychotics should be prescribed for maintenance treatment in bipolar disorder only after unsuccessful attempts have been made to discontinue the drug and other treatments have been considered.

Antipsychotics are frequently used to treat psychotic depression (major depressive episode with psychotic features in DSM-III-R) (Spiker et al, 1986). Typically, they are prescribed in combination with an antidepressant since this combination is the most effective pharmacotherapy. Because the risk of tardive dyskinesia is very small during the first six months of antipsychotic treatment, this is not a concern in treating an acute depression.

Over the last decade, a number of studies have demonstrated the efficacy of antipsychotics in treating patients with borderline personality disorder (Soloff, 1987). The majority of these studies show that antipsychotics diminish anxiety, depressed mood, hostility, and the transient psychotic symptoms occasionally seen in these patients. The doses prescribed are significantly lower—typically 20 to 50 percent of the usual dose—compared to those given to overtly psychotic patients with schizophrenia and/or mania. A variety of antipsychotics have been used in these studies, suggesting that all are likely to be equally effective. Anecdotally, the practice of prescribing antipsychotics to borderline patients in crisis has been increasing over the last fifteen years. The antipsychotic is typically prescribed when the patient is experiencing a time of either overwhelming affect, increased behavioral outbursts (such as self-mutilation, suicidal gestures) that are seemingly uncontainable by psychotherapeutic means alone, or when the patient is becoming fragmented under stress. The usual warnings about tardive dyskinesia apply, thereby suggesting the more intermittent short-term use of antipsychotics in these patients.

Demented patients, such as those with Alzheimer's disease, can be helped somewhat by the judicious use of antipsychotic medications (Raskind, Risse, and Lampe, 1987). They are prescribed for two reasons. The first is to diminish the paranoia, delusions, and hallucinations that are sometimes seen in these patients. When used in this way, the antipsychotics, if prescribed carefully and in low dose (and sometimes very low dose), can be helpful. The second reason is to control behavior in an agitated, difficult-to-manage patient. Unfortunately, when the antipsychotics are prescribed for behavioral control, the possibilities exist for therapeutic abuse in the form of using excessive doses that keep the patient very groggy, with the risk of unwanted and unneeded side effects. The antipsychotics have no effect on the core cognitive dysfunction of the disorder or on the progression of the disease.

Antipsychotics are an integral part of the treatment of Tourette's syndrome, a disorder typically arising in childhood and characterized by tics and other involuntary movements as well as obsessive and compulsive symptoms and attention deficit symptoms in some patients. Among the antipsychotics, haloperidol and pimozide (which is rarely prescribed except in Tourette's syndrome) are used almost exclusively (Erenberg, 1988). The doses prescribed are tiny compared to typical antipsychotic doses. Unfortunately, even at low doses, the usefulness of the medications is limited by both side effects and partial responses. Tardive dyskinesia is a risk with long-term use of the medication, especially since Tourette's is probably a lifelong disorder and the treatment needs to be considered in terms of years. The risk is mitigated somewhat by the low doses prescribed and the possibility of intermittent therapy.

Occasionally, antipsychotics are used in the treatment of drug-induced psychoses (Grinspoon and Bakalar, 1986). Most commonly, the medication is prescribed to decrease the psychotic symptoms of acute drug-induced psychosis caused by phencyclidine (PCP), LSD, or amphetamines. If psychopharmacological treatment is needed (and preferentially, the patient should be treated without medications), antipsychotics can be helpful. The nonsedating, low anticholinergic medications, such as haloperidol or fluphenazine are preferable because they will have the fewest side effects that may interact with the effects of the initial drug. There is some controversy about prescribing antipsychotics to treat PCP-induced psychosis, but they are commonly used. Antipsychotics should *not* be used for treatment of withdrawal syndromes from drugs such as benzodiazepines, barbiturates, or alcohol, even though psychotic symptoms may arise.

Finally, antipsychotics are occasionally prescribed in the treatment of profound generalized anxiety. This is not a generally recommended approach, especially since other antianxiety agents that do not cause tardive dyskinesia are available. Additionally, anxious patients become easily psychologically dependent on medication and changing them to another drug may be very difficult.

## BIOLOGIC EFFECTS

The central scientific observation which ultimately led to the dopamine hypothesis of schizophrenia is that all effective antipsychotics decrease the activity of the neurotransmitter dopamine. Furthermore, with the possible exception of clozapine, the antipsychotics all decrease dopamine activity in the same way—by blocking the dopamine receptor (Pickar, 1986). (There are other ways to decrease dopamine activity. For instance, reserpine works by depleting the dopamine stores in the neuron, not by dopamine blockade.) Of course, the truth of these two findings—that all antipsychotics are antidopaminergic and that these medications are effective in decreasing psychosis—does not necessarily imply a causal link between them. This is comparable to the observation that until recently all cyclic antidepressants caused dry mouth; yet the mechanism of this side effect—anticholinergic blockade—is unrelated to the antidepressant effect of the medications. A more impressive piece of evidence suggesting that the dopamine blockade is related to a medication's capacity to decrease psychosis is that the clinical potency of a neuroleptic (i.e., how many milligrams are necessary to cause a clinical effect) is highly correlated with its affinity for the dopamine receptor (which in turn is a measure of how effectively it blocks dopamine) (Creese, Burt, and Snyder, 1976). Thus, a neuroleptic that is weaker in blocking dopamine may require 600 mg to exert a clinical effect whereas a more powerful dopamine blocker may show the same effect with only 5 mg. Clozapine may be the only antipsychotic that is clinically effective out of proportion to its ability to block dopamine. If clozapine is ultimately shown to be the most effective of the antipsychotics, an explanation of its clinical capabilities would need to involve other neurotransmitters and would make our understanding of antipsychotics more complex and probably more accurate.

A problem with explaining the antipsychotics' effects in schizophrenia solely by their capacity to block dopamine is that the blocking occurs quickly yet the clinical response emerges gradually over a number of weeks. This is analogous to a similar flaw in the monoamine hypothesis of depression and the mechanism of action of antidepressants (see chapters 2 and 9).

If antipsychotics are effective in schizophrenia by blocking dopamine, in which parts of the brain that utilize dopamine is this response mediated? Despite the lack of direct evidence, the sites that seem most likely (as reviewed in chapter 2) are the mesolimbic and mesocortical pathways. These two groups of neurons connect the midbrain with areas of the limbic system that are involved with regulation of affect and cortical regions that mediate cognitive problem solving and stress responses, respectively (Weinberger, 1987).

Another way of understanding the clinical capacities of the antipsychotics is to consider their effects on the midbrain itself. Since this area of the brainstem which utilizes dopamine as a neurotransmitter is vital in modulating sensory input and regulating arousal, the effect of a dopamine blocker may be to allow better discrimination between relevant and irrelevant stimuli. This would result in increasing linear thought (and therefore decreasing loose associations and thought disorder) and in decreasing arousal in a general way (and possibly decreasing paranoia.)

The antipsychotics' ability to block dopamine also explains their most characteristic side effects—the extrapyramidal symptoms and tardive dyskinesia. As discussed in chapter 2, one of the areas that utilize dopamine as a neurotransmitter is the nigrostriatal tract—an area that is central in the regulation of movement. It is known, for instance, that Parkinson's disease, which is structurally characterized by destruction of the nigrostriatal dopamine neurons, is characterized by symptoms similar to those seen as side effects of antipsychotics. The best current treatment for Parkinson's disease is 1-dopa which is metabolized into dopamine and substitutes at least partially for the loss of naturally occurring dopamine. Thus, the extrapyramidal symptoms are sometimes correctly called pseudoparkinsonian symptoms or drug-induced Parkinson's symptoms.

Too much activity in this same area can result in the opposite—too much movement. This is exemplified by Huntington's disease, a hereditary disease characterized in its initial stages by increased movements described as choreiform (from the Latin "choreia" referring to a choral dance) as well as dementia and other neurological symptoms, and is caused by the destruction of the neurons that inhibit movement. These neurons contain GABA which is a major inhibitory neurotransmitter within the central nervous system. Without the proper inhibition, exaggerated movements occur.

Other side effects seen with antipsychotics are caused by the effect of these medications on neurotransmitters other than dopamine (Richelson, 1984). All antipsychotics block dopamine and are therefore able to cause dopamine-blocking side effects. Yet haloperidol causes far more akinesia than does chlorpromazine. The explanation for this is found in the relative capacity of each antipsychotic to also block acetylcholine (i.e., to have anticholinergic activity). The regulation of movement as discussed above is best explained by the balance of activity between dopamine and acetylcholine and not by dopamine activity alone. Thus, increasing dopamine or decreasing acetylcholine will result in the same clinical effect. For instance, prior to the discovery of l-dopa, the most common medications used to treat Parkinson's disease were anticholinergic medications (which are still being used today). All antipsychotics block acetylcholine—but each to a different degree. An antipsychotic with low anticholinergic activity, such as fluphenazine, will cause a great many parkinsonian side effects whereas chlorpromazine, with its strong anticholinergic activity, is relatively devoid of these side effects.

The positive effects of the antipsychotics in treating the disorders (other than schizophrenia) listed above can be understood by their ability to decrease psychosis, arousal, and excessive movements. Whether psychosis is present or not, mania is certainly characterized by increased arousal which can be diminished by antipsychotics. Similarly, the capacity of these medications to have beneficial effects with borderline personality patients in times of crisis or fragmentation can be understood as decreased arousal or psychosis or both. Antipsychotics are effective in Tourette's syndrome in large part because of their ability to reduce movements, possibly in the same area that is involved in Huntington's and Parkinson's diseases.

Among the drug-induced psychoses, the effect of the antipsychotics in reducing symptoms is best understood for stimulants such as cocaine and amphetamines. These drugs exert their clinical effects by releasing and blocking the reuptake of dopamine and norepinephrine (Fischman, 1987). Therefore, dopamine blockers are extremely effective in decreasing the symptoms of amphetamine psychosis. PCP is less well understood. It unquestionably has some dopamine-like activity similar to amphetamines, but it has a host of other biochemical effects as well. Dopamine blockers are therefore less reliably effective in treating PCP psychoses compared to amphetamine-induced states. Although LSD is thought to exert its effects primarily through serotonergic mechanisms, it also enhances dopamine activity as well. A general effect on diminishing arousal may be the best current explanation for the capacity of the antipsychotics to treat PCP and LSD psychoses.

## CHOOSING AN ANTIPSYCHOTIC

Table 12–2 shows the currently available antipsychotics, their trade names, and general dosage ranges. As noted above, they are all equally effective (except for clozapine, which may be more effective) for treating most psychotic states. The currently available antipsychotics belong to six different chemical classes,

TABLE 12–2

*Antipsychotics*[a]

| Generic Name (Trade Name) | Usual Dosage Range (mg/day) |
|---|---|
| *Low Potency* | |
| Chlorpromazine[c] (Thorazine) | 100–600 |
| Mesoridazine[c] (Serentil) | 50–300 |
| Thioridazine (Mellaril) | 100–600 |
| *Middle Potency* | |
| Acetophenazine (Tindal) | 20–125 |
| Chlorprothixene[c] (Taractan) | 50–300 |
| Loxapine[c] (Loxitane) | 10–100 |
| Molindone (Moban) | 10–100 |
| Perphenazine[c] (Trilafon) | 8–64 |
| Thiothixene[c] (Navane) | 5–50 |
| Trifluoperazine[c] (Stelazine) | 5–50 |
| Trifluopromazine (Vesprin) | 25–200 |
| *High Potency* | |
| Droperidol[b,c] (Inapsine) | — |
| Fluphenazine[c] (Prolixin) | 2–30 |
| Haloperidol[c] (Haldol) | 2–30 |
| *Novel Antipsychotics* | |
| Clozapine (Clozaril) | 100–600 |
| *Long-Acting Injectable* | |
| Fluphenazine | |
| (Prolixine Decanoate) | 6.25–25 |
| (Prolixin Enanthate) | every two weeks |
| Haloperidol | 25–100 |
| (Haldol Decanoate) | every four weeks |

[a] Prochlorperazine (Compazine) and pimozide (Orap) are also antipsychotics but are virtually never used to treat psychotic states.

[b] Droperidol is available *only* as an injectable medication for inpatients.

[c] Available in short-acting injectable form.

one of which has three subclasses. Knowing which medication is an aliphatic phenothiazine (chlorpromazine) and which is a thioxanthene (thiothixene) may make for polysyllabic sentences but will not be of help in making practical clinical decisions. Ignore these classifications.

A more meaningful classification system is based on the recognition that some medications require high doses to be therapeutic, cause a great deal of sedation, and result in relatively few extrapyramidal symptoms (EPS). These are called low-potency antipsychotics. Others, referred to as high-potency, are prescribed in small doses, are relatively nonsedating, and frequently cause EPS. Still others, of course, are in the middle. Since high-potency antipsychotics are similar to each other, as are the low-potency drugs, it is not necessary to be familiar with all the antipsychotics. Typically, a skilled psychopharmacologist will be very familiar and experienced with three or four medications and use the others only rarely. I, for instance, prescribe thiothixene a great deal as a middle-potency medication, acknowledging that perphenazine or trifluoperazine would work just as well with the same general side effects.

Most of the commonly prescribed antipsychotics are available in short-acting injectable forms, typically administered intramuscularly (IM) to patients who are acutely psychotic, dangerous, and/or refuse oral medications. As a general rule, when given intramuscularly, the antipsychotic dose is half the oral dose for the same desired clinical effect since IM medication is not metabolized as quickly.

The two available long-acting injectable preparations are appropriate therapeutic options only in the maintenance treatment of schizophrenia. These medications are usually administered deep in the buttocks (less commonly in the arm) and work by releasing the antipsychotic gradually over many weeks. The long-acting antipsychotics are listed in Table 12–2 with their approximate dosage ranges.

In order to decide which antipsychotic to prescribe, the most important considerations are the patient's past experience and potential side effects. Patients who hate haloperidol because they experienced terrible side effects when they took it previously should be given a different antipsychotic. If, for instance, the side effect was severe EPS, a lower-potency drug such as trifluoperazine or thiothixene can be prescribed. If side effects are not the reason for the patient's aversion to a particular medication (as might be the case if the negative feelings about medication are a displacement from his feelings of shame about being psychotic and hospitalized the year before), a different medication that is pharmacologically similar can be employed. A reasonable substitute for haloperidol might be fluphenazine which is, in many ways, indistinguishable. If weight gain has been a significant problem with antipsychotics in the past, molindone, which is least likely to cause this side effect, can be prescribed. Clozapine should *never* be the first antipsychotic prescribed because of the medical risks associated with its use (see below).

## TECHNIQUES FOR PRESCRIBING

Although they are all equally effective, the antipsychotics are not equipotent. In order to solve the problem of discussing the different doses needed for equivalent responses, a uniform potency system had to be established. Since chlorpromazine was the first antipsychotic released, it was arbitrarily used as the reference drug and all other antipsychotics were compared to it. Thus, in the discussion of doses, I will occasionally refer to chlorpromazine-equivalents (CPZ-E), which is the number of milligrams of chlorpromazine equivalent to the dose of that particular antipsychotic. Table 12–3 shows the approximate potency equivalence among antipsychotics. In discussing doses, this section will

TABLE 12–3
*Antipsychotic Dosage Equivalence[a]*

| Generic Name (Trade Name) | Dosage Equivalence |
|---|---|
| *Low Potency* | |
| Chlorpromazine (Thorazine) | 100 |
| Mesoridazine (Serentil) | 50 |
| Thioridazine (Mellaril) | 100 |
| *Middle Potency* | |
| Acetophenazine (Tindal) | 20 |
| Chlorprothixene (Taractan) | 40 |
| Loxapine (Loxitane) | 10 |
| Molindone (Moban) | 10 |
| Perphenazine (Trilafon) | 10 |
| Thiothixene (Navane) | 5 |
| Trifluoperazine (Stelazine) | 5 |
| Trifluopromazine (Vesprin) | 30 |
| *High Potency* | |
| Fluphenazine (Prolixin) | 2.5 |
| Haloperidol (Haldol) | 2.5 |
| *Novel Antipsychotics* | |
| Clozapine (Clozaril) | 50[b] |

[a] In chlorpromazine-equivalents (the number of mg of each drug equal to chlorpromazine 100 mg)

[b] Antipsychotic equivalence for clozapine is poorly established.

focus on using antipsychotics for schizophrenia. Use of these medications for treating other disorders will be described at the end of the section.

When treating acute schizophrenia with antipsychotics, the evidence is clear that optimum response is seen with a daily dose of not more than 700 mg CPZ-E (Baldessarini, Cohen, and Teicher, 1988). This translates to a haloperidol dose of less than 20 milligrams. Despite this, many patients are treated with far higher doses which are not only not helpful but may ultimately cause a decreased response. (See discussion on "clinical window" below.) A reasonable way to start treatment with an acutely psychotic schizophrenic is by prescribing a daily dose of 200 mg CPZ-E, such as haloperidol 5 mg or thiothixene 10 mg. Usually, this is given initially in two or three divided doses, although the antipsychotics have long half-lives and each dose lasts for far longer than twenty-four hours. Divided doses in the initial stages of treatment may utilize the tranquilizing/sedating effects of these medications which are separate from their antipsychotic effect. Once the patient is stabilized on a consistent dose, the medication should be taken once daily at night. The dose can then be raised to the final dose over the next two weeks if the patient does not begin to improve. Since the effects of antipsychotics occur gradually over numbers of weeks, not dissimilar to the effects of antidepressants, there is little rationale for changing doses very frequently except, of course, to decrease side effects. If a patient is having a particularly agitated day early in treatment, an as-needed extra dose of the antipsychotic or the addition of a low-dose benzodiazepine tranquilizer can be given. To raise the daily dose with every increase in symptoms early in the course of treatment is to doom the patient to high dose treatment. This will cause more side effects but will not decrease the psychosis any faster.

Although the warnings about polypharmacy are generally correct—that there are very few reasons to combine two or more medications of the same class—there is one clinical situation in which the simultaneous use of two antipsychotics can be helpful. If a patient is gradually improving on a nonsedating antipsychotic, such as fluphenazine, but is still suffering from insomnia, it is a reasonable option to also prescribe a low dose of a sedating antipsychotic at bedtime, such as chlorpromazine 50 mg for a period of days to weeks.

Unfortunately, there are no good guidelines as to the "correct" psychopharmacological strategies to be used when a patient shows a poor response to an adequate trial of an antipsychotic at an appropriate dose. Raising the dose to much higher than 700 CPZ-E is virtually always tried. Although groups of patients will not generally respond, an occasional patient may. It is important, though, that if the higher dose is not clearly more effective than the lower dose, it should be lowered to its original level. Using one of the injectable antipsychotics in case the patient is not taking the medication or metabolizes the medication very quickly is also sometimes helpful. Switching to another antipsychotic can also be tried. No data exist as to the success rate of this approach. My own experience is rather negative.

Clozapine is an important new option for treatment-refractory patients. Because of the medical risks associated with this medication (discussed later in this chapter), clozapine is recommended *only* for patients who have been unresponsive to at least two—possibly three—antipsychotics at high dose (at least 1,000 CPZ-E for six weeks each), or who could not tolerate the side effects of a number of different conventional antipsychotics despite vigorous treatment of the side effects (e.g., antiparkinsonian agents) (Lieberman, Kane, and Johns, 1989). Clozapine is effective for both acute as well as maintenance therapy. Doses start at 25 to 50 mg daily, increasing gradually to 300 to 500 mg over two to five weeks.

If maintenance, preventive treatment is appropriate, the appropriate doses used are slightly less than those needed for acute antipsychotic treatment. The best recent estimate is that optimum prophylaxis will occur when the maintenance dose is between 300 and 600 mg CPZ-E (Baldessarini et al., 1988). As discussed in more detail in chapter 5, there may be important risk/benefit decisions to be made even within this range, with higher doses decreasing the number of exacerbations and relapses but at the cost of subtle, typically unrecognized side effects that have an adverse effect on quality of life. It would be helpful if we could just lower the dose of maintenance medication until symptoms reappear and know that this is the threshold dose. However, since the effect of maintenance treatment is primarily preventive, the dose could be lowered to subeffective levels and the relapse might not occur for many months, thereby preventing any simple understanding of a minimum effective dose.

It may be useful to think of a "therapeutic window" to help conceptualize the relationship between dose and response for both acute and maintenance treatment but especially for the latter. Figure 12–1 shows this visually. This is analogous to the therapeutic blood level window for antidepressants described in chapter 9. Unfortunately, blood levels of antipsychotics are neither reliable nor meaningful enough to be used clinically. Because of this, Figure 12–1 substitutes dose for blood level. For each patient, at some point on the curve, raising the dose will make the patient worse, generally not by increasing psychosis but by increasing depression or lack of motivation or anxiety or emotional withdrawal. It is vital for all therapists who treat schizophrenic patients to look for evidence of the toxic effects of treatment since they are usually more subtle than the therapeutic effects.

When a patient on maintenance antipsychotic treatment has an exacerbation, the first things to check are whether the patient has been compliant with the treatment regimen and whether street drugs have been used. If these two factors can be ruled out, then raising the dose by 100 to 300 mg CPZ-E for one to four weeks can be very helpful.

**Figure** 12–1 Dose/Response Relationship for Antipsychotics in Schizophrenia

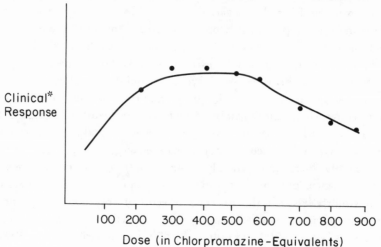

Dose (in Chlorpromazine-Equivalents)

*-Measured by symptoms in acute treatment of lack of relapse
in maintenance treatment

All of the statements made above apply equally when antipsychotics are prescribed for schizoaffective disorder, mania or psychotic depression. Because of the astonishing energy seen in hospitalized manic patients, prodigious doses of antipsychotics are often prescribed, sometimes up to 3,000 mg CPZ-E (or haloperidol 60–70 mg) or more. Patients with borderline personality are usually treated with lower doses, typically in the range of 50 to 200 mg CPZ-E. Antipsychotic doses used to treat Alzheimer's patients are much smaller than those noted above. It is not unusual to see therapeutic benefit (acknowledging the limits of that benefit) at 10 to 50 mg CPZ-E. Similarly, Tourette's patients are treated with haloperidol doses of 0.5 to 5 mg daily (20–200 mg CPZ-E).


SIDE EFFECTS


The difficulties of evaluating and treating the side effects of antipsychotics are notorious. Not only are the side effects subjectively extremely distressing at times, but some of them are difficult to distinguish from the psychopathology of the disorders themselves. An added problem is that schizophrenic patients may have a particularly hard time describing side effects, especially when acutely psychotic and experiencing somatic delusions.

Antipsychotic-induced side effects can be divided into three groups: (1) the acute side effects which include dystonias, the common extrapyramidal side effects (EPS), and the neuroleptic malignant syndrome; (2) nonneurological side effects; and (3) tardive dyskinesia, which only occurs with prolonged use. Table 12–4 classifies the most common side effects typically seen with antipsychotics. Table 12–5 lists the antipsychotic classes by their likelihood of causing each of the major side effects.

## Acute Side Effects

### Acute Dystonia

Typically within hours to days after the beginning of antipsychotic medication, some patients will experience sudden muscle tightening, typically in the neck and/or jaw. These reactions are very frightening but rarely dangerous. They are most likely to occur in young men and in those patients taking high-potency antipsychotics (Gelenberg, 1987). Another acute dystonic reaction is called an oculogyric crisis, in which the eyes involuntarily look toward a certain direction, typically up. If patients are instructed to look elsewhere, they can, but their eyes will gravitate back to their original position when distracted. Both the classic muscle dystonia and the oculogyric reactions can be

TABLE 12–4

*Side Effects of Antipsychotics*

Acute side effects:
    Dystonic reactions
    Extrapyramidal symptoms, including akinesia and akathisia
    Neuroleptic malignant syndrome
Common non-neurological side effects:
    Sedation
    Anticholinergic effects
    Postural hypotension
    Weight gain
Tardive dyskinesia
Others:
    Sexual dysfunction
    Photosensitivity
    Gynecomastia (breast swelling)
    Retinal pigmentation (causing permanent change in vision)
        occurs only with thioridazine in doses over 800 mg daily
    Agranulocytosis (low white blood cell count) occurs with clozapine only
    Seizures (especially with clozapine)

TABLE 12–5

*Antipsychotic Classes and Their Likelihood to Cause Common Side Effects*

| Medication Class Generic Name (Trade Name) | Side Effects | | | |
|---|---|---|---|---|
| | Extrapyramidal Symptoms (EPS) | Sedation | Anticholinergic Effects | Postural Hypotension |
| Low Potency Chlorpromazine (Thorazine) Thioridazine (Mellaril) Mesoridazine (Serentil) | + | + + + | + + + | + + + |
| Middle Potency Acetophenazine (Tindal) Chlorprothixene (Taractan) Loxapine (Loxitane) Molindone (Moban) Perphenazine (Trilafon) Thiothixene (Navane) Trifluoperazine (Stelazine) Trifluopromazine (Vesprin) | + + | + to + + | + + | + + |
| High Potency Haloperidol (Haldol) Fluphenazine (Prolixin) | + + + | + | + | + |
| Novel Antipsychotics Clozapine (Clozaril) | 0 | + + + | + + + | + + + |

+ = Minimal
+ + = Moderate
+ + + = Severe

treated quickly and effectively with diphenhydramine (Benadryl, a common antihistamine) or benztropine (Cogentin). If the dystonia is very disturbing, these antidote medications can be administered either intramuscularly or intravenously. When given intravenously, the dystonia may vanish within 30 seconds to a minute. The prophylactic use of anticholinergic medications, such as benztropine will prevent these reactions to a substantial degree (Arana, Goff, Baldessarini, and Keepers, 1988). Dystonia may occur more than once in the beginning of treatment but almost never thereafter.

### Extrapyramidal Symptoms

The EPS seen commonly with antipsychotics, mimicking the classic symptoms of Parkinson's disease, are akinesia, akathisia, and tremor. The tremor is seemingly less common with antipsychotics than in classic Parkinson's disease and is, of course, easily recognized. Akinesia and akathisia are both common, sometimes difficult to recognize, and important to treat.

Akinesia is the most common and most important EPS. The word literally means "without movement." In its most obvious state, akinesia is characterized by a decrease in spontaneous movement. A patient with akinesia will exhibit fewer of the natural movements that all of us spontaneously exhibit, such as crossing our legs, scratching ourselves, shifting positions in chairs, showing random spontaneous facial expressions. When walking, akinetic patients will have less arm swing than normal, may shuffle, and will look generally stiff. The terms "masked facies" and "wooden appearance" are often used to describe these patients. When people say that someone looks like a "mental patient," they are frequently referring to medication-induced akinesia.

The description of akinesia has thus far concentrated on physical side effects. A more important group of akinetic side effects are those related to psychological symptoms such as lack of motivation and spontaneity, diminished range of affect, even lack of spontaneous thought (Van Putten and Marder, 1987). These are similar, if not identical, to some of the core features of schizophrenia—the negative symptoms. The difficulty in making an accurate diagnosis when the side effects of the treatment mimic the symptoms of the disorder being treated becomes even more pointed when trying to distinguish between post-psychotic depression and akinesia. Compounding the difficulty is the possibility of having both or all three of the these potentially identical-looking syndromes—akinesia, negative symptoms, and depression. It is sometimes necessary to prescribe antiparkinsonian medications at relatively high doses as a diagnostic tool: if the symptoms are relieved, they were probably due to akinesia. If not, they were either negative symptoms or depression.

In understanding akinesia, it is helpful to remember that dopamine blocking, which is assuredly the cause of akinesia, occurs not only in the areas of the brain that regulate movement, but in areas that are involved with affect and cognition too. It should not be surprising, therefore, that in some patients, the side effects can manifest themselves in cognitive/affective slowing as well as physical slowing. In the book *Awakenings*, Oliver Sacks describes patients with post-encephalitic Parkinson's disease who existed in a frozen state for decades until they were given l-dopa (Sacks, 1983). Descriptions of their internal experiences during those years and the changes (some good, some not) after taking l-dopa help to make clear the role dopamine may play in psychological variables such as will and motivation.

Akinesia can be treated in three ways. The most common method is to prescribe antiparkinsonian medications—either anticholinergics or amantadine (see below for details on doses)—which are very effective. Another successful approach is to lower the medication dose. If possible, this is undoubtedly the wisest strategy. Sometimes, however, the side effects disappear coincident with the disappearance of therapeutic effects, thereby precluding this strategy. The third possibility is to switch to a different antipsychotic which causes less akinesia.

There is no consensus as to whether antiparkinsonian medication should be prescribed preventively in the beginning of antipsychotic treatment. The advantage, of course, is the prevention of dystonias, akinesias, and other EPS. But no medication is devoid of problems. Is it worth the dry mouth and constipation that are often induced by the antiparkinsonian medications in order to prevent EPS? My own practice is that when I prescribe high-potency neuroleptics at a moderate dose or higher—say, above 200 mg CPZ-E—I do prescribe prophylactic antiparkinsonian drugs. EPS can be very unpleasant, and I want to prevent my patients disliking a medication that may be very helpful to them. In those cases in which I do not prescribe prophylactic antiparkinsonian drugs, I tell the patients what side effects to look for and give them a prescription for the antidote medication should these side effects occur.

Conflict also exists as to whether patients on maintenance antipsychotics need to remain on antiparkinsonian medications. Although some patients can be withdrawn from their antiparkinsonian medication during maintenance treatment without the re-emergence of akinesia, a great many cannot (Manos, Gkiouzepas, and Logothetis, 1981). My own experience is that cavalierly stopping medications like benztropine during the maintenance phase of antipsychotic treatment causes an increase in symptoms, both psychological and physical, in many patients. It is appropriate to attempt to withdraw antiparkinsonian medications occasionally. This should be done gradually and with patient, therapist, and psychopharmacologist looking for clinical changes.

Akathisia (literally meaning not sitting) is the second of the two very common EPS. Although it is not as socially disabling as akinesia, akathisia is typically more uncomfortable. It is as difficult to diagnose as akinesia and possibly more so. In its classic form, akathisia is described as a motor restlessness in which patients exhibit increased numbers of fidgety, purposeless movements. These movements typically include crossing and uncrossing the legs, rubbing the thighs repeatedly while seated, or shifting position in a chair an unusual number of times. In more severe akathisia, patients will shift continually from foot to foot while standing or seem to walk in place (Van Putten and Marder, 1987). These fidgety movements are typically done unconsciously; if they are pointed out, patients will stop the movement transiently and then resume it when distracted.

Since these movements are observable and differ somewhat from classic manifestations of anxiety, they are relatively easy to diagnose. What is more difficult to diagnose are the akathetic symptoms manifested purely by subjective feelings. Patients may complain of feeling jittery, restless inside, or wired, in the absence of external fidgeting. They may describe feeling unable to relax or not being able to get in a comfortable position when they try to sleep. In an extreme form, patients will note an "indescribable tension." Even an extremely astute clinician with a great deal of experience with schizophrenics and antipsychotics would be hard pressed to distinguish definitively between subjective akathisia and anxiety/agitation. An even more muddled situation arises when the patient is experiencing both anxiety *and* akathisia.

The cause of akathisia is not as well understood as that of akinesia. Although dopamine blocking is thought to be implicated, it is likely that other biochemical systems are also involved. The same general treatment strategies used for akinesia are also helpful for akathisia—lowering the antipsychotic dose, using antidote medications, and switching antipsychotics. Antiparkinsonian drugs, however, are more effective for akinesia than for akathisia (Borison and Diamond, 1987). Because of this, two other medications are sometimes prescribed to decrease akathetic symptoms. First, the group of medications known as beta-blockers, commonly used for hypertension, angina, and migraine headaches, have been shown to be effective for akathisia. Seemingly, the most effective is propranolol (Inderal) which, unfortunately, is also the most likely to cause lethargy and fatigue (Gelenberg, 1987). Propranolol can be used by itself or in conjunction with antiparkinsonian agents. Benzodiazepines such as diazepam and lorazepam, and clonidine, a sedating antihypertensive, are the other two types of medications that are sometimes effective in diminishing akathisia. Neither beta-blockers nor benzodiazepines are effective in treating akinesia.

*Neuroleptic Malignant Syndrome*

The least common and most dangerous of all neuroleptic-induced side effects is the neuroleptic malignant syndrome (NMS), the hallmarks of which are fever and muscle rigidity, typically in combination with mental status changes (e.g., confusion, stupor) and tachycardia (fast pulse). Neuroleptic malignant syndrome typically, but not exclusively, occurs soon after beginning antipsychotic treatment or after raising the dose (Kaufmann and Wyatt, 1987). The use of higher doses of neuroleptics, especially when the dose is rapidly increased, is associated with greater risk for NMS (Keck, Pope, Cohen, McElroy, and Nirenberg, 1989). The exact cause of neuroleptic malignant syndrome is unknown, although decreased dopamine transmission seems central. Once the diagnosis is made, the antipsychotic must be stopped immediately. Medical hospitalization is mandatory. General treatment approaches include decreasing temperature, keeping the patient well hydrated, and treating any intercurrent infections. If these measures are not sufficient, a number of medications have been used with some success. These include dantrolene which decreases muscle rigidity, bromocriptine which increases dopamine, and benzodiazepines (Kaufmann and Wyatt, 1987). Improvement occurs over days to weeks. However, up to 20 percent of patients with neuroleptic malignant syndrome have died (Caroff, 1980). If further antipsychotic treatment following recovery is needed, it is best to wait at least two weeks and, possibly, to use a low-potency antipsychotic (Rosebush, Stewart, and Gelenberg, 1989).

## Other Side Effects

The most common nonneurological side effects seen with antipsychotics are sedation, anticholinergic symptoms, postural hypotension, and weight gain. These side effects are caused by the interactions of the medications with non-dopamine neurotransmitter systems, such as norepinephrine, histamine, and acetylcholine. In this way, they are similar to the antidepressants which cause many of the same side effects. The most common nonneurological side effect is sedation. In general, the higher-potency antipsychotics, such as fluphenazine and haloperidol, are the least sedating although molindone is notably less sedating than other middle-potency medications. There is some accommodation to the sedation but it is rarely complete. Thus, a patient who is initially very sedated from a specific antipsychotic may get less sedated over a period of time, but it may always be somewhat of a problem.

Like the antidepressants, the antipsychotics can cause a cluster of side effects referred to as anticholinergic. These include dry mouth, constipation, urinary hesitation, blurry vision, and possible memory dysfunction. There is an inverse relationship between an antipsychotic's capacity to cause EPS on one hand and anticholinergic side effects on the other (Richelson, 1984). This is understandable since the major treatment for EPS is anticholinergic medication. It is as if some antipsychotics have their own built-in antidote, thereby preventing EPS but causing a great deal of dryness.

Postural hypotension refers to a drop in blood pressure upon standing up or shifting from lying to sitting. The antipsychotics most likely to cause this are the low-potency compounds.

Weight gain can be a terrible problem with all antipsychotics except molindone. The etiology of weight gain is unknown, although appetite stimulation seems to play at least some part in it.

Sexual dysfunction of all kinds is also seen with any of the antipsychotics. Thioridazine is unusual in its capacity to cause retrograde ejaculation in men, in which the ejaculation is directed inward towards the bladder instead of towards the penis.

A number of other side effects are sometimes seen with antipsychotics (see Table 12–4). The most important of these is photosensitivity, which is characterized by an increased sensitivity to the sun's effects, thereby making the patient more likely to be badly sunburned. A high grade sunscreen can be very effective in diminishing the photosensitivity. Chlorpromazine is more likely to cause this side effect than are the other antipsychotics.

Clozapine's side effect profile differs substantially from those of the other antipsychotics. It is similar to the low-potency compounds in the frequency with which it causes sedation, constipation, and postural hypotension. In contrast, however, clozapine produces increased salivation. More than the other antipsychotics, clozapine is also associated with grand mal seizures. The most important and dangerous side effect of clozapine, which limits its use except in treatment-refractory patients, is its capacity to cause agranulocytosis, seen in 1 to 2 percent of those treated, and characterized by a marked decrease in white blood cells that puts the patient at risk for life-threatening infections. As a consequence, clozapine can be prescribed only in conjunction with a mandatory program of weekly blood counts, so that if agranulocytosis occurs, it is discovered quickly—and the medication stopped.

## Tardive Dyskinesia

Tardive dyskinesia (TD) is the most feared of all neuroleptic-induced side effects. And yet, it is not as dangerous as neuroleptic malignant syndrome, not as unpleasant as akathisia, generally not as socially disabling as akinesia. But all of these other side effects will assuredly disappear if the antipsychotic is discontinued. Tardive dyskinesia is the only side effect that is potentially irreversible. In this possibility—spending a lifetime of twitching and grimacing—lies the fear of TD.

TD is not a unitary phenomenon. Its manifestations are varied. In the most common type, the increased movements primarily involve the face. Tongue thrusting, chewing movements, lip smacking, and eye blinking are typical. Another common version is characterized by movements of the extremities described as choreoathetoid (literally dancing without position or place). The fingers move in repetitious writhing patterns that are often extremely subtle. An atypical variety of TD called tardive akathisia may manifest itself by persistent restlessness. More severe types of TD involve the respiratory muscles, causing grunting or odd breathing patterns, or truncal dyskinesias in which the torso moves in thrusting motions. Fortunately, this last type is exceedingly unusual.

In all the TD variations, the movements are involuntary. Often, patients will not even be aware of them. If they are pointed out, patients are usually able to suppress the movements voluntarily for a while. The movements get worse with anxiety or stress and disappear during sleep.

It is difficult to estimate the prevalence of TD in patients on antipsychotics. One reason for this is that varying definitions of TD and different populations studied have produced rates ranging from 0.5 to 100 percent! (Casey, 1987). Another reason is that some schizophrenics have TD-like movements not related to their medication treatment. Loose-fitting dentures, common in the elderly, will cause oral movements similar to TD. Additionally, observers in the preneuroleptic era described movements seen in a number of schizophrenic patients that were identical to those of TD (Cunninghan Owens, Johnstone, and Frith, 1982). The best guess is that tardive dyskinesia (by definition caused by neuroleptics) occurs in 15 to 20 percent of treated patients.

TD never occurs immediately upon exposure to antipsychotics. The risk for developing it starts after six months to a year of treatment. All available antipsychotics confer an approximately equal risk for TD. (Clozapine may be the first exception.) It has been surprisingly difficult for research studies to demonstrate that the length of time on antipsychotics or the daily dose correlates with increased risk for TD. Nonetheless, virtually all psychopharmacologists work on these assumptions. Older age, being female, and having a nonschizophrenic diagnosis (e.g., a mood disorder) may all increase the risk of TD (Kane and Smith, 1982). Surprisingly, short "drug holidays"—stopping the antipsychotic for a few days at a time intermittently—does not decrease the risk; if anything, this rapid on/off dopamine blockade may increase the risk by accelerating receptor supersensitivity which may be the mechanism for TD.

The most common theory of TD is that it occurs because of the effect of chronic dopamine blockade in creating supersensitive dopamine receptors (Casey, 1987). It is known that when a receptor is blocked on a chronic basis (as, for instance, dopamine receptors are with the long-term use of antipsychotics), it becomes supersensitive—that is, it overreacts to whatever stimulation it receives. Thus, the acute dopamine blockade that causes akinesia (decreased movements) can, over a long time, cause tardive dyskinesia (increased movements). Because this theory is inconsistent with a number of clinical and research findings, it is likely that the final explanation will be far more complex.

The most important recent finding about TD concerns its natural history. Everyone's major fear was that not only was it irreversible but that it was progressive, that it would get worse over time. Thankfully, that is true in only a small minority of cases. Even patients who stay on neuroleptics despite TD because of relapses when the antipsychotic is withdrawn will often either show an improvement or show no change in the movements over the ensuing years. For patients who can successfully lower their antipsychotic dose or discontinue the medication altogether, improvement or disappearance of the movements, even after years, is common (Glazer, Moore, Schooler, Brenner, and Morgenstern, 1984).

After investigating a remarkable variety of treatments for TD, it is clear that no drugs are consistently effective. Without question, the most important treatment is prevention: antipsychotics should be prescribed for more than six months only for patients whose need for long-term antipsychotics is clear and well documented. Of course, since there are no treatments even remotely as effective as antipsychotics for chronic schizophrenia, the risk for TD is frequently unavoidable in these patients. The second strategy is to use the lowest dose of medication possible. Once TD is diagnosed, the need for maintenance antipsychotics should be reevaluated. Could the patient be treated with intermittent antipsychotics? If this is possible, the months of time when the patient is off antipsychotics will probably help diminish the TD movements. Also, since anticholinergic medications can make TD movements more prominent (but do not cause them), discontinuing these drugs can be helpful. If the antipsychotic is discontinued, the TD will typically worsen temporarily as a result of the cessation of dopamine blockade.

If the TD is mild, the patient, psychotherapist, and psychopharmacologist can discuss all risks and benefits fully and may decide together to continue treatment as is, since the risks of being off antipsychotics may be far greater than the social disability of the TD movements. If antipsychotics need to be continued but the movements are significant and treatment is necessary, a remarkable array of alternatives exist. Paradoxically, raising the neuroleptic dose will suppress the movements since this will increase the dopamine blockade and thereby diminish the amount of dopamine available to the receptor. At the same time, though, it may simultaneously increase the risk for more long-term movements. Other treatment alternatives include beta-blockers such as propranolol, clonidine, benzodiazepines, and sodium valproate. Cholinergic agonists—those drugs that increase acetylcholine such as choline, lecithin, and deanol—have been tried but without much success (Casey, 1987).

## ANTIPARKINSONIAN MEDICATIONS

Because antiparkinsonian medications are so important in the ongoing treatment with antipsychotics, it is worth looking at the specific choice of medications available. Table 12–6 shows the names, classes, and typical dose ranges of the antiparkinsonian medications. The anticholinergic medications are the most commonly prescribed antiparkinsonian drugs. They are all probably equally effective although benztropine and trihexyphenidyl are the most popular. Trihexyphenidyl is a potentially abusable drug, possibly because of its mild stimulant effect. All of the anticholinergic drugs share the same side effects, such as dry mouth, constipation, urinary hesitation, blurred vision, and decreased memory that are seen with other medications (such as the low-potency antipsychotics or some of the tricyclic antidepressants) with anticholinergic effects. If too high a dose of these medications is taken or if there are additive effects when they are combined with other medications that have their own anticholinergic effects, anticholinergic toxicity can result. This might be the case, for example, in a patient who is being treated simultaneously with chlorpromazine, benztropine, and amitriptyline for schizoaffective disorder, depressed type. Further, since many over-the-counter sedatives and cold remedies contain anticholinergic compounds, the patient could add to the risk without knowing it.

TABLE 12–6

*Antiparkinsonian Medications*

| Generic Name (Trade Name) | Dosage Ranges (mg/day) |
| --- | --- |
| *Anticholinergics* | |
| Benztropine (Cogentin) | 2–6 |
| Trihexyphenidyl (Artane) | 4–15 |
| Biperiden (Akineton) | 2–8 |
| Procyclidine (Kemadrin) | 7.5–20 |
| Diphenhydramine (Benadryl) | 25–100 |
| *Dopaminergic* | |
| Amantadine (Symmetrel) | 100–300 |

Anticholinergic toxicity may be manifested by confusion, overt psychosis with visual hallucinations, incredibly hot dry skin, and very dilated pupils. (In the Renaissance, atropine, which causes significant anticholinergic effects, was used by women for the much desired and admired effect of dilated pupils, thus giving rise to the nickname for atropine—belladonna [beautiful woman].) If anticholinergic toxicity is present, all anticholinergic medications must be discontinued.

The only antiparkinsonian drug that is not anticholinergic is amantadine which is also used as an antiviral medication. It does not cause anticholinergic side effects, but in my experience is less effective than the anticholinergics. Because it is a dopamine agonist, it can aggravate psychotic thinking. Fortunately, this is rare.

# 13

# Electroconvulsive Therapy (ECT); Stimulants

Both electroconvulsive therapy (ECT) and stimulants are infrequently used treatments in modern psychiatry that are often thought of as dangerous, to be used only in desperate situations—and maybe not even then. Inappropriate use of both has certainly occurred, more in the past than recently. As with so many treatments, however, a therapy that is used incorrectly—with the wrong patients or for the wrong reasons—does not accurately reflect the qualities of the treatment but the need for care in its use. ECT and stimulants are important options that can be very effective in specific clinical situations. ECT, in fact, is potentially lifesaving. Although it is technically not a medication, of course, and is used almost exclusively with psychiatric inpatients, ECT is often considered as a treatment option for severe mood disorders. Yet because of its past abuses and the intensity of feelings it engenders, myths, half-truths, and accurate observations about ECT are usually presented in equal proportion when it is discussed. It is therefore vital that all therapists have at least some knowledge of ECT, its appropriate uses, and its side effects.

## ECT

First used in the late 1930s, ECT is among the oldest biologic treatments in psychiatry still currently utilized. Starting with the premise that schizophrenia (dementia praecox as it was then called) and epilepsy were rarely seen together and might therefore be antagonistic, early researchers induced grand mal seizures in schizophrenic patients and noted some clinical response. Initially, the seizures were provoked with medications. Using electric currents to cause seizures began in 1938 and gradually replaced the medications because the new technique was more reliable and controllable. It also became apparent at that time that those with severe depressions were most responsive to this new treatment. Because antidepressants, lithium, and antipsychotics had not yet been discovered and other effective biologic treatments for severe psychiatric disorders simply did not exist, ECT quickly became a popular treatment—and an overused one. Despite increasing safety in its use (the risk of fractures, for example, has been virtually eliminated through the adminstration of short-acting muscle paralyzing medications), ECT fell into increasing disfavor because of its use and abuse as a means of behavioral control and not as a treatment of specific disorders. Several studies over the last fifteen years, however, have helped reestablish ECT as an important option for severe mood disorders and in a few other clinical situations. There is no evidence that ECT is currently used to treat the underprivileged. Rather, those patients most likely to receive it are white, voluntary patients who are covered by private insurance and not by state-subsidized insurance (Thompson and Blaine, 1987).

## Clinical Uses

With only rare exceptions, the proper use of ECT is in the treatment of major mood disorders. Table 13–1 shows the disorders and clinical situations for which ECT should be considered. The most well-validated of these is the treatment of acute delusional depression in which patients are not only severely

TABLE 13–1
*Disorders and Situations for Which ECT Is Beneficial*

| Disorder or Situation | Efficiency Rating |
|---|---|
| *Disorder* | |
| Delusional depression | + + + |
| Major depression with melancholia | + + |
| Mania | + + |
| Major depression, severe, not responsive to antidepressants | + + |
| Schizophrenia, acute; especially with catatonic features | + |
| *Clinical Situation* | |
| Obsessional suicidality | + + |
| Pregnancy with severe mania or depression | + + |
| Severe depression with major medical illness or with intolerable side effects to antidepressants | + + |

+ + + = Definite efficacy
  + + = Probable efficacy
    + = Possible efficacy

THE PSYCHOTHERAPIST'S GUIDE TO PSYCHOPHARMACOLOGY

depressed but also show clear evidence of mood-congruent delusions. The case for ECT in these patients is strengthened by their relatively poor response to antidepressants (Kroessler, 1985). A second important use of ECT is as a treatment for severe depressions, especially those episodes that have not improved from an adequate trial of an antidepressant. In general, the more a patient fits the picture of melancholic depression, the better the response to ECT. Unipolar and bipolar depressions are equally likely to improve (Black, Winokur, and Nasrallah, 1986). Milder depressive conditions such as dysthymic disorder and adjustment disorder with depressed mood do not respond to ECT.

Acute mania is also responsive to ECT (Small et al., 1988). Since other less disruptive treatments for mania, such as lithium, are also available, ECT is rarely used for this purpose. Finally, acute schizophrenia is sometimes treated effectively with ECT. It is most likely to be helpful with relatively acute, rapid onset episodes (Consensus Conference, 1985). Because antipsychotics are very effective for these same patients, ECT is rarely, if ever, given as a first treatment for acute schizophrenia. Among the subtypes, catatonic schizophrenia may respond best, raising the question whether this subtype is truly schizophrenia or an atypical form of a mood disorder (Weiner and Coffey, 1988). Chronic schizophrenia is unlikely to improve with ECT.

In addition, there are three clinical situations listed in Table 13–1 for which ECT may offer particular advantages over other treatments. Despite the lack of controlled trials, a wealth of anecdotal clinical experience indicates that patients who are obsessively suicidal often respond to ECT with a marked decrease in their urges to kill themselves. Typically, these are patients who think of suicide continually and often make repeated attempts at self-destruction with eating utensils, towels, or other means at their disposal. It is not known whether the positive results seen with ECT in these patients are due to its effect on an underlying depression, by interrupting the obsession with self-destruction, or by another undiscovered mechanism. ECT is not an effective treatment for obsessive compulsive disorder.

The other clinical situations for which ECT can be helpful are severe mood disturbances in patients with special medical needs, such as pregnant women or those with severe medical problems. Given the risk of fetal malformation from the use of medications to treat pregnant women, particularly in the first trimester when the most sensitive aspects of fetal growth occur, ECT is sometimes considered to treat severe mania or depression. In mania, frenzied activity and inattention to safety may pose a great risk to the fetus, while anorexia and risk of suicide are fetal risks in depression. (See chapter 8 for discussion of using biological treatments in pregnancy.) Because the medications used in ECT induction last no more than minutes (see below), they are less likely to be of risk than antidepressants or especially lithium, which cross into the placenta and are taken on a daily basis. With minimal alterations in the actual technique of the treatments, ECT is probably safe for both mother and fetus (Nurnberg and Prudic, 1984).

Similarly, depressed patients with medical problems for whom the side effects of antidepressants are dangerous or intolerable are candidates for ECT. Because the more recently released antidepressants generally cause fewer side effects than the older ones, however, a trial of at least one antidepressant is usually undertaken before ECT is seriously considered.

## Mechanisms of Action

Two central statements regarding ECT's mechanism of action can be made: First, its positive effects are due to the electrical seizure caused by the ECT, and not to the magic of the ritual involving anesthesia or from the simple passage of electricity through the brain. Second, despite decades of research into its biochemical actions and attempts to link these with those of antidepressants or other medications, the biological mechanisms by which ECT exerts its therapeutic effects are unknown.

Concerns that ECT's efficacy was due to a placebo or suggestion effect have been laid to rest by a series of double-blind studies comparing real and "sham" ECT. In these studies, patients receiving sham ECT were given all the procedures of ECT—anesthesia, electrodes applied to the head, and so on—except that no current was passed and no seizure occurred. Without question, real ECT is more effective than sham ECT (Janicak et al., 1985). These studies and the observation that ECT worked just as well when anesthesia and muscle-relaxants were introduced (compared to the earlier more frightening and dangerous techniques in which patients were conscious until the time of the actual treatment) also refuted the belief that ECT's effectiveness was related to the sense of punishment or regression induced by the procedure.

Another early concern was that the "mind-scrambling" effect of ECT as exemplified by memory loss (see below) was the essential therapeutic ingredient. This is unlikely to be so, since memory deficits do not correlate with therapeutic response (Sackheim, 1988). Furthermore, the recent changes in ECT techniques have resulted in less memory loss without a diminishment in therapeutic efficacy.

The therapeutic effects of ECT are inherently linked to the induction of a grand mal seizure in the patient, completely analogous to a spontaneously occurring seizure in an epileptic. The differences between an epileptic patient's seizure and that induced by ECT are due to the anticipated, controlled nature of the latter. During ECT, because of pretreatment with muscle relaxants, there are no muscle contractions, and because of control of breathing by the attendant anesthesiologist or nurse-anesthetist, oxygenation continues safely. In the seizures of epilepsy, both muscle contractions and lack of oxygen are potential problems.

If the amount of electricity given during an ECT treatment is insufficient, producing an incomplete seizure (termed a "missed seizure"), it is less effective. Although seizures induced by the absolutely minimal amount of electricity necessary may not always be therapeutic, the use of very high-intensity current, far higher than is needed, will only produce more cognitive side effects (Sackheim, 1988).

Biochemically, the effects of ECT on a variety of neurotransmitters—especially those thought to be involved in mood regulation, such as norepinephrine, serotonin, and dopamine—have been investigated repeatedly. To sum up a whole body of literature, the known effects of ECT on neurotransmitters do not yield a consistent pattern of results and certainly do not help elucidate its mechanism of action (Lerer, 1987).

### Techniques of Administration

First and foremost, if the patient is competent to understand the nature of the procedure, ECT should only be given after fully informed consent, typically after far more extensive discussion than for any other procedure in psychiatry. Each state has slightly different regulations regarding the informed consent procedure and how to proceed with a legally incompetent patient. Overall, however, the vast majority of abuses of the past have been eliminated. Some hospitals even provide videotapes for patients and their families that serve to educate and demystify ECT.

ECT should be administered only by those psychiatrists specifically trained and knowledgeable in its use. Although it is given predominantly to inpatients, it can be used with outpatients who have friends or family who can drive them to and from the hospital for treatments and stay with them for the rest of the day. The actual number of ECT treatments given to an individual patient for a complete course of therapy varies. Typically, six to twelve treatments are effective, although some severely ill patients may require up to twenty. In the United States, ECT is typically given three times weekly, making a total course of therapy last between two and four weeks for the majority of patients. The number of treatments should be determined purely by the patient's response, with the endpoint being clinical remission or a plateau of response. A successful course of ECT should always be followed by continuation treatment with medications to prevent relapse, analogous to the treatment of mania or depression following clinical remission from antidepressants or lithium. (See chapter 3 for discussion of continuation treatment.) Rarely, a patient who relapses on medication is considered for once monthly maintenance ECT.

Before treatment, patients always receive some sort of medical evaluation, with each hospital requiring different tests. General screening blood tests are usual as is an electrocardiogram. Often, back X-rays (to note the presence of old fractures) are taken. Medications that interfere with seizures, such as benzodiazepines, are reduced in dose or discontinued.

The only important technical consideration is whether to use bilateral (on both sides of the head) or unilateral (with the current delivered to the non-dominant, right hemisphere of the brain) ECT. In both circumstances, seizures will occur. Without question, unilateral ECT causes less post-ECT confusion and fewer cognitive deficits (Sachs and Gelenberg, 1988). For some patients, however, it may be less effective. Therefore, a common strategy is to start with unilateral treatment, switching to bilateral after five or six treatments if no improvement is seen.

On the morning of an ECT treatment, the patient has usually fasted for eight to twelve hours. Atropine, a medication that minimizes a transient slowing of the heart rate from ECT, is given. After being taken into a room that is specifically equipped for the ECT procedure, an intravenous line (IV) is inserted through which the patient is given methohexital, a very short-acting barbiturate that induces sleep virtually immediately. Then succinylcholine, a muscle relaxant that prevents the actual physical manifestations of the seizure, is given. During this time, blood pressure and electrocardiogram monitoring is continual while the patient's breathing is insured by the use of a breathing bag and mask handled by the anesthesiologist. The electrodes are then placed on the patient's two temples for bilateral treatment or on the right temple and near the middle of the head for unilateral ECT. After the current is delivered, monitoring for the actual presence of the seizure is done through a variety of means, the most precise of which is the electroencephalogram (EEG, or brain wave test). Since succinylcholine blocks the muscle twitching, there may be no physical evidence that a seizure is occurring. Following the ECT treatment, the patient is observed, first in the recovery room and then on the ward. Patients awaken gradually within minutes to an hour after the procedure.

## Side Effects

Although ECT, as currently practiced in the United States, is not a completely safe procedure, it is a far cry from the early days in the 1940s and 1950s when it was genuinely dangerous. At that time, mortality rates from ECT were significant—one per thousand—and rates of major complications, most commonly fractures, occurred in up to 40 percent of those treated (Consensus Conference, 1985). With the advances in ECT techniques—the use of anesthesia, muscle relaxants, and better control of breathing and oxygenation—the dangers have diminished dramatically. At present, mortality rates are the same as those associated with the use of short-acting barbiturate anesthetics, and fractures have been virtually eliminated. Cardiovascular changes from the procedure are a significant risk only for those who have preexisting cardiac problems.

The major side effects of ECT of current concern to patients and psychiatrists alike are those related to cognition. Seizures in general, and ECT treatments specifically, have clear adverse effects of cognition and memory. The most predictable of these is a post-ECT confusional state that increases with the number of treatments given and with bilateral rather than unilateral placement. Patients awaken from the ECT with confusion and possibly disorientation to time, place, and/or situation which lasts between minutes and a few hours in the vast majority of patients.

Of more concern are the effects of ECT on memory. Both anterograde memory (the ability to learn new material) and retrograde memory (the ability to retrieve previously acquired material) are affected (Sachs and Gelenberg, 1988). As with the acute confusional effects, memory problems increase with more treatments and with bilateral (vs. unilateral) treatments. During the time in which ECT is given and typically for a few weeks thereafter, anterograde memory is decreased in most patients. This deficit gradually diminishes and a return to normal capacity to learn new information is generally evident by two months in most patients and by six months in almost all patients.

Retrograde memory deficits are also maximal right after ECT, improving gradually over weeks to months. Memory for recent events is disrupted more than those related to the distant past. Thus, two weeks after the last ECT treatment, a patient may remember events occurring years before but not what happened two months before. By six months after ECT, the more recent event is likely to be retrievable. Remembering specific events that occurred just prior to the ECT treatments or during the time of the hospitalization, however, may be permanently lost.

Despite the studies that have documented the conclusions just presented, many patients complain that, following ECT, their memory is not as good as it had been previously. A variety of possibilities exist to explain these complaints (Squire, 1985). The most obvious is that the tests used to assess memory function are simply not sensitive enough to document these complaints. Also, it may be that because of the disruption of memory around the time of the ECT, a feeling of discontinuity of experience is translated as memory deficit. Having a time of memory impairment may additionally sensitize patients to normal memory gaps which are then interpreted as secondary to ECT. The effects of recurrent depression on memory may also play a part in these complaints for some patients.

Finally, many patients have heard that ECT causes permanent brain damage. The animal studies that purport to show brain damage have induced far greater numbers of seizures, and in some cases continuous seizures, than are used with ECT. Additionally, ensuring the delivery of oxygen to the brain during seizures, which may be a vital factor in preventing brain damage and is done routinely in modern ECT, is ignored in animal studies. Ongoing work in this area continues, but for now, the evidence is consistent that ECT does not cause permanent brain damage (Sachs and Gelenberg, 1988).

To summarize the current knowledge about the risks of ECT: (1) In contrast to its use in the past, ECT is now a medically safe procedure in which the risk of serious medical complications is very low. (2) Transient confusion predictably occurs but is never a long-term problem. (3) Around the time of the ECT, the ability to learn new material and to retrieve old memories is unquestionably disrupted, but these effects disappear in the overwhelming majority of patients within a few months at most. Some patients, however, continue to complain of memory problems for months and years that cannot be explained by our current knowledge.

## STIMULANTS

Similar to ECT, stimulants are among the oldest biological treatments in psychiatry, having been first developed fifty years ago, initially as a treatment for asthma. Although their current uses are limited, there is still a small but important place for stimulants in modern psychiatry. (They are also prescribed by other physicians as appetite-suppressing drugs for weight loss and in treating narcolepsy, a neurological disorder characterized in part by excessive sleepiness). Unfortunately, a number of psychiatrists refuse to prescribe them in any circumstance because of their abuse potential and because of the government's scrutiny of all prescriptions written for the two most common stimulants, d-amphetamine and methylphenidate.

### Clinical Uses

The only major uses for stimulants in psychiatry are in the treatment of attention deficit disorder (ADD) and occasionally in depressive disorders. For patients with ADD, both children and adults, stimulants are the mainstay of treatment. The evidence for efficacy in children is clear and beyond dispute for both methylphenidate (Ritalin) which is the most commonly prescribed stimulant and dextroamphetamine (Dexedrine). Pemoline (Cylert) is also effective, although possibly less so than the other two. Evidence from controlled studies on the use of stimulants for adults with ADD is less impressive, but this may reflect the greater difficulty in making the diagnosis and/or the presence of associated conditions (such as drug and alcohol abuse) that complicate the condition.

Stimulants are useful in only occasional cases of depression. Certainly, they are never appropriate first treatments for clear, uncomplicated major depressive disorder. However, all psychopharmacologists have seen at least a few depressed patients who either did not respond to or could not tolerate the effects of antidepressants who obtained some benefit from stimulants. In addition, stimulants are sometimes helpful when prescribed simultaneously with cyclic antidepressants if the latter have been ineffective when given alone. There is also increasing use of stimulants in treating depressed medically ill patients (Woods, Tesar, Murray, and Cassem, 1986). These patients do not always have all the same symptoms as those seen in major depressive episode as described in DSM-III-R, but they seem to suffer from some form of depression. Often, the response of these patients to low-dose stimulants is dramatic. Stimulants have also recently been prescribed with benefit to patients with cognitive and affective symptoms related to AIDS (acquired immune deficiency syndrome) (Holmes, Fernandez, and Levy, 1989). Finally, there is evidence that stimulants can be helpful for apathetic geriatric patients (Chiarello and Cole, 1987).

## Mechanisms of Action

Stimulants seem to exert their major effects on brain biology by increasing the functional activity of the catecholamines (see chapter 2), dopamine and norepinephrine. They cause the immediate release of dopamine from the neuron and may also block its reuptake, further increasing its availability (Chiarello and Cole, 1987). Similar, although less consistent, effects are seen with norepinephrine. The result of these actions is that stimulants typically produce increased arousal, decreased fatigue, and a heightened ability to concentrate. Their ability to cause euphoria is inconsistent, as are their effects on increased motor activity (Rapoport et al., 1980). Stimulants reliably decrease appetite and increase pulse rate, effects that are somewhat dose-related.

## Techniques of Administration

Table 13–2 lists the three stimulants used for the disorders previously noted with their typical dosage ranges for both adults and children. d-Amphetamine and methylphenidate are very similar in their therapeutic and side effects. They are both short-lived, lasting between two and five hours, and are equally effective, although individual patients occasionally prefer one or the other. d-Amphetamine is prescribed at half the dose of methylphenidate to achieve the same effect. Because both stimulants are so brief in duration, they are often prescribed two to three times daily. Both medications are available in sustained-release forms which, unfortunately, are not always released as gradually as one would want, thereby limiting their usefulness. Initial doses for stimulants in treating both child and adult ADD are 5 mg twice daily for methylphenidate and 2.5 to 5 mg twice daily for d-amphetamine. Because the effects are seen rapidly, often within the first day, dose adjustments can be made relatively quickly, typically every two or three days. When prescribed for depression, especially for the medically ill, the lowest possible dose, such as 2.5 mg of methylphenidate, is often prescribed first. Dose adjustments are then made carefully on the basis of the initial response.

Compared to the other two stimulants, pemoline is slower in onset of action and longer in duration (Conners and Taylor, 1980). It is also not quite so effective as the other two. Improvement at any dose will be seen more gradually, typically over days to a week. Because it lasts longer, pemoline has a distinct advantage in being effective when given only once daily, typically in the morning. Initial doses of pemoline are 18.75 or 37.5 mg, increased after a number of days or a week by 18.75 mg at a time. (It is not clear why pemoline tablets are available in these unusual potencies.) Reflecting its lesser capacity for

TABLE 13–2

*Stimulants*

| Generic Name | Trade Name | Usual Dosage Range (mg/day) |
|---|---|---|
| d-Amphetamine | Dexedrine | 5–40 |
| | Dexedrine spansules (sustained release) | |
| Methylphenidate | Ritalin | 10–80 |
| | Ritalin-SR (sustained release) | |
| Pemoline | Cylert | 18.75–150 |

abuse, pemoline prescriptions are not scrutinized by government regulatory agencies as are those for d-amphetamine and methylphenidate.

Tolerance to their therapeutic effects with the need for higher doses is generally not seen when stimulants are used to treat ADD. The extent of tolerance when stimulants are prescribed for depression is extremely variable but seems to be higher than for ADD.

### Side Effects

The most common side effects from stimulants are, as expected, related to overstimulation. These include anxiety, irritability, insomnia, headaches, decreased appetite, weight loss, as well as increased pulse and blood pressure. Since the side effects are typically dose-related, they usually diminish if the dose is decreased. Also, tolerance often develops to a number of these side effects, specifically insomnia, the pulse/blood pressure effects, and the diminished appetite. When prescribed for the depressed medically ill, stimulant side effects rarely cause clinically significant problems. When taken in high dose for an extended period of time, stimulants can precipitate an acute paranoid psychosis.

When either methylphenidate or d-amphetamine is prescribed for children, other side effects may be seen. The most important of these are their effects on height. Children taking stimulants show a small (average of less than one inch) decrement in height. If, however, stimulants are withdrawn during adolescence, a growth rebound occurs with the children's final height the same as others (Gittelman Klein and Mannuzza, 1988). If the medications are withdrawn over two summers, the small decrement in height disappears (Gittelman Klein, Landa, Mattes, and Klein, 1988). The concern, then, is for those children who continue stimulant treatment throughout adolescence without interruption because of ongoing ADD symptoms.

Other side effects commonly seen with children are crying spells, lethargy, dysphoric mood, nausea, and abdominal discomfort. Children with Tourette's syndrome, a tic disorder (see chapter 8), may have an exacerbation of their symptoms.

Pemoline causes liver inflammation in an occasional patient, necessitating infrequent checks of liver function.

The final problems with stimulants concerns their potential for abuse. Without doubt, both methylphenidate and d-amphetamine are abusable drugs. For that reason, they need to be prescribed with caution. However, drug abuse and dependence occur as an interaction between a drug and an individual with a particular vulnerability for abusing drugs. Thus, cavalierly prescribing Dexedrine to a former "speed freak" who complains of distractibility is simply not comparable to administering the same medication to a 58-year-old compliant, treatment-refractory patient with depression. In other words, stimulants are useful with the right patients at the right time, but can be dangerous when prescribed unwisely.

# SECTION
## FIVE

# 14

## The Split Treatment Model

### *Interactions Between Psychotherapy and Pharmacotherapy*

**M**ore and more often, therapeutic tasks for patients with psychiatric/psychological disorders are shared by two professionals, the psychotherapist and the pharmacotherapist. Although the interactions between psychotherapy and pharmacotherapy are themselves worthy of discussion, splitting the two treatment modalities adds other, often unexplored factors. The first half of this chapter describes psychotherapy/pharmacotherapy interactions and theoretical aspects of what I call split treatment; the second half is devoted to the more practical issues of finding a psychopharmacologist and working within the split treatment model. Because virtually no research on these topics has been done, in the discussion I rely primarily on clinical observations, theoretical concerns, and practical suggestions.

### EARLY MODELS, EARLY PROBLEMS

If split treatment simply means two professionals performing different therapeutic functions, it is not new. In psychoanalytically oriented hospitals, more in the past than recently, the therapist/analyst would treat the patient in intensive psychotherapy while another physician would be responsible for giving or withdrawing passes, setting behavioral limits, occasionally prescribing medications, and interacting openly with the nursing staff on issues of the patient's behavior. The goal of this split was to avoid disrupting the intimacy or trust of the primary therapeutic relationship by segregating psychoanalysis from other aspects of therapy which were considered of lesser importance and theoretical interest. Thus, even though the therapy was split, no attempt was made to integrate the two treatments.

This legacy of keeping therapies pure and eschewing more integrative approaches to treatment was equally apparent when biological therapies emerged in the 1960s. Early psychopharmacologists displayed the same tendency for dichotomous thinking as had psychoanalysts, but in reverse. Medication treatments for the more "biological" disorders, such as manic-depressive illness and schizophrenia, were thought to be sufficient for maximal improvement, and psychotherapy was relegated to a minor place, at best. As an example, following the establishment of lithium as helpful in treating manic-depressive illness, lithium clinics, composed of patients with mood disorders, most of whom took lithium, were organized (Gitlin and Jamison, 1984). Papers emanating from these clinics described patients who seemingly had no psychological needs and for whom psychotherapy was virtually never necessary. Patients took their lithium, had their doses adjusted, their blood drawn, and otherwise led symptom-free normal lives. Little or no attention was paid to the effects of stressful events or personality variables and their impact on these patients' lives. In similar fashion, books written for the lay public (such as *Moodswings* [Fieve, 1976] were highly successful in describing the extraordinary advantages of lithium, but seemed to imply that bipolar patients had no psychological difficulties. The overly simplistic psychoanalytic model had been replaced by an equally simplistic medical model.

With this tendency to dichotomous thinking, notions that patients might suffer from difficulties that were both biological *and* psychological and might therefore benefit from multimodal treatment were lacking. Thus for patients with marked rapid mood swings, the question posed might be whether they suffered from narcissistic pathology (a "psychological" disorder) or cyclothymia as a variant of bipolar disorder (a "biological" disorder)—but rarely both. With these unimodal formulations, combined treatment was rarely considered. Whatever its other faults, DSM-III, published in 1980, attempted to avoid this dichotomous approach to psychopathology. Its multiaxial format (see chapter 1 in this book) effectively forced readers to think about multiple simultaneous disorders. Thus, the clinician wondering if a patient's mood instability was evidence of cyclothymia or of narcissistic personality disorder could now conceptualize both disorders existing simultaneously—and consider multiple treatments.

Aside from the narrow unimodal models of psychopathology, the other major obstacle to the development of split treatment was a series of fears and prejudices that evolved between psychiatrists and the growing numbers of nonphysician therapists. In large part, these fears resulted from the competition between the two professions for status in the community as well as from the different fees charged. Therapists feared that a consulting psychiatrist might denigrate the therapist's competence and then steal the referred patient by providing psychotherapy as well as psychopharmacological consultation. Psychiatrists were worried that their position at the top of the psychotherapeutic hierarchy was being threatened and therefore placed great emphasis on the different training received by nonphysician therapists. Furthermore, as malpractice suits became a greater source of concern, some psychiatrists felt an increased need for control of the patients with whom they were involved. The split treatment model was a direct threat to control. For example, if a patient in split treatment committed suicide during a time when the patient was in intensive psychotherapy but in maintenance pharmacotherapy (and therefore seeing the psychopharmacologist infrequently), some pharmacotherapists feared that, as a member of the treatment team, they might be held liable for the outcome. Their possible liability might be heightened had the patient overdosed on the prescribed medications. Ignored in these scenarios, of course, was the importance of mutual respect and trust between the two professionals and the need for them to work *together* and not in isolation from each other.

## PSYCHOTHERAPY/PHARMACOTHERAPY INTERACTIONS: THEORETICAL ISSUES

Among the more important concerns for therapists considering having a patient participate in both psychotherapy and medication treatment are those related to the hypothetical negative interactions between the two modalities, whether utilized by one practitioner or two. Of most concern to therapists is that drug therapy will have negative effects on psychotherapy. Specific concerns include the following (Klerman, 1984):

1. Medication use could undermine psychotherapy by promoting an antitherapeutic attitude (negative placebo effect) in both therapist and patient. In this view, taking medication fosters dependency and passivity. It subtly promotes a stance in which the patient waits to be "fixed" by external magic, be it medication or the therapist, thereby discouraging the mutual exploratory active mode that is characteristic of good psychotherapy.

2. Medication-induced reduction of symptoms reduces the motive for continuing patient treatment. Most therapists would agree that an "optimum" level of distress is needed for most successful therapies. If the level is too high, the patient will become overwhelmed; if it is too low, motivation will decrease and defenses will help seal over the underlying problems without resolving the

conflict, thereby making it likely that the same problems will arise at a later time. Because successful pharmacotherapy diminishes symptoms/distress, there is a concern that the patient will then not be sufficiently motivated to continue to explore underlying issues and will terminate therapy prematurely. A further theoretical concern is that the symptom relief seen with pharmacotherapy will lead to symptom substitution, again without any resolution of underlying problems.

3. The introduction of possible medication treatment may produce an altered sense of self in a psychotherapy candidate and provoke a variety of negative feelings in the patient (see below). In terms of its meaning for the therapy, some patients may interpret the suggestion of medication evaluation as implying that they are not appropriate for "pure" psychotherapy and that they are less interesting than other patients. It can be seen as a failure of their capacity to work through issues by themselves, without the crutch of drugs.

As hypotheses, these concerns are individually valid. Medication treatment can have these negative effects with some patients. As pharmacotherapy becomes more popularized in the lay media, more patients are presenting to mental health professionals with the inner conviction that their lifetimes of dysphoria and poor interpersonal relationships are chemical in origin; what they need, they seem to say, is to have their chemical imbalances fixed. Without question, this attitude and a fixation on chemical imbalances as the sole cause of one's misery would indeed undermine any psychological therapies.

Fortunately, this kind of rigid thinking is unusual in the majority of patients. If, in the course of a good psychotherapy, medication is introduced, the psychodynamic meaning of taking pills, of its transference implications, of its possible effects of promoting passivity are all issues that can and should be explored in the treatment. Furthermore, these concerns have been examined, albeit sporadically, in a number of studies (Conte, Plutchnik, Wild, and Karasu, 1986; Beitman, 1988). Whether treating patients with mood disorders, anxiety disorders, or schizophrenia using combined treatment, the evidence can best be summarized as follows: (1) There is no consistent evidence that psychotherapy and psychopharmacology when used together are less effective than either treatment alone; neither a negative placebo effect nor symptom reduction as a motive for discontinuing psychotherapy is found. (2) Combined therapy is found to be as effective or more effective than either treatment alone. Of course, neither the patients treated in these studies nor the types of structured psychotherapies used are necessarily comparable to that of community practice. As such, these studies may not adequately address the concerns of most therapists. Nonetheless, the observation that medication does not diminish the effects of psychotherapy is reassuring.

## THERAPEUTIC SPLIT MODEL

The concerns about psychotherapy/pharmacotherapy interactions just discussed are relevant whether the therapies are provided by one or two professionals. When the two treatments are split, there is another series of considerations. These can be most easily explored by describing the advantages and disadvantages of a therapeutic split treatment model.

### Advantages of the Split Model

1. The therapeutic split keeps the psychotherapy focused on psychological issues. If medications are introduced in the course of an ongoing psychodynamic therapy, it can be disruptive to the already established themes and patterns of therapist/patient interaction. With a treatment model that encourages fantasies, dreams, projections, and transference distortion, asking about side effects and discussing medication dosage adjustments may distract both the patient and the therapist from the psychodynamic work. In a therapeutic split model, the psychopharmacologist can evaluate the efficacy of the medication, and explore side effect issues consistently without fear of disrupting the therapy while the therapist can defer most of the medication questions to the psychopharmacologist. This can be especially useful when a patient has a somatic focus and side effects become a paramount issue. Depressed, somatically preoccupied patients can spend astonishing amounts of time in therapy dwelling on complaints of constipation, dry mouth, dizziness, and fatigue, with the attendant paralysis in addressing psychotherapeutic issues. With a split model, the "medication visit" can be the designated forum for discussing symptoms and side effects. If the therapist and psychopharmacologist establish a good working relationship, the patient's somatic concerns can be contained effectively, allowing more psychotherapeutic work to be accomplished.

2. Similarly, the therapeutic split allows for the different interviewing styles to be used most effectively. The structured, fact-based questions of a medication visit (How well are you sleeping? Are you experiencing any dizziness? Is your mood worse in the morning?) is obviously different from the less directive and more open-ended approach of psychodynamic psychotherapy. Switching back and forth between the directive medical model style and the less structured psychodynamic model as would be inevitable if a single practitioner were doing both treatments might be confusing to the patient and retard a productive working rhythm of psychotherapy.

3. The therapeutic split model may help in the management of an overwhelming or unmanageable transference/countertransference relationship. Pa-

tients with both severe personality disorder (usually narcissistic or borderline) and a concomitant mood disorder, either unipolar or bipolar, are seemingly becoming more common in clinical practice. Managing patients with severe borderline disorder is difficult enough, but when biological instability is also present, the ensuing chaos can be overwhelming and sometimes unmanageable. The impulsivity of bipolar disorder can heighten the potential self-destructiveness of these patients, while psychomotor retardation and depressive fatigue can exacerbate their emotional isolation and despair. In these instances, having two professionals working together can minimize the therapeutic exhaustion that so commonly interferes with the treatment of these patients. This may be of even greater importance in the near future with the general decrease in inpatient psychiatric insurance coverage and the growing numbers of patients who cannot afford hospitalization in times of crisis.

> Brenda was an exhausting patient. At age 41, she had been in psychotherapy for almost twenty years for treatment of her severe borderline personality, with self-mutilation, chronic rage, erratic performances at work and chaotic relationships. The intensity and unremitting nature of her psychopathology and of the overwhelming hostile, dependent transferences that were typical of her psychotherapies often culminated in her therapists feeling overwhelmed and depleted. At these times, either through a conscious resignation from the case or through unconscious countertransference behaviors that made the therapy unworkable, Brenda would be pushed out of psychotherapy and would begin again with a new therapist. Because of her chronic dysphoria that was clearly based in her personality disorder, the presence of a superimposed major depressive disorder and the possibility of adjunctive antidepressant treatment was difficult to ascertain. Nonetheless, a psychopharmacological consultation was ultimately obtained. Over the next four years, despite a minimal response to a variety of medications, Brenda continued to see both her therapist and the pharmacotherapist. The two professionals communicated regularly during this time with much clarification of potential splitting issues and even more mutual commiseration. During this time, it became clear that the presence of a colleague allowed each to tolerate what would have been intolerable if working alone. The therapy proceeded slowly with the psychopharmacologist providing a once monthly visit, medication management, an occasional time when the negative transference would temporarily switch to him, and a source of support to both Brenda and her therapist.

4. Splitting the two treatments allows the patient to be seen simultaneously via the microcosmic, intensive observations of the psychotherapist as well as the

more macrocosmic, broad view of the pharmacotherapist. Therapists working with patients in intensive psychotherapy one to three times weekly will naturally focus on links between the material being presented and the patients' mood. It is remarkably easy for them to miss possible cyclical changes in mood that vary, as an example, by the season of the year. Seasonal patterns would be more easily discovered if the patient were seen once a month in a setting that focused more on symptom patterns and not on psychodynamic issues.

Roberta was being treated by a psychiatrist experienced in psychopharmacology with a combination of psychotherapy and medication for narcissistic personality disorder and atypical depression. Because of her increasing depressive symptoms, antidepressants were prescribed at a time when the focus of the therapy was on the dependent relationship the patient maintained with her husband. Within a month, Roberta was markedly less depressed, made plans for a new career and decided to separate from her husband. Her changes were decisive, even bold, and out of character for her. Two months later, it became clear to both patient and psychiatrist that she was experiencing a pharmacological hypomania, and that many of the changes she made were impulsive and difficult to sustain. Had a second professional who was not involved in the psychotherapeutic issues been prescribing the antidepressants, it is far more likely that he would have noted the hypomania precipitated by antidepressants and intervened to diminish the impulsivity earlier.

Donna was being seen in weekly psychotherapy for severe narcissistic personality disorder and hysteroid dysphoria/atypical depression (see chapter 3). Her psychiatrist, who saw her for both therapy and medication, prescribed an MAO inhibitor as a maintenance treatment. Despite the success of the antidepressant in decreasing depressive responses to rejection, the patient still experienced frequent short-lived mood swings that were easily understandable as psychodynamically based in her narcissistic pathology. Following a series of major stressors in a relationship and at work, these mood swings intensified. The patient was ultimately fired from her job because of emotional instability. A second opinion was obtained at that time, and the pattern of a rapid-cycling Bipolar II disorder that had emerged over the previous six months was diagnosed. Lithium was prescribed with clear benefit, although narcissistic mood swings persisted.

In both these cases, the simultaneous presence of two types of mood swings—"biological"/bipolar as well as psychological/narcissistic—made accurate diagnosis difficult. The psychodynamic pathology so dominated both the overall clinical picture and the content of the therapeutic hour that the emergence of the more severe bipolar mood swings was not diagnosed in either case as early as it might have been. Had the split treatment model been used, it is more likely that the hypomania in the first case and the bipolar mood swings in the second would have been diagnosed sooner and appropriate treatment instituted earlier.

5. The split model is often less expensive for patients than seeing a psychiatrist alone. Initially, the split treatment costs more because of the initial medication consultation and the relatively frequent number of medication visits when doses are being adjusted. Over time, however, the number of medication visits generally decreases to one visit every one to three months. Since psychiatrists tend to charge more than other therapists, the split treatment may ultimately save the patient money. Additionally, insurance companies frequently pay for medication consultations and their follow-up visits at the medical rate, typically 80 percent of usual and customary charges, far more than the rather meager psychotherapy insurance reimbursements.

### Disadvantages of the Split Model

The core disadvantage of the therapeutic split model is the dichotomous nature of the treatment and its effect on retarding the development of an integrated view of the self. This difficulty may be manifested in a variety of ways:

1. The split model may foster resistance to one or the other modalities of treatment. Separating medication treatment from psychotherapy by time, place, and person (i.e., going to different offices at different times to see different professionals) undermines the spirit of an integrated but multimodal treatment. It becomes easier for patients to dismiss psychotherapeutic needs ("the antidepressant will make me all better, so talking about my relationships is a waste of time") or medication needs ("I know I've had three psychotic episodes but now I'm working on the roots of my problems in therapy and I'll never get sick again"). Although similar resistances can occur with just one treating professional, the split is easier when two separate individuals are involved.

2. The split model can exacerbate the splitting seen in patients with primitive defenses. Narcissistic and borderline patients tend to split a single therapist into an omnipotent and a devalued object over the course of treatment. With two treating professionals, the tendency to split them into good and bad objects is heightened. This can result in the psychopharmacologist being seen as the uncaring, withholding, distant bad object who spends too little time with the patient and "throws pills" at him while the therapist is seen as the

caring, engaging, soothing good object. Conversely, the therapist can be seen as the ineffectual, soft, and incompetent bad object while the psychopharmacologist is seen as the powerful, effective keeper-of-the-magic. Because these stereotypes frequently reflect the professionals' unconscious biases, a split between the two professionals can easily occur, with either one (or both) unconsciously undermining the treatment of the other.

> Robert was in twice weekly psychotherapy with Dr. C for his narcissistic personality and in maintenance lithium treatment with Dr. D for cyclothymia. Both were very competent professionals whose styles differed. Dr. C was soft spoken and worked within a psychodynamic framework. Dr. D, on the other hand, was a very talkative clinician who was wary of any approaches reminiscent of classical psychoanalysis but had always worked well with patients in psychotherapy and respected Dr. C's work. As Robert's psychotherapy focused on his anger at various parental figures throughout his life, he began to complain about his therapist to Dr. D. He expressed concern that Dr. C stayed silent at times when he, Robert, was feeling helpless and needed some guidance or reassurance. He expressed appreciation that Dr. D carried a beeper and was more available than his therapist. Dr. D's more open approach, he said, helped him feel more grounded and let him deal better with the world. Although initially Dr. D encouraged Robert to speak directly with his therapist, he was becoming increasingly sympathetic to Robert's complaints about his therapy. He considered suggesting to him that he should seek therapy either with himself or with a more reality-oriented therapist. His feelings made him uneasy and he called Dr. C to clarify the situation. Not surprisingly, Dr. C related that Robert had actually been making unrealistic demands in the therapy, insisting that his therapist see him whenever he wanted and not require him to come to his regularly scheduled appointments, that he lower his fee (for no particular reason), and so on. In retrospect, it was clear that when Robert had complained about his therapist, Dr. D had unconsciously encouraged it because of his own concerns about psychoanalytic techniques. Once the two therapists talked, Dr. D was able to resume a more neutral stance with Robert and the potential for a serious therapeutic rift subsided.

2. The split model can retard the patient's ability to integrate various aspects of himself—the biological/psychological, heredity/environment, mastery-through-understanding/mastery-through-medication dichotomies. Having experiences such as manic episodes, psychotic depressions, or panic attacks and being able to integrate these as part of oneself without being defined by them

("I have manic-depressive illness" vs "I am manic-depressive"), or having them overwhelm all other aspects of identity is difficult. The goal should be to integrate these experiences yet hold them slightly apart to be able to examine, understand and deal with them realistically. Seeing two professionals—"one for my mind and one for my brain" creates a very real obstacle to this type of integration.

3. The limited interaction between the psychopharmacologist and the patient can become a frustrating experience for both. Patients may bring up important material that needs to be explored psychotherapeutically in the midst of a (typically) short medication visit. Since the patient is in therapy with someone else, the pharmacotherapist is always forced to suggest that the patient explore the issue elsewhere, promoting feelings of rejection. Of course, if the patient consistently brings tantalizing psychodynamic material to the pharmacotherapist while the psychotherapy is at a standstill, this may indicate that the patient is frightened of these issues and brings them up only in settings where they cannot be explored.

4. In the split model, it is more difficult to deal with the issues surrounding the potential for suicide and the possibility of overdosing on the prescribed medication. If the psychopharmacologist gives a six-week supply of medication to a stable patient who then becomes suicidal two weeks later, it is the therapist (who has not prescribed the medication) who must then think of how many pills the patient has, whether the patient is safe with the pills at home, and so on. Although theoretically, a shared therapeutic responsibility promotes a more coordinated team approach for both professionals, it also makes it easier for this kind of vital information to "slip through the cracks" to the detriment of patient care.


## PSYCHODYNAMICS OF PSYCHOPHARMACOLOGY


Having a therapist suggest the possibility of a medication consultation, seeing a separate professional, and taking pills to alter the way in which one thinks or feels are all parts of an interaction that can have powerful meanings to a patient—meanings that are rooted in individual sensitivities, past experiences, and transference distortions. Reactions may vary, from extremely positive to sufficiently negative to cause a disruption in therapy. In order to integrate the consultation procedure into the psychotherapy, therapists must be prepared to explore patients' reactions and be alert to covert responses that may be expressed in the days or weeks following the initial discussion. Whatever the response, it invariably will yield rich understandings about the patient's inner life and can be used fruitfully in psychotherapy. Patients' feelings can be divided into responses to the therapist, to the psychopharmacologist, and to the medication itself.

The simple suggestion of a psychopharmacological consultation may provoke a wide range of powerful feelings. Some patients may experience it as a rejection, that their therapist doesn't want to work with them; some may think that they are crazy or that their problems are too overwhelming for their therapist. (Of course, at times, it may be true that the consultation expresses an overwhelmed feeling on the therapist's part or the concern that the patient cannot be contained by talking therapy alone.) Others may feel narcissistically wounded, that they are not "good enough" for psychodynamic therapy and that they've let the therapist down. They may interpret the suggestion as reflecting the therapist's impatience or dissatisfaction with the patient's progress. All of these reactions are rooted in the patient's own self-concept and past experiences with others. As an example, a patient who feels that his parents pushed him away whenever he revealed his inner concerns would be more likely to experience a suggestion for a consultation as a repetition of the earlier parental rejection. Working through these feelings will be useful, not only for the outcome of the consultation, but for the psychotherapy itself.

Responses to the psychopharmacologist may also reflect a combination of realistic appreciation of the physician as well as transference distortions of parental figures. The transference is especially powerful for father figures in view of the societal role physicians have always played. This may in large part determine whether the pharmacotherapist is perceived as warm and nurturing, a figure who will soothe the suffering of the patient with his medications, or as a distant, controlling figure who cares little for the patient's inner life but is simply interested in manipulating behavior through pills. A split transference often develops with the maternal therapist and paternal pharmacotherapist perceived according to the patient's childhood memories. This transference configuration is enhanced with the common situation of a female therapist and a male pharmacotherapist.

Finally, the pills themselves can provoke powerful feelings. Medication may be viewed as a form of control by an external power with subsequent feelings of rage and inner helplessness. If a patient has had previous episodes of psychiatric disturbance treated with psychotropic medications—for instance, recurrent depressions treated with antidepressants—pills may also symbolize the disorder previously treated and may evoke strong feelings of disappointment, denial, or anger. Similarly, a patient whose mother was psychiatrically disturbed and was treated with medication will often see taking medications as tantamount to becoming the hated crippled parent. Conversely, if the patient's own past experience with caregivers or psychopharmacologists has had some positive aspects to it, medications can be thought of as a source of support. At times, pills can become powerful transitional objects with a needed ability to soothe during periods of potential fragmentation (Adelman, 1985).

Understanding and working through these potential distortions often provoked by psychopharmacological consultation can be extremely useful. It is important to remember, however, that some of the reactions to pharmacotherapists may be rooted in a realistic appraisal of the manner in which they treat patients. A patient sensitized to issues of paternal distance and rejection will have an even more difficult and probably unhelpful experience with a distant pharmacotherapist. Knowing a patient's individual sensitivities and working with a psychopharmacologist with some psychological mindedness can make the difference between a successful consultation and a failure.

## PATIENT EDUCATION

Among the more unfortunate legacies of the medical model in psychiatry is the tradition of treating patients like helpless young children, incapable of understanding the nature of their problems and too fragile to be told "painful truths." This has led to the all-too-frequent situation of expecting intelligent, clearminded adults to take their medication compliantly without explanations as to what disorder is being treated, why the medication is being prescribed, what positive effects might be expected, and what side effects should be looked for. Among the many consequences of this paternalistic (in the worst nineteenth-century sense) attitude are patient passivity, patient fear, and retardation in the development of the type of healthy cognitive mastery that strengthens the therapeutic partnership between patient and physician. Moreover, treating patients as children is likely to diminish compliance. Patients who understand the nature of the disorder being treated and the treatment offered are more likely to work productively in an active collaboration. This may result not only in better compliance but in actually improving the overall outcome of treatment (Cochran, 1984).

The tradition of prescribing medication for psychiatric problems and disorders is very recent; acceptance of these medications by society in general is even more recent. As such, patients come to a psychopharmacological consultation with a varied set of truths, half-truths, fantasies, and misconceptions. Therefore, among the tasks inherent in psychopharmacological work is the need to explain to patients the nature of the disorder for which medication may be prescribed and the rationale for treatment. The exact amount of information will differ between patients, based on their desire and capacity to understand the information. Additionally, patients may want and need different amounts of information at different times during treatment. For instance, the optimum amount of information given to a profoundly depressed suicidal patient who has limited ability to concentrate is less than should be given to that same patient when he is no longer suicidal, beginning to emerge from the depression, and able to think clearly. Furthermore, if at a later time the patient is considering the pros and cons of maintenance treatment, additional information must be provided.

A number of books or booklets are currently available that offer clear and readable explanations of the nature of psychiatric disorders and current treatment options. My own feeling is that these books can be extremely helpful but only as adjunctive educational tools. The primary mode of communicating knowledge should still be verbal. Direct discussion is preferable because it allows flexibility in the language used and the amount of detail presented. In addition, the physician is available for clarifications and questions. Most importantly, these discussions help establish the therapeutic partnership between the psychopharmacologist and patient.

The main issues that need to be addressed with the patient (and the referring therapist) are:

1. What is the diagnosis? Given the vagaries of current psychiatric knowledge, a clear unambiguous diagnosis is not always possible. A brief discussion of the two or three major possibilities (e.g., depression or dysthymia or both) can be very useful even without a definitive conclusion.

2. What are the possible treatments and what are the relative advantages and disadvantages of each? In treating anxiety, for example, the topics might include a brief discussion of the benzodiazepines, how they may be safer than prior tranquilizers such as barbiturates, and why Xanax is being recommended over Valium for this particular patient.

3. What are the goals of the medication treatment? Patients frequently have understandable but unrealistic expectations and fantasies. They might expect an antidepressant to be an antiunhappiness pill, or, to "cure" their depressive personality. Conversely, patients need to know that it is realistic to expect a medication to diminish or abolish panic attacks, or diminish the sleep, appetite, and energy symptoms of a major depressive episode.

4. What side effects are common with the particular medication being prescribed? Here too, patients differ in the amount of information they want. For some, knowing the possible, though unlikely, side effects, will heighten their anxiety and somatic preoccupation. Others will feel greater mastery knowing all the potential side effects.

The type of patient who reads the *Physicians' Desk Reference* (PDR) is a particular challenge. The PDR lists virtually all side effects ever reported for any drug. It is *not* a textbook of psychopharmacology and does not make a clear enough distinction between typical and extraordinarily rare side effects. To summarize, the PDR can be terrifying. Only a brave and trusting patient would take an MAO inhibitor after reading the PDR. For patients who do read it, the discussion needs to emphasize the issue of rare versus common side effects and the purpose of the book.

5. How long should the patient stay on the medication? Are there long-term side effects? These questions arise more commonly later on in treatment and are valid and important concerns. It is at these times that the issues of maintenance treatment (discussed further in the individual chapters) are most relevant.

## MEDICATION COMPLIANCE: INTRA- AND INTERPERSONAL FACTORS

It is consistently observed that noncompliance with medication regimens occurs in 25 to 50 percent of psychiatric patients (Blackwell, 1976). Noncompliance can be minor, such as missing occasional doses or mistiming the medication— taking one pill in the morning and two in the evening instead of one pill three times daily. In the majority of these instances, the consequences are trivial. But noncompliance can also be significant, resulting in either missing enough doses to diminish treatment outcome, or taking too much medication with the risk of causing significant adverse effects. Therapists must be cognizant of these issues for two reasons. First, understanding factors related to compliance (and therefore, the ultimate success of the medication) helps in choosing an appropriate psychopharmacologist for any particular patient. Second, when patients are seen in a split treatment, the therapist is often the first to learn about the extent of noncompliance and the reasons for it. Some of these factors (see below) are rooted in irrational fears, beliefs, family interactions, or other psychological and psychosocial factors for which psychotherapeutic work may be fruitful. Thus, for those compliance problems rooted in the patient/psychopharmacologist interaction, the therapist may be able to help the patient interact in a more productive and satisfactory way with the physician.

Reasons for significant noncompliance are varied and often overly determined. Factors related to noncompliance may stem from patient, psychopharmacologist, or patient/psychopharmacologist interaction variables (Docherty and Fiester, 1985). Patients may be noncompliant because of acute symptoms inherent in the disorder being treated or as a result of more long-term character traits. For example, a patient with paranoid delusions may be noncompliant because of the conviction that the medications are poisonous or instruments of mind control, convictions that may vanish once the patient's paranoia diminishes. Denial of illness, seen frequently with mania and schizophrenia, will also diminish compliance.

Other patients have psychological conflicts that affect compliance. These may include negative attitudes towards authority, fears of addiction (out of proportion to the realistic possibility), the assumption that taking medication implies "being crazy," sensitivity about not being in control, or secondary gain from the disorder.

A patient's sociocultural environment will also affect noncompliance through family and cultural attitudes towards medications. A patient whose family is deeply involved with a fundamentalist religion whose followers believe that psychiatric disorders are the work of the devil is at high risk to not take medication correctly, if at all. Similarly, cultural or ethnic factors within a family or a community may promote resistance to treatment for psychological problems in general, and specifically to the use of medications to treat them. Patients from these families will receive significant pressure to not take the prescribed medications. Patients from chaotic families have been demonstrated to comply less well than those from stable, supportive families (Docherty, 1988). Also, patients are sometimes profoundly influenced by uneducated opinions from friends, be they close or distant. All physicians have had the experience of a patient actively resisting a certain medication because a neighbor's brother's friend took a similar medication and had, say, a stroke. Naturally, resistances based on these kinds of distorted information may also mask more deepseated fears.

The psychopharmacologist's approach to the patient can also affect compliance and, therefore, outcome. Patients whose physicians believe in the efficacy of their prescribed treatment, for instance, have better compliance.

But a key component in compliance is the doctor-patient relationship (Docherty and Fiester, 1985). Patient and pharmacotherapist enter the consultation each with his own preconception. Yet they can and do influence each other within the first hour. Ultimately, some congruence of goals, expectations, and working relationship must be achieved for compliant and successful treatment to occur.

Aspects of the doctor/patient interaction that generally (but not always) foster compliance are:

1. Increased active participation by the patient. Patients who feel engaged in the treatment, and not like passive oral receptacles of the doctors' pills,

are more likely to be compliant. Such participation may be fostered by discussing varied side effects among a class of medications and helping to pick the one(s) that would be most tolerable, or finding the easiest way to take the daily dose—all in the morning, for example, or three times daily. This gives the patient a greater sense of control in the treatment.

Patient participation does not imply physician passivity. Excessive physician passivity diminishes compliance. What is needed is active collaboration between an engaged patient and an "expert provider" who can dispense knowledge, experience, and (it is hoped) wisdom as conjoint decisions are made.

2. Congruent expectations between patient and physician. In the first session, patient and physician must clarify treatment expectations—about what the treatment may or may not do, what information the patient may want or need, the structure of treatment (how often will they meet, for how long, costs), how long it will take for the medication to work, side effects, and so on.

3. Good communication between doctor and patient. As noted above, patient dissatisfaction with communication with the doctor can be extremely disruptive to treatment. General guidelines are that communication should be brief, clear, and comprehensible. Too often, physicians alternate between not giving enough information or giving it in technical language that is neither comprehensible nor helpful to a patient in distress.

4. Affective tone. Not surprisingly, it is helpful for patient and psychopharmacologist to work in a context characterized by understanding and caring—the same traits that correlate with successful outcome in psychotherapy. Paranoid or suspicious patients, however, or those who had certain types of poor early parenting may experience excessive warmth as smothering and controlling and react negatively. Sheer volume of warmth and friendliness is less helpful than giving the appropriate amount for any individual patient.

Those aspects of treatment that foster compliance must not be seen as ends in themselves. They are necessary but not sufficient for providing optimal care. The wrong medication given in a warm, empathic manner to an actively involved patient in a collaborative effort is no more useful than is the right medication prescribed by a cold distancing psychopharmacologist to a patient who feels neglected—and who therefore doesn't take the pills as prescribed. Compliance is a necessary component of successful treatment but only if the right treatment is complied with.

## TECHNICAL ASPECTS OF SPLIT TREATMENT

### Choosing a Psychopharmacologist

In a community in which there is only one psychiatrist with psychopharmacological expertise, there are no options. But in many areas, a number of practitioners may be available. On what basis might a therapist pick one or a few psychopharmacologists to work with in a split treatment model? Table 14–1 lists the important considerations for this decision. Some of these are relevant in every case—for instance, a specific competence in prescribing medications. Others may apply only in certain clinical situations.

Although the tasks for which a therapist engages the psychopharmacologist—making an accurate diagnosis, evaluating the patient for possible medication treatment, starting the medication and then monitoring it—are specific skills, it is generally preferable to work with someone whose skills extend beyond psychopharmacology. As noted in some of the cases presented above, the interactions and overlap between Axis I and Axis II disorders can be significant and difficult for the most skilled clinicians. Psychopharmacologists with no skill, interest, or experience in personality disorders may be very capable of prescribing medications correctly, but are at risk to be overly inclusive about whom to treat. They may, for instance, interpret all mood swings as bipolar disorder (ignoring personality mood swings) or miss the often multiple sources of dysphoria in a patient with both a personality disorder and major depression. The aphorism "when you are a hammer, everything looks like a nail" applies. Classic cases of medication-responsive disorders will be diagnosed and treated correctly by even narrowly based practitioners. For the more difficult or sensitive patients, broad-based psychiatric skills will enhance the outcome of the consultation.

TABLE 14–1

*Considerations in Choosing a Psychopharmacologist*

General clinical competence
Acceptance and respect for psychotherapy
Specific psychopharmacological competence
Comfort with the split treatment model
Capacity to communicate with the therapist
Capacity and willingness to educate patients
Personal style

Additionally, some psychopharmacologists with no interest or acceptance of other treatment modalities may have disparaging feelings toward psychotherapy in general, or toward the specific type of therapy in which the patient is engaged. Inevitably, these feelings are communicated to the patient either overtly or covertly with predictable negative consequences.

Overall skill as a psychiatric clinician, however, does not immediately confer sophisticated knowledge of diagnosis and psychopharmacology. It is imperative that the pharmacotherapist you work with have specific competence in this area. A competent clinical psychopharmacologist need not know nor have experience with every medication in every class of treatment. Experience with ten antipsychotics, as opposed to five, will rarely, if ever, translate to useful clinical knowledge. A competent psychopharmacologist, though, will have at least *some* experience with more than one agent in each of the major medication classes.

In addition, the psychopharmacologist must feel comfortable and interested in prescribing medication. All too often, psychiatrists with little interest or skill in psychopharmacology are asked to consult and prescribe medications. The psychiatrist's lack of interest or skill in the area is inevitably transmitted to the patient, and even if medications are prescribed, it is in a haphazard, unthoughtful, and usually unsuccessful manner.

> Arthur had a good response from the antidepressant, desipramine. As he ran out of medication two months after improving, he called Dr. A, his prescribing psychiatrist. Dr. A replied in irritation that Arthur need not call, that he would approve a refill if the pharmacy called. No provision was made for follow-up. The next time Arthur ran out of medication, he simply stopped taking it. Three weeks later, he relapsed back into a depression. When his therapist asked why he had discontinued his medication, he replied that he didn't know how long he was supposed to take the antidepressant and that Dr. A had given him no instructions. Between his lack of information, his sense of being a bother to Dr. A, and his subsequent anger, he had simply stopped the medication.

An interested psychopharmacologist who is unsure of a specific technical point (e.g., how to treat the postural hypotension seen with MAO inhibitors) can easily find the answer by informal discussion with colleagues, reading, or even calling the pharmaceutical firm. Without the interest in clinical psychopharmacology, however, the questions will remain unanswered and the outcome will be less satisfactory than it could have been.

Most psychopharmacologists are reasonably skilled at diagnosing and prescribing for most, if not all, major Axis I disorders, even if they have a specific clinical focus on one syndrome. There may be times, though, when a subspecialist in a specific disorder should be consulted. For instance, skill in treating severe anorexia or bulimia with medication involves not just a knowledge of the medications involved, but an awareness of the medical dangers of antidepressants when used to treat these specific disorders. As noted in chapter 6, treating patients with drug or alcohol abuse is particularly difficult and often requires specialized experience in this area.

Not all psychiatrists feel comfortable working in a split treatment model. They are uneasy about being part of a treatment in which they are not the primary therapists and therefore see the patient infrequently. If a psychiatrist with these concerns works in a split treatment model, boundaries become blurred, patients get confused, and therapeutic work is sabotaged.

> Dr. B, a psychiatrist who is both a psychoanalyst and a competent pharmacotherapist, often received referrals from therapists for psychopharmacological consultations. As he became more interested in psychoanalysis and less in medication treatment, he became more uneasy about his role as a pharmacotherapist to patients in therapy with others. He found himself feeling critical of the referring therapists, thinking frequently of how he would handle aspects of the treatment differently. After at least two different instances in which he accepted patients into therapy who had been initially referred to him for medication evaluation, Dr. B became aware that he had unconsciously sabotaged the previous therapies. At that point, he stopped accepting pharmacological consultations and prescribed only for patients who were seeing him in psychotherapy.

Not all psychiatrists are as self-aware as was Dr. B. A pharmacotherapist who is not comfortable with his role will undermine therapies repeatedly. If this happens with any regularity with a colleague, find another.

Although two professionals should be able to work together without having the same theoretical formulations, it is important that they share somewhat similar languages (or at least understand each other's languages!) in describing psychiatric problems. When communicating with each other, terms such as borderline, psychotic, or depression must refer to the same clinical phenomena. Otherwise, communication may be impaired or, ultimately, avoided, to the detriment of the patient's care.

Among the greatest failings of psychopharmacologists is their lack of attention to patient education. In choosing an appropriate pharmacotherapist for a patient, the match between the patient's anticipated need for information and the physician's capacity and skill to provide it should be considered.

Finally, there are times when the "match" of personal attributes between an individual patient and a psychopharmacologist can either enhance or interfere with successful treatment. These considerations are no different from those relevant to picking a psychotherapist. A dramatic, manipulative patient may work better with a pharmacotherapist who stays slightly disengaged. Conversely, a patient who needs more encouragement or nurturing might work more effectively with a more active practitioner. A schizoid patient may feel threatened by someone who is overly warm, while an obsessional patient may need a psychopharmacologist who has the patience for detailed explanations. As noted above, the quality of the therapeutic alliance between pharmacotherapist and patient will materially affect the therapeutic outcome.

## Finding a Psychopharmacologist in Your Community

Depending on the size of the psychiatric community, there may be one or dozens of competent psychopharmacologists available. The best initial approach to finding a psychopharmacologist is the time-honored one of asking colleagues about their own experiences. Using the criteria listed above, an initial cursory assessment of the strengths and weaknesses of the psychiatrists in your community can be made. If possible, it is helpful to identify at least two psychopharmacologists so that if one is unavailable because of vacation, you already have another known to you who will be able to see your patient. It is also helpful, if possible, to know at least one male and one female pharmacotherapist for those patients who would clearly work better with clinicians of one sex or the other.

Once you have the name of a potential practitioner with whom to work, there are two ways to evaluate whether this will be a successful therapeutic relationship. The simplest way is to refer a patient at an appropriate time and to see how it works out, from your point of view and that of your patient. Some therapists want to meet the psychopharmacologist in person, in order to evaluate the psychiatrist's personality, interest, and style of working. This can be very helpful, but is also time consuming. Many psychiatrists are disinclined to take the time to be "interviewed," especially if their practices are already relatively busy. In addition, the medical model, in which all psychiatrists have trained, virtually never uses the interviewing approach to find specialists for consultation purposes. Thus, a lack of desire to meet with a therapist first may have little to do with the psychopharmacologist's competence with your patient or his capacity to work well with you.

## The Consultation Process

### *The Initial Consultation*

The first step toward a psychopharmacological consultation is to discuss the possibility with the patient. As noted above, the suggestion may be met by a variety of reactions that have important transference implications. With some patients, these issues must be worked out before the actual consultation process can begin. With others, or in times of clinical crisis, the consultation can begin while its meanings are being explored.

Once both therapist and patient agree to pursue a consultation, it is wisest for the therapist to call the psychopharmacologist first. This accomplishes a number of goals: (1) if the therapist and psychopharmacologist haven't worked together before, it serves as an introduction; (2) it establishes the availability of the pharmacotherapist (or if he is unavailable, allows the therapist to restart the process with someone else before the patient calls); and (3) it introduces the patient's name and briefly describes the problem in question to the consultant. In my experience, the level of personal attention the pharmacotherapist gives the patient during the first telephone call increases if the groundwork has been laid by the therapist beforehand. If the two professionals have not worked together previously, it can be helpful to clarify the consultation procedure during this call. How many visits will the consultation take? What are the fees? How much information does the pharmacotherapist want beforehand? This information can then be given to the patient. All too frequently, patients who are referred for psychiatric consultation expect elaborate neurological testing and are disappointed when it is not done. Conversely, some patients expect to be interviewed for fifteen minutes and given medication. A realistic appreciation of the nature of a psychopharmacological consultation is vital for coordinated treatment and patient compliance.

There is no universal method of psychopharmacological consultation. In most cases, though, patients are seen one to three times before a diagnostic decision and recommendation for treatment are made. A patient who presents with a classic melancholic depression or a clear-cut panic disorder can usually be diagnosed within one visit. The 24-year-old patient with borderline personality disorder who has been hospitalized twice and has been on multiple medications (the names of which are frequently forgotten) will usually require more visits and past information.

Unfortunately, there is very little magic in a psychopharmacological consultation. Within the interview, the psychopharmacologist will seek a careful delineation of symptoms and a sense of their timing with an additional emphasis on past psychiatric treatments and family and medical history. An interview that concentrates on eliciting symptoms may offend patients who are accustomed to the more psychodynamic examination of "why?" instead of the more symptom-based questions of "what?" Patients may get confused when the needed answer to the question "when did you start feeling depressed?" involves a time frame—"in May"—and not just "after my mother got sick." Timing and evolution of symptom clusters are vital pieces of diagnostic information. Life events and stressors, although important, are not *as* primary in a psychopharmacological consultation. Therefore, in the beginning of the first interview, some consultants explain that the interview will focus more on "what" rather than "why"; that for the purposes of the consultation—to clarify the nature of the problem, to decide whether medication might be helpful, and, if so, which medication—the "what" questions are vital.

The amount of medical information and number of lab tests needed in a consultation varies among psychopharmacologists and from patient to patient. It is impossible to state specifically in advance the extent and cost of the tests. A young healthy male with insomnia or depression may require only a minimal number of blood tests in order to exclude obvious abnormalities. An older depressed man with a history of heart disease may require consultation with an internist and an electrocardiogram and other sophisticated tests. The lab tests virtually always focus on ensuring the patient's physical health and ruling out medical disorders that may either cause the psychiatric syndrome in question or interact with its treatment. Further details on these tests are presented in the previous chapters. It must be emphasized, though, that no test substitutes for a careful history. Except in unusual cases (e.g., the discovery of a brain tumor on a CAT scan or of overt hyperthyroidism in a patient with anxiety), an accurate clinical history carries more weight than do the less easily interpretable lab tests.

If the consultation requires two or more sessions, the psychopharmacologist may call you after the first one to clarify certain clinical points that remain unclear after meeting with the patient. For instance, in evaluating a depressed patient it is often difficult, but important, to accurately date the course of symptoms: is the patient always depressed, as in dysthymic disorder, with superimposed depressive episodes, or does he have clear periods of normal mood? A depressed patient with the cognitive distortions of his disorder may perceive himself as having been depressed for years or a lifetime. The therapist who has seen the patient over months or years may have seen clear periods of normal mood. This distinction can have important implications in predicting response to antidepressants and evaluating the effect of treatment.

Once the consultant has finished his evaluation, he should communicate his thoughts both to the patient directly and to you via a telephone call. A consultation in which the referring therapist has not been given the conclusions of the consultant (assuming the therapist made the initial contact) has achieved only half its goal and should be considered incomplete. If this happens regularly with any particular consultant, bring it to his attention; if the pattern continues, find another pharmacotherapist for future collaborative work. At the end of the consultation, if the pharmacotherapist recommends medication as an appropriate treatment, he can either prescribe at that time or discuss it with you first. If you have strong feelings that medication should not be prescribed without your input, let him know beforehand, since in the medical model consultants frequently make interventions at the time of the consultation before talking to the referring physician. Written reports are sent by some, but not all consultants. They are time consuming and someone (usually the patient) ends up paying for it. When a written report is needed (e.g., for medicolegal reasons when working with a suicidal patient), let the consultant know. Similarly, it is sometimes recommended that the patient, therapist, and pharmacotherapist all meet together at the end of the consultation. Although this would aid in reducing the possibility of splitting and would enhance communication, it is frequently difficult to arrange and expensive for the patient. If the two professionals are comfortable with the split treatment model, a three-way meeting is unnecessary.

### Working in an Ongoing Split Treatment

If medication is prescribed, the psychopharmacologist will typically see the patient after one to three weeks to evaluate the potential therapeutic effect and to ask about side effects in a more detailed manner than is possible on the telephone. During times of active dose adjustment and clinical change, more contact is needed. Once a patient is on a stable dose of medication, the frequency of contact decreases. Although telephone calls are often necessary to adjust doses or for patients to ask about unusual side effects, they cannot substitute for occasional face-to-face meetings in achieving a solid relationship between prescribing physician and patient. When virtually all the contact between patient and psychopharmacologist is by telephone, it can be easily assumed by the patient (and sometimes correctly!) that the physician is uninterested in the patient or the treatment, a feeling that is likely to have a negative effect on the outcome. Face-to-face meetings will enhance any placebo effect, foster compliance with the medication regimen, and decrease the possibilities of a negative transference with the pharmacotherapist. Together, these translate into a better treatment response.

Meetings between patient and pharmacotherapist typically last between fifteen and thirty minutes. The brevity of the meeting sharpens the boundaries between the psychotherapy sessions and the "med" visits. Seeing two mental health professionals for psychotherapy-length sessions, even if the stated goal of one of them is medication management, invites confusion and "parallel" therapies. With some extremely anxious patients, medication checkups may need to be forty-five minutes in order to answer all of the patient's questions and to allay any fears of the medication. In these cases, it is important that the extended "med" visits focus on the medication treatment.

Because the psychotherapist almost always sees the patient more frequently than the psychopharmacologist, questions pertaining to the medication ("Is the fatigue I feel due to the antidepressant?") are often directed to the therapist. The majority of these questions should be redirected to the pharmacotherapist. Except in the case of profoundly disturbed patients who are incapable of making the call, therapists should not call the psychopharmacologist to relay questions; the patient should call directly. This strengthens the alliance between physician and patient, promotes a more active stance on the patient's part in the treatment and diminishes the chance for a triangulation of the therapeutic relationship. If the patient has characterological issues with parental authority figures, this also allows for an interpersonal experience that, if successful, may be corrective or an important focus for psychotherapeutic treatment if problems arise.

For patients who are in maintenance treatment that may last many months or years, the amount of contact between patient and pharmacotherapist may vary from once a month to every six months. Similarly, it is difficult to suggest an appropriate frequency of contact between the therapist and psychopharmacologist over the course of a prolonged split treatment. What is needed is a balance between the extremes of two parallel treatments done in isolation versus overly enmeshed contact with the other professional. If contact is too infrequent, important observations and insights will not be shared, and the two professionals may push the treatment (and the patient) in opposite directions. Patients are also greatly relieved to know that the two professionals communicate with each other about them on a regular basis. Conversely, too much contact between professionals absorbs too much time, resulting in subsequent resentment on the part of one or both professionals. It may also be a clue to seductive, manipulative pathology on the patient's part, promoting the mobilization and overengagement of "caretakers" around him as he waits passively to be rescued or cured.

Contact between the two professionals should always occur in the following circumstances:

1. When the patient's clinical condition changes acutely. The discussion should focus on the nature of the change and any stressors, if any, that might have precipitated it. A coordinated plan of action can then be agreed upon and implemented.

2. If the patient becomes significantly suicidal. Questions to be addressed include the possibility of hospitalization, frequency of therapeutic contact, and whether the patient has a lethal amount of medication at home if an overdose is attempted. At times, if a suicidal patient is not hospitalized, the therapist (who is likely to see the patient more frequently) can keep the pills in his office, dispensing a week (or less) of medication at a time to the patient. This would drastically decrease the risk in case of an impulsive overdose.

3. When a major change in medications is made. The pharmacotherapist should generally inform the therapist if, for example, the patient is changed from a cyclic antidepressant to an MAO inhibitor because of nonresponse. Minor dosage alterations do not need to be discussed every time.

4. Whenever an important clinical question arises. For instance, trying to distinguish between a mild hypomania, especially if precipitated by antidepressants, and the emergence of true assertiveness is often difficult (as in the case of Roberta, described earlier in the chapter). Similarly, distinguishing between an exacerbation of depressed mood in a patient with both major depression and chronic self-esteem problems and depressive personality is easier with multiple observers.

Cynthia was in psychotherapy, dealing with her feelings of inadequacy and dependency on her mother. Additionally, her recurrent depressions were successfully treated by a pharmacotherapist with desipramine 150 mg daily. Following a threat by her mother to force her to move to her own apartment, Cynthia became frantic and suicidal. When she saw her pharmacotherapist, she asked to be hospitalized, describing hypersomnia and fatigue that had lasted for weeks. She did not mention the fight with her mother nor did she say that the hypersomnia occurred only on weekends when she was home all day with her mother. When the two treating professionals discussed the situation, the therapist clarified the acute and recent nature of the exacerbation as well as the variable course of the vegetative symptoms of depression. Because of this information, it was decided not to increase the antidepressant or to hospitalize the patient but to focus the work on her interactions with caregivers such as her mother and the psychopharmacologist.

5. If there is any evidence that therapeutic splitting has occurred and is not diminishing through psychotherapeutic work. The clearest sign of the split is the patient devaluing the other professional—"he doesn't understand me the way you do" or "she doesn't help me at all"—often accom-

panied by a seductive overevaluation of the professional being addressed. In these situations, a personal knowledge of the other professional helps. If exploring transference implications of the split is not sufficient, it is often helpful for the two professionals to communicate.

Sometimes, two professionals may genuinely disagree as to the precipitant and appropriate intervention when a patient seems to be worse: Is the depressive exacerbation in a patient due to the emergence of early, painful memories being worked through or is it a seasonal mood disorder? It is confusing for patients to be given divergent explanations. At these times, the two clinicians need to confer and to make sure that even with disagreement, information can be presented to the patient in a way that does not undermine either treatment.

# Appendix

## Psychiatric Medications

*Note.* Medications are listed alphabetically in the first column using both generic and trade names. When trade names are listed, however, the reader is instructed to look up the generic name or medication class for other trade names for the same product.

| Name | Trade Name(s) | Medication Class[a] (or Major Use) |
|---|---|---|
| Acetophenazine | Tindal | Antipsychotic |
| Adapin: *see* Doxepin | | |
| Akineton: *see* Biperiden | | |
| Alprazolam | Xanax | BZP antianx/hyp |
| Amantadine | Symmetrel | Antipark, anti-s.e. |
| Amitriptyline | Elavil, Endep | Cyclic AD |
| Amobarbital | Amytal | Barb antianx/hyp |
| Amoxapine | Asendin | Cyclic AD |
| d-Amphetamine | Dexedrine | Stimulant |
| Amytal: *see* Amobarbital | | |
| Anafranil: *see* Clomipramine | | |

[a]Abbreviations: AD = antidepressant; Antianx = antianxiety; Antihist = antihistamine; Antipark = antiparkinsonian; Anti-s.e. = anti-side effect; Barb = barbiturate; BZP = Benzodiazepine; Hyp = hypnotic; Nonbarb = nonbarbiturate; OCD = obsessive compulsive disorder.

| Name | Trade Name(s) | Medication Class[a] (or Major Use) |
|------|---------------|-----------------------------------|
| Antabuse: *see* Disulfiram | | |
| Artane: *see* Trihexyphenidyl | | |
| Asendin: *see* Amoxapine | | |
| Atarax: *see* Hydroxyzine | | |
| Atenolol | Tenormin | Antianx, anti-s.e. |
| Ativan: *see* Lorazepam | | |
| Aventyl: *see* Nortriptyline | | |
| Benadryl: *see* Diphenhy-dramine | | |
| Benztropine | Cogentin | Antipark |
| Biperiden | Akineton | Antipark |
| Bromocriptine | Parlodel | Cocaine abuse |
| Bupropion | Wellbutrin | Cyclic AD |
| Buspar: *see* Buspirone | | |
| Buspirone | Buspar | Antianx |
| Butabarbital | Butisol | Barb antianx/hyp |
| Butisol: *see* Butabarbital | | |
| Calan: *see* Verapamil | | |
| Carbamazepine | Tegretol | Mood stabilizer |
| Catapres: *see* Clonidine | | |
| Centrax: *see* Prazepam | | |
| Chloral hydrate | Noctec | Hypnotic |
| Clordiazepoxide | Librium | BZP antianx/hyp |
| Chlorpromazine | Thorazine | Antipsychotic |
| Chlorprothixene | Taractan | Antipsychotic |
| Cibalith: *see* Lithium | | |
| Clomipramine | Anafranil | Cyclic AD, OCD |
| Clonazepam | Klonopin | BZP antianx/hyp |
| Clonidine | Catapres | Antianx, Tourette's |
| Clorazepate | Tranxene | BZP antianx |
| Clozapine | Clozaril | Antipsychotic |
| Clorazil: *see* Clozapine | | |
| Cogentin; *see* Benztropine | | |
| Cylert: *see* Pemoline | | |
| Cyproheptadine | Periactin | Anorexia nervosa |
| Dalmane: *see* Flurazepam | | |
| Depakene: *see* Valproate | | |
| Depakote: *see* Valproate | | |
| Desipramine | Norpramin, Pertofrane | Cyclic AD |
| Desyrel: *see* Trazodone | | |

| Name | Trade Name(s) | Medication Class[a] (or Major Use) |
|---|---|---|
| Dexedrine: *see* d-Amphetamine | | |
| Diazepam | Valium | BZP antianx/hyp |
| Dilantin: *see* Phenytoin | | |
| Diphenhydramine | Benadryl | Antihist, antianx/hyp, antipark |
| Disulfiram | Antabuse | Alcohol abuse |
| Doriden: *see* Glutethimide | | |
| Doxepin | Adapin, Sinequan | Cyclic AD |
| Droperidol | Inapsine | Antipsychotic |
| Elavil: *see* Amitriptyline | | |
| Endep: *see* Amitriptyline | | |
| Ergoloid mesylates | Hydergine | Memory loss |
| Eskalith: *see* Lithium | | |
| Eskalith-CR: *see* Lithium | | |
| Ethchlorvynol | Placidyl | Nonbarb hypnotic |
| Ethinamate | Valmid | Nonbarb hypnotc |
| Etrafon (combination of amitriptyline and perphenazine) | | |
| Fenfluramine | Pondimin | Childhood autism |
| Fluoxetine | Prozac | Cyclic AD |
| Fluphenazine | Prolixin | Antipsychotic |
| Flurazepam | Dalmane | BZP hypnotic |
| Glutethimide | Doriden | Nonbarb hypnotic |
| Halazepam | Paxipam | BZP antianxiety |
| Halcion: *see* Triazolam | | |
| Haldol: *see* Haloperidol | | |
| Haloperidol | Haldol | Antipsychotic |
| Hydergine: *see* Ergoloid mesylates | | |
| Hydroxyzine | Atarax, Vistaril | Antihist, antianx/hyp |
| Imipramine | Tofranil | Cyclic AD |
| Inapsine: *see* Droperidol | | |
| Inderal: *see* Propranolol | | |
| Isocarboxazid | Marplan | MAO inhibitor AD |
| Isoptin: *see* Verapamil | | |
| Kemadrin: *see* Procyclidine | | |
| Klonopin: *see* Clonazepam | | |

| Name | Trade Name(s) | Medication Class[a] (or Major Use) |
|---|---|---|
| Librium: *see* Chlordiaz-epoxide | | |
| Limbitrol (combination of amitriptyline and chlor-diazepoxide) | | |
| Lithium | Eskalith, Lithonate, Lithotabs, Lithobid, Eskalith-CR, Cibalith-S | Mood stabilizer |
| Lithobid: *see* Lithium | | |
| Lithonate: *see* Lithium | | |
| Lithotabs: *see* Lithium | | |
| Lorazepam | Ativan | BZP antianx/hyp |
| Loxapine | Loxitane | Antipsychotic |
| Loxitane: *see* Loxapine | | |
| Ludiomil: *see* Maprotiline | | |
| Luminal: *see* Phenobarbital | | |
| Maprotiline | Ludiomil | Cyclic AD |
| Marplan: *see* Isocarboxazid | | |
| Mebaral: *see* Mephobarbital | | |
| Mellaril: *see* Thioridazine | | |
| Mephobarbital | Mebaral | Barb antianx |
| Meprobamate | Miltown | Nonbarb antianx/hyp |
| Mesoridazine | Serentil | Antipsychotic |
| Methylphenidate | Ritalin | Stimulant |
| Methyprylon | Noludar | Nonbarb hypnotic |
| Miltown: *see* Meprobamate | | |
| Moban: *see* Molindone | | |
| Molindone | Moban | Antipsychotic |
| Naltrexone | Trexan | Opiate addiction |
| Nardil: *see* Phenelzine | | |
| Navane: *see* Thiothixene | | |
| Nembutal: *see* Pentobar-bital | | |
| Noctec: *see* Chloral hydrate | | |
| Noludar: *see* Methyprylon | | |
| Norpramin: *see* Desipramine | | |

| Name | Trade Name(s) | Medication Class[a] (or Major Use) |
|------|---------------|------------------------------------|
| Nortriptyline | Aventyl, Pamelor | Cyclic AD |
| Orap: *see* Pimozide | | |
| Oxazepam | Serax | BZP antianx/hyp |
| Pamelor: *see* Nortriptyline | | |
| Parlodel: *see* Bromocriptine | | |
| Parnate: *see* Tranylcypromine | | |
| Paxipam: *see* Halazepam | | |
| Pemoline | Cylert | Stimulant |
| Pentobarbital | Nembutal | Barb antianx/hyp |
| Periactin: *see* Cyproheptadine | | |
| Perphenazine | Trilafon | Antipsychotic |
| Pertofrane: *see* Desipramine | | |
| Phenelzine | Nardil | MAO inhibitor AD |
| Phenergan: *see* Promethazine | | |
| Phenobarbital | Luminal | Barb antianx |
| Phenytoin | Dilantin | Bulimia nervosa |
| Pimozide | Orap | Tourette's syndrome |
| Placidyl: *see* Ethchlorvynol | | |
| Pondimin: *see* Fenfluramine | | |
| Prazepam | Centrax | BZP antianxiety |
| Procyclidine | Kemadrin | Antipark |
| Prolixin: *see* Fluphenazine | | |
| Promethazine | Phenergan | Antihist antianx/hyp |
| Propranolol | Inderal | Antianx, anti-s.e. |
| Protriptyline | Vivactil | Cyclic AD |
| Prozac: *see* Fluoxetine | | |
| Restoril: *see* Temazepam | | |
| Ritalin: *see* Methylphenidate | | |
| Secobarbital | Seconal | Barb antianx/hyp |
| Seconal: *see* Secobarbital | | |
| Serax: *see* Oxazepam | | |
| Serentil: *see* Mesoridazine | | |
| Sinequan: *see* Doxepin | | |
| Stelazine: *see* Trifluoperazine | | |

| Name | Trade Name(s) | Medication Class[a] (or Major Use) |
|---|---|---|
| Surmontil: see Trimi-pramine | | |
| Symmetrel: see Amantadine | | |
| Taractan: see Chlorprothi-xene | | |
| Tegretol: see Carbam-azepine | | |
| Temazepam | Restoril | BZP antianx/hyp |
| Tenormin: see Atenolol | | |
| Thioridazine | Mellaril | Antipsychotic |
| Thiothixene | Navane | Antipsychotic |
| Thorazine: see Chlorpro-mazine | | |
| Tindal: see Acetophenazine | | |
| Tofranil: see Imipramine | | |
| Tranxene: see Clorazepate | | |
| Tranylcypromine | Parnate | MAO inhibitor AD |
| Trazodone | Desyrel | Cyclic AD |
| Trexan: see Naltrexone | | |
| Triavil (combination of amitriptyline and per-phenazine) | | |
| Triazolam | Halcion | BZP hypnotic |
| Trifluoperazine | Stelazine | Antipsychotic |
| Trifluopromazine | Vesprin | Antipsychotic |
| Trihexyphenidyl | Artane | Antipark |
| Trilafon: see Perphenazine | | |
| Trimipramine | Surmontil | Cyclic AD |
| L-Tryptophan | | Hypnotic |
| Valium: see Diazepam | | |
| Valmid: see Ethinamate | | |
| Valproate | Depakene, Depakote | Mood stabilizer |
| Verapamil | Calan, Isoptin | Mood stabilizer |
| Vesprin: see Trifluopro-mazine | | |
| Vistaril: see Hydroxyzine | | |
| Vivactil: see Protriptyline | | |
| Wellbutrin: see Bupropion | | |
| Xanax: see Alprazolam | | |

# Further Reading

*General Texts*

For those interested in more extensive reading in current diagnostic categories, the single best text is unquestionably the American Psychiatric Association's *Diagnostic and Statistical Manual of Mental Disorders, Third Edition, Revised* (Washington, DC, American Psychiatric Association, 1987). DSM-III-R is not only the standard for psychiatric diagnosis, but is a very good textbook of psychopathology with excellent definitions of psychiatric symptoms, as well as brief reviews of differential diagnosis, course, prevalence, and familial patterns of the disorders it defines. A more detailed and highly readable text which follows the DSM-III diagnostic system is Jerrold S. Maxmen's *Essential Psychopathology* (New York, Norton, 1986).

Readers who wish to pursue more detailed information on general principles or specific topics in biological psychiatry should consult *Psychopharmacology: The Third Generation of Progress,* edited by H. Y. Meltzer (New York, Raven Press, 1987). It is exceedingly long (184 chapters), technical, and dry, but it is the definitive text in the field, written by the leaders of the profession and covering every topic imaginable.

Textbooks of clinical psychopharmacology written for practicing physicians abound. Readers interested in more detail than is presented in this book might consult A. F. Schatzberg and J. O. Cole's *Manual of Clinical Psychopharmacology* (Washington, DC, American Psychiatric Press, 1986); J. G. Bernstein's *Drug Therapy in Psychiatry, second edition* (Littleton, Mass., PSG Publishing, 1988); or, although it is somewhat dated, *The Practitioner's Guide to Psychoactive Drugs, second edition,* edited by E. L. Bassuk, S. C. Schoonover, and A. J. Gelenberg (New York, Plenum, 1983).

For those interested in the history of modern psychopharmacology, *Discoveries in Biological Psychiatry,* edited by F. J. Ayd and B. Blackwell (Philadephia, Lippincott, 1970), gives a series of fascinating accounts of the initial discoveries by many of the scientists who made them.

## Chapter 1
## Diagnosis and Treatment

In its Introduction and Chapters 1 and 2, DSM-III-R presents an excellent description of its assumptions, multiaxial system, and its correct uses.

A seminal article for those interested in the origins of the diagnostic approach taken by DSM-III-R is "Diagnostic Criteria for Use in Psychiatric Research" by J. P.

359

Feighner, E. Robins, S. B. Guze, R. A. Woodruff, G. Winokur, and R. Munoz in *Archives of General Psychiatry* 26 (1972): 57–63, in which the first set of modern descriptive diagnostic criteria were proposed.

A more vigorous (possibly too much so) and lively defense of psychiatric diagnosis can be found in R. L. Spitzer's "More on Pseudoscience in Science and the Case of Psychiatric Diagnosis" in *Archives of General Psychiatry* 33 (1976): 459–470.

Leon Eisenberg's beautiful essay "Mindlessness and Brainlessness in Psychiatry," *British Journal of Psychiatry* 148 (1986): 497–508, lucidly points out the dangers of reductionistic mind versus body dichotomies.

*Chapter 2*
## Biological Basis of Psychopharmacology

Meltzer's edited text, cited under General Texts, is the best overall reference for this chapter, with many individual chapters covering neuronal function, neurotransmitters and receptors, biological hypotheses of the major psychiatric disorders, and mechanisms of action of psychiatric medications.

Goodman and Gilman's *Pharmacological Basis of Therapeutics, seventh edition,* edited by A. G. Gilman, L. S. Goodman, T. W. Rall, and F. Murad (New York, Macmillan, 1985) has long been the definitive text on cellular function and the effects of medications (not only those used in psychiatry) on these functions.

M. B. Martin, C. M. Owen, and J. M. Morihisa's "An Overview of Neurotransmitters and Receptors," in *Textbook of Neuropsychiatry,* edited by R. E. Hales and S. C. Yudofsky (Washington, DC, American Psychiatric Press, 1987), provides an exceedingly clear exposition of current concepts of neurotransmitter/receptor function along with an excellent review of biological hypotheses of depression, schizophrenia, and panic disorder.

S. Snyder's *The New Biology of Mood* (New York, Roerig/Pfizer, 1988) gives clear readable descriptions of the neurotransmitters involved in regulation of cognition and affect and the limbic system.

A fascinating hypothesis on schizophrenia that presents a "neurodevelopmental" model, in which functional biochemical abnormalities are integrated with developmental issues, is presented in D. Weinberger's "Implications of Normal Brain Development for the Pathogenesis of Schizophrenia" in *Archives of General Psychiatry* 44 (1987): 660–669.

*Chapter 3*
## Mood Disorders

Excellent recent reviews on genetics, diagnosis, and psychotherapy and medication treatments on unipolar depression are found in the section entitled "Unipolar Depression" (section editor M. B. Keller), in *Review of Psychiatry, Volume 7,* edited by A. J. Frances and R. E. Hales (Washington, DC, American Psychiatric Press, 1988).

The section "Bipolar Disorder" (section editors F. K. Goodwin and K. R. Jamison) in *Annual Review, Volume 6*, edited by R. E. Hales and A. J. Frances (Washington, DC, American Psychiatric Press, 1987) provides a similarly fine review of a variety of aspects of bipolar disorder.

F. K. Goodwin and K. R. Jamison's *Manic-Depressive Illness* (Oxford, Oxford University Press, in press) is both comprehensive and thorough, and will immediately establish itself as the definitive book on the topic.

Snyder's *The New Biology of Mood* (New York, Roerig/Pfizer, 1988) provides a fine description of the biological and clinical effects of antidepressants.

Exploring the boundaries of "atypical depression" is the subject of active ongoing research. Therefore, there are no helpful up-to-date reviews available. For an early provocative view of one investigator's experience, see H. Akiskal's "Subaffective Disorders: Dysthymic, Cyclothymic, and Bipolar II Disorders in the 'Borderline' Realm," *Psychiatric Clinics of North America* 4 (1981): 25–46.

## Chapter 4
## Anxiety Disorders and Insomnia

Although now somehat dated in its treatment sections because of the number of recent findings, *Anxiety and the Anxiety Disorders,* edited by A. H. Tuma and J. D. Maser (Hillsdale, NJ, Lawrence Erlbaum Associates, 1985) provides detailed and thorough discussions on most topics related to anxiety, including questions of classification.

An interesting review of the genetics of anxiety and anxiety disorders, which is far more than a compendium of study results, can be found in I. M. Marks, "Genetics of Fear and Anxiety Disorders," *British Journal of Psychiatry* 149 (1986): 406–418.

The section entitled "Panic Disorder" (section editors D. H. Barlow and M. K. Shear) in *Review of Psychiatry, Volume 7,* edited by A. J. Frances and R. E. Hales (Washington, DC, American Psychiatric Press, 1988) is superb, thoughtfully discussing biological and psychological models and treatment in an evenhanded manner.

"Social Phobia: Review of a Neglected Anxiety Disorder," by M. R. Liebowitz, J. M. Gorman, A. J. Fyer and D. F. Klein, *Archives of General Psychiatry* 42 (1985): 729–736, reviews the concept of social phobia as a specific disorder in a lucid manner.

For a review of treatment, both behavioral and pharmacological, see T. Perse, "Obsessive-Compulsive Disorder: A Treatment Review" in *Journal of Clinical Psychiatry* 49 (1988): 48–55.

More detailed information on insomnia can be obtained in the section entitled "Sleep Disorders" (D. J. Kupfer, section editor) in *Annual Review, Volume 4* (Washington, DC, American Psychiatric Press, 1985) and in the entire issue of *Psychiatric Clinics of North America* (Volume 10, December 1987) also entitled "Sleep Disorders" (M. Erman, guest editor).

## Chapter 5
## Schizophrenia and Related Disorders

An excellent comprehensive view of schizophrenia, covering diagnostic issues, genetics, and psychosocial and pharmacological aspects of treatment is available in "Schizophrenia" (N. C. Andreasen, section editor) in *Annual Review, Volume 5,* edited by A. J. Frances and R. E. Hales (Washington, DC, American Psychiatric Press, 1986).

A compelling note of caution on accepting the two-syndrome concept of schizophrenia (which focuses on positive and negative symptoms) too literally is found in M. McGuffin, A. Farmer and I. I. Gottesman's "Is There Really a Split in Schizophrenia: The Genetic Evidence," *British Journal of Psychiatry* 150 (1987): 581–592.

*Chapter 6*
## Disorders of Impulse Control

For using medications to treat either anorexia nervosa or bulimia, the best reference, although quickly becoming outdated, is *The Role of Drug Treatments for Eating Disorders,* edited by P. E. Garfinkel and D. M. Garner (New York, Brunner/Mazel, 1987). Practical suggestions regarding the use of medications as part of an overall treatment plan are succinctly summarized in J. Yager's "The Treatment of Eating Disorders" in *Journal of Clinical Psychiatry* 49[9,suppl] (1988): 18–25.

M. Strober and J. Katz provide an excellent critical overview of the relationship between depression and eating disorders in "Depression in the Eating Disorders: A Review and Analysis of Descriptive, Family and Biological Findings," in *Diagnostic Issues in Anorexia Nervosa and Bulimia Nervosa,* edited by D. M. Garner and P. E. Garfinkel (New York, Brunner/Mazel, 1986).

For the relationship between alcoholism and depression, the best single summary article is M. A. Schuckit's "Genetic and Clinical Implications of Alcoholism and Affective Disorders" in *American Journal of Psychiatry* 143 (1986): 140–147.

"The Pharmacotherapy of Alcoholism" by H. R. Kranzler and B. Orrok in *Review of Psychiatry, Volume 8,* edited by A. Tasman, R. E. Hales, and A. J. Frances (Washington, DC, American Psychiatric Press, 1989), is a recent comprehensive overview of the topic.

*Chapter 7*
## Personality Disorders

H. S. Akiskal, R. M. A. Hirschfeld, and B. I. Yeravanian provide a thoughtful review of the relationship between personality and mood disorders in "The Relationship of Personality to Affective Disorders: A Critical Review" in *Archives of General Psychiatry* 40 (1983): 801–810.

The confusing relationship between borderline personality disorder and mood disorders is best conceptualized by J. G. Gunderson and G. R. Elliott in "The Interface Between Borderline Personality Disorder and Affective Disorder" in *American Journal of Psychiatry* 142 (1985): 277–288.

P. H. Soloff provides a current review of the use of medications in treating borderline personality disorder in "Psychopharmacologic Therapies in Borderline Personality Disorder" in *Review of Psychiatry, Volume 8,* edited by A. Tasman, R. E. Hales, and A. J. Frances (Washington, DC, American Psychiatric Press, 1989).

Although not covered in the chapter, the relationship of platelet monoamine oxidase (MAO) activity and personality is a fascinating topic. A representative paper exploring this topic is "Personality Traits Related to Monoamine Oxidase Activity in Platelets" by L. von Knorring, L. Oreland, and B. Winblad in *Psychiatry Research* 12 (1984): 11–26.

## Chapter 8
## Treatment of Special Age-Groups

Although psychopharmacology is not particularly highlighted, the section on child psychiatry (J. M. Wiener, section editor) in *Review of Psychiatry, Volume 8*, edited by A. Tasman, R. E. Hales, and A. J. Frances (Washington, DC, American Psychiatric Press, 1989) is a fine summary of current thinking.

The best single reference on diagnostic and treatment issues in geriatric psychiatry is M. Jenike's *Geriatric Psychiatry and Psychopharmacology: A Clinical Approach* (Chicago, Yearbook Medical Publishing, 1989).

Aside from not describing the fetal abnormalities seen in conjunction with the use of carbamazepine (first reported in mid-1989), the best two references on the use of psychiatric medications in pregnant women are "The Use of Psychotropic Agents in Pregnancy and Lactation" by J. F. Mortola in *Psychiatric Clinics of North America* 12 (1989): 69–87 and "Treatment Guidelines for Psychotropic Drug Use in Pregnancy" by L. S. Cohen, V. L. Heller, and J. F. Rosenbaum in *Psychosomatics* 30 (1989): 25–33.

## Chapter 9
## Antidepressants

A recent review that highlights both the current use of antidepressants as well as exploring the antidepressants of the future is R. J. Baldessarini's "Current Status of Antidepressants: Clinical Pharmacology and Thereapeutics" in *Journal of Clinical Psychiatry* 50 (1989): 117–126.

For those interested in a rather technical and biologically oriented review of the recent research on how antidepressants work, see G. R. Heninger and D. S. Charney's "Mechanisms of Action of Antidepressant Treatments: Implications for the Etiology and Treatment of Depressive Disorders" in *Psychopharmacology: The Third Generation of Progress,* edited by H. Y. Meltzer (New York, Raven Press, 1987).

## Chapter 10
## Lithium and Other Mood Stabilizers

The ultimate reference on lithium is *Lithium Encyclopedia for Clinical Practice, second edition,* by J. W. Jefferson, J. H. Greist, D. L. Ackerman, and J. A. Carroll (Washington, DC, American Psychiatric Press, 1987), which has short, practical, and readable chapters on every imaginable topic.

Although written for patients, M. Schou's *Lithium Treatment of Manic-Depressive*

*Illness: A Practical Guide, second edition* (Basel, S. Karger, 1983) is an excellent monograph on lithium that would usefully educate professionals as well.

The concept of kindling and its relevance for treating mood disorders is best explained in "Kindling and Carbamazepine in Affective Illness" by R. M. Post, T. H. Uhde, F. W. Putnam, J. C. Ballenger, and W. H. Berrettini, in *Journal of Nervous and Mental Disease* 170 (1982): 717–731; and "Conditioning and Sensitisation in the Longitudinal Course of Affective Illness" by R. M. Post, D. R. Rubinow, and J. C. Ballenger in *British Journal of Psychiatry* 149 (1986): 191–201.

## Chapter 11
## Antianxiety Medications and Hypnotics

Reviews on the benzodiazepine receptor are rather technical and difficult to read. The clearest one I have found is O. M. Wolkowitz and S. M. Paul's "Neural and Molecular Mechanisms in Anxiety" in *Psychiatric Clinics of North America* 8 (1985): 145–158.

The most balanced review on benzodiazepine withdrawal that avoids both minimizing and overdramatizing the problem is "Benzodiazepine Withdrawal: A Review of the Evidence," by R. Noyes, M. J. Garvey, B. L. Cook, and P. J. Perry, in *Journal of Clinical Psychiatry* 49 (1988): 382–389.

## Chapter 12
## Antipsychotics

For those interested in the current refinements of the dopamine hypothesis and how the effectiveness of clozapine, the atypical antipsychotic, has altered scientific thinking, see A. Carlsson's "The Current Status of the Dopamine Hypothesis of Schizophrenia" with commentaries by D. Klein, A. Friedhoff, H. Y. Meltzer, and S. H. Snyder in *Neuropsychopharmacology* 1 (1988): 179–203.

Excellent clinical descriptions of akinesia and akathisia are found in "Behavioral Toxicity of Antipsychotic Drugs," by T. Van Putten and S. Marder, in *Journal of Clinical Psychiatry* 48 [9, suppl] (1987): 13–19.

## Chapter 13
## Electroconvulsive Therapy (ECT); Stimulants

The article on ECT that best summarizes current thinking is "Electroconvulsive Therapy" by Consensus Conference in *Journal of the American Medical Association* 254 (1985): 2103–2108. For those interested in more detail on ECT's mechanism of action, effects on memory, and related topics, see "Electroconvulsive Therapy" (section editors R. M. Rose and H. A. Pincus) in *Review of Psychiatry, Volume 7,* edited by A. J. Frances and R. E. Hales (Washington, DC, American Psychiatric Press, 1988).

"The Use of Psychostimulants in General Psychiatry: A Reconsideration," by R. J. Chiarello and J. O. Cole in *Archives of General Psychiatry* 44 (1987): 286–295, is the best review on the topic.

## Chapter 14
## Split Treatment Model

A detailed review on hypothesized interactions between psychotherapy and psychopharmacology is found in "Ideologic Conflicts in Combined Treatment" by G. L. Klerman in *Combining Psychotherapy and Drug Therapy in Clinical Practice*, edited by B. D. Beitman and G. L. Klerman (New York, Spectrum Publications, 1984).

In "Combined Psychotherapy and Pharmacotherapy for Depression: A Systematic Analysis of the Evidence" in *Archives of General Psychiatry* 43 (1986): 471–479, H. R. Conte, R. Plutchik, K. V. Wild, and T. B. Karasu provide a critical review of the merits of a combined therapeutic approach for depression.

"The Therapeutic Alliance and Compliance with Psychopharmacology," by J. P. Docherty and S. J. Fiester, in *Annual Review, Volume 4*, edited by R. E. Hales and A. J. Frances (Washington, DC, American Psychiatric Press, 1985), thoughtfully reviews the topic.

# References

ADELMAN, S. (1985). Pills as transitional objects: A dynamic understanding of the use of medication in psychotherapy. *Psychiatry, 48,* 246–253.

ADLER, L., ANGRIST, B., PESELOW, E., CORWIN, J., MASKANSKY, R., & ROTROSEN, J. (1986). A controlled assessment of propranolol in the treatment of neuroleptic-induced akathisia. *British Journal of Psychiatry, 149,* 42–45.

AKISKAL, H. S., DJENDEREDJAN, A. H., ROSENTHAL, R. H., & KHANI, M. K. (1977). Cyclothymic disorder: Validating criteria for inclusion in the bipolar affective group. *American Journal of Psychiatry, 134,* 1227–1233.

AKISKAL, H. S., KHANI, M., & SCOTT-STRAUSS, A. (1979). Cyclothymic temperamental disorders. *Psychiatric Clinics of North America, 2,* 527–554.

AKISKAL, H. S., ROSENTHAL, T. L., HAYKAL, R. F., LEMMI, H., ROSENTHAL, R. H., & SCOTT-STRAUSS, A. (1980). Characterological depressions: Clinical and sleep EEG findings separating 'subaffective dysthymias' from 'character spectrum disorders.' *Archives of General Psychiatry, 37,* 777–783.

AMBELAS, A. (1987). Life events and mania: A special relationship. *British Journal of Psychiatry, 150,* 235–240.

AMERICAN PSYCHIATRIC ASSOCIATION. (1987). *Diagnostic and Statistical Manual of Mental Disorders, Third Edition, Revised* (DSM-III-R). Washington, DC: American Psychiatric Association.

ANDERSEN, A. E. (1987). Use and potential of antianxiety agents in the treatment of anorexia nervosa and bulima nervosa. In P. E. Garfinkel & D. M. Garner (Eds.), *The role of drug treatments for eating disorders.* New York: Brunner/Mazel.

ANGST, J. (1973). The course of monopolar depression and bipolar psychoses. *Psychiatrie, Neurologie et Neurochirurgie, 76,* 489–500.

ANGST, J., FELDER, W., & FREY, R. (1979). The course of unipolar and bipolar affective disorders. In M. Schou & E. Stromgren (Eds.), *Origin, prevention and treatment of affective disorders.* New York: Academic Press.

ARANA, G. W., GOFF, D. C., BALDESSARINI, R. J., & KEEPERS, G. A. (1988). Efficacy of anticholinergic prophylaxis for neuroleptic-induced acute dystonia. *American Journal of Psychiatry, 145,* 993–996.

AYD, F., & BLACKWELL, D. (EDS.). (1970). *Discoveries in biological psychiatry.* Philadelphia: Lippincott.

BAILEY, G., & EGAN, J. (1989). Conduct disorders. In A. Tasman, R. E. Hales, & A. J. Frances (Eds.), *Review of psychiatry,* Vol. 8. Washington, DC: American Psychiatry Press.

BALDESSARINI, R. J. (1989). Current status of antidepressants: Clinical pharmacology and therapy. *Journal of Clinical Psychiatry, 50,* 117–126.

BALDESSARINI, R. J., COHEN, B. M., & TEICHER, M. H. (1988). Significance of neuroleptic dose and plasma level in the pharmacological treatment of psychoses. *Archives of General Psychiatry, 45,* 79–91.

BALLENGER, J. C. (1986). Pharmacotherapy of the panic disorders. *Journal of Clinical Psychiatry, 47* (Suppl.), 27–31.

BALLENGER, J. C., BURROWS, G. D., DuPONT, R. L., LESSER, I. M., NOYES, R., PECKNOLD, J. C., RIFKIN, A., & SWINSON, R. P. (1988). Alprazolam in panic disorder and agoraphobia: Results from a multicenter trial. 1. Efficacy in short-term treatment. *Archives of General Psychiatry, 45,* 413–422.

BARABAN, J. M., WORLEY, P. F., & SNYDER, S. (1989). Second messenger systems and psychoactive drug action: Focus on the phosphoinositide system and lithium. *American Journal of Psychiatry, 146,* 1251–1260.

BEIN, H. J. (1970). Biological research in the pharmaceutical industry with reserpine. In F. Ayd & B. Blackwell (Eds.), *Discoveries in biological psychiatry.* Philadelphia: Lippincott.

BEITCHMAN, J. H. (1985). Childhood schizophrenia: A review and comparison with adult-onset schizophrenia. *Psychiatric Clinics of North America, 8,* 793–814.

BEITMAN, B. (1988). Combining pharmacotherapy and psychotherapy: Diagnostic considerations. In F. Flach (Ed.), *Psychobiology and psychopharmacology.* New York: Norton.

BENDZ, F. H. (1983). Kidney function in lithium-treated patients: A literature review. *Acta Psychiatrica Scandinavia, 68,* 303–324.

BERRY, C., SHAYWITZ, S., & SHAYWITZ, B. (1985). Girls with attention deficit disorder: A silent minority? A report on behavioral and cognitive characteristics. *Pediatrics, 76,* 801–809.

BIEDERMAN, J. (1988). Pharmacological treatment of adolescents with affective disorders and attention deficit disorder. *Psychopharmacology Bulletin, 24,* 81–87.

BIEDERMAN, J., LERNER, Y., & BELMAKER, R. N. (1979). Combination of lithium carbonate and haloperidol in schizo-affective disorder: A controlled study. *Archives of General Psychiatry, 36,* 327–333.

BLACK, D. W., WINOKUR, G., & NASRALLAH, A. (1986). ECT in unipolar and bipolar disorders: A naturalistic evaluation of 460 patients. *Convulsive Therapy, 2,* 231–237.

BLACKWELL, B. (1976). Treatment adherence. *British Journal of Psychiatry, 129,* 513–531.

BLAND, R. C., NEWMAN, S. C., & ORR, H. (1986). Recurrent and non-recurrent depression: A family study. *Archives of General Psychiatry, 43,* 1085–1089.

BLEHAR, M. C., & ROSENTHAL, N. E. (1989). Seasonal affective disorders and phototherapy. *Archives of General Psychiatry, 46,* 469–474.

BLOOM, F. E. (1985). Neurohumoral transmission and the central nervous system. In A. G. Gilman, L. S. Goodman, T. W. Rall, & F. Murad (Eds.), *Goodman and Gilman's The pharmacological basis of therapeutics,* 7th Ed. New York: Macmillan.

BOND, W. S. (1986). Psychiatric indications for clonidine: The neuropharmacologic and clinical basis. *Journal of Clinical Psychopharmacology, 6,* 81–87.

BORISON, R. L., & DIAMOND, B. I. (1987). Neuropharmacology of the extrapyramidal system. *Journal of Clinical Psychiatry, 48.* (9, Suppl), 7–12.

BREIER, A., CHARNEY, D. S., & HENINGER, G. R. (1986). Agoraphobia with panic attacks: Development, diagnostic stability, and course of illness. *Archives of General Psychiatry, 43,* 1029–1036.

BREIER, A., CHARNEY, D. S., & HENINGER, G. R. (1984). Major depression in patients with agoraphobia and panic disorders. *Archives of General Psychiatry, 41,* 1129–1135.

BUNNEY, W. E., & DAVIS, J. M. (1965). Norepinephrine in depressive disorders: A review. *Archives of General Psychiatry, 13,* 483–494.

BUNNEY, W. E., & GARLAND–BUNNEY, B. L. (1987). Mechanisms of action of lithium in affective illness: Basic and clinical implications. In H. Y. Meltzer (Ed.), *Psychopharmacology: The third generation of progress.* New York: Raven Press.

BUSTO, U., SELLERS, E. M., NARANJO, C. A., CAPPELL, H., SANCHEZ-CRAIG, M., & SYKORA, K. (1986). Withdrawal reaction after long-term therapeutic use of benzodiazepines. *New England Journal of Medicine, 315,* 854–859.

BYERLEY, B., & GILLIN, J. C. (1984). Diagnosis and management of insomnia. *Psychiatric Clinics of North America, 7,* 773–789.

CADE, J. F. J. (1949). Lithium salts in the treatment of psychotic excitement. *Medical Journal of Australia, 2,* 349–352.

CAMPBELL, M. (1987). Drug treatment of infantile autism. In H. Y. Meltzer (Ed.), *Psychopharmacology: The third generation of progress.* New York: Raven Press.

CAMPBELL, M., SMALL, A. M., GREEN, W. H., JENNINGS, S. J., PERRY, R., BENNETT, W. G., & ANDERSON, L. (1984). Behavioral efficacy of haloperiodol and lithium carbonate: A comparison in hospitalized aggressive children with conduct disorder. *Archives of General Psychiatry, 41,* 650–656.

CAMPBELL, M., SMALL, A. M., PALIJ, M., PERRY, R., POLONSKY, B., LUKASHOK, D., & ANDERSON, L. T. (1987). The efficacy and safety of fenfluramine in autistic children: Preliminary analysis of a double-blind study. *Psychopharmacology Bulletin, 23,* 123–127.

CAMPBELL, M., & SPENCER, E. K. (1988). Psychopharmacology in child and adolescent psychiatry: A review of the past five years. *Journal of the American Academy of Child and Adolescent Psychiatry, 27,* 269–279.

CANTWELL, D. P. (1985a). Hyperactive children have grown up: What have we learned about what happens to them? *Archives of General Psychiatry, 42,* 1026–1028.

CANTWELL, D. P. (1985b). Pharmacotherapy of ADD in adolescents: What do we know, where should we go, how should we do it? *Psychopharmacology Bulletin, 21,* 251–257.

CANTWELL, D. P., & HANNA, G. (1989). Attention-deficit hyperactivity disorder. In A. Tasman, R. E. Hales, & A. J. Frances (Eds.) *Review of Psychiatry,* Vol. 8. Washington, DC.: American Psychiatric Press.

CARLSON, G. A., & CANTWELL, D. P. (1980). Unmasking masked depression in children and adolescents. *American Journal of Psychiatry, 137,* 445–449.

CAROFF, S. N. (1980). The neuroleptic malignant syndrome. *Journal of Clinical Psychiatry, 41,* 79–83.

CASEY, D. E. (1987). Tardive dyskinesia. In H. Y. Meltzer (Ed.), *Psychopharmacology: The third generation of progress.* New York: Raven Press.

CASPAR, R. C., REDMOND, D. E., KATZ, M. M., SCHAFFER, C. B., DAVIS, J. M., & KOSLOW, S. H. (1985). Somatic symptoms in primary affective disorder. Presence and relationship to the classification of depression. *Archives of General Psychiatry, 42,* 1098–1104.

CHARNEY, D. S., HENINGER, G. R., & JATLOW, P. I. (1985). Increased anxiogenic effects of caffeine in panic disorders. *Archives of General Psychiatry, 42,* 233–243.

CHARNEY, D. S., & HENINGER, G. R. (1985). Noradrenergic function and the mechanism of action of antianxiety treatment II: The effect of long-term imipramine treatment. *Archives of General Psychiatry, 42,* 473–481.

CHARNEY, D. S., STERNBERG, D., KLEBER, H. D., HENINGER, G. R., & REDMOND, D. E. (1981). The clinical use of clonidine in abrupt withdrawal from methadone. *Archives of General Psychiatry, 38,* 1273–1277.

CHARNEY, D. S., & WOODS, S. W. (1989). Benzodiazepine treatment of panic disorder: A comparison of alprazolam and lorazepam. *Journal of Clinical Psychiatry, 50,* 418–423.

CHEUNG, H. K. (1981). Schizophrenics fully remitted on neuroleptics for 3–5 years: To stop or continue drugs. *British Journal of Psychiatry, 139,* 490–494.

CHIARELLO, R. J., & COLE, J. O. (1987). The use of psychostimulants in general psychiatry: A reconsideration. *Archives of General Psychiatry, 44,* 286–295.

CHOUINARD, G. (1988). Clonazepam in the treatment of psychiatric disorders. In S. L. McElroy & H. G. Pope (Eds.), *Use of anticonvulsants in psychiatry.* Clifton, NJ: Oxford Health Care, Inc.

CIRAULO, D. A., BARNHILL, J. G., GREENBLATT, D. J., SHADER, R. I., CIRAULO, A. M., TARMEY, M. F., MOLLOY, M. A, & FOTI, M. E. (1988). Abuse liability and clinical pharmacokinetics of alprazolam in alcoholic men. *Journal of Clinical Psychiatry, 49,* 333–337.

COCHRAN, S. (1984). Preventing medical noncompliance in the outpatient treatment of bipolar affective disorders. *Journal of Consulting and Clinical Psychology, 52,* 873–878.

COHEN, L. S., HELLER, V. L., & ROSENBAUM, J. F. (1989). Treatment guidelines for psychotropic drug use in pregnancy. *Psychosomatics, 30,* 25–33.

COLE, J. O., GOLDBERG, S. C., & KLERMAN, G. L. (1964). Phenothiazine treatment in acute schizophrenia. *Archives of General Psychiatry, 10,* 246–261.

CONNERS, C. K., & TAYLOR, E. (1980). Pemoline, methylphenidate, and placebo in children with minimal brain dysfunction. *Archives of General Psychiatry, 37,* 922–930.

CONSENSUS CONFERENCE. (1985). Electroconvulsive therapy. *Journal of the American Medical Association, 254,* 2103–2108.

CONSENSUS DEVELOPMENT PANEL. (1985). Mood disorders: Pharmacologic prevention of recurrences. *American Journal of Psychiatry, 142,* 469–476.

CONTE, H., PLUTCHNIK, R., WILD, K., & KARASU, T. B. (1986). Combined psychotherapy and pharmacotherapy for depression: A systematic analysis of the evidence. *Archives of General Psychiatry, 43,* 471–479.

COOPER, J. E., KENDALL, R. E., & KURLAND, B. J. (1972). *Psychiatric diagnosis in New York and London: Maudsley Monograph No. 20,* London: Oxford University Press.

CORYELL, W., & WINOKUR, G. (1982). Course and outcome. In E. S. Paykel (Ed.), *Handbook of affective disorders.* New York: Guilford Press.

COSTA, E. (1985). Benzodiazepine–GAPA interactions: A model to investigate the neurobiology of anxiety. In A. H. Tuma & J. D. Maser (Eds.), *Anxiety and the anxiety disorders.* Hillsdale, NJ: Lawrence Erlbaum Associates.

COWDRY, R. W. (1987). Psychopharmacology of borderline personality disorder: A review. *Journal of Clinical Psychiatry, 48* (Suppl.), 15–22.

COWDRY, R. W., & GARDNER, D. L. (1988). Pharmacotherapy of borderline personality disorder: Alprazolam, carbamazepine, trifluoperazine, and tranylcypromine. *Archives of General Psychiatry, 45,* 111–119.

CREESE, I. (1985). Dopamine and antipsychotic medications. In R. E. Hales & A. J. Frances (Eds.), *Annual review,* Vol. 4. Washington DC: American Psychiatric Press.

CREESE, I., BURT, D. R., & SNYDER, S. H. (1976). Dopamine receptor binding predicts clinical and pharmacological potencies of antischizophrenic drugs. *Science, 192,* 481–483.

CROW, T. J. (1980). Molecular pathology of schizophrenia: More than one disease process? *British Medical Journal, 280,* 66–68.

CROW, T. J., FERRIER, I. N., & JOHNSTONE, E. C. (1986). The 2 syndrome concept and neuroendocrinology of schizophrenia. *Psychiatric Clinics of North America, 9,* 99–113.

CROWE, R. R. (1974). An adoption study of antisocial personality. *Archives of General Psychiatry, 31,* 785–791.

CROWE, R. R., NOYES, R., PAULS, D. L., & SLYMEN, D. (1983). A family study of panic disorder. *Archives of General Psychiatry, 40,* 1065–1069.

CUNNINGHAM OWENS, D. G., JOHNSTONE, E. C., & FRITH, C. D. (1982). Spontaneous involuntary disorders of movement: Their prevalence, severity, and distribution in chronic schizophrenics with and without treatment with neuroleptics. *Archives of General Psychiatry, 39,* 452–461.

DAVIDSON, J. (1989). Seizures and bupropion: A review. *Journal of Clinical Psychiatry, 50,* 256–261.

DAVIDSON, J. R. T., GILLER, E. L., ZISOOK, S., & OVERALL, J. E. (1988). An efficacy study of isocarboxazid and placebo in depression, and its relationship to depressive nosology. *Archives of General Psychiatry, 45,* 120–127.

DAVIDSON, J., MILLER, R., TURNBALL, C., & SULLIVAN, J. L. (1982). Atypical depression. *Archives of General Psychiatry, 39,* 527–534.

DAVIDSON, J., SWARTZ, M., STORCK, M., KRISHNAN, R. R., & HAMMETT, E. (1985). A diagnostic and family study of posttraumatic stress disorder. *American Journal of Psychiatry, 142,* 90–93.

DAVIS, J. M., KOSLOW, S. H., GIBBONS, R. D., MAAS, J. W., BOWDEN, C. L., CASPER, R., HANIN, I., JAVAID, J., CHANG, S. S., & STOKES, P. E. (1988). Cerebrospinal fluid and urinary biogenic amines in depressed patients and healthy controls. *Archives of General Psychiatry, 45,* 705–717.

DAVIS, J. M., SCHAFFER, C. B., KILLIAN, G. A., KINARD, C., & CHAN, C. (1980). Important issues in the drug treatment of schizophrenia. *Schizophrenia Bulletin, 6,* 70–87.

DELVA, N. J., & LETEMENDIA, F. J. (1982). Lithium treatment in schizophrenia and schizo-affective disorder. *British Journal of Psychiatry, 141,* 387–400.

DENIKER, P. (1970). Introduction of neuroleptic chemotherapy in psychiatry. In F. Ayd & B. Blackwell (Eds.), *Discoveries in biological psychiatry.* Philadelphia: Lippincott.

DEVEAUGH-GEISS, J., LANDAU, P., & KATZ, R. (1989). Preliminary results from a multi-center trial of clomipramine in obsessive-compulsive disorder. *Psychopharmacology Bulletin, 25,* 36–40.

DIETCH, J. T., & JENNINGS, R. K. (1988). Aggressive dyscontrol in patients with benzodiazepines. *Journal of Clinical Psychiatry, 49,* 184–188.

DOCHERTY, J. (1988). Managing compliance problems in psychopharmacology. In F. Flach (Ed.), *Psychobiology and psychopharmacology,* New York: Norton.

DOCHERTY, J., & FIESTER, S. (1985). The therapeutic alliance and compliance with psychopharmacology. In R. E. Hales & A. J. Frances (Eds.), *Annual review,* Vol. 4. Washington, DC: American Psychiatric Press.

DOCHERTY, J., FIESTER, S., & SHEA, T. (1986). Syndrome diagnosis and personality disorders. In A. J. Frances & R. E. Hales (Eds.), *Annual review,* Vol. 5, Washington, DC: American Psychiatric Press.

DOWNING, R., & RICKELS, K. (1987). Early treatment response in anxious outpatients treated with diazepam. *Acta Psychiatrica Scandinavia, 72,* 522–528.

DREIFUS, F., SANTILLI, N., & LANGER, D. (1987). Valproic acid hepatic fatalities: A retrospective review. *Neurology, 37,* 379–385.

DWORKIN, R. H., & CALIGOR, E. (1988). Psychiatric diagnosis and chronic pain: DSM-III-R and beyond. *Journal of Pain and Symptom Management, 3,* 87–98.

EDELSTEIN, C. (1989). *Mood disorders and eating disorders.* Presented at the 142nd American Psychiatric Association Annual Meeting, San Francisco, CA.

ELKIN, I., SHEA, M. T. WATKINS, J. T. IMBER, S. D., SOTSKY, S. M., COLLINS, J. F., GLASS, D. R., PILKONIS, P. A., LEBER, W. R., DOCHERTY, J. P., FEISTER, S. J., & PARLOFF, M. B. (1989). National Institute of Mental Health Treatment of Depression collaborative research program: General effectiveness of treatments. *Archives of General Psychiatry, 46,* 971–982.

ERENBERG, G. (1988). Pharmacologic therapy of tics in childhood. *Psychiatric Annals, 18,* 399–408.

EXTEIN, I. R., & GOLD, M. S. (1988). The treatment of cocaine addicts: Bromocriptine or desipramine. *Psychiatric Annals, 18,* 535–537.

FAWCETT, J. (1989). Valproate use in acute mania and bipolar disorders: An international perspective. *Journal of Clinical Psychiatry, 50* (Suppl.), 10–12.

FAWCETT, J., CLARK, D. C., AAGESEN, C. A., PISANI, V. D., TILKIN, J. M., SELLERS, D., McGUIRE, M., & GIBBONS, R. D. (1987). A double-blind placebo-controlled trial of lithium carbonate therapy for alcoholism. *Archives of General Psychiatry, 44,* 248–256.

FAWCETT, J., EDWARDS, J. H., KRAVITZ, H. M., & JEFFRIESS, H. (1987). Alprazolam: An antidepressant? Alprazolam, desipramine, and an alprazolam-desipramine combination in the treatment of adult depressed outpatients. *Journal of Clinical Psychopharmacology, 7,* 295–310.

FERNSTROM, M. A., KROWINSKI, R., & KUPFER, D. (1986). Chronic imipramine treatment and weight gain. *Psychiatric Research, 17,* 269–273.

FIEVE, R. R. (1976). *Moodswings: The third revolution in psychiatry.* New York: Bantam Books.

FIEVE, R., & PESELOW, E. (1983). Lithium: Clinical applications. In G. D. Burrows, T. Norman, & B. Davies (Eds.), *Antidepressants.* Amsterdam: Elsevier.

FINK, M. (1988). Convulsive therapy: A manual of practice. In A. J. Frances & R. E. Hales (Eds.), *Review of psychiatry,* Vol. 7. Washington DC: American Psychiatric Press.

FISCHMAN, M. W. (1987). Cocaine and the amphetamines. In H. Y. Meltzer (Ed.), *Psychopharmacology: The third generation of progress.* New York: Raven Press.

FLAMENT, M., RAPOPORT, J., BERG, C., SCEERY, W., KILTS, C., MELLSTROM, B., & LINNOILA, M. (1985). Clomipramine treatment of childhood obsessive-compulsive disorder: A double-blind controlled study. *Archives of General Psychiatry, 42,* 977–983.

FRANCE, R. D., HOUPT, J. L., & ELLINWOOD, E. H. (1984). Therapeutic effects of antidepressants in chronic pain. *General Hospital Psychiatry, 6,* 55–63.

FRANK, J. B., KOSTEN, T. R., GILLER, E. L., & DAN, E. (1988). A randomized clinical trial of phenelzine and imipramine for post-traumatic stress disorder. *American Journal of Psychiatry, 145,* 1289–1291.

FREEMAN, P., & GUNDERSON, J. (1989). Treatment of personality disorders. *Psychiatric Annals, 19,* 147–153.

FRIEDMAN, M. J. (1988). Toward rational pharmacotherapy for post-traumatic stress disorder: An interim report. *American Journal of Psychiatry, 145,* 281–285.

FYER, A., LIEBOWITZ, M., GORMAN, J., CAMPEAS, R., LEVIN, A., DAVIES, S. O., GOETZ, D., & KLEIN, D. F. (1987). Discontinuation of alprazolam treatment in panic patients. *American Journal of Psychiatry, 144,* 303–308.

FYER, A. J., MANNUZZA, S., & ENDICOTT, J. (1987). Differential diagnosis and assessment of anxiety: Recent developments. In H. Y. Meltzer (Ed.), *Psychopharmacology: The third generation of progress.* New York: Raven Press.

FYER, A., & SANDBERG, D. (1988). Pharmacologic treatment of panic disorder. In A. J. Frances & R. E. Hales (Eds.), *Review of psychiatry,* Vol. 7. Washington, DC: American Psychiatric Press.

GARDOS, G., COLE, J. O., HASKELL, D., MARBY, D., PAINE, S. S., & MOORE, P. (1988). The natural history of tardive dyskinesia. *Journal of Clinical Psychopharmacology, 8* (Suppl.), 31S–37S.

GARLAND, E. J., REMICK, R. A., & ZIS, A. P. (1988). Weight gain with antidepressants and lithium. *Journal of Clinical Psychopharmacology, 8,* 323–330.

GAWIN, F. H., ALLEN, D., & HUMBLESTONE, B. (1989). Outpatient treatment of 'crack' cocaine smoking with flupenthixol decanoate: A preliminary report. *Archives of General Psychiatry, 46,* 322–325.

GAWIN, F. H., & KLEBER, H. D. (1986). Abstinence symptomatology and psychiatric diagnosis in cocaine abusers: Clinical observations. *Archives of General Psychiatry, 43,* 107–113.

GAWIN, F. H., KLEBER, H. D., BYCK, R., ROUNSAVILLE, B. J., KOSTEN, T. R., JATLOW, P. I., & MORGAN, C. (1989). Desipramine facilitation of initial cocaine abstinence. *Archives of General Psychiatry, 46,* 117–121.

GELENBERG, A. (1987). Treating extrapyramidal reactions: Some current issues. *Journal of Clinical Psychiatry, 48* (Suppl.), 24–27.

GELLER, B., COOPER, T. B., CHESTNUT, E. C., ANKER, J. A., & SCHLUCHTER, M. D. (1986). Preliminary data on the relationship between nortriptyline plasma level and response in depressed children. *American Journal of Psychiatry, 143,* 1283–1286.

GEORGOTAS, A., McCUE, R. E., HAPWORTH, W., FRIEDMAN, E., KIM, O. M., WELKOWITZ, J., CHANG, I., & COOPER, T. B. (1986). Comparative efficacy and safety of MAOIs versus TCAs in treating depression in the elderly. *Biological Psychiatry, 21,* 1155–1166.

GERSON, S. C., PLOTKIN, D. A., & JARVIK, L. F. (1988). Antidepressant drug studies, 1964 to 1986: Empirical evidence for aging patients. *Journal of Clinical Psychopharmacology, 8,* 311–322.

GILLIN, J. C., SPINWEBER, C. C., & JOHNSON, L. C. (1989). Rebound insomnia: A critical review. *Journal of Clinical Psychopharmacology, 9,* 161–172.

GITLIN, M., COCHRAN, S., & JAMISON, K. (1989). Maintenance lithium treatment: Side effects and compliance. *Journal of Clinical Psychiatry, 50,* 127–131.

GITLIN, M., & JAMISON, K. (1984). Lithium clinics: Theory and practice. *Hospital and Community Psychiatry, 35,* 363–368.

GITLIN, M., & PASNAU, R. O. (1989). Psychiatric syndromes linked to reproductive function in women: A review of current knowledge. *American Journal of Psychiatry, 146,* 1413–1422.

GITLIN, M. J., WEINER, D. F., FAIRBANKS, L., HERSHMAN, J. M., & FRIEDFELD, N. (1987). Failure of T₃ to potentiate antidepressant response. *Journal of Affective Disorders, 13,* 267–272.

GITTELMAN, R., MANNUZZA, S., SHENKER, R., & BONAGURA, N. (1985). Hyperactive boys almost grown up. I. Psychiatric status. *Archives of General Psychiatry, 42,* 937–947.

GITTELMAN KLEIN, R. (1987). Pharmacotherapy of childhood hyperactivity: An update. In H. Y. Meltzer (Ed.), *Psychopharmacology: The third generation of progress.* New York: Raven Press.

GITTELMAN, R., & KLEIN, D. F. (1984). Relationship between separation anxiety and panic and agoraphobic disorders. *Psychopathology, 17,* 56–65.

GITTLEMAN-KLEIN, R., & KLEIN, D. F. (1971). Controlled imipramine treatment of school phobia. *Archives of General Psychiatry, 25,* 204–207.

GITTELMAN-KLEIN, R., LANDA, B., MATTES, J. A., & KLEIN, D. F. (1988). Methylphenidate and growth in hyperactive children: A controlled withdrawal study. *Archives of General Psychiatry, 45,* 1127–1130.

GITTELMAN-KLEIN, R., & MANNUZZA, S. (1988). Hyperactive boys almost grown up. III. Methylphenidate effects on ultimate height. *Archives of General Psychiatry, 45,* 1131–1134.

GLAZER, W. M., MOORE, D. C., SCHOOLER, N. R., BRENNER, L. M., & MORGENSTERN, H. (1984). Tardive dyskinesia: A discontinuation study. *Archives of General Psychiatry, 41,* 623–627.

GOLDBERG, S. C., KLERMAN, G. L., & COLE, J. O. (1965). Changes in schizophrenic psychopathology and ward behavior as a function of phenothiazine treatment. *British Journal of Psychiatry, 111,* 120–133.

GOODWIN, F. K., & JAMISON, K. (1984). The natural course of manic-depressive illness. In R. M. Post & J. C. Ballenger (Eds.), *Neurobiology of mood disorders.* Baltimore, MD: Williams & Wilkins.

GOODWIN, F. K., & ZIS, A. P. (1979). Lithium in the treatment of mania: Comparison with neuroleptics. *Archives of General Psychiatry, 36,* 840–844.

GORMAN, J. M., LIEBOWITZ, M., FYER, A., & STEIN, J. (1989). A neuroanatomical hypothesis for panic disorder. *American Journal of Psychiatry, 146,* 148–161.

GREEN, B. L., LINDY, J. D., & GRACE, M. C. (1985). Posttraumatic stress disorder. *Journal of Nervous and Mental Disease, 173,* 406–411.

GREEN, W. H. (1988). Pervasive developmental disorders. In C. J. Kestenbaum & D. T. Williams (Eds.), *Handbook of clinical assessment of children and adolescents,* Vol. 1. New York: N.Y. Press.

GREENBLATT, D. J., HARMATZ, J., ENGELHARDT, N., & SHADER, R. I. (1989). Pharmacokinetic determinants of dynamic differences among three benzodiazepines. *Archives of General Psychiatry, 46,* 326–332.

GREENBLATT, D. J., HARMATZ, J. S., ZINNY, M. A., & SHADER, R. I. (1987). Effect of gradual withdrawal on the rebound sleep disorder after discontinuation of triazolam. *New England Journal of Medicine, 317,* 722–728.

GREENBLATT, D., & SHADER, R. (1987). Pharmacokinetics of antianxiety agents. In H. Y. Meltzer (Ed.), *Psychopharmacology: The third generation of progress.* New York: Raven Press.

GRINSPOON, L., & BAKALAR, J. (1986). Psychedelics and arylcyclohexylamines. In A. J. Frances & R. E. Hales (Eds.), *Annual review,* Vol. 5. Washington DC: American Psychiatric Press.

GROF, P., ANGST, J., & HAINES, T. (1973). The clinical course of depression: Practical issues. In J. Angst & J. Stuttgart (Eds.), *Classification and prediction of outcome of depression.* New York: F. K. Schattauer Verlag.

GROSS, H. A., EBERT, M. H., FADEN, V. B., GOLDBERG, S. C., NEE, L. E., & KAYE, W. (1981). A double-blind controlled trial of lithium carbonate in primary anorexia nervosa. *Journal of Clinical Psychopharmacology, 1,* 376–381.

GUNDERSON, J. G., & ELLIOTT, G. R. (1985). The interface between borderline personality disorder and affective disorder. *American Journal of Psychiatry, 142,* 277–288.

GUZE, S. (1976). *Criminality and psychiatric disorders.* New York: Oxford University Press.

GWIRTSMAN, H. E., GUZE, B. H., YAGER, J., & GAINSLEY, B. Treatment of anorexia nervosa with fluoxetine: An open clinical trial. Submitted for publication.

HALMI, K., ECKERT, D., LaDU, T., & COHEN, J. (1986). Anorexia nervosa: Treatment efficacy of cyproheptadine and amitriptyline. *Archives of General Psychiatry, 43,* 177–181.

HARRIS, M. J. & JESTE, D. V. (1988). Late-onset schizophrenia: An overview. *Schizophrenia Bulletin, 14,* 39–55.

HARTMANN, E. (1977). L-Tryptophan: A rational hypnotic with clinical potential. *American Journal of Psychiatry, 134,* 366–370.

HAURI, P., & SATEIA, M. (1985). Nonpharmacological treatment of sleep disorders. In R. E. Hales & A. J. Frances (Eds.), *Annual review,* Vol. 4, Washington, DC: American Psychiatric Press.

HELZER, J. E., ROBINS, L. N., & McEVOY, L. (1987). Post-traumatic stress disorder in the general population: Findings of the epidemiologic catchment area survey. *New England Journal of Medicine, 317,* 1630–1634.

HENINGER, G., & CHARNEY, D. S. (1987). Mechanism of action of antidepressant treatments: Implications for the etiology and treatment of depressive disorders. In H. Y. Meltzer (Ed.,), *Psychopharmacology: The third generation of progress.* New York: Raven Press.

HENINGER, G., & CHARNEY, D. S. (1988). Monoamine receptor systems and anxiety disorders. *Psychiatric Clinics of North America, 11,* 309–326.

HENINGER, G., CHARNEY, D. S., & STERNBERG, D. (1983). Lithium carbonate augmentation of antidepressant treatment: An effective prescription for treatment refractory depression. *Archives of General Psychiatry, 40,* 1335–1342.

HERMAN, J. B., BROTMAN, A., W., & ROSENBAUM, J. F. (1987). Rebound anxiety in panic disorder patients treated with shorter-acting benzodiazepines. *Journal of Clinical Psychiatry, 48* (Suppl.), 22–26.

HERZ, M. I., SZYMANSKI, H. V., & SIMON, J. C. (1982). Intermittent medication for stable schizophrenic outpatients: An alternative to maintenance medication. *American Journal of Psychiatry, 139,* 918–922.

HESTBECH, J., HANSEN, H. E., AMDISEN, A., & OLSEN, S. (1977). Chronic renal lesions following long-term treatment with lithium. *Kidney International, 12,* 205–213.

HIRSCHFELD, R. M. A., KLERMAN, G. L., CLAYTON, P. J., KELLER, M. B., McDONALD-SCOTT, P., & LARKIN, B. H. (1983). Assessing personality: Effects of the depressive state on trait measurement. *American Journal of Psychiatry, 40,* 695–699.

HOEHN-SARIC, R., McLEOD, D. R., & ZIMMERLI, W. D. (1988). Differential effects of alprazolam and imipramine in generalized anxiety disorder: Somatic versus psychic symptoms. *Journal of Clinical Psychiatry, 49,* 293–301.

HOGARTY, G. E., McEVOY, J. P., MUNETZ, M., DiBARRY, A. L., BARTONE, P., CATHER, R., COOLEY, S. J., ULRICH, R. F., CARTER, M., & MADONIA, M. J.: Environmental/Personal Indicators in the Course of Schizophrenia Research Group. (1988). Dose of fluphenazine, familial expressed emotion, and outcome in schizophrenia: Results of a two-year controlled study. *Archives of General Psychiatry, 45,* 797–805.

HOLLISTER, L. E., MOTZENBECKER, F., & DEGAN, R. (1961). Withdrawal reactions from chlordiazepoxide (Librium). *Psychopharmacologia, 2,* 63–68.

HOLLISTER, L. E., & YESAVAGE, J. (1984). Ergyloid mesylates for senile dementia: Unanswered questions. *Annals of Internal Medicine, 100,* 894–898.

HOLMES, V. F., FERNANDEZ, F., & LEVY, J. K. (1989). Psychostimulant response in AIDS-related complex patients. *Journal of Clinical Psychiatry, 50,* 5–8.

HSU, L. G. K. (1988). The outcome of anorexia nervosa: A reappraisal. *Psychological Medicine, 18,* 807–812.

HYMAN, S. E. (1988). Recent developments in neurobiology: Part I: Synaptic transmission. *Psychosomatics, 29,* 157–165.

HYMOWITZ, P., FRANCES, A., JACOBSBERG, L. B., SICKLES, M., & HOYT, R. (1986). Neuroleptic treatment of schizotypal personality disorders. *Comprehensive Psychiatry, 27,* 267–271.

INSEL, T. R., & AKISKAL, H. S. (1986). Obsessive-compulsive disorder with psychotic features: A phenomenologic analysis. *American Journal of Psychiatry, 143,* 1527–1533.

INSEL, T., NINAN, P., ALOI, J., JIMERSON, D. C., SKOLNICK, P., & PAUL, S. M. (1984). A benzodiazepine-receptor mediated model of anxiety. Studies in non-human primates and clinical implications. *Archives of General Psychiatry, 41,* 741–750.

INSEL, T., & ZOHAR, J. (1987). Psychopharmacologic approaches to obsessive-compulsive disorder. In H. Y. Meltzer (Ed.), *Psychopharmacology: The third generation of progress,* New York: Raven Press.

JABLENSKY, A. (1985). Approaches to the definition and classification of anxiety and related disorders in European psychiatry. In A. Tuma & J. Maser (Eds.), *Anxiety and the anxiety disorders,* Hillsdale, NJ: Lawrence Erlbaum Associates.

JANICAK, P. G., DAVIS, J. M., GIBBONS, R. D., ERICKSEN, S., CHANG, S., & GALLAGHER, P. (1985). Efficacy of ECT: A meta-analysis. *American Journal of Psychiatry, 142,* 297–302.

JANOWSKY, A. J., OKADA, F., APPLEGATE, C., MANIER, D. H., & SULSER, F. (1982). Role of serotonergic input in the regulation of the beta-adrenergic receptor coupled adenylate-cyclase in brain. *Science, 218,* 900–901.

JANOWSKY, A., & SULSER, F. (1987). Alpha and beta receptors in brain. In H. Y. Meltzer (Ed.), *Psychopharmacology: The third generation of progress.* New York: Raven Press.

JEFFERSON, J. (1988). Biologic systems and their relationship to anxiety: A summary. *Psychiatric Clinics of North America, 11,* 463–472.

JEFFERSON, J. W., GREIST, J. H., ACKERMAN, D. L., & CARROLL, J. A. (1987). *Lithium encyclopedia for clinical practice,* 2nd ed. Washington, DC: American Psychiatric Association Press.

JEFFERSON, J. W., GREIST, J. A., CLAGNAZ, P. J., EISCHENS, R. R., MARTEN, W. C., & EVENSON, M. A. (1982). Effect of strenuous exercise on serum lithium level in man. *American Journal of Psychiatry, 139,* 1593–1595.

JENIKE, M. A., SURMAN, O. S., CASSEM, N. H., ZUSKY, P., & ANDERSON, W. H. (1983). Monoamine oxidase inhibitors in obsessive-compulsive disorder. *Journal of Clinical Psychiatry, 44,* 131–132.

JOFFE, R., POST, R. M., ROY-BYRNE, P., & UHDE, T. W. (1985). Hematological effects of carbamazepine in patients with affective illness. *American Journal of Psychiatry, 142,* 1196–1199.

JOHNSTONE, E. C., OWENS, D. G. C., FRITH, C. D., & CROW, T. J. (1986). The relative stability of positive and negative features in chronic schizophrenia. *British Journal of Psychiatry, 150,* 60–64.

JONES, K. L., LACRO, R. V., JOHNSON, K. A., & ADAMS, J. (1989). Pattern of malformations in the children of women treated with carbamazepine during pregnancy. *New England Journal of Medicine, 320,* 1661–1666.

JOYCE, P. R., & PAYKEL, E. S. (1989). Predictors of drug response in depression. *Archives of General Psychiatry, 46,* 89–99.

JUDD, L., & HUEY, L. (1984). Lithium antagonizes ethanol intoxication in alcoholics. *American Journal of Psychiatry, 141,* 1517–1521.

KAHN, R. J., McNAIR, D. M., LIPMAN, R. S., COVI, L., RICKELS, K., DOWNING, R., FISHER, J., & FRANKENTHALER, L. M. (1986). Imipramine and chlordiazepoxide in depressive and anxiety disorders. II. Efficacy in anxious outpatients. *Archives of General Psychiatry, 43,* 79–85.

KALES, A., SOLDATOS, C. R., BIXTER, E. O., & KALES, J. D. (1983). Early morning insomnia with rapidly eliminated benzodiazepines. *Science, 220,* 95–97.

KALES, A., SOLDATOS, C. R., CALDWELL, A. B., KALES, J. D., HUMPHREY, F. J., CHARNEY, D. S., & SCHWEITZER, P. K. (1980). Somnabulism: Clinical characteristics and personality patterns. *Archives of General Psychiatry, 37,* 1406–1410.

KANE, J. M. (1986). Somatic therapy. In A. J. Frances & R. E. Hales (Eds.), *Annual review,* Vol. 5. Washington, DC: American Psychiatric Press.

KANE, J., HONIGFELD, G., SINGER, J., MELTZER, H., & THE CLOZARIL COLLABORATIVE STUDY GROUP. (1988). Clozapine for the treatment-resistant schizophrenic. *Archives of General Psychiatry, 45,* 789–796.

KANE, J. M., & LIEBERMAN, J. A. (1987). Maintenance pharmacotherapy in schizophrenia. In H. Y. Meltzer (Ed.), *Psychopharmacology: The third generation of progress.* New York: Raven Press.

KANE, J. M., QUITKIN, F. M., RIFKIN, A., RAMOS-LORENZI, J. R., NAYAK, D. D., & HOWARD, A. (1982). Lithium carbonate and imipramine in the prophylaxis of unipolar and bipolar II illness: A prospective placebo-controlled comparison. *Archives of General Psychiatry, 39,* 1065–1069.

KANE, J. M., & SMITH, J. M. (1982). Tardive dyskinesia: Prevalence and risk factors. *Archives of General Psychiatry, 39,* 473–481.

KAPLAN, A. (1987). Anticonvulsant treatment of eating disorders. In P. E. Garfinkel & D. M. Garner (Eds.), *The role of drug treatments for eating disorders.* New York: Brunner/Mazel.

KASS, F., SKODOL, A. E., CHARLES, E., SPITZER, R. L., & WILLIAMS, J. B. W. (1985). Scaled ratings of DSM-III personality disorders. *American Journal of Psychiatry, 142,* 627–630.

KASSETT, J. A., GERSHON, E. S., MAXWELL, M. E., GUROFF, J. J., KAZUBA, D. M., SMITH, A. L., BRANDT, H. A., & JIMERSON, D. C. (1989). Psychiatric disorders in the first-degree relatives of probands with bulimia nervosa. *American Journal of Psychiatry, 146,* 1468–1471.

KATON, W., VITALIANO, P. O., ANDERSON, K., JONES, M., & RUSSO, J. (1987). Panic disorder: Residual symptoms after the acute attacks abate. *Comprehensive Psychiatry, 28,* 151–158.

KAUFMAN, C. A., & WYATT, R. J. (1987). Neuroleptic malignant syndrome. In H. Y. Meltzer (Ed.), *Psychopharmacology: The third generation of progress.* Raven Press: New York.

KAVALE, K. A., & FORNESS, S. R. (1983). Hyperactivity and diet treatment: A meta-analysis of the Feingold hypothesis. *Journal of Learning Disabilities, 16,* 324–330.

KAYE, W. (1987). Opioid antagonist drugs in the treatment of anorexia nervosa. In

P. E. Garfinkel & D. M. Garner (Eds.), *The role of drug treatments for eating disorders.* New York: Brunner/Mazel.

KAYSER, A., ROBINSON, D. S., YINGLING, K., HOWARD, D. B., CORCELLA, J., & LAUX, D. (1988). The influence of panic attacks on response to phenelzine and amitriptyline in depressed outpatients. *Journal of Clinical Psychopharmacology, 8,* 246–253.

KECK, P. E., POPE, H. G., COHEN, B. M., McELROY, S. G., & NIRENBERG, A. A. (1989). Risk factors for neuroleptic malignant syndrome: A case control study. *Archives of General Psychiatry, 46,* 914–918.

KEELER, M. H., TAYLOR, C. I., & MILLER, W. C. (1979). Are all recently detoxified alcoholics depressed? *American Journal of Psychiatry, 136,* 586–588.

KELLER, M. B., LAVORI, P. W., KLERMAN, G. L., ANDREASEN, N. C., ENDICOTT, J., CORYELL, W., FAWCETT, J., RICE, J. P., & HIRSCHFELD, R. M. A. (1986). Low levels and lack of predictors of somatotherapy and psychotherapy received by depressed patients. *Archives of General Psychiatry, 43,* 458–466.

KELLER, M., LAVORI, P. W., RICE, J., CORYELL, W., & HIRSCHFELD, R. M. A. (1986). The persistent risk of chronicity in recurrent episodes of non-bipolar major depressive disorder: A prospective follow-up. *Archives of General Psychiatry, 143,* 24–28.

KELLER, M. B., & SHAPIRO, R. W. (1982). "Double depression:" Superimposition of acute depressive episodes on chronic depressive disorders. *American Journal of Psychiatry, 139,* 438–442.

KELLER, M. B., SHAPIRO, R. W., LAVORI, P. W., & WOLFE, N. (1982). Recovery in major depressive disorder: Analysis with the life table and the regression models. *Archives of General Psychiatry, 39,* 905–910.

KENDLER, K. (1986). Genetics of schizophrenia. In A. J. Frances & R. E. Hales (Eds.), *Annual review,* Vol. 5. Washington, DC: American Psychiatric Press.

KENDLER, K. S. (1980). The nosologic validity of paranoia (simple delusional disorder): A review. *Archives of General Psychiatry, 37,* 699–706.

KENNEDY, S. H., PIRAN, N., WARSH, J. J., PRENDERGAST, P., MAINPRIZE, E., WHYNOT, C., & GARFINKEL, P. E. (1988). A trial of isocarboxazid in the treatment of bulimia nervosa. *Journal of Clinical Psychopharmacology, 8,* 391–396.

KLEBER, H. D., & GAWIN, F. H. (1986). Cocaine. In A. J. Frances & R. E. Hales (Eds.), *Annual review,* Vol. 5. Washington, DC: American Psychiatric Press.

KLEIN, D. F. (1964). Delineation of two drug-responsive anxiety syndromes. *Psychopharmacologia, 5,* 397–408.

KLEIN, D. F., GITTELMAN, R., QUITKIN, F., & RIFKIN, A. (1980). *Diagnosis and drug treatment of psychiatric disorders: Adults and children,* 2nd ed. Baltimore, MD: Williams & Wilkins.

KLERMAN, G. (1984). Ideologic conflicts in combined treatment. In B. D. Beitman & G. L. Klerman (Eds.), *Combining psychotherapy and drug therapy in clinical practice.* New York: Spectrum Publications.

KLERMAN, G. L. (1988). The current age of youthful melancholia. Evidence for increase in depression among adolescents and young adults. *British Journal of Psychiatry, 152,* 4–14.

KNIGHTS, A., & HIRSCH, S. R. (1981). "Revealed depression" and drug treatment for schizophrenia. *Archives of General Psychiatry, 38,* 806–811.

KOCSIS, J. H., FRANCES, A. J., VOSS, C., MANN, J. W., MASON, B. J., & SWEENEY, J. (1988). Imipramine treatment for chronic depression. *Archives of General Psychiatry, 45,* 253–257.

KOSLOW, S. H., MAAS, J. W., BOWDEN, C. L., DAVIS, J. M., HANIN, I., & JAVAID, J. (1983). CSF and urinary biogenic amines and metabolites in depression and mania: A controlled, univariate analysis. *Archives of General Psychiatry, 40,* 999–1010.

KRAMER, M. S., VOGEL, W. H., DIJOHNSON, C., DEWEY, D. A., SHEVES, P., CAVICCHIA, C., LITLE, P., SCHMIDT, R., & KIMES, I. (1989). Antidepressants in "depressed" schizophrenic inpatients: A controlled trial. *Archives of General Psychiatry, 46,* 922–928.

KRANZLER, H. R., & ORROK, B. (1989). The pharmacotherapy of alcoholism. In A. Tasman, R. E. Hales, & A. J. Frances (Eds.), *Review of psychiatry,* Vol. 8. Washington, DC: American Psychiatric Press.

KROESSLER, D. (1985). Relative efficacy rates for therapies of delusional depression. *Convulsive Therapy, 1,* 173–182.

KROLL, J., & OGATA, S. (1987). The relationship of borderline personality disorder to the affective disorders. *Psychiatric Developments, 2,* 105–128.

KUKOPULOS, A., MINNAI, G., & MULLER-OERLINGHAUSEN, B. (1985). The influence of mania and depression on the pharmacokinetics of lithium: A longitudinal single-case study. *Journal of Affective Disorders, 8,* 159–166.

LADER, M. (1988). B-receptor antagonists in neuropsychiatry: An update. *Journal of Clinical Psychiatry, 49,* 213–223.

LECKMAN, J., WALKUP, J., RIDDLE, M., TOWBIN, K. E., & COHEN, D. J. (1987). Tic disorders. In H. Y. Meltzer (Ed.), *Psychopharmacology: The third generation of progress.* New York: Raven Press.

LEONARD H., & RAPOPORT, J. (1989) Anxiety disorders in childhood and adolescence. In A. Tasman, R. E. Hales, & A. J. Frances (Eds.), *Annual review,* Vol. 8. Washington, DC: American Psychiatric Press.

LEONARD H., SWEDO, S., RAPOPORT, J., COFFEY, M., & CHESLOW, D. (1988). Treatment of childhood obsessive-compulsive disorder with clomipramine and desmethylimipramine: A double-blind crossover comparison. *Psychopharmacology Bulletin, 24,* 93–95.

LERER, B. (1987). Neurochemical and other neurobiological consequences of ECT: Implications for the pathogenesis and treatment of affective disorders. In H. Y. Meltzer (Ed.), *Psychopharmacology: The third generation of progress.* New York: Raven Press.

LESSER, I. M., RUBIN, R. T., PECKNOLD, J. C., RIFKIN, A., SWINSON, R. P., LYDIARD, R. B., BURROWS, G. D., NOYES, R., & DUPONT, R. L. (1988). Secondary depression in panic disorder and agoraphobia. 1. Frequency, severity, and response to treatment. *Archives of General Psychiatry, 45*, 437–443.

LEVINE, R., HOFFMAN, J. S., KNEPPLE, E. D., & KENIM, M. (1989). Long-term fluoxetine treatment of a large number of obsessive-compulsive patients. *Journal of Clinical Psychopharmacology, 9*, 281–283.

LEVINSON, D. F., & LEVITT, M. E. M. (1987). Schizoaffective mania reconsidered. *American Journal of Psychiatry, 144*, 415–425.

LEVITT, J. J., & TSUANG, M. T. (1988). The heterogeneity of schizoaffective disorders: Implications for treatment. *American Journal of Psychiatry, 145*, 926–936.

LEVY, A. B., DIXON, K. N., STERN, S. L. (1989). How are depression and bulimia related? *American Journal of Psychiatry, 146*, 162–169.

LEWINE, R. R. J. (1988). Gender and Schizophrenia. In M. T. Tsuang & J. C. Simpson (Eds.), *Handbook of Schizophrenia: Volume 3, Nosology, epidemiology, and genetics of schizophrenia.* Amsterdam: Elsevier.

LIEBERMAN, J. A., KANE, J. M., & JOHNS, C. A. (1989). Clozapine: Guidelines for clinical management. *Journal of Clinical Psychiatry, 50*, 329–338.

LIEBOWITZ, M. R., GORMAN, J. M., FYER, A. J., CAMPEAS, R., LEVIN, A. P., SANDBERG, D., HOLLANDER, E., PAPP, L., & GOETZ, D. (1988). Pharmacotherapy of social phobia: An interim report of a placebo-controlled comparison of phenelzine and atenolol. *Journal of Clinical Psychiatry, 49*, 252–257.

LIEBOWITZ, M. R., GORMAN, J. M., FYER, A. J., & KLEIN, D. F. (1985). Social phobia: Review of a neglected anxiety disorder. *Archives of General Psychiatry, 42*, 729–736.

LIEBOWITZ, M. R., KLEIN, D. F., QUITKIN, F. M., STEWART, J. W., & McGRATH, P. J. (1984). Clinical implications of diagnostic subtypes of depression. In R. M. Post & J. C. Ballenger (Eds.), *Neurobiology of mood disorders.* Baltimore, MD: Williams & Wilkins.

LIEBOWITZ, M. R., QUITKIN, F. M., STEWART, J. W., McGRATH, P. J., HARRISON, W. M., MARKOWITZ, J. S., RABKIN, J. G., TRICANO, E., GOETZ, D. M., & KLEIN, D. F. (1988). Antidepressant specificity in atypical depression. *Archives of General Psychiatry, 45*, 129–137.

LIEBOWITZ, M. R., STONE, M. R., & TURKAT, I. D. (1986). Treatment of personality disorders. In A. J. Frances & R. E. Hales (Eds.), *Annual review.* Vol. 5. Washington, DC: American Psychiatric Press.

LIPPER, S., DAVIDSON, J. R. T., GRADY, T. A., EDINGER, T. D., HAMMETT, E. B., MAHORNEY, S. L., & CAVENAR, J. O. (1986). Preliminary study of carbamazepine in post-traumatic stress disorder. *Psychosomatics, 27*, 849–854.

LORANGER, A. W. (1984). Sex differences in age at onset of schizophrenia. *Archives of General Psychiatry, 41*, 157–161.

LUCKI, I., & RICKELS, K. (1986). The behavioral effects of benzodiazepines following long-term use. *Psychopharmacology Bulletin, 22*, 424–433.

LUCKI, I., RICKELS, K., & GELLER, A. M. (1985). Psychomotor performance following the long-term use of benzodiazepines. *Psychopharmacology Bulletin, 21*, 93–96.

LYDIARD, R. B., & BALLENGER, J. C. (1987). Antidepressants in panic disorder and agoraphobia. *Journal of Affective Disorders, 13,* 153–168.

LYDIARD, R. B., & LAIRD, L. K. (1988). Prediction of response to antipsychotics. *Journal of Clinical Psychopharmacology, 8,* 3–13.

MAAS, J. W., KOSLOW, S. H., KATZ, M. M., GIBBONS, R. C., BOWDEN, C. L., ROBINS, E., & DAVIS, J. M. (1984). Pretreatment neurotransmitter metabolite levels and response to tricyclic antidepressant drugs. *American Journal of Psychiatry, 141,* 1159–1171.

MAJ, M. (1988). Lithium prophylaxis of schizoaffective disorders: A prospective study. *Journal of Affective Disorders, 14,* 129–135.

MALCOLM, R., BALLENGER, J. C., STURGIS, E. T., & ANTON, R. (1989). Double-blind controlled trial comparing carbamazepine to oxazepam treatment of alcohol withdrawal. *American Journal of Psychiatry, 146,* 617–621.

MANOS, N., GKIOUZEPAS, J., & LOGOTHETIS, J. (1981). The need for continuous use of antiparkinsonian medication with chronic schizophrenic patients receiving long-term neuroleptic therapy. *American Journal of Psychiatry, 138,* 184–188.

MARDER, S., VAN PUTTEN, T., MINTZ, J., LEBELL, J., MCKENZIE, J., & MAY, P. R. A. (1987). Low and conventional dose maintenance therapy with fluphenazine decanoate: Two year outcome. *Archives of General Psychiatry, 44,* 518–521.

MARDER, S., VAN PUTTEN, T., MINTZ, J., MCKENZIE, J., LEBELL, M., FALTICO, G., & MAY, P. R. A. (1984). Costs and benefits of two doses of fluphenazine. *Archives of General Psychiatry, 41,* 1025–1029.

MARKS, I. M. (1986). Genetics of fear and anxiety disorders. *British Journal of Psychiatry, 149,* 406–418.

MARTIN, M., OWEN, C., & MORIHISA, J. (1987). An overview of neurotransmitters and neuroreceptors. In R. E. Hales & S. C. Yudofsky (Eds.), *Textbook of psychiatry.* Washington, DC: American Psychiatric Press.

MCELROY, S., KECK, P. E., POPE, H. G., & HUDSON, J. I. (1988). Valproate in primary psychiatric disorders: Literature review and clinical experience in a private psychiatric hospital. In S. L. McElroy & H. G. Pope (Eds.), *Use of anticonvulsants in psychiatry: Recent advances.* Clifton, NJ: Oxford Health Care, Inc.

MCELROY, S. C., KECK, P. E., & POPE, H. G. (1987). Sodium valproate: Its use in primary psychiatric disorders. *Journal of Clinical Psychopharmacology, 7,* 16–24.

MCGLASHAN, T. H. (1986). The Chestnut Lodge follow-up study. III. Long-term outcome of borderline personalities. *Archives of General Psychiatry, 43,* 20–30.

MCGLASHAN, T. H., & CARPENTER, W. T. (1976). Post-psychotic depression in schizophrenia. *Archives of General Psychiatry, 33,* 231–239.

MCGRATH, P. J., STEWART, J. W., HARRISON, W., & QUITKIN, F. M. (1987). Treatment of tricyclic refractory depression with a monoamine oxidase inhibitor antidepressant. *Psychopharmacology Bulletin, 23,* 169–172.

MELLINGER, G. D., & BALTER, M. B. (1981). Prevalence and patterns of use of psychotherapeutic drugs: Results from a 1979 national survey of American adults. In G.

Tognoni, C. Bellantuono, & M. Lader (Eds.), *Epidemiological impact of psychotropic drugs*. New York: Elsevier.

MENDELSON, W. (1987). Medications in the treatment of sleep disorders. In H. Y. Meltzer (Ed.), *Psychopharmacology: The third generation of progress*. New York: Raven Press.

MENDELSON, W. (1985). Pharmacological treatment of insomnia. In R. E. Hales & A. J. Frances (Eds.), *Annual review*, Vol. 4. Washington, DC: American Psychiatric Press.

MERIKANGAS, K. R., LECKMAN, J. F., PRUSOFF, B. A., PAULS, D. C., & WEISSMAN, M. M. (1985). Familial transmission of depression and alcoholism. *Archives of General Psychiatry, 42*, 367–372.

MEYER, R. E. (1989). Prospects for a rational pharmacotherapy of alcoholism. *Journal of Clinical Psychiatry, 50*, 403–412.

MILES, P. (1977). Conditions predisposing to suicide: A review. *Journal of Nervous and Mental Diseases, 164*, 231–246.

MITCHELL, J. E., PYLE, R. L., ECKERT, E. D., HATSUKAMI, D., POMEROY, C., & ZIMMERMAN, R. (1989). Response to alternative antidepressants in imipramine nonresponders with bulimia nervosa. *Journal of Clinical Psychopharmacology, 9*, 291–293.

MITCHELL, P. B. (1988). The pharmacological management of bulimia nervosa: A critical review. *International Journal of Eating Disorders, 7*, 29–41.

MITLER, M. M., SEIDEL, W. F., VAN DEN HOED, J., GREENBLATT, D. J., & DEMENT, W. C. (1984). Comparative hypnotic effects of flurazepam, triazolam and placebo: A long-term simultaneous nighttime and daytime study. *Journal of Clinical Psychopharmacology, 4*, 2–13.

MODELL, J. G., LENOX, R. H., & WEINER, S. (1985). Inpatient clinical trial of lorazepam for the management of manic agitation. *Journal of Clinical Psychopharmacology, 5*, 109–113.

MOHLER, H., & OKADA, T. (1977). Benzodiazepine receptor: Demonstration in the central nervous system. *Science, 198*, 849–851.

MOREY, L. C. (1988). Personality disorders in DSM-III and DSM-III-R: Convergence, coverage and internal consistency. *American Journal of Psychiatry, 145*, 573–577.

MORTOLA, J. F. (1989). The use of psychotropic agents in pregnancy and lactation. *Psychiatric Clinics of North America, 12*, 69–87.

MUNJACK, D. J., CROCKER, B., CABE, D., BROWN, R., USIGLI, R., ZULUETA, A., McMANUS, M., McDOWELL, D., PALMER, R., & LEONARD, M. (1989). Alprazolam, propranolol, and placebo in the treatment of panic disorder and agoraphobia with panic attacks. *Journal of Clinical Psychiatry, 9*, 22–27.

NELSON, J. C., JATLOW, P. I., & QUINLAN, D. M. (1984). Subjective complaints during desipramine treatment: Relative importance of plasma drug concentrations and the severity of depression. *Archives of General Psychiatry, 41*, 55–59.

NINO-MURCIA, G., & DEMENT, W. C. Psychophysiological and pharmacological aspects of somnambulism and night terrors in children. In H. Y. Meltzer (Ed.), *Psychopharmacology: The third generation of progress*. New York: Raven Press.

NINO-MURCIA, G., & KEENAN, S. (1988). A multicomponent approach to the management of insomnia. *Annals of Behavior Medicine, 10,* 91–96.

NOYES, R. (1985). Beta-adrenergic blocking drugs in anxiety and stress. *Psychiatric Clinics of North America, 8,* 119–132.

NOYES, R., GARVEY, M. J., COOK, B. L., & PERRY, P. J. (1988). Benzodiazepine withdrawal: A review of the evidence. *Journal of Clinical Psychiatry, 49,* 382–389.

NURNBERG, H. G., & PRUDIC, J. (1984). Guidelines for treatment of psychosis during pregnancy. *Hospital & Community Psychiatry, 35,* 67–71.

OLAJIDE, D., & LADER, M. (1987). A comparison of buspirone, diazepam, and placebo in patients with chronic anxiety states. *Journal of Clinical Psychiatry, 7,* 148–152.

PARE, C. M. B. (1985). The present status of monoamine oxidase inhibitors. *British Journal of Psychiatry, 146,* 576–584.

PATTERSON, J. F., (1988). Akathisia associated with busipirone. *Journal of Clinical Psychopharmacology, 8,* 296–297.

PAUL, S. (1985). *Biochemical neural mechanisms of anxiety*. Kalamazoo, MI: Upjohn.

PAUL, S. M., JANOWSKY, A., & SKOLNICK, P. (1985). Monoamine neurotransmitters and antidepressant drugs. In R. E. Hales & A. J. Frances (Eds.), *Annual review*, Vol. 4. Washington, DC: American Psychiatric Press.

PAUL, S. M., MARANGOS, P. J., & SKOLNICK, P. (1981). The benzodiazepine-GABA-chloride ionophore receptor complex: Common site of minor tranquilizer action. *Biological Psychiatry, 16,* 213–229.

PERRY, J. C. (1985). Depression in borderline personality disorder: Lifetime prevalence at interview and longitudinal course of symptoms. *American Journal of Psychiatry, 142,* 15–21.

PERSE, T. (1988). Obsessive-compulsive disorder: A treatment review. *Journal of Clinical Psychiatry, 49,* 48–55.

PFOHL, B., & ANDREASEN, N. C. (1986). Schizophrenia: Diagnosis and classification. In A. J. Frances & R. E. Hales (Eds.), *Annual review*, Vol. 5. Washington, DC: American Psychiatric Press.

*PHYSICIANS' DESK REFERENCE.* (1989). Oradell, N.J.: Medical Economics Co.

PICKAR, D. (1986). Neuroleptics, dopamine and schizophrenia. *Psychiatric Clinics of North America, 9,* 35–48.

PIRKE, K., PAHL, J., SCHWEIGER, Y., & WARNHOFF, M. (1985). Metabolic and endocrine indices of starvation in bulimia: A comparison with anorexia nervosa. *Psychiatry Research, 15,* 33–37.

PISCIOTTA, A. V. (1982). Carbamazepine: Hematologic toxicity. In D. M. Woodbury, J. K. Penry, & C. Pippenger (Eds.), *Antiepileptic drugs*. New York: Raven Press.

PLENGE, P., & MELLERUP, E. T. (1986). Lithium and the kidney: Is one daily dose better than two? *Comprehensive Psychiatry, 27,* 336–342.

PLOTKIN, D. A., GERSON, S. C., & JARVIK, L. F. (1987). Antidepressant drug treatment in the elderly. In H. Y. Meltzer (Ed.), *Psychopharmacology: The third generation of progress.* New York: Raven Press.

POHL, R., BERCHOU, R., & RAINEY, J. M. (1982). Tricyclic antidepressants and monoamine oxidase inhibitors in the treatment of agoraphobia. *Journal of Clinical Psychopharmacology, 2,* 399–407.

POHL, R., YERAGANI, V. K., BALON, R., & LYCAKI, A. (1988). The jitteriness syndrome in panic disorder patients treated with antidepresants. *Journal of Clinical Psychiatry, 49,* 100–104.

POPE, H. G., & HUDSON, J. I. (1986). Antidepressant drug therapy for bulimia: Current status. *Journal of Clinical Psychiatry, 47,* 339–345.

POPE, H. G., & HUDSON, J. I. (1989). Pharmacologic treatment of bulimia nervosa: Research findings and practical suggestions. *Psychiatric Annals, 19,* 483–487.

POPE, H. G., JONES, J. M., HUDSON, J. I., COHEN, B. M., & GUNDERSON, J. G. (1983). The validity of DSM-III borderline personality disorder. *Archives of General Psychiatry, 40,* 23–30.

POPE, H. G., & LIPINSKI, J. F. (1978). Diagnosis of schizophrenia and manic-depressive illness: A reassessment of the specificity of "schizophrenic symptoms" in the light of current research. *Archives of General Psychiatry, 35,* 811–828.

POST, R. M. (1987). Mechanisms of action of carbamazepine and related anticonvulsants in affective illness. In H. Y. Meltzer (Ed.), *Psychopharmacology: The third generation of progress.* New York: Raven Press.

POST, R. M. INTERVIEW. (1986). *Currents in Affective Disorders, 5,* 5–10.

POST, R. M. (1988). Efficacy of carbamazepine in the treatment of bipolar affective disorder. In S. L. McElroy & H. G. Pope (Eds.), *Use of anticonvulsants in psychiatry.* Clifton, NJ: Oxford Health Care, Inc.

POST, R. M., RUBINOW, D. R., & BALLENGER, J. C. (1984). Conditioning, sensitization and kindling: Implications for the course of affective illness. In R. M. Post & J. C. Ballenger (Eds.), *Neurobiology of mood disorders.* Baltimore, MD: Williams & Wilkins.

POST, R. M., RUBINOW, D. R., & BALLENGER, J. C. (1986). Conditioning and sensitization in the longitudinal course of affective illness. *British Journal of Psychiatry, 149,* 191–201.

POST, R. M., & UHDE, T. W. (1987). Clinical approaches to treatment resistant bipolar illness. In R. E. Hales & A. J. Frances (Eds.), *Annual review,* Vol. 6. Washington, DC: American Psychiatric Press.

POST, R. M., UHDE, T. W., BALLENGER, J. C., CHATTERJI, D. C., GREENE, R. F., & BUNNEY, W. E. (1983). Carbamazepine and its − 10, − 11 − epoxide metabolite in plasma and CSF. Relationship to antidepressant response. *Archives of General Psychiatry, 40,* 673–676.

POST, R. M., UHDE, T. W., PUTNAM, F. W., BALLENGER, J. C., & BERRETTINI, W. H. (1982). Kindling and carbamazepine in affective illness. *Journal of Nervous and Mental Disease, 170,* 717–731.

Post, R. M., Uhde, T. W., Roy-Byrne, P. P., & Joffe, R. T. (1986). Antidepressant effects of carbamazepine. *American Journal of Psychiatry, 143,* 29–34.

Price, L. H., Charney, D. S., & Heninger, G. R. (1986). Variability of response to lithium augmentation in refractory depression. *American Journal of Psychiatry, 143,* 1387–1392.

Prien, R. F. (1987). Long-term treatment of affective disorders. In H. Y. Meltzer (Ed.), *Psychopharmacology: The third generation of progress,* New York: Raven Press.

Prien, R. F. (1988). Somatic treatment of unipolar depressive disorder. In A. J. Frances & R. E. Hales (Eds.), *Review of psychiatry,* Vol. 7. Washington, DC: American Psychiatric Press.

Prien, R. F., & Gelenberg, A. J. (1989). Alternatives to lithium for preventive treatment of bipolar disorder. *American Journal of Psychiatry, 146,* 840–848.

Prien, R. F., & Kupfer, D. J. (1986). Continuation drug therapy for major depressive episodes: How long should it be maintained? *American Journal of Psychiatry, 143,* 18–23.

Puig-Antich, J., Perel, J. M., Lupatkin, W., Chambers, W. J., Tabrizi, M. A., King, J., Goetz, R., Davies, M., & Stiller, R. L. (1987). Imipramine in prepubertal major depressive disorders. *Archives of General Psychiatry, 44,* 81–89.

Quitkin, F. M., Rabkin, J. G., Ross, D., & McGrath, P. J. (1984). Duration of antidepressant drug treatment: What is an adequate trial? *Archives of General Psychiatry, 41,* 238–245.

Rabkin, J. G., Quitkin, F. M., McGrath, P., Harrison, W., & Tricamo, E. (1985). Adverse reactions to monoamine oxidase inhibitors. Part II. Treatment correlates and clinical management. *Journal of Clinical Psychopharmacology, 5,* 2–9.

Raft, D., Davidson, J., Mattox, A., Mueller, R., & Wasik, J. (1979). Double-blind evaluation of phenelzine, amitriptyline and placebo in depression associated with pain. In A. Singer (Ed.), *Monoamine oxidase: Structure, function and altered functions.* New York: Academic Press.

Rapoport, J. L., Buchsbaum, M. S., Weingartner, H., Zahn, T. P., Ludlow, C., & Mikkelsen, E. J. (1980). Dextroamphetamine: Its cognitive and behavioral effects in normal and hyperactive boys and normal men. *Archives of General Psychiatry, 37,* 933–943.

Raskind, M. A., Risse, S. C., & Lampe, T. H. (1987). Dementia and antipsychotic drugs. *Journal of Clinical Psychiatry, 48* (suppl), 16–18.

Rasmussen, S., & Eisen, J. (1989). Clinical features and phenomenology of obsessive-compulsive disorder. *Psychiatric Annals, 19,* 67–73.

Rasmussen, S. A., & Tsuang, M. T. (1986). Clinical characteristics and family history in DSM-III obsessive-compulsive disorder. *American Journal of Psychiatry, 143,* 317–322.

Rasmussen, S. A., & Tsuang, M. T. (1984). Epidemiology of obsessive-compulsive disorder. *Journal of Clinical Psychiatry, 45,* 450–457.

RAZANI, J., WHITE, K. L., WHITE, J., SIMPSON, G., SLOANE, R. B., REBAL, R., & PALMER, R. (1983). The safety and efficacy of combined amitriptyline and tranylcypromine antidepressant treatment: A controlled trial. *Archives of General Psychiatry, 40,* 657–661.

REGIER, D., BOYD, J., BURKE, J., RAE, D. S., MYERS, J. K., KRAMER, M., ROBINS, L. N., GEORGE, L. K., KARNO, M., & LOCKE, B. F. (1988). One-month prevalence of mental disorders in the United States. *Archives of General Psychiatry, 45,* 977–986.

REGIER, D., & BURKE, J. (1987). Psychiatric disorders in the community: The epidemiologic catchment area study. In R. E. Hales & A. J. Frances (Eds.), *Annual review.* Vol. 6. Washington, DC: American Psychiatric Press.

REICH, J. (1986). The epidemiology of anxiety. *Journal of Nervous and Mental Diseases, 174,* 129–136.

REICH, J., NOYES, R., & TROUGHTON, E. (1987). Dependent personality disorder associated with phobic avoidance in patients with panic disorder. *American Journal of Psychiatry, 144,* 323–326.

REICH, J., NOYES, R., & YATES, W. (1989). Alprazolam treatment of avoidant personality traits in social phobic patients. *Journal of Clinical Psychiatry, 50,* 91–95.

RIBLET, L. A., EISON, A. S., EISON, M. S., TAYLOR, D. P., TEMPLE, D. L., & VAN DER MAELEN, C. P. (1984). Neuropharmacology of buspirone. *Psychopathology, 17* (Suppl.3), 69–78.

RICE, J., REICH, T., ANDREASEN, N. C., ENDICOTT, J., VAN EERDEWEGH, M., FISHMAN, R., HIRSCHFELD, R. M. A, & KLERMAN, G. L. (1987). The familial transmission of bipolar illness. *Archives of General Psychiatry, 44,* 441–447.

RICHELSON, E. (1984). Neuroleptic affinities for human brain receptors and their use in predicting adverse effects. *Jounral of Clinical Psychiatry, 45,* 331–336.

RICKELS, K., CASE, W. G., & DOWNING, R. W., (1982). Issues in long-term treatment with diazepam. *Psychopharmacology, 18,* 38–41.

RICKELS, K., CASE, W. G., DOWNING, R. W., & FRIEDMAN, R. (1986). One year follow-up of anxious patients treated with diazepam. *Journal of Clinical Psychopharmacology, 6,* 32–36.

RICKELS, K., CASE, W. G., DOWNING, R. W., & WINOKUR, A. (1983). Long-term diazepam therapy and clinical outcome. *Journal of the American Medical Association, 250,* 767–771.

RICKELS, K., CHUNG, H. R., CSANALOSI, I. B., HUROWITZ, A. M., LONDON, J., WISEMAN, K., KAPLAN, M., & AMSTERDAM, J. D. (1987). Alprazolam, diazepam, imipramine, and placebo in outpatients with major depression. *Archives of General Psychiatry, 44,* 862–866.

RICKELS, K., FOX, I. L., GREENBLATT, D. J., SANDLER, K. R., & SCHLESS, A. (1988). Clorazepate and lorazepam: Clinical improvement and rebound anxiety. *American Journal of Psychiatry, 145,* 312–317.

RICKELS, K., & SCHWEIZER, E. (1987). Current pharmacotherapy of anxiety and panic.

In H. Y. Meltzer (Ed.), *Psychopharmacology: The third generation of progress.* New York: Raven Press.

RICKELS, K., SCHWEIZER, E., CASE, W. G., & GARCIA-ESPANA, F. (1988). Benzodiazepine dependence, withdrawal severity, and clinical outcome: Effects of personality. *Psychopharmacology Bulletin, 24,* 415–420.

RICKELS, K., SCHWEIZER, E., CSANALOSI, I., CASE, W. G., & CHUNG, H. (1988). Long-term treatment of anxiety and risk of withdrawal: Prospective comparison of clorazepate and buspirone. *Archives of General Psychiatry, 45,* 444–450.

RIES, R. K., ROY-BYRNE, P. P., WARD, N. G., NEPPE, V., & CULLISON, S. (1989). Carbamazepine treatment for benzodiazepine withdrawal. *American Journal of Psychiatry, 146,* 536–537.

RIFKIN, A., QUITKIN, F. M., CARRILLO, C., BLUMBERG, A. G., & KLEIN, D. F. (1972). Lithium in emotionally unstable character disorder. *Archives of General Psychiatry, 27,* 519–523.

RIFKIN, A., & SIRIS, S. (1987). Drug treatment of acute schizophrenia. In H. Y. Meltzer (Ed.), *Psychopharmacology: The third generation of progress,* New York: Raven Press.

ROBINS, E. (1986). Completed suicide. In A. Roy (Ed.), *Suicide,* Baltimore, MD: Williams & Wilkins.

ROBINS, L. (1987). The epidemiology of antisocial personality. In R. Michels & J. Cavenar (Eds.), *Psychiatry,* Philadelphia: Lippincott.

ROBINS, L., HELZER, J., WEISSMAN, M., ORVASCHEL, H., GRUENBERG, E., BURKE, J. D., & REGIER, D. A. (1984). Lifetime prevalence of specific psychiatric disorders in three sites. *Archives of General Psychiatry, 41,* 949–958.

ROBINSON, D. S., & KURTZ, N. M. (1987). Monoamine oxidase inhibiting drugs: Pharmacologic and therapeutic issues. In H. Y. Meltzer (Ed.), *Psychopharmacology: The third generation of progress,* New York: Raven Press.

ROBINSON, D. S., NIES, A., RAVARIS, C. L., IVES, J. O., & BARTLETT, D. (1978). Clinical pharmacology of phenelzine. *Archives of General Psychiatry, 35* 629–635.

ROBINSON, R. G. (1987). Depression and stroke. *Psychiatric Annals, 17,* 731–740.

ROFFWARG, H., & ERMAN, M. (1985). Evaluation and diagnosis of the sleep disorders: Implications for psychiatry and other clinical specialties. In R. E. Hales & A. J. Frances (Eds.), *Annual review,* Vol. 4, Washington DC: American Psychiatric Press.

ROSEBUSH, P. I., STEWART, T. D., & GELENBERG, A. J. (1989). 20 neuroleptic challenges after neuroleptic malignant syndrome in 15 patients. *Journal of Clinical Psychiatry, 50,* 295–298.

ROSENTHAL, N. E., SACK, D. A., GILLIN, J. C., LEWY, A. J., GOODWIN, F. K., DAVENPORT, Y., MUELLER, P. S., NEWSOME, D. A., & WEHR, T. A. (1984). Seasonal affective disorder: A description of the syndrome and preliminary findings with light therapy. *Archives of General Psychiatry, 41,* 72–80.

ROSENTHAL, N. E., SACK, D. A., SKWERER, R. G., JACOBSEN, F. M., & WEHR, T. A. (1988). Phototherapy for seasonal affective disorders. *Journal of Biological Rhythms, 3,* 101–120.

Ross, H. E., Glaser, F. B., & Germanson, T. (1988). The prevalence of psychiatric disorders in patients with alcohol and other drug problems. *Archives of General Psychiatry, 45*, 1023–1031.

Rounsaville, B. J., & Kranzler, H. R. (1989). The DSM-III-R diagnosis of alcoholism. In A. Tasman, R. E. Hales, & A. J. Frances (Eds.), *Review of psychiatry*, Vol. 8, Washington, DC: American Psychiatric Press.

Roy, A. (1986). Suicide in schizophrenia. In A. Roy (Ed.), *Suicide*, Baltimore, MD: Williams & Wilkins.

Ryan, N. (1989). Major depression. In C. G. Last & M. Hersen (Eds.), *Handbook of child psychiatric diagnosis*, New York: Wiley.

Ryan, N. D., Puig-Antich, J., Ambrosini, P., Rabinovich, H., Robinson, D., Nelson, B., Iyengar, S., & Twomay, J. (1987). The clinical picture of major depression in children and adolescents. *Archives of General Psychiatry, 44*, 854–861.

Sachs, G., & Gelenberg, A. (1988). Adverse effects of electroconvulsive therapy. In A. J. Frances & R. E. Hales (Eds.), *Review of psychiatry*, Vol. 7, Washington DC: American Psychiatric Press.

Sackheim, H. (1988). Mechanisms of action of electroconvulsive therapy. In A. J. Frances & R. E. Hales (Eds.), *Review of psychiatry*, Vol. 7, Washington DC: American Psychiatric Press.

Sacks, O. (1983). *Awakenings*. New York: Dutton.

Salzman, C. (1987). Treatment of agitation in the elderly. In H. Y. Meltzer (Ed.), *Psychopharmacology: The third generation of progress*, New York: Raven Press.

Salzman, C. (1988). Use of benzodiazepines to control disruptive behavior in inpatients. *Journal of Clinical Psychiatry, 49* (Suppl.), 13–15.

Satel, S. L., & Nelson, J. C. (1989). Stimulants in the treatment of depression: A critical overview. *Journal of Clinical Psychiatry, 50*, 241–249.

Scharf, M. B., Fletcher, K., & Graham, J. P. (1988). Comparative amnestic effects of benzodiazepine hypnotic agents. *Journal of Clinical Psychiatry, 49*, 134–137.

Schatzberg, A. F., & Cole, J. O. (1986). *Manual of clinical psychopharmacology*, Washington, DC: American Psychiatric Press.

Schou, M. (1986). Lithium treatment: A refresher course. *British Journal of Psychiatry, 149*, 541–547.

Schou, M. (1988). Effects of long-term lithium treatment on kidney function: An overview. *Journal of Psychiatric Research, 22*, 287–296.

Schuckit, M. A. (1986). Genetic and clinical implications of alcoholism and affective disorder. *American Journal of Psychiatry, 143*, 140–147.

Schuckit, M. A. (1983a). Anxiety related to medical disease. *Journal of Clinical Psychiatry, 44*, 31–36.

Schuckit, M. A. (1983b). Alcoholism and other psychiatric disorders. *Hospital and Community Psychiatry, 34*, 1022–1026.

SECUNDA, S., KATZ, M., SWANN, A., KOSLOW, S., MAAS, J., CHUANG, S., & CROUGHAN, J. (1985). Mania: Diagnosis, state measurement and prediction of response. *Journal of Affective Disorders, 8,* 113–121.

SHAPIRO, E., SHAPIRO, A. K., INLOP, G., HUBBARD, M., MANDELI, J., NORDLIE, J., & PHILLIPS, R. A. (1989). Controlled study of haloperiodol, pimozide, and placebo for the treatment of Gilles de la Tourette syndrome. *Archives of General Psychiatry, 46,* 722–730.

SHAW, E. D., MANN, J. J., STOKES, P. E., & MANEVITZ, A. Z. A. (1986). Effects of lithium carbonate on associative productivity and idiosyncrasy in bipolar outpatients. *American Journal of Psychiatry, 143,* 1166–1169.

SHEAR, K. (1986). Pathophysiology of panic: A review of pharmacologic provocative tests and naturalistic monitoring data. *Journal of Clinical Psychiatry, 47* (suppl), 18–26.

SHEAR, K., & FYER, M. R. (1988). Biological and psychopathologic findings in panic disorder. In A. J. Frances & R. E. Hales (Eds.), *Review of psychiatry,* Vol. 7. Washington, DC: American Psychiatry Press.

SHEEHAN, D. V., BALLENGER, J., & JACOBSEN, G. (1980). Treatment of endogenous anxiety with phobic, hysterical and hypochondriacal symptoms. *Archives of General Psychiatry, 37,* 51–59.

SIEVER, K. J., & KLAR, H. (1986). A review of DSM-III criteria for the personality disorders. In A. J. Frances & R. E. Hales (Eds.), *Annual review,* Vol. 5, Washington, DC: American Psychiatric Press.

SIMEON, J. G., & FERGUSON, H. B. (1985). The use of antidepressant and anxiolytic medications. *Psychiatric Clinics of North America, 8,* 893–907.

SIRIS, S. G., MORGAN, V., FAGERSTROM, R., RIFKIN, A., & COOPER, T. B. (1987). Adjunctive imipramine in the treatment of postpsychotic depression: A controlled trial. *Archives of General Psychiatry, 42,* 533–539.

SIRIS, S.G., VAN KAMMEN, D. P., & DOCHERTY, J. P. (1978). Use of antidepressant drugs in schizophrenia. *Archives of General Psychiatry, 35,* 1368–1377.

SITLAND-MARKEN, P. A., RICKMAN, L. A., WELLS, B. G., & MABIE, W. C. (1989). Pharmacologic management of acute mania in pregnancy. *Journal of Clinical Psychopharmacology, 9,* 78–87.

SKOLNICK, P., MONCADA, V., BARKER, J., & PAUL, S. (1981). Pentobarbitol has dual actions to increase brain benzodiazepine receptor affinity. *Science, 211,* 1448–1450.

SMALL, J. G., KLAPPER, M. H., KELLAMS, J. J., MILLER, M. J., MILSTEIN, V., SHARPLEY, P. H., & SMALL, I. F. (1988). Electroconvulsive treatment compared with lithium in the management of manic states. *Archives of General Psychiatry, 45,* 727–732.

SNAITH, R.P. (1987). The concepts of mild depression. *British Journal of Psychiatry, 150,* 387–393.

SNYDER, S. H. (1988). *The new biology of mood.* New York: Roerig/Pfizer.

SOLOFF, P. (1987). Neuroleptic treatment in the borderline patient: Advantages and techniques. *Journal of Clinical Psychiatry, 48* (Suppl.), 26–30.

SOLOFF, P. H., GEORGE, A., NATHAN, R. S., SCHULZ, P. M., & PEREL, J. M. (1986A). Paradoxical effects of amitriptyline on borderline patients. *American Journal of Psychiatry, 143*, 1603–1605.

SOLOFF, P. H., GEORGE, A., NATHAN, R. S., SCHULZ, P. M., ULRICH, R. F., & PEREL, J. M. (1986B). Progress in pharmacotherapy of borderline disorders: A double-blind study of amitriptyline, haloperidol and placebo. *Archives of General Psychiatry, 43*, 691–697.

SPIKER, D. G., PEREL, J. M., HANIN, I., DEALY, R. S., GRIFFIN, S. J., SOLOFF, P. H., & COFSKY-WEISS, J. (1986). The pharmacological treatment of delusional depression: Part II. *Journal of Clinical Psychopharmacology, 6*, 339–342.

SQUIRE, L. (1985). The question of long-term effects. In *Electroconvulsive Therapy*, NIH Consensus Development Conference, NIH, Bethesda, Md.

SQUIRES, R. F., & BAESTRUP, C. (1977). Benzodiazepine receptors in rat brain. *Nature, 266*, 732–734.

STANLEY, M., & MANN, J. J. (1988). Biological factors associated with suicide. In A. J. Frances & R. E. Hales (Eds.), *Review of Psychiatry*, Vol. 7, Washington DC: American Psychiatric Press.

STARKMAN, M., ZELNICK, T., TESSE, R., & CAMERON, O. G. (1985). Anxiety in patients with pheochromocytomas. *Archives of Internal Medicine, 145*, 248–252.

STEINER, M., HASKETT, R., & OSMUN, J. (1980). Treatment of premenstrual tension with lithium carbonate. *Acta Psychiatrica Scandinavia, 61*, 96–102.

STRAUSS, J. S., & CARPENTER, W. T. (1974). The prediction of outcome in schizophrenia. II. Relationships between predictor and outcome variables: A report from the WHO International Pilot Study of Schizophrenia. *Archives of General Psychiatry, 31*, 37–42.

STROBER, M. (1989). Bipolar depression. In G. Last & M. Hersen (Eds.), *Handbook of child psychiatric diagnosis*, New York: Wiley.

STROBER, M., & CARLSON, G. (1982). Bipolar illness in adolescents: Clinical, genetic and pharmacologic predictors in a three-to-four year prospective follow-up. *Archives of General Psychiatry, 39*, 549–555.

STROBER, M., & KATZ, J. (1986). Depression in the eating disorders: A review and analysis of descriptive, family and biological findings. In D. M. Garner & P. E. Garfinkel (Eds.), *Diagnostic issues in anorexia nervosa and bulimia nervosa*, New York: Brunner/Mazel.

STROBER, M., MORRELL, W., BURROUGHS, S., LAMPERT, C., DANFORTH, H., & FREEMAN, R. (1988). A family study of bipolar I disorder in adolescence: Early onset of symptoms linked to increased familial loading and lithium resistance. *Journal of Affective Disorders, 15*, 255–268.

SZYMANSKI, L. S., RUBIN, I. L., & TARJAN, G. (1989). Mental retardation. In A. Tasman, R. E. Hales, & A. J. Frances (Eds.), *Review of Psychiatry*, Vol. 8, Washington DC: American Psychiatric Press.

TALLMAN, J. F., THOMAS, J. W., & GALLAGHER, D. W. (1978). GABA-ergic modulation of benzodiazepine binding site sensitivity. *Nature*, *274*, 383–395.

TASK FORCE ON THE USE OF LABORATORY TESTS IN PSYCHIATRY. (1985). Tricyclic antidepressants—blood level measurements and clinical outcome: An APA task force report. *American Journal of Psychiatry*, *142*, 155–162.

TAYLOR, J. L. & TINKLENBERG, J. R. (1987). Cognitive impairment and benzodiazepines. In H. Y. Meltzer (Ed.), *Psychopharmacology: The third generation of progress*, New York: Raven Press.

THOMPSON, J. W., & BLAINE, J. D. (1987). Use of ECT in the United States in 1975 and 1980. *American Journal of Psychiatry*, *144*, 557–562.

THOMPSON, J. L., MORAN, M. G., & NIES, A. S. (1983). Psychotropic drug use in the elderly. *New England Journal of Medicine*, *308*, 134–138.

TORGERSEN, S. (1979). The nature and origin of common phobic fears. *British Journal of Psychiatry*, *134*, 343–351.

TORGERSEN, S. (1983). Genetic factors in anxiety disorders. *Archives of General Psychiatry*, *40*, 1085–1089.

TSUANG, M. T., WOOLSON, R. F., & FLEMING, J. A. (1979). Long-term outcome of major psychoses. I. Schizophrenia and affective disorders compared with psychiatrically symptom-free surgical conditions. *Archives of General Psychiatry*, *39*, 1295–1301.

UHDE, T. W., STEIN, M. B., VITTONE, F. J., SIEVER, L. J., BOULENGER, J. P., KLEIN, E., & MELLMAN, T. A. (1989). Behavioral and physiologic effects of short-term and long-term administration of clonidine in panic disorder. *Archives of General Psychiatry*, *46*, 170–177.

UHDE, T., VITTONE, B., & POST, R. (1984). Glucose tolerance tests in panic disorder. *American Journal of Psychiatry*, *141*, 1461–1463.

UHLENHUTH, E. H., BALTER, M. B., MELLINGER, G. D., CISIN, I. H., & CLINTHORNE, J. (1983). Symptom checklist syndromes in the general population: Correlations with psychotherapeutic drug use. *Archives of General Psychiatry*, *40*, 1167–1173.

VAN KAMMEN, D., BUNNEY, W. E., DOCHERTY, J. P., MARDER, S. R., EBERT, M. H., ROSENBLATT, J. E., & RAYNER, J. N. (1982). d-Amphetamine-induced heterogenous changes in psychotic behavior in schizophrenia. *American Journal of Psychiatry*, *139*, 991–997.

VANDEREYCKEN, W. (1987). The use of neuroleptics in the treatment of anorexia nervosa patients. In P. E. Garfinkel & D. M. Garner (Eds.), *The role of drug treatments for eating disorders*, New York: Brunner/Mazel.

VAN PUTTEN, T., & MARDER, S. (1987). Behavioral toxicity of antipsychotic drugs. *Journal of Clinical Psychiatry*, *48* (Suppl.), 13–19.

VAN PUTTEN, T., & MAY, P. R. A. (1978A). "Akinetic depression" in schizophrenia. *Archives of General Psychiatry*, *35*, 1101–1107.

VAN PUTTEN, T., & MAY, P. R. A. (1978B). Subjective response as a predictor of outcome in pharmacotherapy: The consumer has a point. *Archives of General Psychiatry, 35,* 477–480.

VESTEGAARD, P. (1983). Clinically important side effects of long-term lithium treatment: A review. *Acta Psychiatrica Scandinavia, 67* (Suppl. 305), 11–33.

VESTEGAARD, P., AMDISEN, A., & SCHOU, M. (1980). Clinically significant side effects of lithium treatment: A survey of 237 patients in long-term treatment. *Acta Psychiatrica Scandinavia, 62,* 193–200.

WALSH, B. T. (1987). Psychopharmacology of bulimia. In H. Y. Meltzer (Ed.), *Psychopharmacology: The third generation of progress,* New York: Raven Press.

WALSH, B., GLADIS, M., ROOSE, S., STEWART, J. W., STETNER, F., & GLASSMAN, A. H. (1988). Phenelzine vs. placebo in 50 patients with bulimia. *Archives of General Psychiatry, 45,* 471–475.

WEHR, T. A., & GOODWIN, F. K. (1987). Can antidepressants cause mania and worsen the course of affective illness? *American Journal of Psychiatry, 144,* 1403–1411.

WEHR, T. A., SACK, D. A., ROSENTHAL, N. E., & COWDRY, R. W. (1988). Rapid cycling affective disorder: Contributing factors and treatment responses in 51 patients. *American Journal of Psychiatry, 145,* 179–184.

WEINBERGER, D. (1987). Implications of normal brain development for the pathogenesis of schizophrenia. *Archives of General Psychiatry, 44,* 660–669.

WEINBERGER, D. R., & KLEINMAN, J. E. (1986). Observations on the brain in schizophrenia. In A. J. Frances & R. E. Hales (Eds.), *Annual Review,* Vol. 5, Washington DC: American Psychiatric Press.

WEINER, R. D., & COFFEY, C. E. (1988). Indications for use of electroconvulsive therapy. In A. J. Frances & R. E. Hales (Eds.), *Review of psychiatry,* Vol. 7, Washington, DC: American Psychiatric Press.

WEISS, G. (1985). Hyperactivity: Overview and new directions. *Psychiatric Clinics of North America, 8,* 737–753.

WEISS, R. D., & MIRIN, S. M. (1989). The dual diagnosis alcoholic: Evaluation and treatment. *Psychiatric Annals, 19,* 261–265.

WEISSMAN, M. M., & MERIKANGAS, K. R. (1986). The epidemiology of anxiety and panic disorders: An update. *Journal of Clinical Psychiatry, 47* (Suppl.), 11–17.

WEISSMAN, M. M., WICKRAMARANTE, P., MERIKANGAS, K. R., LECKMAN, J. F., PRUSOFF, B. A., CARUSO, K. A., KIDD, K. K., & GAMMON, G. D. (1984). Onset of major depression in early adulthood. Increased familial loading and specificity. *Archives of General Psychiatry, 41,* 1136–1143.

WENDER, P. (1988). Interview. *Currents in Affective Illness, 7,* 5–12.

WENDER, P., REIMHERR, F. W., & WOOD, D. R. (1981). Attention deficit disorder ("Minimal brain dysfunction") in adults: A replication study of diagnosis and drug treatments. *Archives of General Psychiatry, 38,* 449–456.

WENDER, P. H., REIMHERR, R. W., WOOD, D., & WARD, M. (1985). A controlled study of methylphenidate in the treatment of attention deficit disorder, residual type, in adults. *American Journal of Psychiatry, 142,* 547–552.

WENDER, P., WOOD, D., & REIMHERR, F. (1985). Pharmacological treatment of attention deficit disorder, residual type (ADD, RT, "minimal brain dysfunctions," "hyperactivity") in adults. *Psychopharmacological Bulletin, 21,* 222–231.

WHEATLEY, D. (1980). Trazodone in depression. *International Pharmacopsychiatry, 15,* 240–246.

WIDIGER, T. A., & ROGERS, J. H. (1989). Prevalence and comorbidity of personality disorders. *Psychiatric Annals, 19,* 132–136.

WINGARD, C. (1961). Is there any legitimate medical use for the compounds of lithium? *Journal of the American Medical Association, 75,* 340.

WOLKOWITZ, O. M., RAPAPORT, M., & PICKAR, D. (IN PRESS). Benzodiazepine augmentation of neuroleptics. In B. Angrist & S. C. Schultz (Eds.), *Neuroleptic augmentation for refractory patients,* Washington, DC: American Psychiatric Press.

WOODS, S. W., TESAR, G. E., MURRAY, G. B., & CASSEM, N. H. (1986). Psychostimulant treatment of depressive disorders secondary to medical illness. *Journal of Clinical Psychiatry, 47,* 12–15.

WRAGG, R. E., & JESTE, D. V. (1989). Overview of depression and psychosis in Alzheimer's disease. *American Journal of Psychiatry, 146,* 577–587.

WYATT, R. J. (1986). The dopamine hypothesis: Variations on a theme. II. *Psychopharmacology Bulletin, 22,* 923–927.

WYATT, R., KAROUM, F., SUDDATH, R., & HITRI, A. (1988). The role of dopamine in cocaine use and abuse. *Psychiatric Annals, 18,* 531–534.

YAGER, J. (1988). The treatment of eating disorders. *Journal of Clinical Psychiatry, 49* (9, Suppl.), 18–25.

ZANARINI, M. C., & GUNDERSON, J. G. (1988). *DSM-III Disorders in Families of DIB Borderlines.* Presented at the 141st American Psychiatric Association Annual Meeting, Montreal, Quebec.

# Index